BUYING GAY

COLUMBIA STUDIES
IN THE HISTORY
OF U.S. CAPITALISM

COLUMBIA STUDIES IN THE HISTORY OF U.S. CAPITALISM

Series Editors: Devin Fergus, Louis Hyman, Bethany Moreton, and Julia Ott

Capitalism has served as an engine of growth, a source of inequality, and a catalyst for conflict in American history. While remaking our material world, capitalism's myriad forms have altered—and been shaped by—our most fundamental experiences of race, gender, sexuality, nation, and citizenship. This series takes the full measure of the complexity and significance of capitalism, placing it squarely back at the center of the American experience. By drawing insight and inspiration from a range of disciplines and alloying novel methods of social and cultural analysis with the traditions of labor and business history, our authors take history "from the bottom up" all the way to the top.

Capital of Capital: Money, Banking, and Power in New York City, 1784–2012,
    by Steven H. Jaffe and Jessica Lautin
From Head Shops to Whole Foods: The Rise and Fall of Activist Entrepreneurs,
    by Joshua Clark Davis
Creditworthy: A History of Consumer Surveillance and Financial Identity in America,
    by Josh Lauer
American Capitalism: New Histories, by Sven Beckert and Christine Desan, editors

BUYING GAY

How Physique Entrepreneurs
Sparked a Movement

DAVID K. JOHNSON

Columbia University Press *New York*

Columbia University Press
Publishers Since 1893
New York ˜ Chichester, West Sussex
cup.columbia.edu
Copyright © 2019 Columbia University Press

Library of Congress Cataloging-in-Publication Data
Names: Johnson, David K., author.
Title: Buying gay : how physique entrepreneurs sparked a movement /
    David K. Johnson.
Description: New York : Columbia University Press, [2019] | Series: Columbia
    studies in the history of U.S. capitalism | Includes bibliographical references
    and index.
Identifiers: LCCN 2018033079 (print) | LCCN 2018037924 (ebook) |
    ISBN 9780231548175 (e-book) | ISBN 9780231189101 (cloth : alk. paper)
Subjects: LCSH: Gay men—United States—History. | Gay erotica—United
    States—History. | Bodybuilding—Periodicals—United States—History. |
    Gay consumers—United States—History. | Gay business enterprises—
    United States—History. | Gay rights—United States—History.
Classification: LCC HQ76.3.U5 (ebook) | LCC HQ76.3.U5 J583 2019 (print) |
    DDC 306.76/620973--dc23
LC record available at https://lccn.loc.gov/2018033079

Columbia University Press books are printed
on permanent and durable acid-free paper.

Printed in the United States of America

Cover design: Noah Arlow

CONTENTS

PREFACE

I FIRST DISCOVERED physique magazines in the attic of a gay rights activist from the 1960s. While perusing yellowing government documents and organizational meeting minutes on fading onion-skin paper, my eyes were drawn to copies of magazines called *Drum, Physique Pictorial,* and *MANual* full of images of nearly naked men.

While they were more attractive than the dull, typewritten correspondence in the adjacent files, I felt guilty for being distracted from what I thought to be my real goal—documenting the important struggle between the federal government and gay men and lesbians in 1950s and 1960s America. After all, I was researching a book on the federal government's Cold War purge of suspected homosexuals as threats to national security—how we were allegedly part of a communist conspiracy to take over American society—and how gay activists had organized to protest such discriminatory policies. These physique magazines, I told myself, were fluff, to be enjoyed after the work was done. It was the 1990s, and I accepted the historical profession's and society's definition of what is of historic importance and what is pornography, of what is political and what is commercial entertainment. But I have come back now to give them a second look and see how they might change our understanding of that history. And I am not alone in that search.[1]

Soon after my discovery, physique photography was enjoying a veritable renaissance outside the academy as art galleries and museums hosted retrospective exhibitions[2] and art house publishers such as Taschen,[3] Janssen,[4] and others[5] produced increasingly lavish books chronicling the lives of Bob Mizer, George Quaintance, Lon of New York, and other beefcake photographers and artists. Tom of Finland got his own nonprofit foundation and several clothing lines.[6] And a few intrepid scholars had begun to take physique magazines seriously as historical artifacts. Film scholar Thomas Waugh argued in his important book on gay visual culture, "Our most important political activity of the postwar decades . . . was not meeting or organizing or publicly demonstrating but consuming." But this interest was confined mainly to art historians who focused on the physique imagery, ignoring what they sometimes dismissed as "unrelated editorial content," and the wider commercial network in which these items circulated.[7] Some queer theorists and cultural critics were openly hostile, seeing in them only evidence of racism, self-loathing, or the closet.[8] I saw a puzzling disconnect between popular appreciation for these physique pioneers and academic dismissal, if not outright distain. I began to wonder why historians of the LGBT community had minimized their significance.

As early as 1982 Dennis Altman alerted us to the central role that commercial enterprises have played in the development of gay community. "One of the ironies of American capitalism," he wrote, "is that it has been a major force in creating and maintaining a sense of identity among homosexuals." Writing about the same time, John D'Emilio also stressed how the development of urban wage labor capitalism opened a space for men and women attracted to members of their own sex to find one another and forge community.[9] But for Altman, D'Emilio, and most historians since, the commercial scene so important to the development of gay community focused on sites of urban leisure—bars, restaurants, bathhouses, and discos, which were mostly straight owned and operated. Much of the ensuing historiographical debate has been over which was most influential to gay community formation—gay bars as sites of prepolitical resistance or the more formal political organizing of the small homophile movement represented by the organizations ONE, Mattachine, and the Daughters of Bilitis.[10] Neither historians who stressed the role of bars nor those who focused on political organizing gave the realm of consumer culture more than a cursory glance.

One explanation for this oversight is the difficulty in finding sources. While the papers of homophile organizations have been carefully preserved and cataloged, the ephemera of commercial enterprises has tended to disappear. Only recently have academic and community-based libraries begun to collect these materials.[11] But the biases of some of the founders of the field also played a role. Many early historians of the LGBT movement, with roots in a gay liberationist ethos that was explicitly anticapitalist, viewed for-profit enterprises such as physique publishers with skepticism, considering them peripheral to movement politics.[12] Even scholars who focus on the development of gay print media and communication networks favored homophile and nonprofit publications over the more commercial and tawdry world of physiques.[13]

As a result, most scholars and activists who have investigated a "gay market" position it as a post-Stonewall development. Imagining capitalism and activism as antithetical, they see a process of "selling out," a narrative in which a leftist political movement has declined into a market niche, a corporatized arm of the neoliberal establishment.[14] As Lillian Faderman and Stuart Timmons summarized in their history of gay and lesbian Los Angeles, "It is ironic that, in L.A. as elsewhere, gay radicals, who prided themselves on their anti-materialism, were actually responsible for the inception of a new gay consumerism when they made the gay community widely visible."[15]

But what I found as I traveled around the country researching was that the notion of a "gay market" was already enjoying wide currency nearly a decade before Stonewall. It was most clearly visible on the nation's newsstands. A social scientist who examined the largest newsstand in Dayton, Ohio, in 1964 found twenty-five magazines targeting a gay audience—so many that the salesperson had established a special section for what he called his "homosexual magazines." He mixed the magazines of the homophile political organizations, ONE and Mattachine Review, with the far larger cache of physiques.[16] With twenty or more "little queer magazines" on American newsstands, each selling between twenty thousand and forty thousand copies, physique magazines represented a major industry. With a circulation rate ten times that of their homophile competitors, physique magazines were the primary gay media outlet in the nation.[17] By 1963 one physique publisher had fourteen full-time employees and was the largest mail customer at Minneapolis's main downtown postal facility, making it arguably the largest gay-owned and gay-oriented commercial enterprise in the world.[18] One publisher estimated that domestic sales of physique magazines topped nine million per year.[19] Far from an "underground" economy, physique magazines and their associated mail-order businesses were a multimillion-dollar market (see fig. o.1).[20]

Editors of tabloid and mainstream magazines realized the extent of this market whenever they published an article on homosexuality and saw their sales soar.[21] Homophile leaders, too, saw how putting the words "the Homosexual Magazine" on their otherwise demurely titled ONE magazine increased sales.[22] Robert Wood, a gay minister with a regular physique magazine column, identified what he termed "a distinct homosexual market" in photographs, books,

FIGURE 0.1 The most visible site of a gay market in the 1950s was the nation's news-stands. This Times Square news seller established a homosexual section in the upper left corner just above his head to display both physique and homophile publications. He is reading the first issue of *Sports Illustrated*, December 1957.

Courtesy of Getty Images.

greeting cards, cosmetics, and clothing in 1961. He thought it represented a new openness in American culture that was empowering the gay community. "As the gay boys set one style change after another they grow more confident of eventual acceptance, and thus the trend to become even more obvious," Wood observed.[23] Even eighty-year-old Justice Felix Frankfurter of the U.S. Supreme Court used the term "homosexual market" to describe the physique magazines that he and his fellow justices cleared of obscenity charges in 1962.[24]

"It's a movement, not a market"[25] is a catchy queer political slogan, one that suggests a once purely progressive cause has been hijacked by corporate interests. But it ignores a history that clearly shows that the creation of a gay market, by and for gay people, was crucial to the emergence and success of a gay movement. Both involved outreach to and cultivation of an otherwise disparate group of people who share a common interest or identity and providing those customers or members a means of contacting one another. Central to both such commercial and political interests is the development of address lists, the holy grail of both a mail-order business and a political organization. Lists and direct-mail marketing were instrumental to the rise of a New Right in the 1980s, a tactic they learned from Marvin Leibman, a closeted gay man.[26] As John D'Emilio famously noted, before activists could mobilize a community, they first had to create one, and physique entrepreneurs were engaged in that enterprise on a scale homophile activists could only dream of. By making gay desire visible, by marketing it to the masses and defending it from government censorship, physique entrepreneurs helped create a sense of a national gay community.[27]

Further research in memoirs, letters, and novels demonstrates that the taking, exchanging, displaying, and viewing of physique photography and drawings have been central to gay male cultural life. Collecting and displaying these items formed a key element of gay men's sense of identity and served as ways to mark oneself as gay and signal this to others. Victor Banis wrote in 1963 about a gay bar where "the photos pinned to the wall, pictures of nearly nude young men, mostly bodybuilders, identified the bar for what it was, a gay hangout." Gay men placing classified advertisements in mainstream periodicals would note their interest in "physiques" to signal their sexual interest in other men. Most fictional representations of the gay world in the pre-Stonewall era made frequent reference to physique photos or paintings. Fritz Peters's novel *Finistere* (1951), the coming-out story of Michael, a teenage boy at a French boarding school, offers a glimpse inside the apartment of a gay man whom Michael encountered on the streets of Paris. What set the space apart and marked it as gay was the artwork above the couch: "All photographs, and all of men. Some of them had obviously been cut out of physical culture magazines, others were snapshots, mostly of men in bathing suits, in one or two cases entirely nude."[28]

With the taking and sharing of erotic images so central to gay male culture, finding a safe place to develop film became a preoccupation of many gay men. Some physique publishers offered a mail-order photo-developing service. It is no accident that Harvey Milk, the first well-known openly gay male political figure in American politics, got his start as the owner of a gay-friendly camera shop in San Francisco that made most of its money developing film.[29]

In deciding to place physique entrepreneurs and commerce at the center of the story of the development of gay community in the post–World War II period,

I follow the work of a wide variety of scholars studying historical movements where consumer culture played a pivotal role in shaping individuals' sense of self, community, and political engagement. While early scholarship tended to depict the rise of mass consumer culture as an oppressive force limiting the agency of individuals, more recent studies emphasize the potentially liberating aspects of consumer society—how it served as a catalyst to group identity formation and collective resistance.[30] T. H. Breen argues that it was the rise of consumer goods in the colonial era that first tied the American colonists together as an "imagined community" and provided an arena of political protest against their colonial oppressors in the form of product boycotts. Daniel Boorstein documented how mail-order catalogs and Rural Free Delivery knitted Americans together into "consumption communities," further complicating the traditional conceptual separation between social movements and commercial enterprises.[31]

Historians of the African American community increasingly credit the beauty, fashion, and media industries as important sites of resistance to Jim Crow segregation and see the civil rights movement as in part a struggle to gain full participation in the postwar marketplace.[32] More recently Joshua Clark Davis has shown how "activist entrepreneurs" who ran headshops, feminist bookstores, and organic grocers played a key role in supporting an American counterculture, while Bethany Moreton has spotlighted the role that Walmart shoppers and employees played in the creation of a conservative movement.[33]

Both the LGBT and African American civil rights struggles took hold at a time that historian Lizabeth Cohen has labeled a "Consumers' Republic"—a postwar society based on the promise that rising levels of consumer choice would provide not only material security but also greater freedom and equality. It was a time when presidential candidates were hiring advertising firms for the first time and Wendell Smith identified a shift from mass marketing to market segmentation, which encouraged the cultivation of "smaller or *fringe* market segments." Embraced by Madison Avenue, market segmentation led to advertisements targeting particular lifestyles or minority groups, most famously positioning the 1960s "Pepsi Generation" against more mass-market Coca-Cola fans. "As mass markets increasingly splintered, individuals gained more opportunity to express identities through their choices as consumers," Cohen argued. In short, market segmentation and gay identity formation worked to reinforce one another.[34]

But neither the African American nor the gay community waited for mainstream advertisers to discover their respective markets. In 1972 *Advertising Age* declared, "No gay market yet," suggesting the topic was still too hot for large Madison Avenue firms. A few years later Absolut Vodka began offering the first national print advertisements targeting an LGBTQ audience—and earned the community's lasting loyalty. By then it was a decades-old phenomenon well-known to physique publishers, specialty clothing companies, and even observant Supreme Court justices.[35]

For historians of mid-twentieth-century sexual politics, consumer culture has become an increasingly important site for exploring community formation and struggle. Martin Meeker and John Howard began to suggest how a gay communications network developed in postwar America that allowed gay men from small towns to interact not only with each other but with those in the meccas of San Francisco and New York.[36] Elizabeth Fraterrigo's work on *Playboy* and Brian Hoffman's on nudist magazines highlight how such commercial publications fostered a heteronormative sexual liberalism in American culture during the same period.[37] More recently Elizabeth Heineman, looking at Germany, and Stephen Vider and Whitney Strub, on the United States, have focused our attention on commercial enterprises and their formative roles in fostering sexual subcultures. Justin Bengry's extensive scholarship on the United Kingdom has begun to examine what he calls a "history of queer capitalism."[38]

I'm not sure if this constitutes what economist Deidre McCloskey lauded in 2007 as a "new turn in queer studies," one that abandoned assumptions about the evils of capitalism and embraced "the power of the market for good."[39] Many queer studies practitioners remain deeply skeptical of consumption as an avenue for political engagement. Following Lisa Duggan, they see a queer consumer economy as sustaining a "new homonormativity," a politics that supports rather than challenges heteronormative institutions while marginalizing women and people of color.[40] But from a historical perspective, we can no longer consider the gay market, whether viewed as a progressive or a limiting force, as a post-Stonewall creation.

It will not be enough to add gay commercial enterprises to the mix of factors leading to creation of gay identity, community, and resistance. My hope is that it will lead to a breakdown of the binary opposition often assumed by scholars between the "commercial" and the "political" when examining this period. After all, the homophile organizations and the physique enterprises were fulfilling many of the same functions—fostering community, providing legal advice, and fighting censorship, among others. Both groups were engaged in a politics of respectability to appeal to a large, middle-class audience and get around aggressive postal inspectors. Homophile publications did this by avoiding nude images, while physique publishers avoided explicit discussions of homosexuality. But it was a false distinction, since newsstand owners, postal authorities, and much of the public considered them all gay magazines. Despite a professed hostility, homophile groups eyed their commercial counterparts with envy and increasingly borrowed their tactics, first in their sale of gay books, and later in their incorporation of advertising and imagery. As the threat of censorship diminished, the two realms became almost indistinguishable. Although we call it the homophile era, it could just as easily be labeled the physique era.[41]

By combining the study of consumer culture with that of LGBT history, *Buying Gay* significantly alters the way in which we conceive the history of the gay movement. Offering a close examination of how gay entrepreneurs used the marketplace in the 1950s and 1960s to mobilize a constituency and create the notion of "gay power," it shows how gay consumer culture developed sooner than we imagined. It demonstrates how physique entrepreneurs enjoyed a constituency that vastly surpassed that of the tiny homophile political movement and how they had a more national and discursive impact than did the localized gay bar scene. It suggests that the physique and homophile organizations increasingly overlapped in the services they provided, offering an expanded notion of gay activism. It continues the work of moving the focus beyond cities, examining how gay print and mail-order networks linked the rural and the urban. It underscores the vibrancy and openness of the pre-Stonewall era, still often imagined as a time characterized by the closet. Ultimately it shows that gay commerce was not a byproduct of the gay movement but a catalyst to it, thus contributing to our understanding of the role of consumer culture in fostering community and providing avenues for resistance.

Buying Gay also shows that McCarthy-era fears were misplaced. It turns out that the rise of a gay community in the United States was not the result of a communist conspiracy, as some feared during the Cold War. Rather than "Stalin's atom bomb" sent to destroy democratic capitalism, an organized and powerful gay community was aided and abetted by capitalism. As physique entrepreneurs freed themselves from the constraints of censorship, they sparked a movement. Less the spawn of Marx and Lenin, it turns out they were, for better or for worse, more the children of Adam Smith and Alexander Hamilton.

ILLUSTRATIONS

BUYING GAY

INTRODUCTION

ONE DAY in 1959, twelve-year-old David Chapman visited the magazine store in his little Southern California town of Chula Vista. Wandering past the stern-faced men perusing the rack of girlie magazines, he discovered his first issue of *Physique Pictorial*. The magazine was small, monochromatic, and printed on nonglossy paper, yet it still stood out to him. As he later recalled, it featured "a guy on the cover with a fabulous physique and smiling open faced." It was the combination of male muscle and smile that set the magazine apart from serious bodybuilding periodicals. "I knew that I had to pick it up and look at it," he remembered. Inside he discovered that the model's name was John Tristram and that he liked to hang around the pool nearly naked with his similarly clad buddy. The combination of male muscle and camaraderie drew him in. Chapman had to buy it (see fig. 0.2).

Sensing that what he was doing was transgressive, he waited nervously until customers at the counter dispersed. "Somehow even then I knew that good little prepubescent Eisenhower-era boys did not purchase magazines of this ilk." Because the proprietor was blind, there was one more hurdle to surmount—he had to announce what he was buying. *"Physique Pictorial*, sir," he stammered as he put down thirty-five cents. Once safely home, he kept the magazine hidden at the bottom of his cigar box, where he stored his most precious and private possessions.[1]

Across the country in New Hampshire, Paul Monette was a teenage student on scholarship at Philips Academy who worked Sundays as a clerk at the Andover Spa, a soda fountain and magazine stand. He had already amassed a stash of *Strength & Health* but found the models unappealing and "determinedly macho." Then in the summer of 1961 he noticed a new arrival. "Recently the

FIGURE 0.2 John Tristram and Forrester D'Orlac cavorting in Bob Mizer's pool exhibited an engaging homoerotic camaraderie. *Physique Pictorial*, Summer 1958.
Courtesy of Bob Mizer Foundation.

distributor had started sending two copies every month of a pocket-size photo magazine called *Tomorrow's Man*," he recalled. Like countless other scared and excited young men, he knew he had to have it but also knew it was dangerous to admit it. He tucked it inside the pages of *Modern Screen* and took it home. "I don't think we ever *sold* a copy of *Tomorrow's Man* over the counter," he remembered. He assumed that the owner's flamboyantly gay son stole the other copy. What set the magazine apart was "an attitude of showing off, a sassy wink of something I'd never seen before. . . . I was staring at men who wanted to be admired. . . . It was the first clue I ever had that being queer existed out there in the world."[2]

Just down the coast in Rhode Island, Michael Denneny had convinced his mother to buy him copies of *Strength & Health* and began lifting weights in the seventh grade. But an even more transformative event happened in 1957. "I can remember the exact moment when I first saw a Tom of Finland drawing. I was walking up High Street in downtown Pawtucket on the way to the library. There is a big newsstand halfway up. . . . It had a drawing of a shirtless boy on a log coming down a river. It pierced me to the soul." The boy was smiling, and accompanied by a grinning comrade. Both were proudly displaying well-developed chests—and bulges in their pants. Denneny had happened on Finish artist Touko Laaksonen's first cover of *Physique Pictorial*. "I shoplifted that magazine very fast," he recalled (see fig. 0.3).

Many other men remember seeing Tom of Finland's first cover image on newsstands and feeling that it spoke directly to them. "I'll never forget seeing it on the newsstand. And, I have talked to other people who experienced the same thing. It was something new," recalled F. Valentine Hooven. Grasping for an analogy, Denneny offered, "It's like asking people of my generation where were you when Kennedy was shot."[3]

Not content just to rely on the newsstand's supply, Denneny sought out a closer connection to this community. He subscribed to several of the new magazines, which arrived in the mail in brown paper envelopes; luckily his liberal parents considered the mail "sacrosanct" and did not intervene. He, too, sensed that the magazines were different from what he called "real bodybuilding magazines." Model Glenn Bishop appeared so frequently with buddy Richard Alan that Denneny imagined that they were a couple. He read longingly of Grecian Guild conventions held in New Orleans and San Francisco. Aware he was both too young and too poor to attend, he found another means to connect. In the November 1957 issue of *VIM*, his letter was featured in the "First-Class Male" section. Thrilled as he was to see his name in print near those of his favorite models and fellow physique enthusiasts, he knew not to boast about it to his parents. "I was aware they had crossed a line. . . . These little magazines allowed me to develop this internal world of desire and beauty that has animated my life."[4]

FIGURE 0.3 Many men vividly recall seeing this first image by Touko Laaksonen in the spring 1957 edition of *Physique Pictorial*. It was publisher Bob Mizer who gave him the moniker Tom of Finland.

Courtesy of Bob Mizer Foundation and the Tom of Finland Foundation.

For countless men growing up in the 1950s and 1960s, their first recognition of gay culture came not from visiting a gay bar in one of America's port cities, nor from joining one of the few avowedly gay organizations then meeting quietly behind closed doors. Long before they moved to Chicago or New York or heard of the Mattachine Society, they encountered *Physique Pictorial*,

Tomorrow's Man, or *VIM* on their local newsstand. Filmmaker John Waters stole his first *Grecian Guild* from Sherman's Newsstand in downtown Baltimore; novelist Edmund White found his first copies in a Cincinnati bookshop; art collector Charles Leslie, in a Rexall drug store in Deadwood, South Dakota.[5]

These magazines appeared nearly everywhere thanks to the structures of capitalism—major commercial magazine distributors insisted that a newsstand or drugstore accept all its offerings. Some newsstands got around this mandate, keeping objectionable material off the shelves and claiming it never sold, but most complied.[6]

Physique magazines were just the most visible embodiment of what in postwar America was emerging as a new market niche. Gay men could buy gay-themed books, send homoerotic greeting cards, play suggestive records at parties, display physique artwork on their walls, and order the latest Greenwich Village fashions. They could participate in this extensive commercial network of book sellers, photographers, publishers, and other entrepreneurs from anywhere in the country simply by getting on the mailing list for catalogs targeting gay men. Reading these magazines and purchasing these goods put them in contact with a national, even international, gay community. More than an "imagined community," it was a form of mail-order activism.

What made it activism was the risk these men took in buying and the producers took in distributing these materials. For Paul Monette it was simply an embarrassing reprimand from his father when his stash of both *Playboy* and *Tomorrow's Man* was found. "There's nothing wrong with those girlie magazines. That's perfectly natural," his father declared, "but the homosexual ones . . . that's not good." For fifteen-year-old Jerry Weiss it was a brush with the law. After one of his usual purchases of *Tomorrow's Man* in Manhattan, he made the mistake of perusing the magazine in public. When a New York City police officer saw him reading one on a subway platform, he confiscated it.[7]

But for hundreds, if not thousands, of others, it meant arrest, expensive trials, loss of jobs, even jail time. The U.S. Post Office considered most of the magazines and photographs that circulated in this network to be a violation of the Comstock Law of 1873 against sending obscene materials through the U.S. mail. Postmaster General Arthur Summerfield and thousands of postal inspectors took this mandate extremely seriously. Inspectors would not only monitor magazine content but infiltrate mailing lists with false names, raid production facilities, and intimidate and prosecute customers. They were supported in their efforts by local police, who enforced state and municipal censorship laws, as well as by organized "antismut" groups, such as Citizens for Decent Literature. Working with federal prosecutors, the Post Office considered any of the magazines that appealed to a homosexual market to be obscene. Most revealed no more skin then *Esquire* or *Playboy*, which the courts had ruled mailable, but they were objectionable because, as one prosecutor put it, they "promote homosexuality in American society."[8]

In a way the prosecutor was correct—by putting homoerotic images out into the marketplace, connecting those who enjoyed viewing them, and publicly defending their right to do so, these entrepreneurs promoted the formation of a self-conscious minority community. The development of this gay commercial network in the 1950s and 1960s and its role in American culture and politics are the subject of this book. It tells the story of how gay entrepreneurs responded to and cultivated a gay market long before the Stonewall Riots of 1969. It chronicles their struggles with both mainstream bodybuilding magazines and the U.S. Post Office, which tried to shut them down. It shows how they created a space for gay men to find one another that became central to gay cultural formation and the winning of gay legal rights. Selling gay materials at newsstands or through the mails, these twentieth-century capitalists helped create community and a site for resistance.[9]

WHAT IS A PHYSIQUE MAGAZINE?

Fitness and bodybuilding magazines were an outgrowth of the turn-of-the-century physical culture movement, a response to a crisis in masculinity in a rapidly urbanizing and industrializing America. As traditional markers of masculinity such as land or independent business ownership became less accessible to white, middle-class men, new markers of masculinity took hold—such as playing sports and developing the muscular male body. By the turn of the twentieth century, college football reached a mass audience, the Olympic Games had been revived, and Bernarr Macfadden had begun building a health and fitness empire publishing *Physical Culture* magazine. Eugene Sandow, known as "the perfect man," became the first international bodybuilding superstar. Photographs of his nearly naked body circulated in magazines and postcards all over Europe and North America.[10]

By the 1930s a host of physical culture magazines catered to and profited from this interest in developing the male body. A tension developed between weight lifting and a newer subfield of bodybuilding that many longtime participants denigrated for its focus more on aesthetics then strength. The first American Athletic Association (AAU) Mr. America contest in 1939 was a reluctant addition to the weightlifting competitions, and it remained an overlooked stepchild to the "iron game." Bob Hoffman, considered the "father of American weightlifting" and publisher of the flagship magazine *Strength & Health*, resisted the new interest in bodybuilding and Mr. America contests, associating these with feminine narcissism. Weightlifters called the artistic poses favored by bodybuilders "sissy stuff." They made fun of bodybuilders' emphasis on pectoral and lateral muscles, which were mostly for show, and their neglect of shoulders and legs, which were more for strength. Hoffman derided them as "Boobybuilders" and "mirror athletes." Only Joe Weider's magazine *Your Physique* and his competing International Federation of BodyBuilders (IFBB) championed this new subfield, and the rivalry between these two promoters and publishers embodied this tension between the older, more traditional field of weightlifting and the newer realm of bodybuilding.[11]

As historians such as George Chauncey have shown us, gay men in the early twentieth century were adept at appropriating urban public spaces for their own purposes, whether bars, public parks, Turkish baths, or the Young Men's Christian Association (YMCA).[12] The gyms, contests, and magazines surrounding bodybuilding were another such public space that gay men actively, if cautiously, appropriated. The proliferation of bodybuilding contests, both local and national, depended on a large gay fan base. Bob Mizer, a gay photographer who frequented Muscle Beach in Los Angeles, said it was an "open secret" that gay men made up a large portion of the audience at Mr. California, Mr. America, and the myriad other bodybuilding competitions. They sat through the lengthy traditional weightlifting competitions in anticipation of the bodybuilding segments usually held at the end of the evening.[13]

Since the serious weightlifting crowd was uninterested in bodybuilding, they gladly ceded the organizing of these contests to others. At one Mr. East Coast contest, the chairman of the planning committee, the chairman of the judging committee, the musical entertainer, and many of the photographers were all gay men. Bodybuilding contestant Dan Lurie said, "It was well known that most of the prominent photographers at that time such as Earle Forbes, Lon Hanagan, and Al Urban were gay."[14] They started running ads in the back of *Strength & Health* offering "undraped" photos of young athletes. By the early 1950s several of these photographers had launched their own magazines. Bob

Mizer was the first with his *Physique Pictorial* in 1951, quickly followed by Irv Johnson, owner of a gym in Chicago, who started *Tomorrow's Man*, and then a gay couple who met at the University of Virginia, Randolph Benson and John Bullock, debuted the *Grecian Guild Pictorial*.

What set these magazines apart from their mainstream competitors was hard to define, but customers like David Chapman, Paul Monette, and Michael Denneny responded in droves. Physique magazines invited and often depicted men gazing at other men, at a time when a mere glance between men was dangerous.[15] They focused on more "natural" or "classical" builds rather than serious weightlifting competitors. They offered coded references to the Grecian way of life, a chance to be part of "the limited aesthetic group who appreciate the glorification of the male body."[16] And they included drawings by physique artists such as Quaintance, Etienne, and Tom of Finland of all-male spaces such as the Roman baths, Western dude ranches, or Scandinavian logging camps.

"Those guys of yours are the sexiest, happiest characters around!" wrote Jim Edwards, an adoring fan, about the images Etienne marketed as "Merry Bachelors." "The situations portrayed in your drawings, the looks in the eyes and *smiles* on the faces and the OUTLINES in the crotch are ten times more suggestive and bold and stimulating as a simple anatomical study of the naked male would be." Edwards was attracted less by the degree of nudity in these magazines than by the hopeful attitude of camaraderie and freedom they inspired. "You're making me begin to believe in a world of leather jackets, broad shoulders and motorcycles that you portray so well." He also imaged a day when censorship would end and "the bare truth will prevail."[17]

Young men were not the only ones to notice these new gay magazines. The editors of mainstream bodybuilding magazines felt these new competitors cut into their bottom line and sounded the alarm. *Strength & Health* warned of a "flood of undersized booklets featuring the male physique in all stages of nudity" targeting "the 'swish' trade." In an article headlined "Let Me Tell You a Fairy Tale," the editors argued that these "homosexual magazines" were being marketed by people whose sole interest was profit, that they were outselling "the regular" physical culture magazines, and that they were contributing to juvenile delinquency. They proposed that any bodybuilder whose photo appeared in these "trashy magazines" be barred from AAU competitions. *Iron Man* penned a similar attack on "the homosexual element" that had "infiltrated" the sport, calling for a cleanup campaign of gyms, contests, and magazines. It proposed a ban on all advertisements of nude physique photography, even while noting these were the most lucrative of advertisements. Physique cover boy Richard Alan joined the chorus, denouncing the fan base that had sent him thousands of letters while purchasing his images, bathing suits, and supplements. "I found out first hand what it was that these boys wanted . . . very few of these 5,000 [letter writers] trained with weights. They were all of the element that is giving weight training its biggest black eye—homosexuals."[18]

Soon the nation's tabloids picked up the story. *Rave*, a bimonthly that called itself the "National Humor Magazine," ran an article in 1957 on "Who Pins Up Pin-Up Boys?" *Rave* editors were shocked to learn that women rarely bought magazines such as *VIM*, *Tomorrow's Man*, or *Body Beautiful*. "Beefcake journals are just plain fruitcake for a huge assortment of swivel-hipped nuts and screwballs," the editors concluded, noting the skimpiness of the posing straps, the salaciousness of the articles, and clothing advertisements for men only. To a typically suggestive *Tomorrow's Man* headline, "Are Bodybuilders Oversexed?," *Rave* editors responded, "Yes! For each other!" A gay man from Artesia, California, wrote in to confirm *Rave's* suspicions and defend his fellow physique magazine subscribers. "You people ought to wise up to the fact that the 'Gay World' is here to stay," he defiantly admonished *Rave*. Fellow tabloid *Hush-Hush* suggested that the coy titles *Physique Pictorial* and *Manorama* might better be replaced with "Queersville Quarterly" or "The Faggot Gazette" (see fig. 0.4).[19]

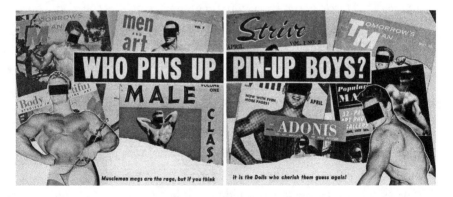

FIGURE 0.4 *Rave's* September 1957 issue revealed to readers that women rarely bought physique magazines. "Beefcake journals are just plain fruitcake for a huge assortment of swivel-hipped nuts and screwballs," editors warned, noting that "gay boys" of Greenwich Village were avid consumers.

Courtesy of University of Washington Libraries, Special Collections, UW39458–9.

Soon more mainstream news sources understood what these magazines represented and let their readers in on the secret. *Sports Illustrated* joined the attack, warning its readers of the "lunatic fringe" that had infiltrated the wholesome field pioneered by Charles Atlas, a sport that had begun as a "a way to get yourself a girl" but now had become "a way to get something quite the opposite." A front-page story in the *New York Times* documenting a perceived rise in overt homosexuality in the city pointed to a proliferation of "the so-called bodybuilding publications" on newsstands, which were "peddling outright homosexual pornography in text and illustration."[20]

The association between gay men and bodybuilding became generalized in American culture. Some observed that barbells had replaced chintz and lavender curtains as accessories in gay homes and plush gyms were the new homosexual hangout. Family physicians were known to warn teenage boys away from lifting weights because of the likelihood of encountering homosexuals.[21] A slew of books and movies from the postwar years portray bodybuilders as narcissistic, unathletic, and of suspect sexuality. When the narrator of the novel *Muscle Beach* (1959) asks a gym owner to explain the bodybuilding community of Venice Beach, he is told, "Well, a large section of them are sexually abnormal. They primp the way a woman primps, and for the same reason." The pulp novel *Muscle Boy* (1958) offered a more sinister assessment of the "beefcake kings," suggesting that behind the veil of athleticism lurked a depraved world of sex perversion and blackmail.[22]

In the film *Muscle Beach Party* (1964), a group of carefully coifed and oiled musclemen threaten the wholesome heterosexual teenage fun of Annette Funicello and Frankie Avalon. Director William Asher accentuates their campiness by having them wear skimpy pink swimsuits as they compete for the title of "Mr. Galaxy" under the direction of Coach Jack Fanny, played by comedian Don Rickels. Constrained by the Hayes Code, which forbade outright mention of homosexuality, Asher pointed most overtly at the sexuality of these bronzed bodybuilders when he positioned Coach Fanny directly in front of the "Mr. Galaxy" contest sign, obscuring the middle letters. The resulting screen image suggested they are competing for the title "Mr. Gay."[23]

The association between bodybuilding and homosexuality in popular culture endured into the 1970s, broken only by the rise of Arnold Schwarzenegger and the popularity of the book and the film *Pumping Iron* (1977), which brought a new image to the sport. According to most accounts, it was the Austrian bodybuilder who inaugurated a fitness revolution and made "working out" at the gym an American popular obsession. But these accounts neglect how George Butler—through whose lens America first discovered Schwarzenegger—had serious trouble getting his book published because of the sport's gay stigma. The editor-in-chief of Doubleday canceled his contract, explaining that "no one in America will buy a book of pictures of these half-unclothed men of dubious sexual pursuits." Before the book made the best-seller list, the *New York Times* dismissed it as "fag bait." Schwarzenegger may have normalized bodybuilding for a general audience, but first he had to heterosexualize it.[24]

Today, physique magazines are often seen as a quaint relic of a time when all things gay remained in the closet. To modern eyes, they seemed to hide behind the worlds of fitness and bodybuilding, engaging in a sort of masquerade or alibi. Calling their audience a "secret public," Christopher Nealon claims that no one—including judges asked to rule on their legality—could determine who the real audience was for these magazines. Thomas Waugh similarly claims that the gayness of these magazines "was an open secret that everyone shared but *didn't articulate*" (emphasis added).[25]

In fact, almost all jurists who looked at these magazines concluded explicitly that they were produced for homosexuals and largely bought by homosexuals. Mainstream muscle magazines never tired of articulating how homosexuals were infiltrating and corrupting a wholesome sport. What we now see as a culture of the closet hiding behind the he-man sport of weightlifting was at the time perceived as an expansive subculture threatening the sport. Interest in physical culture was not a ruse behind which gay men hid but a way for them to express their desires and find each other. Far from being in the closet, gay men's place in bodybuilding was part of public discourse—the subject of frequent editorials, pop culture depictions, and discussions in both mainstream and gay circles.

But to say that physique magazines represented the closeted nature of homosexuality in the postwar years is only one of the misunderstandings surrounding the genre. They are also generally viewed as static. Most studies are based on only the best-known magazine, *Physique Pictorial*, with a smattering of examples from one or two others.[26] Such studies provide no sense of how this genre changed and developed over the tumultuous decades between 1950 and 1967 as physique publishers interacted with various legal frameworks, distribution networks, and consolidation strategies. With all the attention on just a few photographers and artists like Bob Mizer and Tom of Finland, the complexity of the market has been obscured. The company that became the largest distributor of physique magazines is almost unknown today, and its pivotal court victory in 1967 largely ignored.

Part of the reason for this static portrayal has been the lack of sources, since research libraries did not collect these periodicals. This situation began to change in the 1990s as both community-based gay and lesbian archives and academic archives specializing in the new field of sexuality studies began to preserve them. The research terrain was further transformed as these magazines again became consumer items sold on eBay and discussed in online blogs. And in just the past few years, as commercial online databases have become available, a systematic review of nearly the entire corpus of physique magazines—numbering hundreds of issues and thousands of pages—has become possible for the first time.[27]

Related to this static perception of physique magazines is the tendency to view them in isolation, not as part of and interacting with a larger network of gay consumer culture, including books, artwork, greeting cards, gay bar guides, and clothing. The typical physique magazine consumer also subscribed to one of the many mail-order gay book services, bought swimwear through the Ah Men catalog, sent gay greeting cards to his friends, and displayed an Athletic Model Guild calendar on his wall. Even if he did not do any of these things, he was influenced by advertising that suggested he could. Subscribing to a physique magazine would allow him to purchase gay novels from the Winston Book Club, decorate the living room with a Quaintance statue or painting, whip up a meal with *The Gay Cookbook*, or play suggestive records or physique films at parties.[28]

Finally, these physique magazines are generally understood to be apolitical. Their increasingly close, if always contentious, relationship to the homophile political movement of the time is largely ignored, along with their key role in winning some of the first gay rights legal victories. The end of censorship in the late 1960s is often seen as a gift from the Supreme Court bestowed on these magazines, or the result of a general tide of 1960s liberalism. Beyond its historical vagueness, this interpretation takes away all agency from the publishers, who were under near constant harassment from a phalanx of postal inspectors, who represented the federal government's oldest law enforcement agency.

Physique entrepreneurs faced a zealous antismut campaign waged by the U.S. Post Office, part of a cultural crusade to attack an increasingly open and organized gay movement, of which physique magazines were an integral part. They had to confront postal authorities' underhanded tactics, which included disingenuous claims that physique entrepreneurs targeted children, and extra-legal "educational visits" to harass physique customers, particularly vulnerable teachers. Many lost their struggle with the Post Office and were forced out of business, their stories largely forgotten and undocumented. Only when these gay entrepreneurs organized into large conglomerates with nationwide distribution systems were they able to acquire the resources that enabled them to fight back and win in the courts.[29]

Despite common perceptions, physique magazines were not closeted about their gay market, not frozen in time, and not isolated from the rest of gay political and consumer culture. They were perceived as gay magazines by nearly everyone involved in their production or reception and they grew more openly gay over time. What emerges from my study is a picture of these magazines as part of a larger network of consumer cultural production that was integral to the development of a homophile movement and to legal struggles that culminated in the federal court rulings in 1962 and 1967 that allowed open homo-eroticism and frontal male nudity. I see these legal victories as the end of an era and the beginning of a new one, as important as the better-known Stonewall Riots of 1969.[30]

PHYSIQUE CONSUMERS

Today we know physique magazines through the idealized images of Tom of Finland and other artists whose work has been exhibited in galleries and immortalized in gay bars and magazines throughout the world. This nostalgic vision has given us a narrow, distorted view, allowing us to imagine that they held up an impossibly idealized model of the gay male body. Some have accused them of contributing to a kind of "body fascism" that encouraged self-hatred among gay men who failed to live up to these standards. But to contemporary viewers, what set gay physique magazines apart from their mainstream competitors was their inclusion of a variety of body types. Indeed one of the criticisms leveled against these "little queer magazines" by their more straight-laced competitors was that their models looked emaciated. One satirical set of drawings contrasted the grim "old school" weightlifter with the "new school" bodybuilder, whose lithe body was covered in a luxurious cape and bejeweled posing strap (see fig. 0.5).[31]

This differing aesthetic sense was largely a response to popular demand. "Thousands of letters have convinced us that the average collector is more

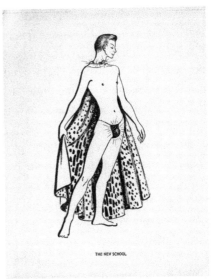

FIGURE O.5 These anonymous drawings, appearing in GYM in June 1959, acknowledged and satirized the shift that physique magazines represented away from the traditional sport of weightlifting toward "natural" or "classical" builds with an emphasis on costumes and posing straps.

Courtesy of University of Washington Libraries, Special Collections, UW39456-7.

interested in the more moderately developed body than the extremely muscular type," Bob Mizer explained. Indeed, the proliferation of gay physique magazines ushered in a broader aesthetic than that exemplified by traditional weightlifting magazines. It was partly by offering more diverse body types and poses that they distinguished themselves as gay. By gleefully soliciting the desires of other men, they were not aping heterosexual masculine norms but subverting them. Jennifer Evans labels this new physique aesthetic "queer beauty," suggesting that in this formative period it acted as a "crucial strategy of resistance and community building."[32]

Publishers encouraged identification and intimacy between models and customers by offering them opportunities to participate in the physique world. Magazines were happy to publish the words, images, or artwork of customers, through either letters to the editor, a club directory, or a more formalized contest. Lionel Kilfoyle was no bodybuilder and not conventionally handsome, but he managed over a three-year period to get his photograph published in

Tomorrow's Man, Grecian Guild Pictorial, and *VIM.* Imploring the Grecian Guild to use his full name and address, he wrote, "I'm trying to get a studio underway. I also need lots & lots of fans and friends. I get very lonely, so introduce me warmly once again to your readers."[33] *Fizeek Art Quarterly* frequently featured the work of customers and other amateur artists. "Just the fact that you have made it possible for a person to become known outside his immediate environment is enough to make one jump for joy," enthused one such artist.[34] Indeed, the barriers to entry to the physique world were low, with customers and models often becoming commercial photographers themselves, further encouraging a sense of group identification.

While this sense of community and identification may have been easier for those whose appearance conformed to the standards of the conventional physique model, it was by no means limited to them. A *Physique Pictorial* reader from Philadelphia confessed that he was sickly and therefore would never have a defined physique. Nevertheless, he reveled in the vision of health, happiness, and camaraderie he found in Mizer's magazine. "Whenever I get the latest issue of *Physique Pictorial* it's like having a wonderful friend visit me—even better, it's like a group of friends. I sense a generous warmth and good feeling."[35] Glenn Carrington, an African American social worker and a graduate of Howard University, lived in Harlem and socialized with a group of self-described "weightlifting" friends; they attended bodybuilding contests, subscribed to physique magazines, and took pictures of one another in physique-inspired poses, suggesting a sense of identification with the mostly white models.[36] Michael Denneny knew that the world of the poised, muscled models was worlds away from the working-class homes and dirt yards of Pawtucket, Rhode Island, yet he remained "riveted" by them (see fig. o.6).[37]

Despite a relative climate of friendship and inclusion, exclusions persisted. The Grecian Guild, founded by two men from the rural South, was perhaps the most racially exclusive. Bob Mizer, famous for featuring blonde Californians, can also be criticized for fostering Jim Crow as he literally segregated his black models into an "All Negroe Album." And yet the very first issue of Mizer's magazine featured black models, and his editorials highlighted parallels between police harassment of physique photographers (for obscenity) and people of color (for anything). Mizer expressed opposition to capital punishment because he saw how it fell disproportionately on the poor and racial minorities, highlighting the case of Jess Neal, a black youth in Utah shot by a firing squad for a murder conviction that was the result of perjured police

FIGURE 0.6 Glenn Carrington's photograph of a circle of "weightlifting friends" in Harlem suggests that although most physique models were white, their admirers were more racially diverse.

Courtesy of the Schomburg Center for Research in Black Culture, New York Public Library.

testimony.[38] He also featured racially mixed models, arguing that the strength of America was in its mixing of races and cultures.[39]

The real culprits in physique racial exclusion appear to have been the customers. Physique publishers, nearly all white, universally complained that images of African American men didn't sell in 1950s and 1960s America. Given the state of segregation throughout the United States in this period—both de jure and de facto—and the absence of such images in mainstream media sources, this is not a surprise. So what is more remarkable than their purported exclusion is their inclusion, despite the financial disadvantage. As Dave Martin said about his welcoming of African Americans into his photography studio, "It certainly wasn't for the money. The pictures didn't sell—no one wanted them. I wouldn't even list them in catalogs. I took them to please myself, for the sheer beauty of the male body."[40] Indeed, the same pressures of capitalism that facilitated community formation also limited participation in it.

As a mail-order based medium, physique magazines represented a more integrated setting than many gay bars at the time. Unlike much of America in the 1950s and 1960s, the U.S. mail was not segregated. Some men of color wrote in to complain of the lack of models of color, but this also suggests that they were already regular customers. "I have just been introduced to your magazine and

I plan to become a regular subscriber, as I enjoy it very much," enthused a reader of *Grecian Guild Pictorial* from Harlem. Perhaps the most racially inclusive physique studio was Kris of Chicago, comanaged by Domingo Orejudos, a Chicagoan of mixed Italian and Philippine heritage. Kris featured a number of models of color, including Johnny Menendez, Joe Harris, Tom Cowans, and Jay Young.[41]

The mails served as an important conduit for communication between physique publishers and their customers—in both directions. We know that readers wrote thousands of letters to their favorite magazines, physique artists, photographers, and models.[42] One minister placed a notice in an unnamed physical culture magazine offering counseling and claimed he received letters from one thousand "avowed homosexuals . . . some even sent pictures in various stages of undress."[43] Though nearly all such correspondence has been lost to history, one of the few batches of letters that has survived—from Thor Studios in Chicago—demonstrates a keen desire on the part of gay men to use these commercial studios to make connections with others like themselves.

Thor Studios sold drawings of muscular lifeguards, workmen, and motorcyclists—usually in pairs or groups, engaged in highly suggestive play. Drawn by a variety of artists, including writer and tattoo artist Samuel Steward, they appeared under the penname "Thor," in publications such as *Tomorrow's Man* and *Der Kreis*. Though exhibiting less talent, they included the sort of highly charged homoerotic settings made famous by the better-known work of Quaintance, Etienne, and Tom of Finland.[44] Despite its relative obscurity, this one physique studio received over two hundred letters between 1953 and 1955 that have survived, thanks to Alfred Kinsey, who was in communication with many physique entrepreneurs and considered customer correspondence a window into their sex lives.

These Thor customer letters reveal that while some customers seemed to play the game and claim to be professional artists needing nude figure studies, most let Thor know of their (homo)sexual interests. Some liberally dropped the term "gay," still mostly an in-group code word; others expressed their admiration for "the Greeks" as well as the "baskets" in Thor's drawings; others simply described preferring men to women. At least one forthrightly wrote, "I am homosexual." They talked of sharing Thor's images with their "pals" and "lots of friends, and good friends, too" adding "do you get what I mean?" to underscore the sexual suggestion. "I intend to use these to liven up the party when I have a group of the boys in my set over for drinks," enthused a writer from

Washington, D.C. One writer claimed to be writing for a whole group of friends in Roseburg, Oregon, "a private art class made up of all male members." A writer from Canada more forthrightly ordered ten prints as "Secretary for our 'Homo-Club.'"

Correspondents often wanted to meet "Thor" when they visited Chicago, but they also wanted to exchange information about "the gay spots of the city." Many expressed frustration with the way the larger society, their families, or the Post Office impeded their desires. "My folks would disown me if they knew what I was after but nevertheless I want what I want," declared a defiant admirer from Millville, New Jersey, referring to his desire either for physique art, for other men, or both. A reader from Wausau, Wisconsin, had Thor's motorcycle series framed on his bedroom wall. They all wanted a more intimate connection to someone who shared their desires. As John Pazdernik from St. Louis wrote, "I feel sure that our friendship will be interesting and enjoyable to both of us. When I wrote the little letter with my order I was taking a stab in the dark as to your feelings, desires, etc. When I was looking at your catalog, I kind of had a hunch that from the way you sketched the imprint of the most beautiful part of the male body, I thought that you had a certain desire and liking for that part of the body for it was sketched too perfect."

Summarizing the sentiments of most of his fellow customers, Carlos Maña from Evanston, Illinois, wrote, "I feel that I know you through your drawings."[45]

Participants in this network joined a homoerotic fantasy world where their desires were normalized without being stigmatized or even labeled. While the magazines clearly served many who openly identified as gay, they also catered to fans who merely thought of themselves as fellow "physique enthusiasts" misunderstood by their families and mainstream society. Wendell from a farm in rural Illinois wrote, "I have to live with my family, and none of them understand my desire for physique photos. . . . Everyone in this community would consider my interest as utterly crazy."[46] Physique photography allowed them to express their interest in other men's bodies and feel that others shared the same excitement. It promoted a collective identity among people who may not have considered themselves gay even if, or because, that collective identity did not carry a label.

For some customers, physique magazines provided a gateway into gay culture, particularly as censorship victories were achieved and they began including more information about that culture, such as book reviews and travel tips. And the lives of the models depicted in the magazines often mirrored that movement into the gay world. John Kehr first wrote from his farm in Oxford, Ohio, in 1956 to *Tomorrow's Man*, which featured his image along with those of other readers. A year later he was named Grecian of the Month. "John is no muscle-bound musclehead; he is, instead, a successful young businessman," *Grecian Guild Pictorial* noted, providing readers with his R.F.D. address in Ohio. The next year he was featured in a John Palatinus mailer as "a popular" New York model who lived alone in Greenwich Village, frequented the theater, and cavorted on the dunes at Jones Beach. Even if partly fictional, this and many similar profiles suggested to thousands of readers a fantasy entry narrative into an urban gay world.[47]

Beyond the images and the merchandise, what the publishers were really providing their customers was contact, both real and imagined, with other customers. In postwar America, physique magazines used the U.S. mail and neighborhood newsstands to provide an analog version of what today we call social media. Like Facebook, physique publishers offered an interactive space where customers could publish letters, enter contests, and submit photographs. Like Google, they provided business directories so customers could find photograph studios, book services, and gay bars. Like Grindr, they eventually developed pen-pal clubs to allow customers to interact directly. As with all social media companies, their customer lists were their most valuable commodity; and as those lists grew, they sold that information to other businesses, widening the network (see fig. 0.7).[48]

The one group almost entirely excluded from the physique world were women. Women participated in this world of gay consumer culture only through the many mail-order book services, including the Daughters of Bilitis's own specialty book service. Indeed the physique world was in some ways predicated on the absence of women, which is how it constituted itself as a homoerotic space. Mainstream fitness magazines began to feature women only as a way to differentiate themselves from their queer counterparts. Lesbian media companies and publishing houses developed much later than those of gay men and were often rooted in 1970s feminist and gay liberation political activism.[49] Rather than being centered on images, some of the first national lesbian businesses grew up around music production. Olivia Records, founded in 1973 as the first woman-centered recording company, was organized as a nonhierarchical collective where workers were paid according to need. It would later expand to offer concerts and lesbian cruises and vacation packages to create safe space for lesbian culture to flourish.[50]

NEARLY EVERYBODY READS...

FIGURE 0.7 This anonymous drawing, for sale through mail order, acknowledges how physique magazines created an "imagined community" of readers who enjoyed viewing the male body.

Courtesy of the Gay, Lesbian, Bisexual, Transgender Historical Society.

Although lesbians certainly took and shared erotic photographs of each other, such practices do not seem to have been as central to lesbian culture as they were to gay male culture. There is little history of lesbian erotica being mass-produced or marketed until the age of desktop publishing in 1984, when *Bad Attitude* and *On Our Backs* appeared on newsstands.[51] As women, lesbians generally experienced lower earning power than gay men, making the creation of a lesbian market a later development. This chronology, resulting in the relative dominance of gay male consumer culture in the early formation of a gay community, provides a potential answer to why the movement, from its inception, was dominated by white men. It may help explain why gay white men perceived that they constituted the movement, since they had created the market on which it depended. As Alexandra Chasin has argued, "The capitalist market makes possible, but also constrains, social movements."[52]

THE PHYSIQUE ERA

Buying Gay tells the story of the rise and decline of physique magazines, a period from 1951 to 1967 that I label the physique era. It looks at the men behind the magazines, cameras, and mail-order catalogs and examines how their businesses functioned, why some became successful while others fell by the wayside, and why it took over fifteen years before they won their First Amendment rights.

It is the story of two southern gentlemen who met at the University of Virginia in 1947 and started not only a lifelong relationship but also a physique photography studio and magazine that popularized the notion of a homoerotic Greek past. It is the story of a New York advertising executive who pioneered the notion of niche marketing of gay books in the 1950s. It is the story of Elsie Carlton, a straight woman who ran one of the nation's first gay mail-order book clubs. It is the story of Postmaster General Arthur Summerfield, who had members of the first gay pen-pal service arrested and sent its founders to prison. It is the story of two gay men from the Dakotas who started a mail-order company in the early 1960s that became the gay Sears Roebuck catalog, offering magazines, books, bar guides, records, clothing, and a pen-pal service to gay men throughout the country. And it is the story of Lynn Womack, who consolidated the field into a physique publishing empire—including his own distribution network, printing plant, and legal library—allowing him to win a landmark First Amendment victory at the U.S. Supreme Court, paving the way for a vibrant gay print and commercial world that could help sustain a movement.

1

EMERGING FROM THE MUSCLE MAGAZINES

Bob Mizer's Athletic Model Guild

There is a world-wide fraternity of men interested in [male] nudes, but
it is so loosely organized that one cannot easily find his way around it.
—Manuel boyFrank, 1944

WHEN TWENTY-FOUR-YEAR-OLD Bob Mizer began marketing
photographs of men in posing straps in 1946, he was already
on a crusade.

He was tired of police harassment in Pershing Square—a well-known meeting spot for gay men in downtown Los Angeles—where he socialized with
friends nearly every day during high school. They gossiped about their fellow
Pershing Square regulars—the effeminate belles, the butch trade, and some in
between. But in 1940 he wrote in his diary of a crackdown: "vice clean up is
tightening . . . Lillie is really serious about cleaning up the city," using a slang
term common in gay circles for the police.

He also made weekly visits to the nearby Los Angeles Central Library and
was tired of reading psychology books on the danger posed by "sexual variants"
such as himself and his friends. "Anything you could read anywhere showed
how pernicious a thing this was . . . [how] you would deteriorate into a mass of
trembling flesh if you did these things," he later complained.

He was also tired of arguing with his Mormon mother, who vociferously
objected to his transgender friend Rodney—later known as Daisy—who was
bullied at school for wearing pink girls' slacks and having plucked eyebrows.
Delia Mizer called Rodney a "pansy" and labeled his sexual proclivities "against
all the laws of nature." Her son responded angrily, using a very different

vocabulary, one that drew on notions of legal equality and civil rights: "Most people are just obeying their impulses," he retorted. "Should they be denied the right to fulfill their instincts?"

As a young man, Mizer had already identified the many ways society looked down on "temperamental people" like him and his circle of Pershing Square friends. More important, he was also clearly determined to do something about it—to confront the legal, medical, and religious prejudices that so viscerally affected his life.

One Sunday night in March 1940 he was on the telephone listening to Rodney describe his sexual exploits from the night before. Someone else on his party line was also listening in—a common occurrence at a time when only the rich had private telephone lines. Using vulgar language, the eavesdropper expressed his contempt for such people. Mizer had had enough. He channeled his anger into his diary that night: "My aim in life will be to create tolerance among mankind and especially to vindicate the decent, spiritual Urning," using a nineteenth-century term for men attracted to other men. He was beginning to articulate the sense of defiance that had been building up inside him. Soon his rudimentary efforts to create tolerance made it into print. "This week I made my column risqué," he noted of his writing in the Polytechnic High School newspaper. "All of my gay friends are included." Even as an eighteen-year-old high school student, Mizer demonstrated a willingness to defy convention and assert his desires. He had also developed the ability to publicly affirm his gay friends—if in a coded way that perhaps only they would understand.

Mizer's ambition was to be an author. He was not just a columnist but an editor of his high school's award-winning newspaper—considered one of the top ten in the country by the Columbia University School of Journalism. He had begun creative writing in grammar school and published several short stories. He was also a voracious reader, checking out popular psychology and sexology books like *Outwitting Our Nerves* and *Sexual Power* on his weekly runs to the Los Angeles Public Library. He so identified with Boris Barisol's biography of writer Oscar Wilde, subtitled *The Man, the Artist, the Martyr*, that he labeled his own 1940 diary "Bob Mizer: The Man, the Thinker, the ?" One of his teachers suggested that his skills at writing, shorthand, and typing would easily land him a steady job as a court reporter. But Mizer wanted to write his own book. He would call it "How You Can Help the Homosexualists" and would target younger gay men whose worldview had not yet formed.[1]

Although he never published such a book, writing would occupy much of his life, as he penned hundreds of feisty editorials denouncing censorship, puritanism, and prejudice for his magazine *Physique Pictorial*, which he published for over twenty years. Not unlike the book he hoped to write, *Physique Pictorial* offered help and comfort to tens of thousands of gay men in Cold War America. As the editor of the first large-circulation American magazine targeting gay men, Mizer found a way to help the community he had found at Pershing Square. In the pages of his path-breaking magazine, Mizer honed the skills he first tried out in his high school newspaper—thumbing his nose at the authorities while speaking up for his friends (see fig. 1.1).

In postwar America, a commercial network of gay physique photographers and magazine publishers emerged from the contests and magazines

FIGURE 1.1 Bob Mizer started his physique photography business in 1946 soon after he graduated from high school. A few years later he launched *Physique Pictorial*, the first magazine targeting a gay male audience.

Courtesy of the Bob Mizer Foundation.

surrounding the physical culture movement. Bob Mizer was neither the first nor the only gay man to capitalize on his community's interest in physique photography. But he became the center of a network that served to connect, inspire, and politicize that subculture. He drew on an older tradition of gay photographers marketing their products through an underground market or in the back pages of mainstream fitness magazines. But with the founding of *Physique Pictorial* in 1951, he opened this tradition to public scrutiny and a new level of visual and discursive engagement. He was joined by Irv Johnson, the owner of a gym in Chicago, who began publishing *Tomorrow's Man* in 1952, and by Randolph Benson and John Bullock, a gay couple who met at the University of Virginia, who began publishing *Grecian Guild Pictorial* in 1955. Together they created a new genre of small magazines that would help serve and unite gay men throughout the country.

The social world Mizer constructed with his gay high school friends at Pershing Square was central to his budding role as a pioneering gay entrepreneur. "The number of faggots cruising around here is legion," remembered the writer Hart Crane. But the number of available sexual partners was only part of the appeal. "Here are little fairies who can quote Rimbaud before they are eighteen," he observed, suggesting how the space also offered an education in gay cultural codes. It was through connections made there that Mizer not only discovered a sense of community and a sense of oppression but also learned about a central feature of gay male culture: photography of the nude male.[2]

While still in high school, Mizer went to a party at his friend Sydney Phillip's place, where three gay friends posed in the nude for "artistic studies" that the host photographed. "It was terribly cute to see them rush to hide in the bathroom whenever a knock was heard at the door," Mizer noted of the models' skittishness. Featured in one of the first entries in his 1940 diary, the night clearly made an impression. A few months later Mizer himself posed for another gay photographer and became "enthused about barbell exercising."[3]

Weightlifting led Mizer to another formative influence: *Strength & Health*, the preeminent physical culture magazine published by Bob Hoffman in York, Pennsylvania. Mizer began reading the magazine in high school when he started lifting weights—he purchased his barbells through its back pages. He enjoyed the bodybuilding photos and articles but was particularly intrigued by the monthly "S & H Leaguers' Page," a pen-pal service for those who wanted to exchange letters and photographs. Members often described their hobbies and interests, which included not only bodybuilding and physique photographs but often music, ballet, and theater. In April 1945 Mizer placed the following notice, hoping to connect with other leaguers; he included his home address, which would become the legendary home of his physique studio: "Bob Mizer, 1834 West 11th St., Los Angeles, Cal. is interested in photography and creative writing, and promises an immediate answer and exchange of photos to all who write. He uses a York barbell and other training appliances and hopes that we will allot more space to the league notes, as he enjoys reading this department and writing to other leaguers."[4]

The response was overwhelming—Mizer received over three hundred letters from fellow S & H Leaguers, some of whom remained lifelong friends. Others leaguers reported similar responses from their notices. One received such a flood of mail—but to the wrong address—that the Post Office requested he issue a correction immediately. Mizer later praised this service for allowing "lonely bodybuilders and others" not only to correspond but also to form "long-lasting and fruitful" friendships. His positive experience with the S & H Leaguers' Page offered a pivotal lesson, demonstrating to Mizer the desire of men who enjoyed physique photography to connect with each other.[5]

After high school graduation he worked as an office clerk and typist for the Texas & Fort Worth Railroad, but in his spare time he also began to help out at various Los Angeles photography studios, learning how to pose models, position lighting, and develop film. In the summer of 1945, during the final days of World War II, Mizer was full of excitement as he made plans over the establishment of what he was already calling "my business." He was honing his craft by apprenticing at Frederick Kovert's Hollywood studio. "I am helping him in my spare time in order to decide whether or not to come into the studio to work." Kovert was a former silent movie actor who had become one of the more daring and well-known photographers of nude men. Mizer was one of numerous young men working for Kovert, doing much of the photography that bore his name. Mizer often brought models there, used his darkroom, and even posed himself. He could do none of this at home, since his mother, who ran a rooming house, did not approve of his interest in photographing nearly naked men. Still, he found Kovert to be controlling and difficult to work with.[6]

Soon he bought his own camera and started to frequent Muscle Beach and bodybuilding competitions to find models. Muscle Beach in Santa Monica— not far from the home he shared with his mother near downtown Los Angeles— was the center of the postwar interest in bodybuilding and beefcake. It was the perfect place to meet bodybuilders who were anxious to be photographed.

"I modeled for Bob Mizer in 1947, '48," Ben Sorensen remembered. "Bob came down to Muscle Beach and just talked to people, you know? He invites us up. Of course everybody's interested, when they're bodybuilding, in getting some free pictures." It was Bob McCune, another bodybuilding champion Mizer photographed, who convinced Mizer to submit his photos to *Strength & Health*. Editor John Grimek, himself a well-known bodybuilding champion, encouraged Mizer to submit more work. "Yours are as good as others," Grimek told the budding photographer when they met at one of the bodybuilding competitions in Los Angeles.[7]

Mizer called his business the Athletic Model Guild (AMG) and offered his first advertisements in *Strength & Health* in 1946, where they competed for attention with similar advertisements from other gay photographers, such as Alfonso Hanagan, know as "Lon of New York." Hanagan had first become interested in physique photography when he became enthralled with images of bodybuilder Tony Sansone, who marketed his own photographs. After moving to New York in 1936 to pursue a career in music, he met Sansone and began to socialize with and photograph him and his friends. By the 1940s his physique photographs were being featured on the cover of *Strength & Health* and bodybuilders began seeking him out, hoping to appear on a magazine cover. As payment, the magazine gave him free ad space in the back of the magazine. It was this mutually profitable world of photographers, bodybuilders, and magazine publishers that Mizer would enter, then help to transform.[8]

When Mizer began marketing physique photography to a gay audience, he joined a field with deep roots in gay culture. The taking, sharing, and selling of such images had been central to gay culture for well over a half century by the time Mizer discovered it. Wilhelm von Gloeden began selling photographs of nude young men he posed in classical staging in Taormina, Sicily, in the 1890s. He developed a large following in cosmopolitan circles, especially among cultivated gay men. Some of his more restrained images appeared in European journals that were popular within the Aesthetic movement, while his nudes circulated through an underground market. Oscar Wilde and other gay notables made pilgrimages to his studio.[9]

In addition to such high art, images of nearly nude men circulated in the context of the physical culture movement, starting with images of Eugene Sandow in the 1890s. By the 1920s nude photos were widely marketed in the back of both art and physical culture magazines. Physical culturist John Hernic offered nude photos in the back of *Art Magazine* in the 1920s and *Strength &*

Health in the 1930s. "These photos will be a source of inspiration to you in your training for a well developed body," Hernic's ad promised, providing a small image of a muscled and oiled young man with a prominent posing strap—a pouch hanging off a string that covered only the genitals, the most revealing item of clothing a model could wear.

Collector Robert Mainardi identifies Hernic as a "mail-order pioneer," but his Apollo Art Studios was soon joined by others. To earn a living during the Depression, brothers Fred and William Ritter photographed themselves and their fellow physical culturists who trained at a New York City YMCA. They developed their own photos and sold high-quality images for $1 apiece. Film historian Thomas Waugh labels them "the first gay generation of physique photographers."[10]

Nude figure studies were only one of the many items available for sale in the back pages of these magazines. There were advertisements for barbells, food supplements, clothing, figure studies, and more. Indeed, most magazines were simply vehicles to sell products. Bob Hoffman founded the York Barbell Company a year before he founded his magazine *Strength & Health* and admitted the periodical was really a means to sell equipment. Both Hoffman and his main competitor Joe Weider distributed their fitness magazines at a loss, seeing them as a way to sell more barbells. Some of the first famous body-builders were similarly engaged in marketing products. Eugene Sandow—considered the world's most perfect man—performed on the vaudeville circuit, published books on physical culture techniques, and marketed postcards of his own image. As much a brand name as a bodybuilder, Sandow opened a chain of vegetarian restaurants, sanatoriums, and hotels that by the 1920s made him a millionaire. Bodybuilding promoter Bernarr Macfadden also constructed a commercial empire around the sport that included health retreats, restaurants, beauty contests, book sales, lectures, and mail-order fitness courses. Right from the start, bodybuilding was a lucrative business, the centerpiece of a network of consumer items.[11]

A legend has developed that Mizer's first business plan was to serve as a referral service between models and the studios that required their services. According to this legend, the talent agency model failed, but Mizer discovered, as if by accident, that the photographs were more lucrative than the modeling connections. This unsubstantiated story implies that his idea of marketing photos to gay men was *sui generis*. It cuts Mizer off from the long tradition of gay men taking, exchanging, and purchasing such photographs, beginning in the late nineteenth century. One of the sources of the legend was Wayne Stanley, a Mizer protégé who inherited Mizer's business and who self-servingly asserted that AMG was "the first photographic studio of the young male physique," ignoring Von Gloeden, Hernic, the Ritter Brothers, Lon of New York, Kovert, and many others. Mizer's diaries suggest that photography was key from the beginning and that he considered himself to be part of a field of physique photographers from at least 1946. While a pioneer in many ways, Mizer did not create the genre.[12]

Although the selling of physique-type photographs was not new, in the post–World War II era such imagery was becoming a much more visible component of American culture. Men had only recently started appearing shirtless in public. While European men had begun going topless on beaches soon after World War I, one-piece men's bathing suits emerged in the United States only in the 1930s. Some called them "Depression suits," suggesting that the shirt disappeared owing to lack of funds. As more and more proud male bathers defied convention by exposing their chests, the media began to talk of a "no shirt movement." Some beach communities such as Atlantic City, New Jersey, pushed back and banned topless male bathing. Responding to the changing beach regulations, clothing manufacturers offered detachable tops for their swimsuits. Representing the shifting cultural sands, their advertisements often featured one shirtless male and another with trunks and a tank top. According to David Chapman, by 1937 the controversy was settled, as most of the nation's beaches allowed men to appear shirtless.[13]

World War II brought images of shirtless sailors and soldiers into American homes and theaters. In covering the war, New York magazines and Hollywood films soon reflected the trend toward displays of the male chest. A cover of *Look* magazine in 1942 featured a shirtless image of Muscle Beach denizen John Kornoff, the U.S. Army's first physical trainer. Cannon Towel advertisements in *Life* featured soldiers bathing in the South Pacific wearing nothing but one of its products. Within a year of the war's end, as Mizer started marketing his photo albums, Sidney Skolsky, sitting across town in Swab's drugstore writing his nationally syndicated gossip column, coined "beefcake" to refer to Hollywood's liberal use of Guy Madison's physique. Madison had been discovered by gay Hollywood agent Henry Willson, who also named and popularized gay actors Tab Hunter and Rock Hudson. Skolsky dubbed the bevy of male actors posing in bathing suits a "beefcake brigade," and this new term for displays of young, pulchritudinous male flesh took hold. Willson was a frequent client of physique photographer Lon of New York but was now bringing that same look to Hollywood. So the popularization of "beefcake" imagery and terminology, from their very origins, had a gay inflection.[14]

But if male torsos could increasingly be seen on American beaches and in popular periodicals after World War II, they were still considered taboo in town. Men would continue to be subject to arrest for appearing shirtless on many city streets and in parks into the early 1960s. They were particularly vulnerable to such arrest if they did so in a known gay cruising area, reflecting the tensions in American culture over male nudity and its homoerotic implications. A seventeen-year-old Harvey Milk remembered being charged with indecent exposure in the summer of 1947 for baring his chest in a secluded gay cruising area of Central Park, even as men with families did exactly the same on the more public grassy lawns. Being grouped among "the men without their shirts" was one of Milk's first visceral experiences of antigay oppression.[15]

As interest in the male physique increased during the postwar period, Mizer's *Physique Pictorial* would catch the beginnings of a cultural wave. Yet he would also feel the wrath of law enforcement that tried to shut his business down, even before it was formally on its feet. He and his magazine would be caught up in legal disputes over the sexual meaning of such displays of male flesh. For the next two decades, Mizer would place himself at the center of this battle.

POSTAL INSPECTOR VISIT

On July 23, 1945, Mizer had his first of many encounters with federal law enforcement authorities. After leaving work as usual at the Texas & Fort Worth Railroad and bicycling by the library on Pershing Square to exchange some books, Mizer arrived home to find postal inspectors waiting for him. They searched his room, found "dirty pictures," and took him to their offices for questioning. Mizer somehow escaped arrest, but a few months later Kovert's studio was also raided, resulting in headlines in the *Los Angeles Examiner*. Intimately involved in the resulting legal drama, Mizer attended court with Kovert, who pleaded guilty to possession of obscene materials, and drafted a letter for Kovert's customers seeking their support. Not even the intimidating tactics of the Post Office and the court system seem to have deterred the twenty-three-year-old Mizer. "Spent evening on [Athletic Model] Guild calls and letters," he wrote in his diary, just two days after being what he described as "probed" by postal inspectors. Rather than serve as a deterrent, Mizer's encounter with federal postal authorities seemed to increase his resolve and suggests how his struggle with the forces of censorship formed a central component of his business. Mizer would face arrest again in 1947 and 1954 in connection with his business, each encounter with the authorities sharpening his sense of outrage.[16]

Mizer began his business in 1946 by producing and distributing mimeographed "albums" to sell his beefcake photographs, copying the standard operating procedure followed by Kovert of Hollywood, Lon of New York, and many other such photographers.[17] He would send customers who responded to his advertisements in *Strength & Health* a one-page sample of photo albums, from which they could select the models and images they wanted to purchase. However, Mizer's early albums went beyond providing the necessary marketing information. Mizer peppered his albums with news and commentary on the physique world—biographies of models, bodybuilding contest results, and warnings about Post Office crackdowns. As with his earlier writings in high school and his later editorials in *Physique Pictorial*, Mizer constructed a narrative that drew customers and models into the same enlightened circle of upstanding physique enthusiasts and supporters of free speech, while casting public censors and moralists into the darkness.

Starting with Forrester Millard in 1946—the first featured model in his premier "Album A"—Mizer constructed a fantasy narrative about his models that encouraged a sense of identification between them and his target audience of middle-class gay men. At the same time, he cleaned up the description of his interactions to avoid any hint of illegality. Although Mizer would print on almost every mailing and magazine he produced that he neither took nor sold nude photographs, he took nudes of Millard and of most every subsequent model. A native of New Mexico, Millard was only sixteen at the time Mizer photographed him, though Mizer fudged his date of birth to make him seventeen.

Publicly, Mizer lauded Millard as the ideal model who had control of every muscle due to hours posing before a circle of mirrors. Privately, Mizer complained that Millard was narcissistic to the point of being "completely entranced with his own physical beauty." Vanity had led Millard to quit school and be supported by his mother and a girlfriend. "In the album bulletins I try to be truthful—but naturally I must show jurisprudence in what truth I tell," Mizer wrote a correspondent at the time. "I would doom a models popularity if I announced he was married with two kids. . . . Most of my models over 23 are married or are permanently shacking up with their common-law wives."

So the biography Mizer constructed for Millard centered on discipline, Horatio Alger upward mobility, and a hint of homosexual camaraderie. "Laughed at because he was skinny, Forrester rapidly developed a magnificently defined body which became the envy of his former tormentors," Mizer wrote. Mizer replaced mention of his real-life girlfriend with "training companion" John Miller, who had won top honors at a recent AAU contest. They posed for Mizer's first duos, a homoerotic format that set Mizer and other gay physique photographers apart from their mainstream colleagues. Dark-featured Millard and blonde Miller looked like the perfect gay couple. They hoped to open a gym together, Mizer told his clients suggestively. The image of Millard and Miller on a settee with overlapping arms, hands touching, appeared in *Strength & Health* and became a signature AMG photo. Millard was later called "almost the touchtone for AMG's fame" (see fig. 1.2).[18]

FIGURE 1.2 Forrester Millard and John Miller, *Physique Pictorial*, June 1954. Bob Mizer signaled that *Physique Pictorial* would offer something different by featuring images of two men in posing straps, their arms draped over one another.

Courtesy of the Bob Mizer Foundation.

To counter the perception of both gay men and bodybuilders as degenerates, Mizer's biographical notes gave his models middle-class respectability, highlighting not only their physical attributes but also their alleged intellectual and professional ambitions. Not only was model Johnny Murphy tops in the "muscle game," but his business courses at Woodbury College were preparing him to become a business executive. "In anything he does, he will not content himself with being just average—he must be the best," Mizer gushed.

From the feedback he received to his many customer questionnaires, Mizer had a keen sense of what his audience liked and the "psychological effect" of his photos. As he told a colleague, "A picture is rarely unpopular if the model looks directly into the lens (and hence seems to be looking at the person observing the picture) as naturally they feel identification with him." Not only in his lighting and posing but also in his editorial content, Mizer made sure that his largely middle-class audience could identify with the models he was offering them, assuring them that they were "from upper-level homes."[19]

While seeking to bond models and customers in a circle of mutual camaraderie and respectability—what he called "the few . . . who demand freedom of expression"—Mizer also used his albums to make a detailed and careful analysis of censorship efforts by people he derided as "philistines," "moralists," and "unaesthetic law enforcement officers."[20] Mizer had gotten nowhere in his attempts to reason with censorship authorities. He and his fellow Los Angeles area physique photographers petitioned the Post Office to allow the use of the mail for nude photography. Postal authorities responded that they were forced to forbid such mail by local civic organizations and church groups that feared such products would fall into the hands of children. Mizer offered a clever countersuggestion: photographers could send nude photographs care of the local postmaster in every city, where they could then be claimed by the recipient with proper proof of age. His proposal went unheeded.[21]

Mizer had been in business less than a year when he first arrested, but it was not for sending nudes through the mail. Mindful of postal inspectors, he had sold nudes only to walk-in customers at his studio near downtown Los Angeles—what amounted to just 10 percent of his business. But when one of those customers, thirty-six-year-old Mexican-born Texan Pasquel Barron, became embroiled in a Post Office obscenity investigation, he admitted to obtaining nudes from Mizer, and the Post Office quickly forwarded the information to the local district attorney. Mizer was arrested in 1947 for contributing to the delinquency of a minor, James Maynor, one of his first models, a seventeen-year-old. The district attorney uncovered a network of teenage body-builders centered on Muscle Beach, many of whom had been brought to Mizer's studio by William Petty, a physical education instructor employed by the city of Santa Monica to organize athletic activities and performances. Petty and another photographer were also arrested.[22]

Unable to afford an attorney, Mizer was convinced by a public defender to plead guilty to the misdemeanor charge—he admitted to photographing Maynor in the nude. But in his plea to avoid prison and receive probation, Mizer insisted that he operated a legitimate business. He stipulated that he had consulted with attorneys and obtained signed release statements from his models or their parents. To distinguish his from previous such enterprises that operated underground, Mizer granted the court access to his meticulous records concerning both customers and models. He freely admitted to being a homosexual and to "attend[ing] several meetings of other types of such individuals in Lafayette Park"—a possible reference to gay social or fraternal organizations. Friends and neighbors testified to his good conduct and character—they described him as a photographer and artist who never smoked, drank, or got entangled in the law. The district attorney countered that Mizer's business was "pandering only to the tastes of lustful homosexuals." Several of his models, including John Miller, featured in AMG's early advertisements, confessed to engaging in oral sex with Mizer.

In denying his request, the probation officer emphasized that Mizer showed no remorse for his activities and was an admitted homosexual. He labeled his business of photographing teenage boys in the nude "a vicious and deliberate crime." Mizer was sentenced to six months at a work farm in Saugus, California. As with his interrogation by postal inspectors in 1945, the time he spent in Saugus seemed to steel his will. He felt abused by a legal system that was persecuting him for his lack of shame in being gay and operating a business that catered to his fellow homosexuals. He would later caution his readers to remain silent if arrested and never admit to any guilt, lest they find themselves "railroaded to prison" like he felt he was. As he wrote to his mother from Saugus, "I feel more strength now than ever before, but this strength, this driving energy, shall be carefully bridled and directed with wisdom. . . . ambition is everything."[23]

Mizer's tone and focus on the forces of censorship turned darker after his 1947 arrest. By 1950 he reported on a "witch hunt" at Muscle Beach, where one Sunday all the photographers were arrested and further photography forbidden.

"Los Angeles and California is in a stage of sex hysteria," he warned, with the state legislature passing sex laws "which only stop short of outlawing the double bed."[24] He chastised "those too stupid and prurient-minded" to understand and appreciate the need for nude art. "These same philistines are mischievously at work to undermine other basic rights of the individual," he wrote. He recommended that readers join the American Civil Liberties Union (ACLU) or the American Sunbathing and Health Association, a nudist organization. "The only successful way to fight these frustrated reactionaries is through national organization." Fighting the forces of censorship through collective action was clearly on Mizer's mind.[25]

Mizer closely followed and reported on the legal struggles of other physique photographers, even though raising such issues threaten to scare away more timid customers. Whenever possible, he noted what he saw as rays of hope, such as a "progressive Federal Judge" in Chicago who ruled in 1947 that photographs of nude males by Al Urban were not obscene. He noted that most magazines and photographers "in the field" had almost always beaten their prosecutions, but "only at damaging expense." These small victories failed to establish a clear national legal precedent, nor did they silence the local churches, parent teacher organizations, and other "moralist groups" behind censorship efforts. Mizer quickly identified the pattern of obscenity prosecution that would continue for the next twenty years: censors won at the local or lower-level courts but then lost on appeal. Physique photographers would have to work together to establish a large war chest to fight the censors and establish a national precedent.[26]

PHYSIQUE PICTORIAL

So when Mizer began publishing *Physique Pictorial* in 1951, he envisioned it as a collective effort—a catalog of merchandise from a variety of gay photographers and other vendors facing exclusion from mainstream fitness magazines. The first few issues were "advertising booklets," offered to subscribers for free—a "gift" underwritten by participating businesses. Like the mainstream fitness magazines, Mizer figured that photograph sales would more than pay for the magazine, as barbell sales financed mainstream fitness magazines. He wanted to bring gay physique photographers into closer alliance and thereby more effectively fight the forces of censorship. First called *Physique Photo News*, it would take advertisements from the back of *Strength & Health* and give them a new, safer, and more prominent home of their own.[27]

Under pressure from postal authorities, mainstream fitness magazines were beginning to refuse ads for undraped nudes. Warning that "queers" had "obtained a particularly vicious hold on our bodybuilding game," *Iron Man* instituted a policy refusing ads with models wearing anything less than swim trunks and threatened even stricter rules in the future. *Strength & Health* had faced censorship efforts over a cover image that had been taken in the nude and later retouched with a posing strap. The managing editor of *Strength & Health* warned Mizer that his advertisement photos were becoming "less athletic and more risqué" and threatened to bar him from the magazine. While Mizer pledged to cooperate, he saw the writing on the wall. "We are anxious to get our own magazine strong enough that in a few years time we can thumb our noses at the physique magazines," he wrote to a trusted adviser.[28]

The first issue represented the combined effort of six physique photography studios, but most of the others soon opted out. "Bruce [Bellas] was so frightened that he decided not to be represented in the next issue," Mizer recalled. To avoid postal inspectors, Bellas preferred to travel from city to city selling his images in person to select clients. Russ Warner also demurred, having already been summoned to Washington for an arduous hearing before postal inspectors over his nude photos with inked-in pouches. "The only people who would want photos of men were gay people," the postal inspectors confided to him, and their threat to "get every one of them" left him skittish. Even Mizer feared repercussions since "it will look dangerously like an organization which might effectively resist the postal distaste for physique work." Postal authorities may not have viewed it as a threat, but such organizational power was clearly at the forefront of Mizer's thinking.[29]

Mizer's efforts at consolidation drew inspiration from the most prominent scholar and writer on the subject of sex in America. Like other early activists for gay rights, Mizer had read Alfred Kinsey's *Sexual Behavior in the Human Male* and considered it pivotal for his understanding of homosexuality as a naturally and frequently occurring variation of human activity. "Dr. Kinsey's first book was the most important one in my whole life," Mizer wrote to a colleague, "and for it I owe him a debt I could probably never repay."[30]

As an avid collector of materials to document American sexual culture, Kinsey became a regular Mizer customer, and the two quickly established an active correspondence that lasted nearly until Kinsey's death in 1956. On his many visits to Los Angeles, Kinsey met with Mizer and conducted sexual histories of his fellow physique photographers and models. Mizer even forwarded his frequent customer questionnaires to Kinsey for tabulation, thereby offering him indirect access to his customer base. In return, Kinsey offered strategic advice about how best to combat postal authorities.

Because of his own struggles with postal and customs authorities over shipments of erotic materials to his institute at Indiana University, Kinsey had developed relationships with prestigious law firms specializing in the First Amendment. It was he who suggested that physique publishers could win at the appellate level if they could find a way to sustain and finance their legal cases. "I have suggested before that all of you photographers should band together and employ the very best attorney that you can in the L.A. area to advise you and to handle individual cases," Kinsey wrote to Mizer in 1951, just as Mizer was establishing *Physique Pictorial*. Kinsey suggested that photographers of female nudes had tried to do this but never succeeded at forming a united group. While Mizer never formally organized his fellow physique photographers, he and his magazine served as a de facto central bureau of information, connecting customers, photographers, and publishers.[31]

Tapping into an underserved gay market, Mizer's business flourished. As Mizer later remembered, "there was not such a thing at the time as a magazine that showed a variety of young, youthful models—not supermen—which is what most people wanted." Through his customer questionnaires, Mizer knew what his clients wanted: less information on weightlifting and exercise and more models. One twenty-two-year-old customer from Winchester, Massachusetts, remarked how Mizer's models were becoming "more youthful, slimmer and more suggestively posed" and encouraged him to be upfront about it—not to "hide all this under the general category of art photography," a common claim of photographers offering undraped nudes. As he wrote to Mizer, "It appears to me that by the constant polls you all seem to be taking so that you may satisfy your customers, you are catering more and more to the homosexual trade." Models, too, knew what Mizer was up to. "I think Bob was, um, interested more in the gay magazines than the bodybuilding ones," remembered model Ben Sorensen. "I'm straight, but that didn't bother me at all. Everybody at the gym knew what they were doing with the photos."[32]

Within a year of establishing AMG, Mizer reported a gross monthly income of $700—annualized, this amounted to nearly three times the average family income of 1947. Mizer had hired his brother as a full-time employee and had nearly $2,000 in savings. His mailing list already contained customers from "practically every country in the world," according to the district attorney who prosecuted his case. "It grew like Topsy—a little bit each time," Mizer remembered.[33] He soon began offering a "Nickle Plan," similar to a monthly book club, where customers would regularly receive photographs from each new AMG album. Wishing to respond to the particular desires of his customers, he allowed them to specify what types of models and photographs they preferred *not* to receive: "models over or under ages, races, slender or very heavy weights, poses with girls, models in clothing or part clothing such as Levis, models in trunks, portraits." Mizer was already engaging in specialization, acknowledging the particular sexual desires, fetishes, and prejudices of his customers.[34]

Although *Physique Pictorial* could increasingly be found on select newsstands, Mizer's initial sense of it as a catalog of merchandise for subscribers endured. He recalled that although magazine wholesaler Lou Elson began to distribute it in New York after a year or two on the market, newsstand sales did not substantially increase total circulation. "Its circulation was horrible. It was very hard to get. Most newsstands didn't carry it," remembered Chuck Renslow, then a fellow physique photographer in Chicago. Mizer himself called his newsstand circulation "quiet select." Continually struggling to find a newsstand distribution network, he mostly sold *Physique Pictorial* by subscription. But he was proud of his independence—unwilling to bow and scrape to distributors or advertisers. In addition to working with a few wholesalers, Mizer sent copies himself to select newsstands. "Tell your dealer about this and give him our address," he suggested to readers, trying to get them actively involved in increasing circulation. When *Physique Pictorial* did manage to appear on newsstands, it sold out almost immediately.[35]

In 1963 AMG tried to diversify and modernize by offering a large-format, color magazine called *Young Adonis* to supplement the black-and-white *Physique Pictorial*. It was a sell-out wherever it was sold, but again Mizer had trouble getting it on newsstands. The distributor wrote Mizer a two-page letter describing the magazine's "sins." Although Mizer promised future issues would feature new offerings, including a fashion section handled by model Mark Nixon, it was the only issue Mizer offered.[36]

FROM GUILD TO NETWORK

Mizer's choice of the term "guild" to refer to his business started a trend among physique photography studios. Don Whitman founded the Western

Photography Guild in Colorado in 1947 and soon had advertisements next to AMG's in the back of *Strength & Health*. In Metairie, Louisiana, a group of physique photographers and artists launched the Southern Guild. And in Portsmouth, Virginia, George U. Lyon and Charles E. Smith started Underwood Photographic Guild. The word "guild" could refer to any association of people with a common goal but historically referred to a group of craftsmen or merchants who exerted some control over their trade. As an avid reader, Mizer was probably well aware that medieval guilds were famous for regulating entry into a profession and often exerted considerable power in city government. His choice of words suggests his aspirations to unite, protect, and empower those involved in the physique field. It was the same term Harry Hay would use as he began organizing the Mattachine Society as a gay political group across town a few years later.[37]

In keeping with the spirit of a guild, Mizer cooperated with and promoted the work of other photographers. He would share or sell mailing lists to competitors and alert readers when new physique magazines were launched or studios opened. *"Physique Pictorial* is not a closed enterprise and any legitimate studio can be represented in it," he promised. By 1954 he regularly included a directory of photographers, artists, and models selling merchandise—a custom followed by many later physique magazines. He was happy to note when individual models offered their own photos directly to readers. When he had a disagreement with a physique artist, he let readers know that the artist's work could now be found in a competing magazine.[38]

As the number of physique studios catering to gay men proliferated, Mizer's magazine functioned like a Better Business Bureau. Mizer barred advertisements from studios who were known to be unreliable, gave bad service, or sold illegal material (although he included photos with "inked" pouches, indicating the original photograph was in the nude.) He threatened to publicly denounce photographers who were territorial and unwelcoming to new talent in their area, and he was quick to publicly reprimand photographers who did not reciprocate his courtesies.[39] Mizer also warned readers of offers from the "get-rich-quick boys" promising special pictures available only to a few "intimate friends." Given the Post Office's vigilance, he knew that studios selling nudes would not last long. "Every mailing list is peppered with postal inspectors and their collaborators," he cautioned. After sending in an exorbitant fee, the customer might receive nothing. He encouraged readers to confess their stories of being victimized by such schemes.[40]

Envisioning a constantly widening network of producers and consumers, Mizer sought to place himself at its fulcrum. Soon he was offering a host of consumer items—artwork, slides, viewers, and "garments for athletes" including jeans, T-shirts, bathing suits, and the ubiquitous posing straps. *Physique Pictorial* functioned as a nexus for finding, producing, selling, and admiring male photos. Other studios described AMG as a one-stop shopping experience: "one of the largest photo guilds in the country and supplies about everything a photo collector or bodybuilder wants: movies, garments, thousands of all sizes of photos, color slides, and many other works of art." The network grew increasingly international as Mizer featured photographs by Arax of Paris and models wearing trunks from Vince of London. He soon had agents in Belgium, France, Denmark, the United Kingdom, and Japan. By 1962 Mizer sponsored European tours for physique enthusiasts, "to photograph local athletes, and to visit famous clubs of special interest."[41]

Mizer encouraged not only other physique photographers but a new and growing group of physique artists in his magazine. AMG became a generative center that showcased the work of talented young painters and sketch artists who then developed their own followings that often eclipsed Mizer's own popularity.[42] In 1957 he introduced an unknown artist who "depicts the healthy robust youth of the forests of Finland," who would later reach international renown as "Tom of Finland." But it was an artist from Virginia, George Quaintance, who created what Mizer called a "vogue" that was widely imitated.[43]

Quaintance had begun taking photographs and drawing sketches of male nudes under the tutelage of Lon of New York. He had worked drawing bodybuilding champions for the cover of Joe Weider's *Your Physique*, but it was when he started painting for Bob Mizer's new magazine that his career took off. Set either at a dude ranch in Arizona, where he lived, or at a bath in ancient Greece, Quaintance's paintings created the kind of playful environment of easy male camaraderie that Mizer sought to foster through his magazine. And like Mizer, Quaintance considered his homoerotic artwork to be "a crusade for the rights of the feelings" of his customers. "I too feel that I crusade in my attempt to supply, or satisfy, a deep emotional hunger in the inner lives of my customers," he explained to a homophile leader. Soon his mailing list of ten thousand active buyers around the world surpassed that of Mizer. He offered not only physique paintings but prints, photographs, and sculptures, expanding his business to a four-man operation. "It grew too fast. . . . I'm trying to adjust myself to all the confusion," he wrote at the time. Those who met him as he toured the country selling his artwork describe a flamboyant artist who loved wearing western gear, turquoise jewelry, and showing off his young Mexican American lover and frequent model, Eduardo.[44]

What distinguished Quaintance's artwork was not just the invitation to view nearly naked men but the excitement of seeing them looking at each other, as Michael Bronski has argued. One of Quaintance's first cover images for *Physique Pictorial* demonstrates how groundbreaking those gazes were. "Morning in the Desert" featured four ranch hands around an outdoor bath dressing and preparing for work. One naked bather is standing, his genitals covered only by soapsuds. Another naked man lies below him in a tub of water, looking directly up at the other's body. But for the cover of the magazine, to pass postal censors, Quaintance shifted the man's head to the left, so his gaze no longer fell longingly on his fellow naked male bather. Like his better-known successor, Tom of Finland, Quaintance constructed a "network of looks" that included and invited those of the viewer, furthering the sense of homoerotic identification.[45]

Mizer's growing network of photographers, artists, and other physique-related businesses used a language of friendship and camaraderie that further encouraged a sense of community. Seattle physique artist William MacLean set up a studio and invited new and emerging physique artists to market their work through him. This offer featured a photograph of the very handsome artist hanging images in his exhibit space, noting suggestively that he was "a very eligible bachelor" and therefore "his studio is a gathering place for the young social set and many a party is hosted there."[46] London model Clive Jones sold his images directly and promised to handle orders personally. "Clive would like to hear from his many friends in America" and promised to send a catalog of images of himself and his "buddies" in London.

Mizer offered slides of physique models intended to be projected on a wall or screen for group viewing. One of MacLean's more reproduced drawings showed a group of men admiring AMG slides and imitating the poses of the models. When Mizer began making physique film shorts, he called for readers to submit script ideas, giving members yet another way to participate. He offered suggestions on where to buy a good, inexpensive projector and soon began renting the films at a quarter of the price of purchasing one. In words and images, he encouraged readers to share the experience of watching physique films. "Imagine what a hit these films would be at your next party or gathering of friends who are physical culture enthusiasts!" Indeed, much of the allure of participating in this network, whether as a producer or as a consumer, was the sense of community it offered (see fig. 1.3).[47]

Mizer's own rhetoric helped to solidify that sense of community. Boasting that his magazine lacked "mass appeal," he explicitly signaled his targeting of a minority population, what he called "the limited aesthetic group" who appreciated the male body. Mizer was borrowing a gay discourse developed in the late nineteenth century, a period he knew well from his reading of Boris Brasol's biography of Oscar Wilde. As art historian Christopher Reed argues, "The Wilde trials seemed to reveal homosexuality as the secret behind the enigmatic passions of the Aesthetes, tainting the entire movement, all of its products, and even the idea of aesthetic sensitivity."[48]

Indeed, the modern identities of "the homosexual" and "the artist"—both considered manifestations of innate predispositions—developed nearly

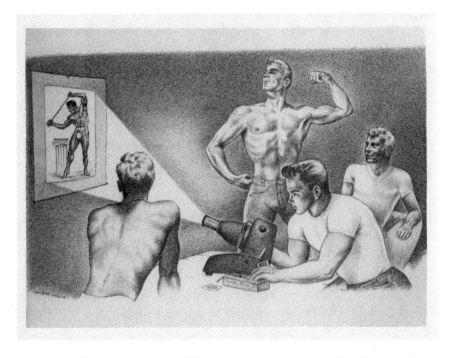

FIGURE 1.3 *Home Show* (1957) by William M. MacLean Studios of Seattle, one of many physique art studios marketing artwork to gay men. Showing a group of young men enjoying Bob Mizer's slides and identifying with the models, the drawing illustrates the social networks that formed around physique images.

Courtesy of Rare and Manuscript Collections, Cornell University Library, George Fisher Papers #7437.

simultaneously in the nineteenth century, as both creating art and committing sodomy moved from activities to ways of being. "Artistic" quickly became euphemistic slang for "queer." Painter Paul Cadmus remembered how the association had transferred to the American scene by the 1930s. "The word homosexual was never used," he remembered. "They just said, 'He's an artist.'" American psychiatrists, too, described men suspected of homosexuality as "aesthetic in temperament." Thus when Mizer adopted this language, praising Quaintance for his "neo-aestheticism" and imagining his audience as "the limited aesthetic group," he was signaling to and helping to construct a distinct gay identity among his readers.[49]

"THE TV SHOW THAT MADE AMERICA GASP!"

Physique Pictorial's increasing circulation came with its own risks. Its presence on Los Angeles newsstands soon caught the attention of Paul Coates, a conservative columnist for the afternoon tabloid the *Los Angeles Mirror,* known for exposing what he considered to be the seamier side of life in Southern California—prostitutes, repo men, drug addicts, and shoplifters. In 1954 Coates used his local television program *Confidential File* on KTTV to alert his audience to the "unpleasant fact" of homosexuality in Los Angeles. It was the first prime-time television program to broach the topic and helped propel Coates's show into national syndication. Coates featured footage of a Mattachine Society meeting with well-dressed men and women drinking coffee and eating cookies. He also gave his audience a glimpse inside a gay bar. But he ended the show by holding up a copy of *Physique Pictorial* as a shocking example on city newsstands of the publications catering to homosexuals. According to one tabloid, it was "the TV show that made America gasp!"[50]

Working closely with the local Parent Teacher Association (PTA), Coates couched his programming as a crusade to warn families of the dangers homosexuals posed to children. He followed up with three newspaper columns devoted exclusively to the presence of gay magazines on the city's newsstands. Although concerned about the homophile magazine *ONE,* which billed itself as "The Homosexual Magazine," he noted that its editors at least made an effort to avoid the lurid. *Physique Pictorial,* however, was "thinly veiled pornography" that appealed to sex criminals and sadists. Coates claimed that this "*Esquire* for men who wish they weren't" featured images of men in chains being beaten and stabbed—a sensational reading of Mizer's photographs with swords and chains as props. He highlighted the case of one of Mizer's teenage models from Muscle Beach—an active church member engaged to be married, he noted—who complained of unwanted homosexual solicitations after his photo appeared in *Physique Pictorial*. There were dozens of such dangerous photographers, Coates warned. "It's big business in our town."[51]

Leveraging his connections to the powerful Chandler media family, Coates orchestrated an all-out assault on Mizer's business. After Coates's columns appeared, a phalanx of local government officials descended on Mizer's business. Police began to intimidate newsstands where his magazine appeared. City regulators inspected his home, and health officials tested his pet monkeys for diseases. The former model featured in Coates's column sued Mizer for invasion of privacy.

Most ominously, the story brought a plainclothes Los Angeles Police Department vice officer to his door asking to buy nudes. Mizer demurred, offering him only his usual catalogs of men in posing straps. Undeterred, Detective Philip Barnes asked who of the many other photographers featured in his magazine might offer nudes. Mizer again demurred, but Barnes had already visited the studio of Lyle Frisby, a young, up-and-coming Mizer protégé whose images Mizer often included in his magazine. More accommodating, Frisby sold him "inked" nude photos, where the posing straps could be easily rubbed off.

Coates proudly covered the sting operation in a subsequent column. To again sensationalize the threat posed to children, he noted ominously that Frisby's Los Angeles studio was located just 250 yards from an elementary school. Both Frisby and Mizer were promptly arrested for possessing and distributing lewd photographs—a violation of the Los Angeles municipal code—allowing Coates's newspaper series to end on a note of civic triumph.[52]

Frisby was easily convicted and spent time in prison. The prosecution of Mizer, however, was more complicated, since the focus of the charge was "aiding and abetting" the sale of lewd pictures. Detective Barnes testified that Mizer told him he could obtain nudes from any of his advertisers, but he failed to note this in his initial report. Mizer denied the claim, testifying that he told detective Barnes that nudes were illegal and unavailable in Los Angeles and that he personally advised all photographers not to deal in nudes. Either way, there was little evidence to link Mizer directly with Frisby's nude photos. Seeing the weakness of the "aiding and abetting" argument, the prosecutor argued that Mizer's own photos were obscene because they displayed both "scenes of brutality and torture" and "the uncovered rump." Mizer's lawyer, Herbert Selwyn from the ACLU, argued that Mizer's posing-strap images were no more lewd than those in classical statuary or in movies such as *Garden of Eden*, a film set in a nudist colony then screening in area theaters. He called it "the first uncovered rump case" in memory.

But as in almost all trials of physique photographers, the real issue was less the explicitness of the photos than the sexual orientation of their audience. Displaying his real concern, the judge told Selwyn, "These are nothing but pin-up pictures for homosexuals." To feed the judge's suspicions, the prosecutor displayed a copy of *Confidential* magazine at trial with the blaring headline "America on Guard! Homosexuals, Inc." Trying to further associate Mizer with the homosexual cause, he concluded his cross-examination by asking, "Do you also publish the magazine known as *ONE*?" The judge sustained Selwyn's objection but enjoyed a "hearty chuckle." He found Mizer guilty and sentenced him to ninety days in prison.[53]

Mizer appealed his conviction, telling Kinsey he was willing to put a substantial dent in his bank account and solicit help from nudist and other groups. He convinced a British magazine to publicize the case. "It is odd that when I am one of the few physique photographers who does not deal in nudes that I should be picked out as the one who must fight for their legality," he complained to Kinsey, who thought he was singled out because of the size of his business. Mizer was the aggressive entrepreneur who took the physique business from the back pages of fitness magazines to the cover of his own magazine, openly challenging postal inspectors. Predictably, Mizer's conviction was overturned on appeal. "You have done very well to stand up for your legal rights," Kinsey congratulated him. But Mizer, concerned about the effect such news might have on the field of physique photography, did not gloat. "I am keeping news of our victory quiet because I think some of the photographers in our field need a bit of a deterrent to keep them in line."[54]

Mizer and Barnes squared off again a year later, this time in a televised congressional hearing. Mizer and Frisby became fodder for Senator Estes Kefauver's traveling hearings on the alleged problem of juvenile delinquency in America, part of his bid to enhance his presidential aspirations. Kefauver got Benjamin Karpman, the chief psychotherapist at St. Elizabeths Hospital in Washington, D.C., to testify that exposure to pornography at an early age could turn someone gay. Barnes described how he had confiscated pornographic materials from major national distributors Edward Mishkin and Irving Klaw. Some of the material was on display in posters lining the walls of the hearing room.

"Have you had any occasion to investigate cases wherein the use of male models might be used?" Kefauver asked—a delicate way to invoke homosexual erotica. Barnes outlined the case of Frisby and Mizer, pointing out that Mizer happened to be in the audience. Exaggerating the success of his efforts, he claimed he had confiscated $10,000 worth of materials from Frisby, that both men had been convicted of obscenity, and that Mizer's sentence had been overturned only because of a technicality. He highlighted the danger they posed to the public by noting the proximity of the school and the youth of the models.

Kefauver commended Barnes's efforts and noted what a difficult job he had, given how the courts and the legislatures continually failed to provide the tools he needed. Barnes impressed on the committee the need for a national agency to coordinate the efforts of local law enforcement to stamp out pornography. At the conclusion of the hearing, Senator Kefauver offered anyone who had been named the opportunity to correct inaccuracies. Detective Barnes looked squarely at Mizer, egging him on. Mizer contemplated speaking up but, aware of the presence of journalists and television cameras, decided instead to offer a written statement, his preferred form of communication.[55]

In the pages of *Physique Pictorial*, Mizer denounced the hearings as "the grossest obscenity of public trust" he had ever witnessed. He accused Barnes of perjuring himself in his claims about Mizer's case. Within a year, however, Mizer enjoyed some *schadenfreude* when he revealed that Barnes was sent to prison for molesting his stepdaughter. He was also delighted to tell readers that Kefauver's chief counsel, James Bobo, was forced to resign after admitting to hosting private screenings of stag films for a Memphis fraternity. It all reinforced Mizer's conviction that the legal system was corrupt and that those who were most obsessed with fighting prurience were hypocrites.[56]

Like many self-appointed guardians of American morality, Coates viewed both the Mattachine Society and the Athletic Model Guild as threats. But the reactions of the two organizations differed markedly. In 1953 Coates gave the Mattachine Society its first negative press coverage by suggesting that it had ties to communism. Coates's accusation caused a crisis in the organization, which led to the resignation of the original founders, many of whom had been members of the Communist Party USA. The organization was restructured and membership fell off. Historian John D'Emilio called it a "retreat to respectability," a turn away from political activism toward internal self-help tactics.[57]

Coates's assault on Mizer was even more aggressive—involving the Los Angeles Police Department, a powerful U.S. senator, and backstage efforts to influence his obscenity trial—yet Mizer changed his operating procedures only slightly. He decided to tone down the "brutality" aspect of his images, eliminating props such as whips or chains. But on the issue of the "uncovered rump," Mizer stood his ground. "Bob has defied them," Kinsey noted of Mizer's refusal to succumb to a Post Office ultimatum barring nudes seen from behind. He also continued his feisty editorials, despite Kinsey's suggestion that he tone them down. "Certain principles I will not back down on," Mizer defiantly told Kinsey.[58]

Each of Mizer's encounters with law enforcement politicized him, and he, in turn, sought to politicize his readers. To supplement his personal experience, he read widely in popular and scholarly texts on censorship and sought to convey that knowledge to his readers. He noted that those who were opposed to physique magazines were organized into groups such as the National Organization for Decent Literature and had the ear of local and national politicians. He pointed out how local newspapers pressured newsstands and magazine distributors to discontinue all physique magazines. He urged readers to organize. When one reader suggested ignoring the censors, Mizer compared him to the Jews in Germany who "ignored the menace of Hitler."

Putting the issue in the context of human rights, Mizer called for a collective and activist opposition. "The censor is a bully and will back down if we all stand up to him." It was a theme he returned to frequently, asserting that putting one's head in the sand would not make the problem go away. He repeatedly implored customers to join the ACLU. "It's *Your* America," he reminded readers, and politicians and police were "your servants." He implored readers to write their representatives and local newspapers to defend freedom of expression. Otherwise, he warned, a state-controlled media will emerge that would be the envy of Hitler. According to his alarmist rhetoric, the ACLU was the only thing standing between the status quo and totalitarianism.

Mizer's editorials on censorship even seeped into model descriptions. He described Sonny Star, a lean model lounging by the pool, as being from Fargo, North Dakota, where a federal censorship trial was taking place. He railed against police corruption and governmental injustice so often that readers tired of his many editorials—one counted eight in a thirty-two-page

issue—and complained of all this "doomsday talk." Many just wanted information on where to purchase forbidden materials.[59]

IRON MAN BETRAYAL

As *Physique Pictorial* and other physique magazines that emphasized the "aesthetic approach" flourished, they increasingly came into conflict with what
Mizer called " 'hard-core' muscle magazines" or "old-school muscle books" that
had fallen on hard times. He knew that their harsh critique of new magazines
like his had alienated "the great bulk" of their readership. But he still encouraged readers to support these magazines and their veteran writers. "We cannot
afford to lose them from the field," he generously noted.[60] Mizer had gotten
his start through the support of these editors and was not prone to burn bridges.

Mizer had an especially close relationship with *Iron Man*, founded by weightlifter Peary Rader in Nebraska in 1933. Mizer had contributed enough photographs to be listed as one of *Iron Man's* "staff photographers" in 1949. Some of
Mizer's first catalog advertisements appeared in its back pages, and Rader had
even printed the first issue of *Physique Pictorial*. But under pressure from the
Post Office, Rader refused to print subsequent issues. Fearing the loss of his
second-class mailing privileges, he then stopped running physique photography advertisements. And in 1956 he published a scathing editorial denouncing
the "homosexual element" that had infiltrated bodybuilding and ruined its reputation. He called for a comprehensive "crusade" to clean up the sport, including a ban on nude or G-string photographs, fewer bodybuilding contests, and
more manly poses. He attributed the immorality that had seeped into bodybuilding to increasing "commercialism," emphasizing that his concerns were
not only moral but also financial. Mizer felt sorry for *Iron Man*. "I doubt if many
copies would be sold to those solely interested in the weightlifting results."[61]

This attack from his former supporter and printer caused Mizer to pen his
first editorial on "Homosexuality and Bodybuilding." Claiming to have less
familiarity with the subject than the editors of *Iron Man* and others who seemed
so preoccupied with it, Mizer first resorted to a version of the schoolyard taunt,
"It takes one to know one." He did so by quoting one of the most famous closeted homosexuals in 1950s America. A London reporter had recently asked
Liberace—in the midst of a legal struggle with a tabloid that had outed him—"Is
your sex life normal?" Fully composed, Liberace hastily replied, "Yes, is yours?"

In many ways, Liberace and Mizer were in parallel situations. Both offered the public fairly open representations of gay life, but without the label. But because of their popularity, they had caught the attention of the media and were being tarred with the sin of homosexuality. But Mizer went beyond Liberace's taunt to frame the question in terms of civil rights. "We wonder if really good people show prejudice against any minority group," he wrote, comparing such prejudice to that against a particular religion, race, or political party. This effectively made Peary Rader the one guilty of immorality and repositioned the debate on homosexuality within the realm of minority rights. Most important, he referred readers to the homophile groups Mattachine Society and ONE for more factual information.[62]

Mizer's mailbox must have been full after this unusually frank editorial. He noted that readers clamored for him to reprint letters, demonstrating their desire to connect to each other, to see who else was out there reading *Physique Pictorial*. Mizer printed only four responses. One called Mizer "naïve" for not realizing that all bodybuilders are in some way homosexual, since they are so obsessed with the male body. Another expressed the opposite view, that such "he-men" could not possibly be sissies. But the most unusual letter came from the mother of four male bodybuilders—three of them married with children, the youngest openly gay. She described his difficult coming-out process, psychiatric consultations, and much anguish. But she then painted the picture of a happy, healthy gay domesticity. "John lives with another young man who shares his interests, both are highly successful in films, are 'accepted' everywhere." She thanked Mizer for his sympathetic attitude.

Mizer could not print any letters from openly gay readers for fear of confirming the concerns of censors. But he gave readers clues that he received many such letters. He noted that many had written in anonymously to "unburden [their] frustrations" and "project [their] own motives to us." Although such personal, confessional letters could not be shared, Mizer assured readers that he would send them to a "psychological research group for study," a probable reference to the Kinsey Institute.[63] While Mizer had to be cautious about the content of his magazine to appease censors, his readers were often more explicit. Mizer considered many of the letters he received to be so salacious or incriminating that he did not want to keep them in his home in the event of a "purge" by authorities.[64]

Art historians have documented the lasting impact that Bob Mizer's physique photography had on Western visual culture, influencing the work of such artists as Francis Bacon, Robert Mapplethorpe, and Andy Warhol. British painter David Hockney famously said, "I came to Los Angeles for two reasons: The first was a photo by Julius Shulman of Case Study House #21, and the other was AMG's *Physique Pictorial*." Dozens of high-end coffee table books attest to the lasting appeal of the artistic vision of Bob Mizer and his fellow gay physique photographers. But Mizer's business model was as generative as his photography. His business acted as a key catalyst for a gay consumer culture network, encouraging and popularizing many other gay mail-order businesses.[65]

Although often portrayed as something of a bumbling loner, Mizer was at the center of an increasingly sophisticated gay network and came to be a leader of an effort to unite and defend the rights of gay men. It was a dream shared with early gay activist Manuel boyFrank, who, through his involvement in an early underground gay pen-pal club, had seen the potential power in gay men's interest in physique photography. Mizer, too, had an early sense of the depth of a gay market, through his work with Kovert's studio and his classified advertising in *Strength & Health*. He also had a great sense of the dangers involved. Each time Mizer had come under attack, he had come back more determined and open about his intentions. Neither the Post Office, nor the local vice police, nor vigilante journalists, nor mainstream muscle magazines deterred him. Over the course of his career he tried various tactics: reasoning with authorities, cautioning his fellow photographers, fanning the flames of outrage, and encouraging collective action. He had been on a crusade since high school to stand up and make the world a better place for his fellow homosexualists, and *Physique Pictorial* was his vehicle.[66]

Mizer saw Alfred Kinsey as a hero and collaborator in this crusade because he saw Kinsey's scientific work as a vehicle for increasing tolerance. "One of the greatest values of your present work will be to allow at least the ones who read it to realize they are not uniquely perverse because of either their overt or desired behavior," he wrote to Kinsey. "Many a man will be able to hold his head a little higher and square back his shoulders and know he is not disgustingly 'abnormal' merely because he is gifted with more healthy, vital sex powers than his sanctimonious moral condemner." But what Mizer wrote so admiringly of Kinsey also applied to his own life's work. Mizer took inspiration from his academic friend and advisor, offering the same message of healthy normality in a more visually accessible format, reaching a much wider audience. He provided images to substantiate Kinsey's scientific treatise.[67]

Like his mentor, Mizer was something of a workaholic, shooting still or moving film nearly every day of his life. But his ambitions were not monetary.

Although by the end of his life he had expanded his home-studio property in Los Angeles to include several adjoining homes and a pool, it was never lavish. It became a sort of dormitory or homeless shelter for wayward models. Friends remember him in later years wearing glasses held together with tape and string. After his death in 1992, friends found hundreds of thousands of dollars in cash stuffed in film cans—proceeds never invested, or given much thought. Mizer's ambitions had not changed from the time he was in high school. He took pride in knowing his readers considered the arrival of his magazine like "a visit from an old friend." And since that old friend "always brings new friends with him," he hoped it offered his readers the sense that they were part of a large, welcoming community similar to the one he had discovered in Pershing Square. As he told his readers, he hoped all who read his magazine carefully—who "take the trouble to study" it—would take away a message of "hope and inspiration."[68]

Hope was the message that Noel Gillespie found in *Physique Pictorial* when he discovered it as a teenager. He remembered it as "a gay-oriented oasis" in a Cold War desert of prudery and macho conformity. He considered Mizer less a salesman than "an old friend and confidante" because of all his "chatty remarks" among the model images. Gillespie praised Mizer's editorials on the "anti-nudity, anti-gay, anti–free speech attitudes" of the period. He recalls how he eagerly anticipated each new issue for both Mizer's "latest fresh-faced discoveries *and* his candid—and for the period, courageous—commentaries." Beyond this special bond with Mizer, he also felt linked to his fellow subscribers through their occasional letters to the editor, which he thought made *Physique Pictorial* "more a friendly resource than a mere sales catalogue."[69]

Hope was exactly the message that a young David Hurles understood when he encountered *Physique Pictorial* on newsstands in Cincinnati in 1957. "I came face to face with the awesome and wonderful knowledge of a place somewhere different from any place I yet knew," Hurles later wrote. He remembered following Mizer's exploits closely, noticing when he put in a swimming pool in 1956. "His pictures, magazines and films turned us on. But more than that, they gave us hope," Hurles eulogized at the time of Mizer's death in 1992. Hurles later became a Mizer protégé and went on to produce his own magazine. "Bob revealed the evidence which made us certain that what we desired and needed did, in fact, exist."[70]

2

SELLING GAY BOOKS

Donald Webster Cory's "Business with a Conscience"

Faggots buy books.
—Hubert Selby, Jr., 1966

I N THE summer of 1949 editor Brandt Aymar developed an innova-
tive marketing campaign for a daring novel that would become
Greenberg Publishers' big fall book. Nial Kent's *The Divided Path* told
the coming-out story of Michael—his adolescence in a small town, his attempts
to date women, his feelings of difference, and his mostly unrequited love for
Paul, "his dream companion," with whom he first experienced "the real meaning of desire." After a long and contemptuous friendship, the two men part
when Paul proposes marriage to their mutual friend Elinor. Giving up all hope
of a life with Paul, Michael moves to New York City, where he comes out into
"the twilight world" of gay bars and private parties. By the end of the novel, as
Paul and Michael are about to be reunited, Michael has a tragic car accident.
In the final scene, the gay hero grasps Paul's hand from inside the car wreck-
age, signaling that he is still alive. Readers are left to imagine their possible
future together.

Because it ended on "a note of hope," Greenberg marketed *The Divided Path*
as "the most forthright homosexual novel of the century." Noting that previous books with this "theme" inevitably ended in tragedy, Greenberg launched
a contest with $400 in cash prizes seeking customer input. "Many will think
this should not happen. We want your opinion, because your opinion, along
with those of many other readers, may establish a new writing trend in novels
on this subject." Announced in trade journals, college newspapers, and other

periodicals, the contest rules asked: "Should Michael, the hero, whose development inevitably sent him into the twilight world, live or die, and why? Should he finally find happiness with Paul, or marry Elinor, whom he also loves? How would you end this novel?"

Although Greenberg's publicity materials labeled the ending "controversial" and anticipated opposition, it was simultaneously signaling to a gay audience that this was a book for them (see fig. 2.1).[1]

The contest was the centerpiece of a multifaceted marketing strategy envisioned by Greenberg editor Brandt Aymar to target what he saw as a burgeoning gay market. "Rapidly growing interest in the subject of homosexuality has made novels on this theme a big seller," he noted in his publicity materials. He knew that Gore Vidal's *The City and the Pillar* sold over thirty thousand

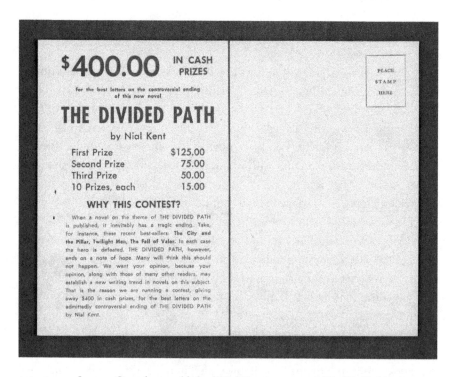

FIGURE 2.1 In 1949 Greenberg published Nial Kent's gay novel *The Divided Path.* Greenberg's marketing program featured a contest for the best letter about the book's "controversial ending."

Greenberg Publisher Records, Courtesy of Rare Book & Manuscript Library,
Columbia University in the City of New York.

copies in 1948, even with a tragic ending and a cover that gave no hint of its contents. The ending of *The Divided Path* was marginally more hopeful, but Aymar thought that with a targeted marketing campaign, they could reach a wider audience. He commissioned a suggestive dust jacket featuring an effeminate man gazing longingly at a more conventionally gendered man, his arm draped over the other's shoulder. Hoping to start a "whispering campaign," he sent complimentary copies to select individuals in the largest U.S. cities so people could "show it at gay bars and talk it up." He also targeted the bookstores where Greenberg's recent reprint of the 1930s gay novel *Twilight Men* had sold well. Aymar made sure to send notices about the contest to all their male clerks, assuming many might be gay (see fig. 2.2).[2]

The contest was a great success—receiving five hundred entries, the majority of which advocated a happy ending for Paul and Michael, a sequel to the novel, and more "open and intelligent" discussion of homosexuality. Twenty percent of the letters were from women. The thirteen winners not only received cash awards but also got their names and addresses printed in the publishing trade press. Most important, it created a tremendous amount of advance buzz about the book. As one bookseller from rural western Pennsylvania wrote, "I am almost certain of the success of the book, and of the contest, for there is a real interest in this type of novel today." Jim Kepner, who was then manager of Books on Telegraph Hill in San Francisco and would go on to become editor of *ONE* magazine, not only entered the contest but also recommended *The Divided Path* highly to his customers.

Although critical reception was generally negative, the book was widely reviewed, including in the *New York Times Book Review*, which found it a poor addition to the "psychopathic shelf, homosexual division." Despite hostile reviews from the mainstream press, sales of the book remained brisk—within a month it was the firm's best seller, and by spring it was selling five hundred copies a day. By the summer of 1950 it was in its third printing and Nial Kent was sailing to France to write his second novel. His proud literary agent was confident that he was the harbinger of a new literary trend. By 1955 it had sold over 130,000 copies.[3] Customers and retailers wanted more. "Do you have any other 'gay' books by Nial Kent?" inquired the owner of a commercial lending library in Massachusetts. "Customers have been after me to get a few 'so-called' gay books."[4]

Much has been written about the rise of the postwar gay novel and Greenberg's pivotal role in "breaking the silence" about homosexuality. Jim Kepner

FIGURE 2.2 Part of Greenberg's marketing campaign for *The Divided Path* included cover art that highlighted the homosexual relationship between the two male characters.

Greenberg Publisher Records, Courtesy of Rare Book & Manuscript Library, Columbia University in the City of New York.

remembers *The Divided Path* and *Quatrefoil* as gay novels that "broke the mold" by rejecting the usual Freudian analysis. Victor Banis, who would author a slew of gay-themed novels in the 1960s, recalls that *The Divided Path* was the first place he saw the word "gay" used to mean homosexual. Cultural critic Michael Bronski, growing up a few years later, wondered how his view of gay life might have evolved differently if he had found *The Divided Path* rather than the harsher portrayals of James Baldwin's *Another Country* or John Rechy's *City of Night*. "The gay revolution began as a literary revolution," argues Christopher Bram.[5]

As revolutionary as the content of these books might have been, so was the way they were marketed. Bryant Aymar not only discovered and promoted many first-time gay authors but also compiled one of the first mailing lists of homosexual consumers. Indeed, the marketing and content of the books reinforced one another, as both signaled the rise of a new gay market.

Greenberg's publicity campaign for *The Divided Path* in 1949 would propel Greenberg and other publishers to release gay-themed books that sold so well that they caught the attention of the U.S. Post Office, which sought to suppress them. The ensuing struggle between mainstream publishers with a profitable market for gay books and powerful government censors created the context that allowed enterprising gay entrepreneurs like Brandt Aymar to launch a new type of business: gay mail-order book services. By identifying, reviewing, distributing, and sometimes even printing gay fiction and nonfiction books, these businesses became a centerpiece of an increasingly rich gay consumer culture network. Before homophile groups started to organize gays and lesbians, commercial publishers such as Greenberg were identifying, cultivating, and quantifying the extent of a gay market. Publishing gay books did more than just break the silence about homosexuality, as important as that was. It created a business model that offered support to community-building efforts nationwide.

THE CORY BOOK SERVICE

By 1949 Greenberg had a fairly long history of publishing gay books. Founded in the 1920s by Jae Greenberg, a graduate of the Columbia School of Journalism, it had published two of the most prominent gay novels during New York's Depression-era "pansy craze"—André Tellier's *Twilight Men* in 1931 and Richard Meeker's *Better Angel* in 1933. Greenberg also published an abridged translation from the German of Anna Elisabet Weirauch's lesbian novel, *Scorpion* (now perhaps most remembered for being translated by Whitaker Chambers, a former Soviet spy who later publicly accused Alger Hiss of being a spy as well). Greenberg's more well-known nonfiction list included many important best-selling titles in sexuality studies, such as *Freud: His Dreams and Sex Theories*

(1949) and Ilsley Boone's *Joys of Nudism* (1934). "Pioneer publisher of popular books on mental hygiene, psychology, and psychoanalysis" was how Greenberg would be remembered.

But it was the work of openly gay editor Brandt Aymar that marked the true innovation in publishing. In 1948 Aymar persuaded Greenberg to reprint *Twilight Men*, which was so successful it went through two print runs. Soon he would find new gay fiction to publish.[6]

When *The Divided Path* was published, Aymar, thirty-eight years old, was not just an editor but Greenberg's vice president. He graduated from Yale in 1933 and got his start as an account executive for several New York advertising agencies. In the clubby, Ivy League world of Madison Avenue, he came under the tutelage of Harford Powel, a major figure in the worlds of publishing and advertising. Former editor of both *Harper's Bazaar* and *Collier's*, Powel had founded an advertising agency that handled publicity for Gimbels and Macy's department stores. He lectured and wrote frequently on advertising and direct mail, becoming an official with the Institute of Public Relations. Powel was also an accomplished novelist and nonfiction writer who, by 1935, was a Greenberg author. Taking on Aymar as a junior partner, together they edited an anthology of popular fiction for Greenberg. During World War II, Powel was called to Washington to direct the drive to persuade Americans to buy Defense Bonds. The younger Aymar served as an ensign in the U.S. Coast Guard Reserve and returned after the war to become Greenberg's managing director. He would remain in publishing until his death at eighty-six, applying much of the expertise on advertising and direct mail he learned from Powel (see fig. 2.3).[7]

Aymar was openly gay—some even said "obvious." He handled all aspects of Greenberg's promotion of gay books, including cultivating authors, review of manuscripts, and marketing plans. "Brandt has the final say-so on all homosexual stuff they do," wrote James Barr, one of his authors. Exhibiting a clear entrepreneurial bent, Aymar did more than shepherd authors through the publishing process. He also edited or coedited over a dozen popular anthologies under his own name, continuing the lessons Powel had instilled. A yachtsman and author of several books on boating, he later moved to a waterside home in Islip on Long Island to indulge his passion. But his financial success and considerable influence did not ensure popularity, especially with struggling young writers. Barr in particular did not appreciate Aymar's sexual flirtations, nor the "greed and snobbery" he saw reflected in his lavish décor and personal yacht.

FIGURE 2.3 Greenberg vice president Brandt Aymar oversaw the first corporate marketing campaign that explicitly targeted a gay market, including an "H" list of customers interested in gay books.

Greenberg Publisher Records, Courtesy of Rare Book & Manuscript Library, Columbia University in the City of New York.

The disgruntled Barr thought he abused his position and enjoyed a "harem of helpless ushers at his beck and call."[8]

It was Aymar's idea to create a list of customers—nicknamed the "H" list—who were interested in books on homosexuality. The list became the center of its publicity campaigns for a growing list of gay fiction and nonfiction. Aymar sent special advance publication announcements to this list and followed up with mailers asking not only for an opinion of the book but also for the names and addresses of friends with similar interests.

The Divided Path contest provided several hundred names and addresses, including those of an eighteen-year-old single man living on Chicago's North Side and a sixty-six-year-old bank teller living with his mother and brother in the family home in Franklin, Indiana. Many had literary interests, including a bookdealer, a biographer, a poet, and a theater director. Some would become future leaders in the homophile movement. Jim Kepner entered the contest. So did Earle Aikin, in whose small apartment in Washington, D.C., the Mattachine Society of Washington would later have its first official meeting and discuss how to end federal government policies excluding gay men and lesbians from public service. Leroy Ebert, then an art student at the Layton School of Art in Milwaukee, would become a collector of physique photography and artwork, his many scrapbooks ending up in the Beinecke Library at Yale.[9]

This cross-section of Americans from small towns and big cities all found themselves first connected through Greenberg's H list, what may have been the largest national list of consumers of gay products in 1949—the closest to a national list of gay or gay-friendly people in the country.

Sure of a ready audience for gay books and eager to build on the success of its gay marketing campaign for *The Divided Path*, Aymar looked for first-time authors who were also writing on this theme. The contest had generated not only an expanded list of customers but also several new manuscripts. In the summer of 1949 James Fugate, a twenty-seven-year-old Kansas rancher and oilfield roustabout, sent Greenberg a manuscript about a love story between two navy ensigns. The story drew from his real-life experience in the navy and in the oilfields of the Southwest. Writing with a "commercial rather than an artistic goal," Fugate had studied writing at the University of Oklahoma and would later move to Hollywood to try his hand at screenwriting.

By the next year Greenberg was marketing Fugate's book as *Quatrefoil*—and Fugate as James Barr. As part of the marketing blitz, Aymar compiled a "special list" of over seventy-five gay bars in U.S. and Canadian cities that would receive complementary copies—one of the first national compilations of gay bars. The list included piano bars such as the Cadillac Lounge in Cleveland, female impersonation cabarets such as Miami's Jewel Box, and gentlemen's hotel bars such as San Francisco's Top of the Mark. Aymar marketed *Quatrefoil* as "one of the best homosexual novels published." Although reliable sales figures are difficult to find, rumor had it that it sold better than Gore Vidal's *City and the Pillar* or Truman Capote's *Other Voices, Other Rooms*, perhaps because of both the happy ending and the targeted Greenberg marketing campaign.[10]

Greenberg followed up later that year with *The Invisible Glass*, a novel by "Loren Wahl," a gay writer from California who served in World War II and wrote of an interracial gay relationship again set in the U.S. military during the war. It was another big success, reprinted in an Avon paperback edition that sold over 100,000 copies.[11]

Then in 1951 Greenberg offered Donald Webster Cory's *The Homosexual in America*, the first nonfiction insider view of the gay community. Not since the Kinsey Report a few years earlier had a nonfiction book on sexuality received such attention—and unlike Kinsey's, this book was aimed at a general readership. To publicize the book, Greenberg sent out six thousand advertising circulars in advance of publication. Aymar arranged cooperative advertising in local markets with interested local booksellers, such as the Georgian Book Shop in Atlanta—"booksellers to the South"—which ran a large advertisement in the *Atlanta Journal-Constitution* and bought a hundred copies. Pickwick Bookshop on Hollywood Boulevard—known for having an unlabeled gay book section—displayed a stack of copies in its large display window. In New York, Cory was a guest on *Psychologically Speaking* on WEVD radio. In a brilliant feat of cross-promotion, Greenberg persuaded *Pageant Magazine* and *People Today* to feature stories about the book and its author on their covers.[12]

All this publicity paid off. The first printing sold out in ten days. Thousands of letters from readers poured in expressing thanks "for speaking up, for saying what had to be said." Letters came in from all over the world, "from homosexuals for the most part and occasionally from their mothers or friends," Cory later wrote. A reader from Chicago had seven friends who would encourage others to buy and read Cory's book. A librarian at the University of Houston distributed a memo suggesting the book to deans and departments all over campus. Paul Britton of Rivera, California, wrote to congratulate Cory on his courage to speak up for "my people" and to pledge his "cooperation and services in any project or plan you may have in the future." After reading Cory's book, Norman Mailer famously exclaimed in print, "I found myself thinking in effect, 'My God, *homosexuals are people, too.*' " It remained one of Greenberg's best-selling books for years, was reprinted seven times, and was translated into French and Spanish. It was, in short, a publishing phenomenon.[13]

The Homosexual in America was a clarion call for what Cory termed "the unrecognized minority" to assert itself. Cory was one of the first to proclaim that gay people constituted a minority group similar to African Americans and Jews—language that Bob Mizer would pick up and use in his editorials. But unlike these other groups, Cory argued, gays had the choice of hiding their difference. Only when gay people spoke up openly about their difference would any lasting change happen. "In the millions who are silent and submerged," Cory wrote, "I see a potential, a reservoir of protest, a hope for a portion of mankind." Cory himself became the most well-known gay spokesperson in America. Budding homophile activists such as Barbara Gittings in Philadelphia and Frank Kameny in Washington read his book and tried to put his words into action. Because the book was so widely read and so influential in politicizing so many individuals who became leaders in the homophile movement, Cory is often referred to as the "father of the homophile movement."[14]

But Greenberg's remarkable lead in gay publishing came to an abrupt halt later that year when, at the urging of the Post Office, the assistant U.S. attorney in Maryland indicted both Jae Greenberg and Brandt Aymar on obscenity charges. Although none of their three recent gay novels—*The Divided Path* (1949), *Quatrefoil* (1950), and *Invisible Glass* (1950)—contained explicit sex scenes, in the eyes of postal inspectors, any suggestion of homosexual behavior was considered obscene.

Greenberg hired attorneys who succeeded in getting the case transferred to New York, where it dragged out for four years. To avoid a trial, and the possibility of a year in prison, Greenberg finally pled guilty, paid a $3,000 fine, and signed an affidavit agreeing to pull the books from the market. Meanwhile, it had published a second book by James Barr, *Derricks*, which ran into censorship issues in Idaho and Detroit. Under advice of counsel, it also stopped selling *Derricks*. Without a trial, the Post Office had effectively intimidated Greenberg out of the market. The publisher's retreat put a serious pall over the publishing of gay books in the United States for several years. "They are frightened about proceeding with any publication programs" with gay books, Cory wrote to Alfred Kinsey. With the Post Office indictments, what had been Greenberg's most promising new market niche became a quagmire.[15]

Gay book publishing hit another roadblock when newspapers started running stories about Senator Joseph McCarthy's charges that homosexuals had infiltrated the State Department and posed a threat to national security due to their alleged unique vulnerability to blackmail. Several reviews of Greenberg's gay novels made reference to homosexuals' newfound political notoriety in Washington. One suspicious reader wondered if his courageous letter of praise to Cory would become part of "a national file of degenerate homo bastards" that would be used in a coming federal roundup. Greenberg authors also felt the heat. Because of stipulations in their contracts, the authors had to cover the costs of litigation with the Post Office, eating up their royalties. James Fugate reported that he made only $5,000 on *Quatrefoil*, even though it sold thirty-five thousand copies. Now it seemed the entire market might dry up. As Fugate wrote of his dwindling hopes of screenwriting in Hollywood, "Believe it or not, they don't like writers that prefer homosexual themes. . . . Blame the State Department."[16]

It was in the midst of Greenberg's legal troubles with censorship that Cory and Aymar decided to join forces and offer an alternative source for gay books. The Cory Book Service (CBS) was the first independent business devoted exclusively to selling books of interest to a gay audience. Building on Greenberg's H list and the flood of mail that Cory received in response to his book, it possessed a formidable mailing list. It sent out an initial solicitation letter expecting a 2 to 3 percent response rate. To its amazement, 40 percent of those on the list agreed to join the new book club. The first book offered by the Cory Book Service, British writer Angus Wilson's novel *Hemlock and After*, sold over a thousand copies. Within a year CBS had two thousand active subscribers.[17] If, in writing *The Homosexual in America*, Cory saw a potential political protest in the homosexual minority, teaming up with Aymar allowed him to see a moneymaking opportunity (see fig. 2.4).

Functioning like a book club, the Cory Book Service selected one gay-themed book of fiction or nonfiction every month and offered extensive and detailed reviews. Cory promised to provide "the best in modern literature" on "the problem of the homosexual" and to make it easily accessible and inexpensive. He was particularly successful at working with foreign publishers, who sometimes offered bulk discounts. Subscribers who ordered four or more books got one free. CBS featured many hard-to-locate foreign titles, such as Christopher Isherwood's novel *The World in the Evening* or Anglican minister Derrick Bailey's *Homosexuality and the Western Christian Tradition*. Thanks to Aymar's insider contacts, the club was able to offer advance notice of new publications, autographed copies of select books, and occasionally featured books by fellow subscribers—all ways of forging an intimate connection between readers, authors, and the book service. It offered Mary Renault's renowned novel *Charioteer* "exclusively for us," five years before it was published in the United States. Combining one "Monthly Selection" along with a slew of supplementary books, CBS offered over sixty books in its first sixteen months of operation.[18]

In fashioning their mail-order book service, Cory and Aymar drew on a decades-long history of mail-order book sales. Since 1926 Harry Sherman's

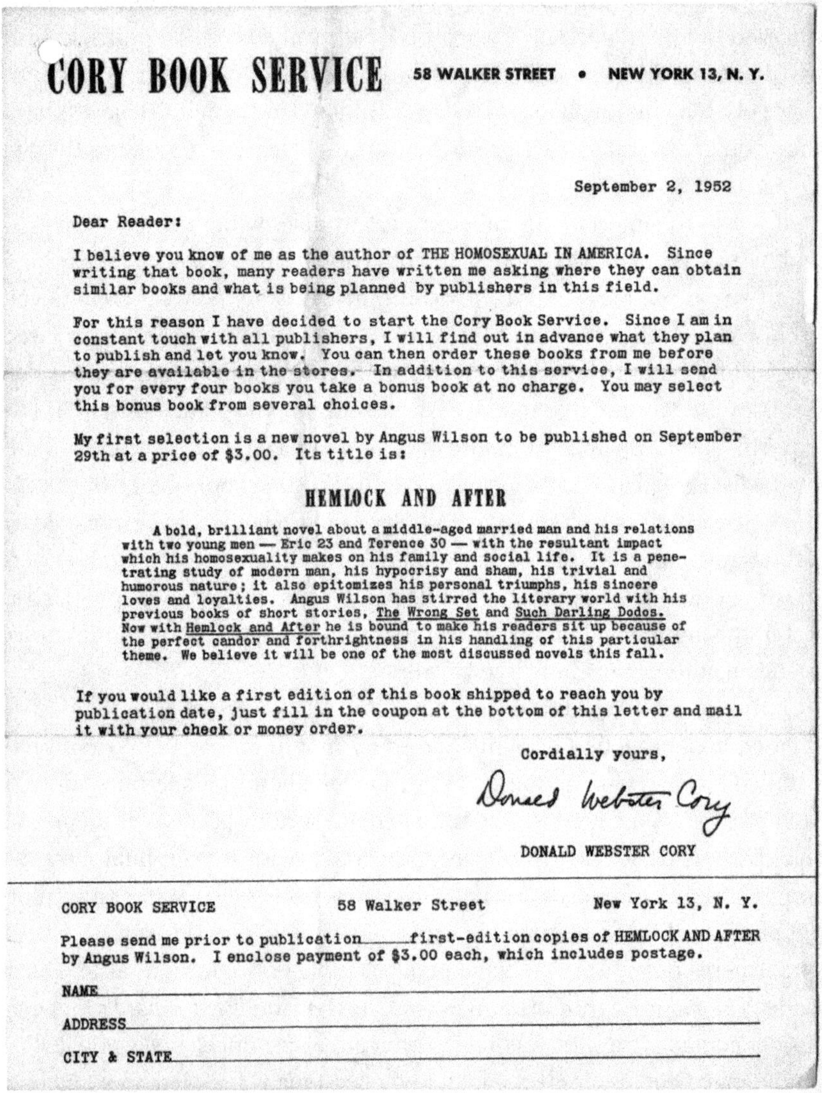

CORY BOOK SERVICE 58 WALKER STREET • NEW YORK 13, N. Y.

September 2, 1952

Dear Reader:

I believe you know of me as the author of THE HOMOSEXUAL IN AMERICA. Since writing that book, many readers have written me asking where they can obtain similar books and what is being planned by publishers in this field.

For this reason I have decided to start the Cory Book Service. Since I am in constant touch with all publishers, I will find out in advance what they plan to publish and let you know. You can then order these books from me before they are available in the stores. In addition to this service, I will send you for every four books you take a bonus book at no charge. You may select this bonus book from several choices.

My first selection is a new novel by Angus Wilson to be published on September 29th at a price of $3.00. Its title is:

HEMLOCK AND AFTER

A bold, brilliant novel about a middle-aged married man and his relations with two young men — Eric 23 and Terence 30 — with the resultant impact which his homosexuality makes on his family and social life. It is a penetrating study of modern man, his hypocrisy and sham, his trivial and humorous nature; it also epitomizes his personal triumphs, his sincere loves and loyalties. Angus Wilson has stirred the literary world with his previous books of short stories, The Wrong Set and Such Darling Dodos. Now with Hemlock and After he is bound to make his readers sit up because of the perfect candor and forthrightness in his handling of this particular theme. We believe it will be one of the most discussed novels this fall.

If you would like a first edition of this book shipped to reach you by publication date, just fill in the coupon at the bottom of this letter and mail it with your check or money order.

Cordially yours,

Donald Webster Cory

DONALD WEBSTER CORY

CORY BOOK SERVICE 58 Walker Street New York 13, N. Y.

Please send me prior to publication ______ first-edition copies of HEMLOCK AND AFTER by Angus Wilson. I enclose payment of $3.00 each, which includes postage.

NAME ______

ADDRESS ______

CITY & STATE ______

FIGURE 2.4 Building on the H mailing list established by Greenberg and the success of his book *The Homosexual in America*, Donald Webster Cory established the Cory Book Service in September 1952, the first commercial book club targeting a gay market.

Courtesy of ONE Archives at the USC Libraries.

Book-of-the-Month Club had been making select new books easily obtainable through the mails. Since then a host of specialized book services had proliferated. In 1943 Sears, Roebuck & Company expanded its already huge assortment of products and services to offer the People's Book Club to its mostly rural female readers. And publishers with highly specialized booklists had long used direct mail to reach their customers. But the book service that may have served as a model for Aymar and Cory was started by Hugo Gernsback, the publisher of *Sexology*, a popular tabloid magazine featuring titillating articles under the guise of "science." He ran an associated mail-order service called the New Book Company, which by 1950 had a mailing list for those who "expressed interest in our homosexual theme books," many published by Greenberg.[19]

Cory and Aymar also drew on the physique mail-order business, which they knew well. Cory's taste in men was reportedly "mostly hunks, studs, and weightlifters" and he had even invested in a "weightlifting firm" where he had friends.[20] Knowing that physique artists and photographers held the largest gay-oriented customer lists, Cory reached out to George Quaintance, who by then was something of a gay celebrity. Quaintance Studios sold homoerotic paintings, sculptures, and physique photographs to a worldwide following of more than ten thousand buyers. His images, which often graced the covers of *Physique Pictorial*, were so popular that they were plagiarized and made into gay greeting cards.

Although Quaintance declined to rent his mailing list to the Cory Book Service, he did agree, out of admiration and respect for Cory, to put a favorable mention of the service in his customer correspondence. Cory assumed that there would be "considerable duplication" between their two lists, signaling an overlap in interests. He later found a physique publisher to provide a mailing list of five thousand names, for which they paid "a great deal" and got a positive response of eleven hundred recipients—a phenomenal 20 percent response rate. Through compiling, sharing, and renting customer lists, the gay business network was growing.[21]

More than a moneymaking opportunity, Cory's effort to distribute gay books was, from the beginning, an act of political resistance—a confrontation with the U.S. Post Office and local censorship efforts. The few historical treatments of the Cory Book Service assume that the indictment of Greenberg Publishers and the drying up of the domestic market meant it ran out of books to sell.[22] But Aymar and Cory started their book service as a way around the censorship problems. And since they were still relying on the U.S. mails for distribution, it was not without risk. They hoped that by demonstrating the market for gay books, they would encourage more publishing in the field. In 1953, for example, Cory proudly announced that Dial Press was bringing *David the King* back into print. If necessary, Aymar and Cory planned to publish or reprint gay work that publishers refused. In 1955 they tried to work with James Barr to republish his works.[23] Far from a victim of censorship, as some historians have suggested, the Cory Book Service represented the beginnings of a campaign against the Post Office and the forces of censorship.

Although a commercial enterprise, the Cory Book Service formed an integral part of the burgeoning homophile movement. It functioned in ways similar to that of a gay political or social service organization. By making literature on homosexuality readily available to the public, Cory believed he was helping to break the silence on homosexuality and thereby improve the lives of gay men and lesbians. This was a philosophy shared by Mattachine, which also saw more public discussion of homosexuality—even by psychiatrists who considered it to be an illness or religious leaders who considered it sinful—as better than silence. In *The Homosexual in America*, Cory had singled out gay literature, particularly the kind published by Greenberg, as a key to changing public understanding. He even ended the book with what he touted as the most extensive bibliography of gay and lesbian novels ever published. "It can enlighten, encourage, and offer a suggestion for the ultimate solution of the individual's dilemma," Cory argued. "It can impart knowledge and insight for the benefit both of the public at large and the homosexual in particular. . . . It can show all readers that the invert's life is not that of a hopeless person doomed to defeat."[24]

The Cory Book Service was only one of the ways that Cory tried to leverage the success of his book to help create social change. As perhaps the most famous homosexual in America, he soon was corresponding with Alfred Kinsey and hosting regular meetings of gay men in New York. At that time, New York City had no formal gay organization. The Mattachine Society, established in Los Angeles just the previous year, had no branches outside of California. The Veterans Benevolent Association, a group of gay World War II veterans that formed to protest their Blue Discharges, was by then largely a social organization. So Cory started hosting a "discussion group" with scheduled speakers, meeting chairmen, and a mailing list. This semiformal organization held meetings mostly in private apartments.[25]

The Reverend Robert Wood remembered attended a meeting in May 1952 with over forty gay men in attendance, but most would share only first names. "It was mostly discussion . . . sharing experiences . . . exchanging information and getting gripes off their chests," Wood recalled. They would discuss professionals and retailers who were especially sympathetic or homophobic. "Bloomingdales was always very supportive of gay fellows, had a lot of gay employees. So Bloomingdale's was a popular place to shop," he noted, summarizing the conversation.[26] By 1952 Cory was encouraged by what he saw happening in New York and what he heard about in California. "I think we are witnessing the beginning of group identification," he told Kinsey, whom he scheduled to appear before the group. Foreseeing a "very courageous drive toward organization," Cory was positioning himself to be at its center.[27]

As part of the effort to raise his profile in New York and create a space for like-minded people, Cory opened a storefront version of the Cory Book Service called The Book Cellar on East 56th Street near 2nd Avenue. Founded in April 1953, it was the first bookstore tailored to the gay market. Gore Vidal and other gay authors occasionally did book signings. Cory described it as a "small but very personal place" that he hoped would become both a local and a national destination. "We sincerely hope that whenever you're in the neighborhood—whether from around the corner or as far away as Texas, California, or Alaska, you'll drop in and make yourself at home." Cory was soon selling greeting cards as well. "We are certain that we could sell a great many of your cards," he assured George Quaintance.[28]

Soon Cory was involved in organizing on a national scale. Indeed, without his help, ONE magazine, the first major homophile news and education source, might never have gotten off the ground. When members of the Mattachine Society in Los Angeles decided in 1953 to found a magazine, Cory agreed to serve as a contributing editor, to advertise the magazine to Cory Book Service members, and even to sell subscriptions to ONE on commission. "With the lifting of taboos on discussions of homosexuality," Cory told his readers, "there is a need for a magazine that will help everyone understand better the enormous problems concerned with this subject." He anticipated that 50 percent of his members would subscribe.

ONE's founder Jim Kepner later acknowledged Cory's key role. "When readers flooded [Greenberg] with all sorts of personal requests and problems, Cory started . . . the Cory Book Service, the first known book club for gays," Kepner later wrote. "Its mailing list helped, a few months later, to get ONE Magazine launched." Having agreed to provide the editors of ONE access to his extensive mailing list, Cory then proposed that the two organizations jointly publish an anthology of gay writing. The association was so close that Cory even contemplated a merger of the two organizations.[29]

Although now almost absent from the historical record, the Cory Book Service was one of the key organizations of the early gay movement. A few years later, when four lesbian couples in San Francisco founded the Daughters of Bilitis, the first lesbian organization, they knew to contact not only the Mattachine Society and ONE, Inc., but also the Cory Book Service.[30] And although CBS is the least well known of the three organizations—all founded within approximately two years of each other—it and its business model were instrumental in sustaining the other two.

While Cory and CBS could serve to help the fledgling homophile movement, he could also retard its growth. Because of his prominence in New York, members of the Mattachine Society in California began courting Cory for access to his mailing list. In the fall of 1954 Cory held lengthy meetings with Wallace de Ortega Maxey, a representative of the Mattachine Society in Los Angeles, about establishing a chapter in New York. At first Cory cordially agreed to facilitate contacts, but he canceled the arrangements at the last minute. He had gotten wind of plans by West Coast activists to start selling books. "I am informed by people out here," he told Maxey, "that ONE and Mattachine and others are setting up a competitive book service."

Cory felt betrayed. In an angry screed to ONE editors, Cory asserted, "it was originally agreed that any names turned over to you be for the purpose of sending the magazine and appealing for funds for the magazine, and for no other purposes." He called their plan to establish a competing book service "most unethical" and "absolutely inexcusable." He not only cut off negotiations with Mattachine but also threatened to cancel all his support for ONE magazine and publicize his withdrawal of support to his readers. Without Cory's help, it would be two more years before Mattachine was established in New York. Cory would remain skeptical of homophile organizations for the rest of his life.[31]

Cory saw this competitive move on the part of Mattachine as harmful not only to his business interests but to the fledgling movement as well. As a business owner, he had a strong entrepreneurial bent, as evidenced in his many other business and publishing ventures.[32] But Cory was both an entrepreneur and an activist and saw no conflict between these roles. He saw his book service as serving the gay community in a way complementary to Mattachine and *ONE*. Having two book services would be "divisive of the forces," he wrote. It would anger his "readers" and make the procurement of publisher discounts more difficult. Indeed, Cory's inclination was to consolidate efforts, not further divide them. And Cory was not the only one to see overlap between the roles of Mattachine, *ONE*, and the Cory Book Service. Leveling charges of "separatism," others in the gay community questioned the need for three independent institutions—a social service organization, a magazine, and a book service. With the movement still in gestation, what type of institutions it might need and what form they might take were open questions.[33]

Selling gay books and organizing for change were seen as complementary goals. The popularity of Cory's own book and the hundreds of people that it encouraged to be open and comfortable about their sexuality had demonstrated the power of books not only to change people's lives but also to foster a movement. "[Cory] really wanted to change the world, he really wanted to make it easier for people of diverse orientations," recalled Elsie Carlton. People who either had no gay connections in their small towns or might be afraid to go into a store and buy a gay book were able to forge these connections through the mail. More than gay bars, which were all local, and the small meetings of Mattachine members in California and later New York, the Cory Book Service held the potential to unite gay men and women from all over the country.[34]

Given the increasing difficulty with gay publishing, customers considered the Cory Book Service to be not just a business but a lifeline to gay culture. As a result, it generated an extremely loyal and devoted following. Subscribers wrote in so frequently with personal stories and pleas for help that Cory wearied of the task of keeping up with the correspondence. Complaining about being "deluged with mail," Cory noted that "my correspondence is from all over the world, in many languages and I answer every letter without aid of secretary or subsidy."[35] More than merely a business, it provided a sense of community, what one contemporary observer described as "a sense of *belonging*." It was "a receptacle for complaints, a shoulder to weep on, a help for people in trouble."[36] When the book service changed ownership and its fate was rumored to be in question, *Mattachine Review* rushed in to assure readers that the new owners were not only of "the highest integrity" but also equally "devoted to the cause."[37]

Cory's power as the proprietor of a service that "specializes in books by and about homosexuals" also caught the attention of the Federal Bureau of

Investigation. Within a month of the opening of his bookstore on 56th Street, an informant told the FBI about his "book-of-the-month type of club" for homosexuals, suggesting that this made him a "bad influence among the homosexuals in New York City and the vicinity." The informant was himself gay and had attended one of Cory's local gatherings. As he told his FBI handler, "[Cory's] activity among the homosexuals tends to encourage homosexuality rather than to reduce it." The FBI, however, apparently took no action.[38]

"LESLIE WINSTON'S" BOOK CLUB

Cory's customers were loyal and dedicated, but the feeling was not always reciprocated. Cory harbored personal conflicts over his sexuality—he was a homosexually active man who simultaneously maintained his marriage to his wife. He used the pseudonym "Donald Webster Cory" for his gay publications and business interests rather than his real name, Edward Sagarin. He increasingly came under the influence of psychologist Albert Ellis, who believed that homosexuals could be taught to adjust to a heterosexual way of life. As Cory became less convinced that homosexuals deserved equal treatment, he began to find the correspondence with his customers burdensome. As Toby Marotta remembered, "By 1954 . . . Cory had sold the book service and let it be known that he wanted nothing to do with groups intent on persuading people that homosexuals were as well-adjusted and respectable as heterosexuals."[39] So Cory's sale of the book service and bookstore, far from evidence of a decline in the market for gay books, expressed his own inability to fully embrace the progressive impact of his own commercial enterprise.

Despite his ambivalence toward his business, Cory did not want to see it disintegrate. "You don't start an enterprise that takes so much emotion, so much experience and effort, and become willing to let it die," explained the woman to whom Cory eventually sold the business. But still bitter over the earlier betrayal, he did not want to see it become a part of Mattachine, despite their close association and natural affinity.

Cory initially sold the business in 1954 to editor and publisher Arthur Richmond, who continued it under the same name, with Cory still very much involved. When Richmond died suddenly of a heart attack a little over a year later, Tony Segura of Mattachine New York wanted to save the business and offered to buy the mailing list from Richmond's widow. Cory once again vetoed any direct connection between Mattachine and the business he had launched. He instead sold it to Elsie L. Carlton, a straight woman he had met through Jewish publishing and progressive political circles.[40]

A forty-five-year-old suburban housewife and mother in Farmingdale, Long Island, Elsie Carlton was an unlikely successor to Cory. Although she had some familiarity with selling books through her brother's publishing business, she knew little about the gay community. When she met Cory and his friends in the Mattachine Society, she did not know they were "fegelah"—the derogatory term for homosexuals she knew from other Jewish kids growing up in New York City. She saw them merely as civic-minded "do-gooders" like herself. She first learned of the discrimination they faced as gay men when Tony Segura complained that no civic group would host a Mattachine representative as speaker. As an officer in the local chapter of the National Conference of Christians and Jews, Carlton thought she could easily get him a speaking slot. "These were liberal women's groups, they would have a speaker on any subject," she recalled. She had successfully brought in Rose Russell of the New York City Teachers Union, a target of Senator Joseph McCarthy. "But I could not get a man of Mattachine to appear. That was a great lesson for me. That was humiliating" (see fig. 2.5).

With the transfer to Elise Carlton, Cory decided it was time to remove his name from the business. Richmond had used Cory's name and even his signature on book service newsletters, but this had caused confusion—especially when it was announced that the owner had died, and hundreds of condolence letters poured in for Cory. So Carlton searched for her "Betty Crocker" —an emblematic persona for her book service that would convey the right image. She liked the name Leslie, with its ambiguous gender. Imagining most of the customers to be gay men, she was uncertain how they would feel about doing business with a woman. The marketing jingle "Winston tastes good, like a cigarette should" was then a popular tune often heard on radio and television. So she settled on the pseudonym Leslie Winston and called her business the Winston Book Service. She hoped it conveyed the image of a "suave and cultured gentleman" to customers who yearned for such an identity.[41]

In 1957, with the Cory Book Service transferred to her name, Carlton set up offices in a commercial office building in downtown Hempstead, Long Island, not far from her home in Farmingdale. She had a separate shipping department, and help from college students, professors, and Mattachine members in putting out the newsletter. Her children pitched in too, helping run the

FIGURE 2.5 Elsie Carlton ran the Cory Book Service, renamed the Winston Book Club, from 1957 to 1967. A suburban housewife on Long Island involved in many liberal causes, she considered her monthly newsletters and voluminous correspondence with gay and lesbian customers a "mitzvah"—a good deed done from religious duty.

Courtesy of Bonnie Carlton Barker.

Pitney-Bowes postage meter. She expanded the size of the newsletter and the number of offerings. Under her stewardship the business flourished, reaching a mailing list of five thousand customers by 1959. As one Mattachine member commented, "she probably has as extensive a [gay interest] mailing list as exists."[42]

Carlton took her role as newsletter writer so seriously that she submitted several of them to the annual Bread Loaf Writers' Conference in Middlebury, Vermont, and was accepted into the prestigious program, which nourished the careers of other would-be writers such as Julia Child and Joan Didion. "I want this to be the very best newsletter that I can write. . . . I want to do a good job for the people," she told the selection committee. She used her clout to help get gay books reprinted and became an agent for authors such as James Barr, whose novels Greenberg had shelved. Barr described Carlton as "a dear lady of great good humor who became my special chicken soup for several years."[43]

Despite her business success, Carlton remained primarily a suburban housewife and mother with a business on the side. Neither her family nor her community encouraged her to focus on the business. "Betty Friedan based her investigations on women like me," Carlton observed, referring to educated suburban housewives whose desire to work outside the home was stymied by societal expectations. She used the thousands of dollars a newsletter generated to supplement the relatively meager income of her husband Roland Carlton, whose Asperger's syndrome limited his business success. "I had a tiger by the tail. It was a valuable piece of property," she observed, speculating about what she might have done if more actively engaged. "Anyone who used it judiciously could really make a staggering amount of money."[44]

Through the business, Carlton became good friends not only with the local "men of Mattachine," as she affectionately called them, but also with many customers from around the country. To reflect this growing feeling of community, she changed the name of her enterprise to the Winston Book *Club*. She received piles of mail from gay men and women wanting help, advice, or reassurance. "The Winston People," as she called them, became much more than customers. "I was writing a love letter, I was not writing a newsletter," Carlton said of her monthly book service brochures.

Beyond routine business correspondence, responding to individual letters of anguish and turmoil took up more of her time. "I began to write to these guys in Oshkosh, Wisconsin, and Eureka, California, saying 'I want you not to be afraid. . . . you are O.K.'" She called these her "spine letters." As with Cory before her, the increasing time spent on correspondence negatively affected the business. Although she sold hundreds of copies of books featured in the newsletter, "Had I not become involved with the victims, it would have become thousands." But Carlton believed in the Jewish concept of "mitzvah"—of doing good deeds. She never forgot the lesson her father had taught her: we have to make the world safe for everyone, and then it will be safe for the Jews. Indeed, she wrote privately that she considered the book service to be "a business with a conscience."[45]

Winston's direct support for Mattachine of New York was of inestimable value. "I gave scads of money to the Mattachine Society," Carlton boasted. Although she financed many Mattachine events, including a major annual convention at New York's Hotel Commodore in 1961—held in conjunction with the American Psychiatric Association, which Mattachine hoped to influence— her role remained hidden. "I didn't have the good sense to put 'Winston Book Service' on the back of the chairs," she later lamented. She did have a small speaking slot at the convention to report on her experience with "Homosexual John Doe: Citizen, Consumer, Friend." Carlton also underwrote much of the *New York Mattachine Newsletter*, with several pages of book reviews and adver- tisements featured in its primitive, eight-page mimeographed format. Matta- chine expressed its appreciation by directing members to Winston to purchase books and sending volunteers out to Winston's Long Island headquarters to stuff envelopes. She earned the title of "Mattachine's long-time friend and advisor." As she recalled near the end of her life, "I sat at a picture window and watched the world change for the gay population, and I had the extraordinary privilege of helping to do it."[46]

Carlton even made public appearances on behalf of the gay and lesbian com- munity. In 1961 she appeared on one of the first radio talk shows on homosexu- ality on New York's WEVD. Discussing "How Normal Are Lesbians?" she joined Daughter of Bilitis research director and out lesbian Florence Jaffy along with Lee Steiner, a psychologist and friend to the homophile movement. Carl- ton later participated in public demonstrations for women's reproductive rights along with William Baird, founder of Parents Aid Society, which provided free birth control clinics. "A champion of the underdog and liberal to her very core," according to her daughter, Carlton saw her work for the gay and lesbian com- munity as a natural extension of her tireless advocacy for women, the Jewish community, and the Democratic Party.[47]

The Winston Book Service established links not only to homophile politics but also to the physique world. Arthur Richmond, during his brief tenure, tried to diversify offerings. He corresponded with several physique artists and even did a test run to one thousand names on a physique mailing list, which unex- pectedly flopped. "Don't know why it didn't work," Richmond confessed. "We tried lamps, perfume, and cards," Richmond wrote to a friend, but the many complicated orders did not significantly increase revenues. "So painfully we stick to books," Richmond lamented. Bob Mizer did refer readers of *Physique Pictorial* to Winston when he featured the suggestive cover art from a pulp novel it was selling. Though unsuccessful at integrating these two fields, the attempts demonstrated an understanding of a gay market beyond books. It was an idea much more successfully pursued a few years later by Guild Press.[48]

After Elsie Carlton sold Winston Book Service in 1967 to Russell Hoffman, a fellow advocate for women's reproductive rights, the newsletter increasingly resembled a modern gay magazine that fused book reviews, physique imagery, and homophile news. In 1967 the Winston newsletter announced the first sex reassignment surgery at Johns Hopkins, the first official recognition given to a university gay organization, and a major antiobscenity victory in the U.S. Court of Appeals. After polling its readers, it also began to offer physique and nudist magazines and "The Gay Baedeker" travel guide—to "places which have gained a reputation for hospitality and acceptance."[49] This was only one of the many ways in which gay book selling and physique publishing had by then begun to merge.

BOOK SERVICES: THE MODEL GAY ENTERPRISE

The Cory and Winston Book Services served a growing homosexual market from 1952 through 1969. Not only did they thrive as commercial enterprises, but they also played a crucial role in supporting homophile activist organizations on both the East and West Coasts.[50] Perhaps even more important, their business model was copied by nearly a dozen similar mail-order book services. At some time every major homophile organization in the United States cashed in on the trend and established its own book service, including the Mattachine Society, ONE, Inc., and the Daughters of Bilitis (DOB).[51] As Cory had feared, ONE, Inc. was the first to establish a book service in 1955. In the midst of Greenberg's censorship struggles, ONE decided to print James Barr's play *Game of Fools*, touting that it was "published by homosexuals." As requests for more titles came in, ONE, Inc. launched the ONE Book Service, which, out of continuing deference to Cory, was designed to accommodate "Western residents." By 1959 it sold $6,000 worth of books. Selling gay books became the model gay enterprise within the homophile movement.[52]

Howard Frisch founded Village Books in 1956 with an emphasis on what he timidly called "Special Fiction," a term that functioned as code for gay. His mail-order business was an outgrowth of his Christopher Street store specializing in theater art books and memorabilia.[53] Frisch's selections were the most highbrow in the field, perhaps because of his close association with Harvard-educated gay bibliographer Noel I. Garde (a.k.a. Edgar H. Leoni), author of a 1940s underground guide to gay bars and books and the definitive 1959 bibliography, *The Homosexual in Literature*, one the first offerings by Village Books. By then it was using the word "homosexual" to describe characters and soon started offering Tom of Finland drawings as a bonus to subscribers.[54]

The Daughters of Bilitis was a late and somewhat reluctant entrant into the book-service field. Editors of the lesbian group's publication, *The Ladder*, rejoiced when Leslie Winston reactivated the Cory Book Service. But "after much soul-searching," and in response to popular demand from friends and subscribers, DOB ventured into the book business in May 1960. It was designed to offer lesbian fiction and nonfiction that the other commercial gay book services neglected. Among its first offerings were autographed copies of Jeannette Howard Foster's *Sex Variant Women in Literature* and two novels with happy endings by Artemis Smith. But it also offered books that dealt largely with male homosexuality, such as Rev. Robert Wood's *Christ and the Homosexual*—the first examination of the church's approach to homosexuality in the United States.

DOB's brochures were mostly primitive mimeographed sheets, and its modest profits came from a small "handling charge" of twenty cents per book. The most unique innovation of DOB was to produce its own 45 rpm records by noted lesbian newsletter writer Lisa Ben, advertised as "the Gayest Songs on Wax." Cleo (Glen) Bonner and Helen Cushman, an interracial lesbian couple in Oakland, ran the book service. Bonner went on to become president of DOB and thus the first woman of color to head a national gay organization.[55]

Hal Call, head of the Mattachine Society in San Francisco, had the most ambitious plans for his book service. He published gay fiction with his Pan-Graphic Press and then offered those and other books through the Dorian Book Service, which by 1960 was publishing an expansive Dorian Book Service Quarterly. It was designed not only to bring in revenue to support Mattachine but also to demonstrate to publishers the market for gay books. Call also saw it as part of the "freedom to read" movement that was confronting the forces of censorship. In advertising Robert Wood's *Christ and the Homosexual*, he urged customers to buy multiple copies to get the word out. Noting that mainstream periodicals refused to carry advertising for the book and mainstream retailers wouldn't stock it, he suggested that customers buy copies for their clergyman, lawyer, and "favorite professor journalist" as a form of activism (see fig. 2.6).[56]

Seeing that the Dorian Book Service was twice as profitable as the *Mattachine Review*, Hal Call had larger goals. In March 1963 he acquired Cosmo Book Sales, another gay enterprise that tried to link the publishing and

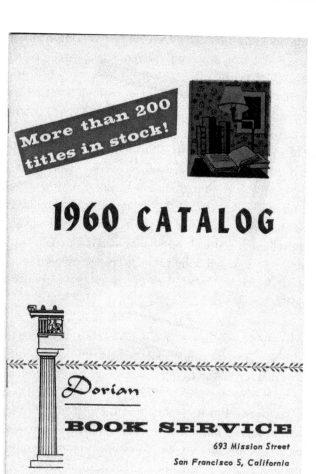

More than 200 titles in stock!

1960 CATALOG

Dorian

BOOK SERVICE

693 Mission Street
San Francisco 5, California

FIGURE 2.6 By 1960 gay mail-order book services proliferated as homophile organizations saw them as a way to enhance their revenue stream while educating the public. The Mattachine Society of San Francisco's Dorian Book Service 1960 catalog featured hundreds of titles.

Courtesy of the Gay, Lesbian, Bisexual, Transgender Historical Society.

physique worlds. It was run by J. D. Mercer (a.k.a. Harrison M. Kleinschmidt), the author of *They Walk in Shadow,* a rambling exposé of the homosexual world—a format that by the early 1960s had become nearly its own genre. Mercer had unsuccessfully pitched it to Greenberg in 1951, just as they came out with Cory's *Homosexual in America.* Meanwhile, Mercer, like Cory, had started selling books himself and even managed to form a sort of association with George Quaintance, acquiring the remaining inventory of Quaintance Studios after the artist's death.[57]

Using Cosmo Book's ten-thousand-name mailing list, Call hoped to turn "sleeping Dorian" into a business powerhouse and open storefronts in San Francisco and Los Angeles. Call believed that they were the only ones on the West Coast of any size specializing in this market in a "prestige manner." He saw no reason for Pickwick and a few others to have a corner on the gay book market.[58] In March 1967 Call partnered with Bob Damron and another man to open the Adonis bookstore on Ellis Street with eight hundred titles. It featured books, magazines, paintings, physique art, gay greeting cards, records, sculptures, novelties, and gifts. Promotional material touted it as a "gay supermarket." Adonis represented a transition from the mail-order world of gay book selling pioneered by Donald Webster Cory to the gay liberation era of brick-and-mortar bookstores.[59]

Craig Rodwell's opening of the Oscar Wilde Memorial Bookshop in New York's Greenwich Village in 1967 is often seen as the first in a long line of commercial bookstores that served the LGBT community. Some historians of gay liberation argue that before Rodwell's pioneering efforts, there was a complete lack of access to gay books. But he was neither the first nor the most extensive purveyor of gay literature. Because he excluded material he considered exploitative, his modest offering of a few dozen volumes paled in comparison to that available through the Guild Press, the Dorian Book Service, or Adonis in San Francisco.[60]

Gay and lesbian bookstores have long been acknowledged as important community-building centers. Rodwell envisioned his store as an arm of the homophile movement—he had unsuccessfully tried to get the Mattachine Society to open a storefront location that could double as a bookstore. It was from this "bookshop of the homophile movement" that he encouraged people to "Buy Gay" and launched a newsletter attacking mafia control of gay bars.[61] In Washington, D.C., Lambda Rising opened in Dupont Circle in 1974 and sponsored that city's first gay and lesbian pride celebrations. Stores such as Lammas Women's Books in Washington, D.C., and Women and Children First in Chicago have offered important support to feminist and lesbian communities since the 1970s. They all hosted author readings, community bulletin boards, and other events.

But they were not the first to try to serve and unite the LGBT community by providing access to literature. More than a decade before such well-known bookstores were founded, Donald Webster Cory and Brandt Aymar pioneered the idea of marketing gay books through the mail. But their role in creating a market for gay books while supporting the homophile cause has been mostly forgotten.[62] Cory was one of the first to identify a potential "reservoir of protest" in the vast hidden homosexual subculture, but he also saw there a commercial market, and a way to foster change. Partnering with Aymar, whose H list first made concrete the very notion of a gay market, he inaugurated a wave of gay book selling that became a key component of a growing gay commercial and homophile movement. Not only the father of the homophile movement, Cory also helped launch one of the first gay commercial enterprises. His idea of gay book services helped to demonstrate a gay market, overcome the forces of censorship, and sustain budding homophile organizations, providing a model for the future. Embracing the commercial world while increasing gay visibility, they were businesses with a conscience.

Gay book services not only proliferated but became increasingly enmeshed in a network of gay commercial and homophile organizations whose interests were parallel. What united gay book services, physique publishers, and homophile organizations was their interest in reaching and expanding a gay market. Commercial outfits such as Greenberg and the Cory Book Service wanted to get customers excited about their offerings. They wanted their loyalty—and their addresses. The customers, in turn, felt a connection with these businesses beyond that of simply offering a useful product. Greenberg may have been the first to establish a gay mailing list, but soon such lists were being traded, rented, borrowed, and sold. And the larger they grew, the more influence they could wield. Gay mailing lists were a powerful tool that promised both economic and political power. But when infiltrated by postal inspectors, they also posed a grave threat to publishers and customers alike.[63]

3

THE GRECIAN GUILD

Imagining a Gay Past, and Future

Almost the first thing that any homosexual does, when called upon to offer any serious defense of homosexuality, is to draw upon the glorious example of the manly Greek warriors and athletes who apparently practiced homosexual love openly and without shame.
—ONE magazine, 1961

I N 1955 a small physique photography studio in Charlottesville, Virginia, made a big announcement. For several years, the Grecian Guild had been one of dozens of such businesses that contributed photographs and competed for advertising space in Tomorrow's Man, Physique Pictorial, and similar magazines. They had built up a customer base that appreciated the "classical naturalness" of their models, which were drawn not from bodybuilding competitions but from the student population at the University of Virginia. The only other feature that distinguished the Grecian Guild from its rivals was that many of the models posed outside, against the backdrop of the nearby Blue Ridge Mountains.

But in August 1955 the Grecian Guild took out full-page, two-color advertisements in Tomorrow's Man and VIM heralding "something new for the Physique World." It was launching a new magazine for "bodybuilders, artists, and lovers of the body beautiful. . . ." The inclusion of "lovers" in this list of usual muscle magazine customers was suggestive, but otherwise the advertisement remained vague, the ellipsis only hinting at future content. Readers were warned that they'd be sorry "and then some" if they missed this opportunity (see fig. 3.1).[1]

To those who responded to the advertisement, the first issue of Grecian Guild Pictorial in the autumn of 1955 fulfilled its promise of newness. Featuring a

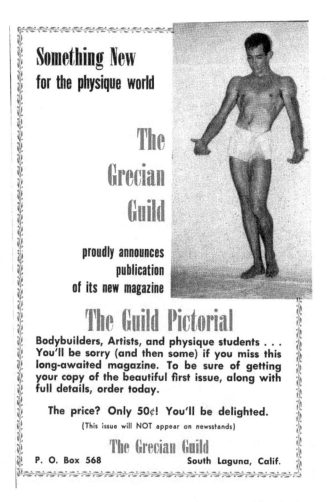

FIGURE 3.1 This advertisement in *VIM* in August 1955 alerted the physique world to a new publication, the *Grecian Guild Pictorial*, and featured model and cofounder John Bullock. The image, with arms outstretched in welcome, also appeared in the magazine's inaugural issue.

bright pink cover with the delicate head of Myron's statue of a discus thrower from fifth-century Athens, the magazine offered membership in a fraternal order of men dedicated to the appreciation of the beauty of the male body. Members from around the nation would meet at annual conventions and return home to form local chapters, creating spaces where "fellow Grecians could gather regularly to pursue those interests which bind us all together in one great brotherhood." The founders planned summer camps and other gatherings for physique artists and photographers to sketch and paint using live models. But more than an opportunity for artistic creation, the guild offered an idyllic vision of male camaraderie: "a place of our own where contests and physique shows can be held and where we can sun and swim and pursue the ways of health and happiness" (see fig. 3.2).

Realizing their vision was utopian, the founders challenged readers to join in the effort to make their plan a reality. "Is this only a dream?" they asked. "Maybe. But maybe not. It can come true IF there are enough of us!" Readers were asked to send a photograph of themselves along with a membership fee.

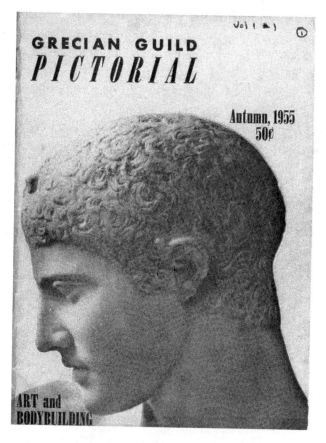

FIGURE 3.2 The first issue of the *Grecian Guild Pictorial* was bright pink, at a time when "gay as pink ink" was a common expression in gay circles. Invoking the values of classical Greece, it promised membership in a fraternal order of men dedicated to the appreciation of the male body.

In return they would get an official membership certificate and a photo of a Grecian Guild model. It would be the beginning of what promised to be a bright future of exchanges with men like themselves. "There is a great day coming," they promised.[2]

The Grecian Guild had a vision of the future, but one that was intrinsically linked to its sense of the past. "The ancient Greeks were a great deal wiser and more sophisticated than most of us today," the founders lamented. "We have retrogressed, in this sense, to a period far beyond the dark ages." Their vision was to return to the values of ancient Greece, where, they asserted, "the body of a muscular, graceful, well-proportioned youth was among the most admirable of all things."[3] The Grecian Guild was not just selling a product, not just offering membership in a fraternal order—it meant to "propagate a philosophy" of Hellenism.

Dating back to at least the nineteenth century, some would argue back to the Renaissance, this nostalgic invocation of ancient Greece had a long history among men attracted to other men as a way to create a folklore of a collective past and legitimize admiration for the male body. Writers from Johann Wincklemann to Walter Pater to Oscar Wilde had made similar arguments. Gay photographers from Wilhelm von Gloeden to Bob Mizer had long invoked the ancient world to normalize their interest in the male nude by including a Greek column or posing their models to imitate classic sculpture.[4]

The Grecian Guild took this classical trope and made it the center of its mission. It promised to take a homoerotic Hellenism developed in elite nineteenth-century literary circles and democratize it into both a commercial venture and a membership organization. It represented a new community-building effort around a centuries-old queer interest in the male physique. More than other efforts, it looked to the future by studying the past.

GRECIAN GUILD FOUNDERS

The Grecian Guild was the brainchild of two white southerners, a gay couple who met while they were students at the University of Virginia. Randolph Benson, the publication director and business manager, was a native of the small farming community of Mint Spring, Virginia. After studying for the ministry and serving in the U.S. Navy during World War II, he was elected to Phi Beta Kappa at the University of Virginia and graduated with a degree in English.

Finishing just one year after the war ended, Benson stayed on for two more years at UVA to get a master's degree in sociology, writing on issues of the history of family and marriage in Virginia.

It was in 1947, while in graduate school, that he met a handsome undergraduate, John Bullock, also from a small farming community—Rowland, North Carolina. One document outlining the history of the guild suggests that they may have met at the university gym. Bullock had served as an artist in the U.S. Army's 1st Armored Division and would become the magazine's art director. His artistic bent and lack of interest in farming had alienated him from his father, who owned hundreds of acres in Rowland—a "plantation" according to his niece—much of it farmed by sharecroppers. He stayed at UVA for only two years, dropping out to follow Benson after Benson finished his thesis and began looking for a teaching assignment.

They spent the next few years moving frequently as Benson secured short-term teaching assignments and worked on his Ph.D. degree at Louisiana State University. It was an uneven partnership, not unlike the Grecian model of an older *erastes* and a younger *eromenos*. "Randy was something of a father figure to John," recalled a member of Bullock's family. Not only was Benson five years older, but he had a more dominant personality. But the magazine and photo studio business complemented each of their strengths and allowed them to work together. It was a partnership that would last sixty years and take them to residences in California, Arizona, and Louisiana; but they would return to Virginia often, always considering it their home.[5]

It was from Charlottesville that they launched a modest physique photography studio in 1953. By then Bullock had begun training as a bodybuilder and photographer and was thus comfortable on both sides of the camera. They recruited models not from Muscle Beach or bodybuilding contests but from the local student population. Advertisements in the back of *Tomorrow's Man* and *VIM* were successful at bringing in not only money but also fan mail. Customers enjoyed the boy-next-door quality of their models. They also appreciated the ideals that Benson and Bullock began to articulate in their photo catalogs about the male body. "How can we become members?" many of them asked. As with Mizer's early success in running a personal advertisement in *Strength & Health*, it seems that this enthusiastic response from the gay reading and buying public convinced Benson and Bullock to expand. After joining the migration to Southern California—what Bob Mizer called the "mecca of bodybuilders and physique photographers"—they launched their own publication.[6]

More than other physique entrepreneurs, the founders of *Grecian Guild Pictorial* used their own lives and images to sell their vision. The first issue featured their names prominently above the table of contents, with Randolph Benson listed as "Publications Director" and John F. Bullock Jr. as "Art Director." One of the first photographs readers encountered was of John Bullock posing with his arms outstretched in a gesture of welcome. Here he used the alias "Jeff Allen," so readers did not immediately know it was one of the guild founders greeting them. But over the next few years in their more private newsletters for Grecian Guild members, Benson and Bullock displayed photos of themselves—both professional headshots in suits and ties and physique photos in swimsuits at the beach—and signed their real names. Whereas Bob Mizer rarely used his name and never his image, Benson and Bullock more clearly identified themselves to readers and more clearly identified themselves with the product. Guild conventions offered special opportunities to meet the founders and hear about their plans. As practitioners of the Grecian ideal, their personas, and their implied relationship, were an integral part of the brand (see fig. 3.3).

Considering how closely they associated themselves with the magazine, it is ironic how little we know about them. Unlike Bob Mizer, who became something of a legend in his time, was interviewed and filmed extensively in the 1970s and 1980s, and left behind a diary and a warehouse full of materials, Benson and Bullock quickly faded from the scene. After selling the magazine in the late 1950s to Lynn Womack, they disappeared from the physique and homophile worlds. They returned to Virginia and became educators—Benson taught sociology at Roanoke College and Bullock taught art in a local high school. No one knew about their previous lives as physique magazine publishers; they left no papers and were never interviewed about their roles. All that we know of them is from slips of information in other people's archives. Indeed, most previous writings on *Grecian Guild Pictorial* have assumed it was a Lynn Womack creation.[7]

We do know that their elite university education at the University of Virginia was transformative. It was not only where they met and formed a lifelong partnership but also where they discovered a sense of themselves as gay men, developed models for community building, and conceived of what would become the Grecian Guild. While at UVA, Benson was a member of Sigma Chi, what *Life* magazine called in a profile from 1950 "one of the biggest, oldest, and most solid" of fraternities. Benson clearly borrowed from the fraternity model in structuring the guild around a national organization with local chapters, a

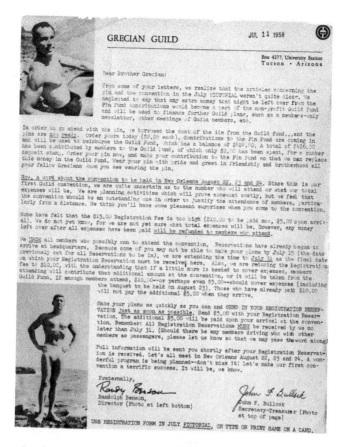

FIGURE 3.3 In a letter to their brother Grecians, cofounders Randolph Benson and John Bullock discuss ideas for a convention of the Grecian Guild planned for New Orleans in 1958, one of three such gatherings they hosted.

Courtesy of ONE Archives at the USC Libraries.

creed, a chaplain, and membership pins analogous to pledge pins. Even their later mailing address ("University Station, Tucson, Arizona") invoked the university experience. "America's only fraternity of bodybuilders, artists and physique students," the magazine would boast. More than merely a membership club, the Grecian Guild represented a brotherhood.[8]

The Grecian Guild was not unique among gay organizations in borrowing aspects of a fraternal organization. Harry Hay's Mattachine Society, founded in Los Angeles just a few years earlier, also drew on the fraternal model. It was after discussions with other gay men at a beer bust at the University of

Southern California that Hay first proposed an organization he wanted to call the International Bachelors' Fraternal Order for Peace & Social Dignity. When he later settled on the name Mattachine for his organization, Hay borrowed the term from Renaissance fraternities of unmarried men or "fool societies" who performed satires of religious and political figures behind masks. Hay's initial written plans for Mattachine stressed that "membership and inter-Order activity shall be Masonic in character" and would include insignia and pins to differentiate ranks within the organization. Hay made sure that early meetings included an initiation ceremony and membership oath and often used fraternal language in referring to his "gay brothers" and "gay sisters."

Hay had become familiar with such fraternal rituals from his undergraduate days at Stanford, where he was involved in the rush process, at least until he came out publicly as gay. During the postwar years, secret fraternal organizations were enjoying a resurgence, and according to historians Lillian Faderman and Stuart Timmons, "Hay believed that such a structure provided both privacy and a sense of brotherhood that would not only defuse fear but would also appeal to homosexuals and encourage organizing." Many gay men certainly perceived it as a fraternal organization. While historians often stress Hay's Communist Party USA background and his borrowing of that organization's secret cell structure, Mattachine also clearly drew on the fraternal model.[9]

THE LURE OF ANCIENT GREECE

The university experience also structured their decision to call themselves "Grecians." Thomas Jefferson's university was known to feature a classical education— its Classics Department was founded at the same time as the university, in 1812—so undoubtedly both men came in contact with the literature, history, and mythology of the ancient world. Oxford began structuring education around classical texts in the nineteenth century as an antidote to the coarseness and materialism of modern capitalism, and as Linda Dowling has shown, this focus on a Hellenistic tradition contained the potential for the construction of a "homosexual counterdiscourse."[10]

It was in such classes that many gay men first encountered affirming notions of homosexuality. For Alan Helms, it was a course at Columbia University in the 1950s. "I was thrilled when one day in Humanities (we were discussing some ancient Greek or other), the professor said, 'Of course, gentlemen, we're all aware that men sometimes experience erotic attraction for other men.'" The encounter gave him ammunition for the homophobia he encountered, even in that classroom. "I knew from the murmurs & shifting chairs that the other guys were acutely uncomfortable with such an idea," he remembered. "Never mind: Aristophanes knew better than they, & Aristophanes was right."[11]

Benson and Bullock shared their nostalgic view of ancient Greece with legions of homoerotically inclined men educated at elite universities. Their experiences were strikingly similar to those of another southern aristocrat, William Alexander Percy, who, at Sewanee: The University of the South, discovered both the idiom of Greek love and a community of like-minded men. Percy considered Sewanee "Arcadia" since it was both the site of his sexual awakening and where he learned a Hellenistic language in which he could express his homoerotic feelings. Percy became a respected lawyer and pillar of white, Jim Crow–era society in Greenville, Mississippi, but was also a lifelong bachelor who published homoerotic poetry. "I am Greek, all Greek; I know the loveliness of flesh and its sweet snare," he confessed in one of his many Hellenistic poems. As he openly acknowledged in his best-selling autobiography, *Lanterns on the Levee: Recollections of a Planter's Son*, "the Greeks practiced bisexuality honestly and simply without thought or condemnation." Like the Grecian Guild founders, Percy looked nostalgically back to a time and place he considered more hospitable.[12]

Like many Americans, Benson's understanding of antiquity was influenced by Paul Brandt's influential study *Sexual Life in Ancient Greece*.[13] Brandt was a German classical scholar whose book became the standard work on homosexuality in the ancient world. Translated into English in 1932, it was widely circulated and reprinted, including a 1953 edition by Barnes and Noble. It offered such a spirited defense of modern-day homosexuality based on Brandt's understanding of the Greek experience that some scholars have dismissed it as "homosexual chauvinism."[14] When making the claim that homosexuality was neither abnormal nor unnatural but "basic in the species," Alfred Kinsey footnoted Brandt's assertions about the near ubiquity of homosexual practices in ancient Greece. Both Benson and homophile leader Jim Kepner credit Brandt with helping them see parallels between ancient Greek gyms and male beauty contests and modern bodybuilding contests. Benson quoted Brandt extensively in the pages of the *Grecian Guild Pictorial*.[15]

Brandt was one of many gay or bisexual men in the late nineteenth century who published scholarship on same-sex sexual relations in ancient Greece to counteract the concurrent scientific classification of homosexuality as a sign of mental or physical degeneration. They used the example of the centrality of homosexual relations to ancient Athenian life to call for decriminalization of same-sex relations in modern Europe. Brandt, for example, worked with Magnus Hirschfield's Scientific Humanitarian Committee in advocating for repeal of the Prussian Paragraph 175 criminalizing homosexual relations. Similarly, John Addington Symonds addressed his early study of "Greek Love" squarely to contemporary psychiatric and legal experts. In A *Problem in Greek Ethics*, Symonds called attention to how in ancient Athens "we have the example of a great and highly-developed race not only tolerating homosexual passions, but deeming them of spiritual value." As D. H. Mader argues, "Far from a means of evasion, allusions to the Greeks were a tool for valorization in a strategy for social acceptance."[16]

In calling themselves "Grecians," Benson and Bullock were self-consciously invoking this long tradition of referencing classical Greece as a way to announce that they valued and defended homoeroticism. As they explained in a lengthy essay in the first issue of *Grecian Guild Pictorial*, they were not Greek nationals, nor even descendants of Greeks—nothing so literal. Asserting that words are important, they articulated the almost postmodern notion that interpretations vary according to a reader's "knowledge, experience, and prejudices." They were confident that their readers shared their particular cultural perspective and therefore might not even need an explanation. "Since you who read this are manifestly interested in the male body as an object of admiration and respect in its highest form," Benson and Bullock wrote, "perhaps you already understand why we are the GRECIAN Guild." They knew they were preaching to the choir, engaging in a sort of insider language. Their invocation of ancient Greece was less a cover or alibi to hide behind than a way to signal to other like-minded men. To many of their gay readers, the name Grecian Guild was not a fig leaf to justify the illicit but a wink of the eye to signify a common desire.[17]

Benson and Bullock could assume this knowledge on the part of their readership, since by the 1950s the association between homosexuality and ancient Greece was well entrenched in American culture. Those who did not benefit from an elite classical education found other sources with similar information. As an eighteen-year-old in Chicago, Mr. S. discovered Plato's *Symposium* and *Phaedrus* while researching a term paper at the public library. "Great was my surprise and joy when I for the first time saw an exact statement of my own feelings," he later wrote. Craig Rodwell received the same lesson in 1960 from a psychiatrist he was forced to see after an arrest in Chicago with an older man. "The psychiatrist ... was very reassuring and told [me] about ancient Greece," he remembered.[18] Novels with gay themes or characters often provided a primer on ancient

Greek myths and a veritable pantheon of homosexual heroes. Blair Niles's *Strange Brother* follows Mark Thornton, a gay man who rejects the gay subculture in New York centered on drag balls and fairies, preferring to work on compiling an anthology of "Comrades and Lovers," which drew heavily on the writings of Edward Carpenter. He dreamed of ancient Greece, where he believed "the love of man for man had reached its pinnacle of beauty." Such novels were widely available at commercial rental libraries then popular in American cities.[19]

Perhaps the most widely available source of this affirming argument about the role of homosexuality in ancient Greece was a series of five-cent pamphlets marketed by Emanuel Haldeman-Julius as his Little Blue Books. A socialist publisher based in Kansas, Haldeman-Julius marketed cheap versions of literary classics as well as practical how-to guides for the masses. An atheist and an early practitioner of companionate marriage who appended his wife's name to his own, Haldeman-Julius fancied himself the Voltaire of his generation, preaching toleration in a culture "stifled by prejudice, sham, and superstition." Among the most popular of the 1,800 pamphlets he offered were volumes in the "Rational Sex" series with such innocuous titles as *What Every Married Man Should Know* and *What Every Married Woman Should Know*.[20]

In 1927—the one year for which sales statistics are available—*Homosexual Life* and *Sex Life in Greece and Rome* were among the firm's best sellers, together selling over 100,000 copies. Total sales of Little Blue Books reportedly exceeded 500 million copies, gaining Haldeman-Julius the moniker "the Henry Ford of literature."[21]

Jim Kepner recalls seeing these books advertised in his hometown newspaper in 1942. He ordered twenty pamphlets for a dollar and included titles on *Homosexual Life* (#692) and *Homosexuality in the Lives of the Great* (#1564) in the mix, hoping no one would notice his true reading interests. He learned that "among the Greeks the conception of love was distinctly homosexual. As one authority puts it, men fell in love with each other. Yet the Greeks were certainly not an effeminate, unmanly or degenerate race." Kepner took away an affirming message about his budding sexuality. "Whatever my problem or condition, it was shared with Michelangelo, Leonardo, all the old Greeks," he reasoned.[22]

Invoking ancient Greece had become integral to both private and public political arguments in favor of homosexual rights. In his famous letter to an American mother concerning her gay son, Sigmund Freud argued in 1935 that homosexuality was no vice, illness, or crime and that persecuting homosexuals was a great injustice. "Many highly respectable individuals of ancient and modern times have been homosexuals," Freud offered by way of proof, "several of the greatest among them (Plato, Michelangelo, Leonardo da Vinci, etc.)." In a coming-out letter in 1945, a Kansas man reassured his parents that there was nothing wrong with his attraction to other men. "The ancient Greek civilization," he counseled them, was "practically based on it and its civilization flourished." Writing in 1961, the editor of ONE argued that "almost the first thing that any homosexual does, when called upon to offer any serious defense of homosexuality, is to draw upon the glorious example of the manly Greek warriors and athletes who apparently practiced homosexual love openly and without shame."[23]

Benson was a devoted reader of ONE and may have drawn inspiration from its marshaling of the models of Greece and Rome to bolster its claims for gay rights. The same year he founded his magazine, ONE ran a six-part series of excerpts of speeches from Plato's Symposium.[24] "I've been a ONE man since the first issue," Benson proudly told editors as he implored them to continue his subscription despite frequent relocations. "And I *must* have every issue," he insisted. "Blessings on you for all the *great* work you're doing!" he wrote in the margins of another subscription renewal. Whether they drew their inspiration from university coursework, novels, pamphlets, or homophile publications, Benson and Bullock were making an implicit argument for social justice that had become commonplace.[25]

Benson and Bullock used their magazine to feature men who shared their nostalgic look back at antiquity. Physique artist George Quaintance had already developed a following through the pages of Physique Pictorial and Tomorrow's Man, but he developed a particularly close relationship with Benson and Bullock. All three were from prominent southern farm families, and all three had relocated to Arizona. Perhaps it was this special affinity that prompted Quaintance to step out from behind the canvas and speak to his audience for the first time in their magazine. He would answer the "constant stream of letters and questions that come to me daily from admirers of my work in all parts of the world."

In the pages of Grecian Guild, Quaintance opened up about how he suffered as a child with feelings of difference and isolation as an artistic boy raised surrounded by farmers. "Naturally I grew up in a dream world," he related, in a narrative that resonated with gay men raised in straight families. His isolation pushed him to read history, and his imagination allowed him to identify with the characters and events he found there. "I came to feel and to know all the past great events and the many lives I was sure I was mixed up with in some way through a thousand years of History." He wasn't sure if this understanding came from his books, his dreams, or even what he believed to be his former lives. Whatever its source, he felt that we all have "a background of knowledge that has nothing to do with our parents or our direct ancestry." Although Quaintance's understanding verged on the paranormal, he was describing a sense of an imagined common cultural past, one not conveyed by one's immediate family. It was a vision in harmony with the mission of the Grecian Guild, which also posited a collective, imaged past distinct from one's biological ancestry. But rather than rely on scholarly argument or historical exegesis, Quaintance *felt* a visceral commonality with the past (see fig. 3.4).[26]

Quaintance —

America's greatest physique artist tells his own story.

PICTORIAL readers and Guild members have deluged us with requests for more of the works of the great artist, Quaintance. We proudly presented herewith representative examples of his work, as well as the accompanying autobiography, in the artist's own words, which we know will be of outstanding interest to each of our readers. There is

QUAINTANCE, the distinguished American physique artist. We are proud to claim this great artist as a charter member of the Grecian Guild.

inspiration here for all—inspiration from the great spirit and mind and heart of a great man. Bodybuilders will see in Quaintance's work

"Neptune's Children," new sculpture figures by Quaintance designed to hang on any flat surface. They may

FIGURE 3.4 In the Spring 1956 issue, *Grecian Guild Pictorial* featured the life and work of popular physique artist George Quaintance. "I too feel that I crusade in my attempt to satisfy a deep emotional hunger in the inner lives of my customers," Quaintance professed.

His emotional link with the past led him, after becoming an enthusiastic Grecian Guild member, to complete two paintings set in the ancient world, *Baths of Ancient Rome* and *Spartan Soldiers Bathing*. But the painting he featured in the first issue, which Benson described as "Grecian," was much simpler. It was not a typical image from Greek mythology; its pond of lily pads was more oriental than classical. What made it particularly "Grecian" were the two men, alone, nearly naked, gazing at one another. A blond man leans against a column, nude save for a fine cloth that cascades down to the ground, where a nude, dark-haired man is reclining suggestively, his buttocks exposed to the viewer. The two men are connected literally through the cloth but more intently through their eyes. The standing man gazes longingly at the supine man below him; indeed, his gaze seems fixed on the man's exposed penis, hidden from the viewer (see fig. 3.5).

Quaintance named the painting *Idyll*, a reference to nostalgic poems describing scenes of pastoral or rustic life. In the ancient Greek context, it referenced poems by Theocritus, many addressed from an older man to his younger beloved, hoping that they will stay friends always, "as of yore Patroclus and Achilles swore." More broadly, idyllic describes an Arcadian paradise— precisely the sort of place Benson and Bullock hoped their organization would create.[27]

MASCULINE COMRADES

By invoking a past that was imagined as a golden age for homoerotic desire, the Grecian Guild was engaging in the construction of a collective memory, a practice common to virtually all social groups. They were "inventing tradition," to borrow the phrasing from Eric Hobsbawn. Or as George Chauncey argues about gay men in the 1920s, "By imagining they had collective roots in the past, they asserted a collective identity in the present."[28]

But it was a particular sort of gay utopia they constructed—one of masculine, mostly white, beauty. Even if it was a halcyon notion of days gone by, it offered a language and an imaginary space that stood in sharp contrast to one of the few other common spaces for gay men—the gay bar—and its language of camp. This particular vision of a masculine, heroic homosexuality was favored by men either not connected to urban gay male culture or disdainful of it. For men such as Alan Helms at Columbia, these classical texts affirmed

FIGURE 3.5 George Quaintance's painting entitled *Idyll* (1952) appeared in the first issue of the *Grecian Guild Pictorial*. Although most of Quaintance's images were set in the American West, after he became a charter member of the Grecian Guild several invoked the homoeroticism of the classical world.

his own experience—his passionate relationship with another undergraduate male, neither of them connected to the gay subculture. To Helms, they were "masculine men who loved men," two halves of the same former self, as explained by Aristotle, not gender-bending queers.[29]

All the early gay physique magazines shared this rejection of gender deviation and effeminacy and instead helped to construct a new vision of gay masculinity. Lon of New York's photographs nearly always contained an iconic classical white column. His motto was "You can love a man, and you can still be a man." Known for images of masculine beauty, Lon also photographed drag queens and was known privately for his camp sensibility—his day job was as a church organist, a long-standing gay stereotype. But his physique images offered no hint of effeminacy.[30]

Bob Mizer, too, like many young gay men coming of age, made a concerted effort to avoid appearing effeminate. He recorded in his diary his efforts to make "my walk more masculine, a deeper, richer voice, changed manners." He was not trying to hide his homosexuality, but he wanted to give it another valence. And in his amazingly candid magazine editorials, Mizer refuted the common assumption that "sissy" and homosexual were synonymous, again pointing to how "homosexuality was the standard way of life among the rugged Greek warriors." Moving beyond such historical references, Mizer cited new social science research, probably Kinsey: "According to researchers of our own current time [homosexuality] is no rarity among such masculine occupations as truck drivers, cowboys, military men, policemen, and many others." Benson made a similar, if more implicit, claim, noting that Grecian Guild readers lived throughout the country and were employed in all occupations, including teachers, office workers, and business executives. They did not differ from "the great majority of Americans," he noted.[31]

This tension between the campy world of gay bars and a more masculine Grecian ideal played out in gay novels of the period. Nial Kent peppered *The Divided Path* with longing references to a lost ancient Greek homoeroticism. The main character, Michael, a precocious but lonely child, took refuge in books, where he learned how his hero Alexander the Great had cut off his hair in mourning his beloved Hephaestion. Michael created an imaginary friend with whom he ventured out at night to dig for antiquities at the site of ancient Troy and swear eternal friendship at the tomb of Achilles. He grew up with what he called the "Greek ideal," where an older partner was the "Inspirer" and the younger the "Hearer." He longed to find someone who shared his ideals, but when he moved to New York and began traveling in gay social circles, Michael was disturbed to find queens calling one another "she," exchanging recipes at parties, and hopping from bed to bed. "So this is what had happened to the Greek ideal of passionate attachments between men," he lamented.[32]

Language about Greek heroes was one of the few ways to talk about same-sex love that did not rely on camp. *ONE* magazine editor Ross Ingersoll lamented the heterosexual assumption that attraction to a man is necessarily a female characteristic and all the effeminizing labels that have therefore been applied to gay men: "Belle, queen, Nellie, fairy, girl, auntie, mother, and so on." He was frustrated by how "we just don't have a word that conveys the idea that a man may be a homosexual but is a man for all that." To fill this gap, he notes how gay men would raise the "glorious example of the manly Greek warriors and athletes" as an alternative discourse of manly same-sex desire. Walt Whitman and his poetic celebration of masculine camaraderie may have been the only other literary reference point for such manly love of comrades. One of Lon of New York's photo catalogs, for example, quoted "The full-spread pride of man is calming and excellent to the soul" from Whitman's famous "I Sing the Body Electric."[33]

This search for a more masculine homosexual model was part of what historian Craig Loftin calls the "anti-swish prejudice" among middle-class homophile leaders and rank-and-file members within the postwar gay community. Frequent articles, editorials, and reader comments complained that the hands-on-hips, limp-wristed swish was damaging to the movement. Some even offered advice on how to cure a tendency toward effeminate mannerisms, voice, or gate. Loftin sees this as the reaction of a rising educated, middle-class gay community separating themselves from the more working-class pansies and fairies, who in the decades before World War II were the more visible segment of the community. While those communities centered around bars and other sites of urban leisure, the more masculine-identified gay men of the postwar period found community through a network of gyms, physique magazines, homophile organizations, and other nonbar settings. Loftin argues that physique magazines and homophile organizations worked together to "reinforce an explicitly masculine postwar iconic representation of male homosexuality." Many of the gay pulp fiction writers of the period, particularly Carl Corley from rural Mississippi and James Barr from Kansas, depicted gay male characters who were decidedly butch.[34]

Most physique magazines, with a far-flung, mostly rural constituency and an emphasis on masculine camaraderie, fitness, and outdoor activities, represented an alternative to urban gay bars. Based on Grecian Guild membership application statistics, the majority (55 percent) of its most devoted readers lived outside of a major metropolitan area, which suggests the guild was dominated by rural members without ready access to gay bars, cafes, or bathhouses. "Over half our members live in smaller cities, towns, and rural areas," Benson noted. "They live almost everywhere—Novelty, Ohio; Nowatta, Oklahoma; Truth or

Consequences, New Mexico; Agana, Guama; Bangkok, Thailand." The founders also seem to have held an anti-urban bias. "I hate cities . . . Period," Benson wrote a colleague. Benson and Bullock spent the majority of their lives in small college towns, moving between Charlottesville, Laguna Beach, Tucson, and Roanoke.[35]

According to a contemporary observer, none of the major physique photographers was particularly fond of alcohol. Mizer, despite being clearly enmeshed in a gay social circle in Los Angeles, did not frequent gay bars. Noting how the new shift from weightlifting to bodybuilding had increased the popularity of gyms, Mizer wrote, "Let us hope that soon gymnasiums will be as popular as cocktail bars are now."[36]

The physique world was a type of alternative social space to gay bars, distinct for its emphasis on the desire to consume visual images rather than the desire to consume alcohol—and for its embrace of a masculine ideal that eschewed camp. While both social spaces were organized around the alibi of commodity consumption, the physique world was in many ways more directly tied to the male body and same-sex desire.

GRECIAN CHAPLAINS

While the Grecian Guild rejected the gay bar as a potential site for socialization, it embraced the Christian Church. Indeed, one of the more striking features of the guild was its invocation of religious language and the voices of Christian ministers, even as it touted the values of pagan antiquity. The guild promoted several bachelor ministers who gave spiritual advice, offered personal counseling through the mail, and formed their own guild chapter. Featured as a Grecian of the Quarter, Rev. Robert H. Coleman, Episcopalian missionary from Baltimore serving in Japan, appeared in two contrasting photographs—one in a clerical collar and one in a posing strap. "The body and the spirit are two parts of the whole," the thirty-three-year-old bachelor minister reminded his fellow Grecians.[37]

By putting religion in the foreground and giving a prominent voice to Christian ministers, Grecian Guild Pictorial set itself apart from other physique magazines. Bob Mizer, for example, who grew up in a very strict Mormon household, was openly hostile to fundamentalist religious faith, which he saw as allied with the forces of censorship. Benson, however, embraced the

Methodist faith of his parents and as a teenager even felt a calling to the ministry. Following in the footsteps of his grandfather, the Rev. Robert Campbell, a well-known Methodist clergyman, Benson passed the examinations to become an assistant minister at the age of nineteen. In the summer of 1940 he served as a substitute minister to a number of Virginia congregations. After his service in World War II, however, he abandoned clerical training and matriculated at the University of Virginia to study English. But he did not abandon his faith. When he founded the Grecian Guild, he proudly described himself as a member of the Episcopal Church, while his partner John Bullock described himself as a member of the Presbyterian Church. Their devotion to their faiths seems to have been lifelong.[38]

This attempt to harmonize Grecian values and Christianity also drew on a long history. Renaissance figures such as Marsilio Ficino, who first translated and popularized the writings of Plato, may have condemned sodomy as a sin, but Ficino considered Socratic love between two men the highest form of friendship. Neo-Platonist thinkers believed that the carnal desires could be purified in keeping with Christian teachings. Perhaps the main character in E. M. Forster's *Maurice* put it best after discovering Plato's *Phaedrus*: "He saw there his malady described exquisitely, calmly, as a passion which we can direct, like any other, towards good or bad." Maurice felt that Plato not only understood him but offered "a new guide for life." The Grecian Guild chaplains took this long-standing tradition within elite Hellenistic circles and gave it a wider audience.[39]

The Reverend Robert Wood was a charter member and early contributor to the magazine who became friends with Benson and Bullock. A 1951 graduate of Oberlin Graduate School of Theology, Wood had just become pastor at the First Congregational Church in Spring Valley, New York. While struggling to locate a parish position, he had worked in Manhattan promoting religious films by day and cruising the bars and streets of Greenwich Village at night looking for a lover. He was also looking for another way to meet men. An avid reader of physique magazines, he had arranged to meet Quaintance on one of his forays to New York to sell paintings, and the two had a tryst that resulted in a lasting friendship. Wood considered it one of the few "meaningful ties" he maintained from "the quagmire of [New York's] mad gay life, most of which was so without purpose or constructive good."

Wood also attended the study groups Donald Webster Cory organized in New York in the wake of the success of his book *The Homosexual in America*.

Wood was inspired by Cory's pioneering first-person analysis of the gay community but lamented his lack of attention to religion. With encouragement from Cory, Wood dedicated himself to finding a way, both in his life and his writing, to integrate a homosexual orientation and the Christian faith. Serving as a chaplain for the Grecian Guild allowed Wood his first opportunity to minister to gay men on a large scale (see figs. 3.6 and 3.7).[40]

Wood offered spiritual exercises for Grecians to practice along with their physical ones. He suggested readers join a Bible study group and learn a verse of scripture each week. Among the many readers who took Wood's advice seriously was Edward Hildebrand of Upper Darby, Pennsylvania. A fifty-year-old

FIGURE 3.6 Rev. Robert Wood served as a chaplain for the Grecian Guild, offering spiritual exercises to members to accompany their physical ones. Author of the book *Christ and the Homosexual* (1961), Wood sought to reconcile a homosexual orientation and the Christian faith.

Courtesy of the Congregational Library & Archives, Boston.

FIGURE 3.7 Grecian Guild chaplain Robert Wood (*standing*) on the beach in Provinc-etown, Massachusetts, which was a gay vacation mecca as early as the 1940s.

Courtesy of the Congregational Library & Archives, Boston.

Lutheran church organist, Hildebrand admitted that "My interest in the *Pictorial* derives from the fact that I am homosexual." He had stopped playing the organ because he had gotten into some embarrassing situations with some young men in the congregation. "I prefer to rigidly control my natural inclination in order to avoid scandal," he explained. Wood congratulated him on admitting his sexual inclinations and suggested that 90 percent of "gay fellows" managed to avoid scandal and enjoy meaningful homosexual relationships.

Wood counseled him not to equate all physical relationships with sin, which for Wood was anything that disrupts one's relationship with God. In educating Hildebrand, Wood was practicing the sort of pastoral care that a few years later he would turn into the pathbreaking book *Christ and the Homosexual.*[41]

On a summer trip back East from Tucson, Benson and Bullock visited Wood at his parsonage in Spring Valley. "We discussed way into the night the values, merits, dangers, opportunities of such an idea as the Guild," Wood recalled. "I was greatly impressed by their sincerity, high character, general competence, vision, etc.," he wrote to friends. Aware that many gay men felt adrift, having been rejected by their families and churches, Wood thought the guild offered the possibility for a "sense of belonging to something worthwhile." A newly ordained Episcopal minister from Los Angeles agreed with Wood's assessment. "I think a magazine like *Grecian Guild Pictorial* can serve a good purpose," wrote Rev. Roland Thorwaldsen, complimenting Wood on his recent article. "It can teach a homosexual to have respect for himself and his fellows. It can furnish him with a set of ideals that he can use in forming a constructive attitude about his condition." The two ministers shared stories about the need to organize Protestant clergy to reach out to homosexuals and provide them with a spiritual home, and they saw the guild as serving an analogous function. It represented an alternative to what they both perceived as the tawdriness and superficiality of gay bars, what Wood described as the "labyrinth of gaiety" centered on buying the latest fashions and nightly cruising.[42]

Both Wood and Benson were critical of much of American religious doctrine and its obsessive focus on puritanism. Wood, who frequented S&M parties and leather bars in New York, was certainly no prude. Both men favored accepting one's desires and channeling them into constructive relationships. Benson published a lengthy attack on puritanism under the obvious pseudonym "Rev. Thorman Alderson." The article confronted the idea that the Grecian Guild's classical framework was mere window dressing for displaying handsome models. It asserted that the values of ancient Greece had much to offer a country ravished by high levels of crime, alcoholism, divorce, and racial strife. A return to Greek values would restore harmony to the individual and end unnecessary suppression of both desires and emotions. "Where you find the body neglected, despised or considered an object of shame, there you have puritanism. Where you find human emotions beaten down, stifled or scorned as signs of weakness, there you have puritanism." It called for a liberation from this way of thinking, a respect for "all sides of the human personality . . . every part of man's nature." Benson also created a Grecian pledge, which asked members to affirm, "I live a life that is open, for I have nothing to hide in darkness nor in secret." It was a message that must have resonated with gay men taught to feel shame about their desires and to hide their emotions. More than a message, the author called it "a movement of enormous practical value."[43]

In keeping with a fraternal model, the Grecian Guild tried to encapsulate its ideals in a simple creed. Reprinted in nearly every issue, the creed underwent frequent revisions that illustrate the tension between homoerotic Hellenism and more mainstream Christian ethics. In its original incarnation it highlighted active dedication to reanimating the values "first perceived and perfected by the people of ancient Greece." The later version did not mention ancient Greece until the end, only to note that the guild passively "honors" those high ideals. The original creed pledged allegiance to "pure beauty of art, particularly as it is embodied in the human physique at its best." This paean to "pure beauty" echoed the nineteenth-century Aesthetic movement and its cult of beauty for its own sake. It was removed from the revised version in favor of "all beauty" and "worthy art"—language at once both more general and more qualified. Beauty had also figured prominently in the original list of Grecian values: "truth, honor, beauty, God and native land." Already an eclectic mix of ancient Grecian and modern Christian ideals, the list became much more conventional in its final revision: "God, truth, honor, purity, friendship and native land." God was prioritized while beauty was replaced by "purity" to provide a moralizing counterweight to any implied decadence.[44]

GROWING AND CONNECTING

The surest sign that *Grecian Guild Pictorial* represented something new was the response it received from its competitors. Within months of its launch, *VIM* editor Bill Bunton, claiming to be "nauseated" and "disgusted," ran a two-page attack against the new magazine that *VIM* parodied as the "Gilded Greek." Noting the models' lack of muscular development, the editors compared them to undernourished escapees from a concentration camp. They also ridiculed the plans to create a brotherhood by holding national conventions, likening it to a "trade union."[45]

Nine months later, *VIM* ran a four-page satirical diatribe against the upstart, calling it "Rollicking Romans Pictorial." This time the editors were more explicit about their moral objections, suggesting that the group's "Credo for Public Consumption" was hiding nefarious activities under the guise of "Art(?) and Bawdy-building." VIM saw the attributes of antiquity differently than did Benson and Bullock. Rather than the ideals of masculine beauty, it saw "debauchery, promiscuity, corruption, and moral pollution." VIM parodied the Grecian Guild membership application, where members were asked to identify themselves as a bodybuilder, artist, or student. To this list VIM added a fourth option—"just looking." It changed the categories "married" and "single" to "married?" and "whatever for?" And to the request for a personal photograph it asked, "What the heck do you want a picture of me for?" (see fig. 3.8).[46]

It was just the kind of publicity—hinting at sexual scandal—a struggling new magazine could only dream of. Watching from California, Bob Mizer credited the attacks with raising the magazine out of virtual obscurity into national prominence. Although it must have stung to see his own image in a posing strap singled out for ridicule, Benson was so thrilled with the free publicity that he wrote VIM a thank-you. The guild had received nearly a thousand inquiries and only two complaints. Benson's only regret was that his critics hadn't included his address. VIM readers wrote in to denounce the editors for their cowardice. Some canceled their memberships in high dudgeon and warned that VIM was "on the way out." VIM claimed to be happy to see them go but also suggested that the letters were curiously similar in language, hinting that the Grecian Guild may have orchestrated a letter-writing campaign. Whether or not he was responsible for all the mail, Benson certainly knew how to capitalize on the publicity. He placed advertisements in other magazines encouraging readers to subscribe to see "What's all the fuss about?"[47]

It may have been the free publicity that got readers' attention. It might have been the pink cover, at a time when "gay as pink ink" was a common in-group expression. Readers may have responded to the promise of fraternal fellowship, the Grecian values, the Christian outreach, or just the photographs. But they responded in droves. Membership grew rapidly, and the magazine quickly stepped up publication from quarterly to bimonthly. According to contemporary accounts, within a year Benson and Bullock were printing twenty-five thousand copies of each issue and boasted to friends that the magazine was outselling all other physique magazines.[48]

By the third issue they had members from forty-five of the then forty-eight U.S. states. Displaying a map of the United States and state membership figures, they turned recruiting other members into a matter of state pride. The

ROLLICKING ROMANS

PICTORIAL

Oh, what fun all the members of the International Order of Rollicking Romans had at our recent convention. On the right is a picture of a Rollicking Roman happily rollicking. However, seconds after this shot was snapped, said Rollicking Roman was pulled into the deep and devoured by two unidentified sharks (see background). The culprit responsible was a member of a rival guild who caught our heroic RR off balance as shown above. Now wasn't he an old meany!

AN EXTRA SPECIAL VIM SUPPLEMENT

ART (?) and BAWDYBUILDING

FIGURE 3.8 The *Grecian Guild Pictorial* was so popular and overt in its appeal to a gay readership that its competitors launched several satirical attacks. The September 1956 issue of *VIM* derided it as "Rollicking Romans Pictorial" and suggested that ancient Greece was a model of "debauchery, promiscuity, corruption and moral pollution."

map graphically illustrated their national reach, mimicking a similar map in the pages of *ONE*. Benson and Bullock believed it was "destined to become a great national organization" if it won the support of all who shared its ideals. The desire for connection was palpable. "I hope that it will not be long until local chapters of the Guild can be formed," wrote an early subscriber who enjoyed sketching the male physique. When George U. Lyon from Portsmouth,

Virginia, offered to form a Virginia chapter, Benson printed his address to facilitate contact. Soon he and Bullock would routinely print the names and addresses of letter writers. The idea of establishing local chapters was so popular they warned readers that "unauthorized individuals" were forming chapters without acquiring the requisite charter. Even teenagers were trying to join. Promising that he lived by the Grecian creed by developing his brain and his body, a fourteen-year-old who trained with his "buddy" in suburban Montreal suggested the formation of a "junior Guild" for those under age.

Readers seemed to appreciate that *Grecian Guild Pictorial* represented something new, and not just in the sort of models it featured. A costume and fashion designer from Ohio wrote to say, "I have long felt the need for such a group, but had little hope of ever finding one." A frequent reader of physique magazines from Texas complimented the guild on "great strides toward the freedom we all want." A reader from New York was the first to use the term "movement" to describe the guild's organizational efforts: "May I commend you highly for initiating a movement that has been needed in this country for many years." A writer from Tampa echoed the sentiment, suggesting that it seemed less like a commercial enterprise and more like a "crusade" or "the voice of a larger movement."[49]

Readers saw this as part of a movement because of the ways in which *Grecian Guild Pictorial* allowed them to connect with each other. Expanding on the muscle magazine practice of offering short model profiles, Benson featured a "Grecian of the Month" and not only noted where readers could buy his photos but also provided the selected brother's address and encouraged members to write.

The men featured were usually shown both in street clothes—often a suit and tie—and in a physique posing strap. They represented the sort of well-rounded ideals of the guild—someone who balanced development of the body with the successful development of the intellect and career. Few of them had any attachments to women; most were affirmatively listed as "bachelors." Ronnie Lewis, a typical Grecian of the Month, was "a splendid young man of high ideals and fine character." He not only developed a fine physique as a top gymnast but also managed his own touring company. Readers might have recognized him as the winner of a photo contest in *Tomorrow's Man* a few years earlier.[50] Another Grecian of the Month, Freddie Regan, had allegedly overcome both polio and tuberculosis through a strenuous health and weightlifting regime and now attended college. Again, careful readers might have recognized him as a featured model of Bob Mizer. "All types of people interest him and Freddie is a good mixer," Benson noted flirtatiously. They mentioned that he had recently appeared in *The Masterpiece*, a physique film by Apollo Films in New York. They did not mention that he appears naked.[51]

Providing the address of the Grecian of the Month was just one of the ways the Grecian Guild facilitated connections between members. Benson and Bullock routinely published the street addresses of correspondents, chaplains, and nearly anyone else featured in the magazine. "I have made some wonderful friendships through the Guild," wrote sixty-two-year-old Frank H. Ordway from Worcester, Massachusetts, as he renewed his membership for a second year.[52] Artist Patrick Flanagan from Indianapolis complained, "Since you printed my letter and photo in the *Pictorial*, I have received so much mail from *Pictorial* readers that it has been impossible for me to answer it all." The Post Office, too, noticed the mail circulating between members and the magazine's surreptitious way of making that happen. Convinced that this was a conduit for obscene materials, postal inspectors asked Benson to stop publishing addresses.

Readers, however, wanted more ways to connect with each other. "Do you have any pen-pal directory whereby members could further inspire each other?" inquired Tom Robinson of Salt Lake City, who included a photo of himself flexing in a swimsuit. The editors confronted a common problem in the physique and homophile worlds: everyone wanted a list of members to facilitate contacts, but few were willing to be listed, for fear of being visited by a postal inspector (see chapter 4). In 1961, with the stated goal of promoting state and local chapters, the guild took the extraordinary step of producing and distributing a formal Grecian Guild Directory with almost three hundred names and addresses. Though many members chose not to be listed, the editors hoped that the publication of the directory would demonstrate that their fears were groundless.[53]

Benson and Bullock originally dreamed of creating more than a magazine for subscribers; they hoped to create a social space for members to interact, what they called "a place of our own." When Benson floated the idea of a national convention, so many members wrote in for details that he had to ask readers to stop making inquiries. Soon plans were underway for a meeting in the summer of 1957, and anticipation was high. "Have you heard any details about the Convention next summer?" Rev. Thorwaldsen wrote to Rev. Wood that winter. Like other guild members, Thorwaldsen needed to know so he could plan his summer vacation and find a temporary replacement at work.

Since no such gatherings had ever been held, the prospect stirred great speculation throughout the physique and homophile worlds. Rev. Thorwaldsen hoped they were preparing a program to create "scientific and sociological respectability" and suggested a panel on "Christian Evaluation of the ideals of the Grecian Guild." He worried that otherwise it might turn into "Muscle Beach Circus."[54] VIM magazine editors imagined something more salacious. Satirizing Benson's initial vision, they foresaw men wearing diaphanous togas and "indulg[ing] in the various activities that bound members together, whatever those activities might be." Speculation only increased when the guild mailed out a call for a national convention at the Hotel Colorado in Glenwood Springs scheduled for that June.

Nestled in the Colorado Rockies, the Hotel Colorado was one of the grand Gilded Age resorts built to take advantage of the nearby mineral springs. Brothers who came alone would be assigned roommates, if they wanted, and the guild would coordinate carpooling. Plans included speeches by guild leaders, a "Mr. Grecian" contest, swimming, and small discussion groups on physical culture, art, and photography. But the call also came with a warning: "ANY CONDUCT NOT BECOMING A GENTLEMAN AND A GRECIAN WILL NOT BE PERMITTED." This stipulation caught the attention of the editors of ONE magazine. "Maybe it's obvious what that's all about, but what is the Grecian Guild all about?" the editors joked.[55]

Despite all the interest, this first attempt at a national convention failed owing to the perennial plight of small organizations—lack of financial support. Benson and Bullock had asked members to contribute to a Guild Fund, a nonprofit entity to fund conventions and other activities, but members were not as generous as they had hoped. Combined with a $15 convention registration fee, the plan may have been too expensive. The location was also too remote. Neither Colorado nor any of its adjacent states had many members. While relatively close to Benson and Bullock's Tucson home, Colorado was several days' journey from the bulk of the membership on the East and West Coasts. It may also have been too rural, offering little in the way of big-city entertainment options. So Benson and Bullock canceled this attempt at a central, national convention and decided to focus on smaller regional conventions for the East, the West, and the Midwest.[56]

Over the next few years Benson and Bullock succeeded in holding at least three conventions—all in major cities. They were highly structured events that showcased local physique artists, bodybuilders, and other entrepreneurs. The first took place the following summer at the Hotel Monteleone in New Orleans.

It was a modest success, with sixteen members attending, all "high-type" men, according to Benson's report to members. It featured a discussion of physique art, diet and health tips, a lesson in physique photography, an address by an Episcopalian minister, and the appearance of the recent winner of the Mr. New Orleans bodybuilding title.

The next summer's convention in San Francisco drew thirty-five members. Those who could not afford a room at the Sir Francis Drake host hotel were directed to contact a Grecian member who handled rooms at the YMCA, or stay with a local Grecian in his home. The event featured a fashion show sponsored by The Chess Man, a clothing store on Powell Street, an art show, and a screening of Pacific Films physique films. With plenty of physique models on hand from three different California physique studios, it was inevitable that one of them, Mel Fortune, won the Mr. Grecian contest. Members convened at Tad's Steak House, home to the famous $1.09 workingman's steak dinner, for a banquet.[57]

Plans to hold a regional convention in New York in August 1960 were canceled, but in 1964 physique photographer Troy Saxon in Kansas City hosted what seems to have been the third and final convention. Some contemporary correspondence suggests that there may have been more. "I am still quite interested in when you will have another convention here on the west coast," Robert Collins wrote to the guild, "I have never been to any of them but do have friend [sic] who have, they always come home raving for weeks."[58]

Benson and Bullock hoped that big national or regional conventions would inspire members to return home and organize local Grecian Guild chapters. One of their most enthusiastic supporters followed through. Dick Moore was a flight attendant for Northwest Airlines based in Minneapolis who was one of the few who attended the first New Orleans convention. Tall, blonde, slim, and in his twenties, he served as a model for one of the physique photography presentations. Not a muscleman, he represented the kind of "classical naturalness" the guild had always featured. A later Grecian of the Month profile gushed about his "warm friendliness, happy disposition, and engaging personality." Fully enmeshed in the physique world, he submitted photos and enthusiastic letters to numerous publications.[59]

With help from the guild's mailing list, Moore returned from the New Orleans convention to Minneapolis to establish the "alpha" chapter of the Grecian Guild, complete with elected officers, a chaplain, and monthly meetings in private homes featuring exercise demonstrations, physique movie showings, and a social hour. He traveled to the second convention in San Francisco to receive the formal charter from Benson, who told members the moment was one of his most gratifying experiences. He was hopeful that this small group could be the germ of more organizing. A photo that appeared in the *Grecian Guild Pictorial* showed nine white members of the Minneapolis chapter posing in the living room of a comfortable two-story house, many in jackets and ties. One member traveled over a hundred miles to attend meetings—underscoring the rural character of the membership and the extreme desire for fellowship.[60]

As two elite white southern men raised in the Jim Crow South, Benson and Bullock had a sense of community that did not readily include men of color. None of their own studio images was of minorities, and their magazine merits the charge unfairly leveled at all physique magazines as "pages of whiteness." When analyzing demographic statistics about their members, they did not even include race or ethnicity as a category. The accompanying collage of images was entirely white. And their easy assertion of an affinity with ancient Greece was racially exclusionary, as Scott Bravmann has argued.[61]

But in 1959, when a new subscriber from Harlem wrote to complain that *Grecian Guild Pictorial* "seldom if ever prints physique shots of Negroes," they made sure to include an image of black bodybuilder Joe Harris by Kris Studios of Chicago, known for the diversity of its models under the influence of cofounder Dom Orejudos. Suggesting they took the hint, the next issue included Latino model Emilio Mercedes. But such inclusions were tokenism at best.[62]

DANGER AHEAD

At the height of its distribution by the American News Company, Benson was printing fifty-five thousand copies of *Grecian Guild Pictorial* and making a profit of $4,000 per issue, as much as a professor's annual salary. Subscriptions, which required no intermediary, brought in twice that. He also sent six hundred copies of each issue to Dominique of London for distribution in Europe. Merchandising and advertising added at least another $1,000 per issue. The money was so tempting that Benson decided to diversify and offer a second physique magazine. Debuting in December 1956, *TRIM* offered photos and content similar to the *Grecian Guild Pictorial*, but without the explicit appeal to a brotherhood of supporters or the values of ancient Greece. Within a year it had a circulation of over thirty thousand.[63] Such success prompted others to enter the market. Five of the biggest physique photography studios joined up to offer *Fizeek*, an updated magazine offering images of America's top physique stars. It claimed to be part of a "new trend in the cultural presentation of the Male form." Thoroughly modern, it made fun of classical tropes. "The boy in the toga becomes the boy in polished cotton," the publishers promised, "this is *our* time, and we speak in our tongue: Let us glory in it."[64] Joe Weider, publisher of the mainstream bodybuilding magazine *Your Physique*, had diversified his offerings to include *Adonis* and *Body Beautiful*, overseen by one of his gay editors, Hal Warner, to appeal to the growing gay market.[65] Grecian Guild was soon competing for space on newsstands with over a dozen similar magazines. Benson and Bullock considered *Grecian Guild Pictorial* to be the leader in the field, but it was an increasingly dense field. Some saw an ominous "overproduction of physique titles."[66]

In 1955 Mizer scanned the newsstands and proudly noted dozens of magazines similar to his *Physique Pictorial* "catering to the artistic presentation of the physique." In the five years since he began publication, he had seen a new interest in physical culture "sweeping the world." Mizer hoped this melding of art and physical culture might become a sort of universal language of brotherhood that would unite men across the Cold War divide. Like Benson and Bullock, he was not only looking hopefully into the future but also imagining a return to an Arcadian past. "Perhaps not since the days of Ancient Greece has there been such a new awakening to the joys of a beautiful and healthful body."[67]

Although fairly cautious in its approach, the Grecian Guild still had fights with censors. Just as Benson and Bullock were launching *Grecian Guild Pictorial* in the summer of 1955, the American News Company (ANC), major distributor of magazines in the United States for decades, threatened to refuse to distribute physique magazines with models wearing less clothing than would be acceptable on a public beach—so no posing-strap photos.[68] Somehow, *Grecian Guild Pictorial* succeeded in winning ANC distribution, but it occasionally ran into trouble with local censors. It had been temporarily banned from newsstands in several cities owing to local cleanup campaigns, including Detroit, Chicago, and San Antonio. "Fuddy-duddies" had given local distributors and newsstands hell, Benson wrote to a colleague, for nothing more than prominent "baskets."

The consensus of news dealers was that the magazine was the most attractive and professional looking of all the physique magazines. They saw how Benson and Bullock had built a reader base that was "peculiarly loyal and devoted."[69] Not wanting to lose their national distribution, Benson and Bullock choose their images conservatively and advised other physique publishers to do the same. By the late 1950s, even in private correspondence, Benson would refer coyly to "personal pix," afraid even to use the word nude. He knew that Dave Martin was in jail for selling nudes in California. "Some of the newer guys resort to these pix to get business rolling, but they usually get caught and that's the end of them," he wrote.[70]

In the summer of 1957 the situation became more chaotic when ANC unexpectedly collapsed, sending magazines scrambling for alternative ways to reach newsstands. Founded in 1864, ANC had boasted about surviving the Great Chicago Fire and the San Francisco earthquake without any interruption in service.[71] Its sudden demise, Benson explained to a friend, felt as if General Motors had folded. With the company under investigation for antitrust violations, speculators apparently realized that its real estate holdings had become more lucrative than its magazine sales.

Getting national distribution was always a key hurdle to physique magazine sales. But now they would be vulnerable to the whims of more localized distribution networks, which might refuse such controversial magazines, because of either personal taste or pressure from local conservative groups or the Post Office. Bob Mizer reported that a citizens' group in Hollywood convinced newsstands to remove the September 1957 issue of VIM because of a photo of a man holding a fishing pole in a manner too suggestive of a phallus. Seeing "chaos in the field," Benson found a temporary replacement distributor, only to have it drop all physique titles. VIM missed several months of publication. Lou Elson's Tomorrow's Man, the most widely circulated physique magazine, was forced to limit production and offer huge discounts to wholesalers and newsstands. Even the mighty Weider empire was forced to discontinue Adonis and Body Beautiful, victims of the dual assault of censors and the demise of the American News Corporation. As one outside observer predicted, "all physique publications are on the brink of total ruin."[72]

As physique magazines became scarce on newsstands, Benson decided to make an appeal to readers. Warning of "Danger Ahead!" he explained the precarious financial situation of most physique magazines in the wake of the ANC collapse. Proclaiming Grecian Guild Pictorial "the acknowledged leader of the entire physique movement," he appealed for readers to become members of the guild and support the Guild Fund. Readers would help ensure the continuation of guild conventions and newsletters and even "hasten the great day when all these dreams come true . . .," employing the utopian rhetoric and the suggestive ellipsis that he had used in launching the project three years before. If they failed to support the Grecian Guild, he predicted the demise of all physique magazines. He positioned himself as "a beacon of light in the darkness" of American puritanical culture and "the guardian of the rights of all in the physique field"—including publishers, photographers, collectors, and readers.[73]

With his business in a slump and his distributors in arrears, Benson decided to retreat from newsstand sales and focus more on subscriptions and the membership organization. He sold off his new publication, *TRIM*, which had only just begun to gather a following, and focused on *Grecian Guild Pictorial* subscribers. It was during this period that they targeted their efforts toward organizing Grecian Guild conventions. By 1960 Benson and Bullock had sold both of their magazines to Lynn Womack, who would be arrested and tried on obscenity charges for sending *Grecian Guild Pictorial* through the U.S. mail.

It seems that Benson and Bullock were quietly forced out of the business by postal authorities. They were likely victims of Postmaster General Arthur Summerfield's crackdown on physique studios that would soon be grabbing headlines throughout the country (see chapter 4). Like many gay men caught up in that crackdown, Benson wrote an urgent letter to ONE asking that his name be removed from all their files because of "rather severe complications of a personal nature." He praised them for their "rugged courage" and lamented that giving up his subscription was like giving up a cherished friend. Unlike Womack and others who would follow in their footsteps, Benson and Bullock retreated into the closet.[74]

Scared by the close encounter with postal authorities, Benson took the opportunity to return to graduate school, finally earning a Ph.D. degree in sociology from Louisiana State University in 1966. In the 1970s he served as chair of sociology at Roanoke College, building it into a department with a national reputation, as he had earlier done with his magazine. Each year the department honors an outstanding senior with the C. Randolph Benson Sociology Award. Bullock became a much-loved art teacher at a nearby high school in Salem, Virginia, and served on the Roanoke City Arts Commission. When Benson's health problems became too great for him to teach, the couple retired to St. Petersburg, Florida. As longtime companions often do, they died within two weeks of each other in 2006. They chose to be buried in adjacent plots in an Episcopal cemetery in Charlottesville, the town where they first met, and where they founded a small physique photography studio. None of their family or academic colleagues knew of their earlier lives as publishers of one of the most popular physique magazines of the 1950s. Like so many other gay commercial ventures in this period, their story was almost lost to history.[75]

The Grecian Guild was not alone in adopting a Hellenistic model, but it is revealing that its most serious and sustained articulation in 1950s physique culture should have originated with two southern men educated at the University of Virginia. It suggests how this model invoked a particular racialized and gendered politics, a politics of respectability we often associate more with the homophile press of the period.

The model would proliferate in the 1950s and 1960s as a myriad of physique magazines and photo studios catering to gay men adopted language and imagery invoking the ancient world. Dozens used it in their choice of name. Joe Weider's *Adonis* and Bob Mizer's *Young Adonis* are two of the most prominent magazines that employed this trope, but so too did photo studios such as Richard Fontaine's Apollo Productions, George Haimsohn's Plato, Konstantine's Spartan, Stuart Rosenberg's Troy Saxon, and Anthony Guyther's Vulcan. Clark Polak's Trojan Book Service and the Mattachine's Dorian Book Service continued the trend. A homophile group that formed in Orange County, California, in 1962 called itself Dionysus, and a gay social membership group in Hollywood in 1964 called itself Romans.[76] With Greek language and imagery nearly ubiquitous in this field, it was no accident that the first major physique film—shot on 16 mm film with sound and screened in theaters—should be *Days of Greek Gods* (1954). In this film, three well-known bodybuilders are looking for a way to spend the afternoon. Since one has just read a book about Greek mythology, the three begin to imitate the poses of Hercules, Apollo, and Narcissus.[77]

Scholars often dismiss physique references to ancient Greece as a mere ruse or rhetorical framework—a "classical alibi" or "discourse of validation"—to avoid censorship. But an examination of the lives of the founders, contributors, and members of the Grecian Guild tells a different story. The Grecian Guild was instrumental in helping a community of men struggling to find a discourse to explain and valorize their sense of themselves, particularly men outside of urban gay enclaves. Benson and Bullock took a discourse about ancient Greece that gay men had been using for nearly a hundred years and gave it mass distribution. They used it like gay men used references to "the Greeks" or Mary Renault novels—as a way to signal their homosexuality. It was a rallying cry that brought in customers and helped them imagine a better world. As historian and biographer Benjamin Wise argues about the way Alexander Percy used the language of Hellenism, it was "a way of speaking out and covering up at the same time."[78]

Invoking classical traditions in order to make an argument for gay rights has been largely forgotten in the twenty-first century, as such a line of argumentation has become politically and historiographically problematic. Indeed, much of modern LGBT historical scholarship and queer theory has asserted that a homosexual identity is a creation of a modern, capitalist world—that homosexual behavior in ancient cultures was understood in very different terms from the way it is today. Invoking classical antiquity also smacks of a Western bias that privileges European ancestry over other cultural and historical influences. Such arguments also raise the specter of pederasty and pedophilia—or at least age-discordant relationships—that play into the hands of gay rights opponents who relentlessly use the argument that gays recruit children to fight gay rights measures. The last time that classical texts figured prominently in a major gay rights legal case—Colorado's Amendment 2 case in 1993—they were offered by conservatives to support a natural law position and to demonstrate millennia of animus toward homosexuality.[79]

Despite these changes in cultural understandings and sensibilities, the use of the classical Greek trope to name gay organizations, periodicals, and commercial ventures continued for decades, even when the need for an alibi had eroded if not disappeared. The lambda or lowercase Greek "L" became one of the primary symbols of the 1970s gay liberation movement. During this same period Seattle's largest gay organization was the Dorian Group, and a Jacksonville, Florida–based gay magazine called itself David—a reference to Michelangelo's Renaissance statue—an indirect link to the classical tradition. Like the Grecian Guild, David offered membership in a fraternal organization with features such as a book club, a travel service, conventions, and even legal aid. As an online website, it continues to serve as one of Atlanta's premier LGBT news and entertainment sources. Even in the twenty-first century, the gay and lesbian bookstore in Barcelona, Spain, was named "Librería Antinous" and an LGBT rights group of Slovenia is "Ganymedes." However naïve, politically insensitive, or historically inaccurate these references are, the lure of an ancient Greek idyll endures.[80]

Beyond a discourse of Hellenism, the Grecian Guild's attempt to form community among physique enthusiasts would also be continued by other organizations. This hunger to connect remained largely at the level of a virtual or imagined community during the physique era, but it animated physique enterprises large and small. The little-known Frontier Athletic Club, for example, published only a primitive mimeographed newsletter, *The Mighty—Happy and Healthy*, which offered news about its "clubhouse" near the Mexican border outside Tijuana where members could enjoy physique photography and other outdoor activities for just a $1 membership fee. With dreams of forming branches in every state, Director George Greig described it as "a world circling friendship organization."[81]

The H&H Club, formed by physique models Richard Harrison and Bob Hoover, similarly offered a primitive newsletter that featured a "correspondence corner" with personal ads and guides to gay bars and restaurants in San Francisco. The club planned to hold a convention at a Los Angeles hotel, where club members could photograph leading physique models in posing sessions and have the opportunity to "get acquainted." Such early attempts at forming community would be carried out more successfully only later, after larger physique enterprises consolidated their efforts and removed the barriers and risks they confronted in postwar American society.[82]

While severely limited by the forces of censorship, the desire to create opportunities for customers to correspond, meet, and get acquainted attests to the palpable wish of gay men to connect with each other during this period. If few members attended a Grecian Guild convention, the possibility of doing so resonated widely.[83] As a teenage *Grecian Guild* subscriber in Pawtucket, Rhode Island, Michael Denneny read the articles so carefully that he underlined the important parts. "That was a proto-political organization, the agenda was very clear to me, and I think to everybody else who joined," Denneny remembered. And all the talk of meetings, pins, and local chapters got him excited about the prospect of meeting others like himself. "We were very poor, but I remember there was a big meeting in New Orleans, and I really wanted to go to that." Even though the Grecian Guild's organizational plans were not fully realized, it made those desires visible. "These magazines were really important to me," Denneny recalled. "They brought this whole possible world into being, which I'm not sure I could have visualized otherwise."[84]

4

"I WANT A PEN PAL!"

Postmaster General Arthur Summerfield
and the Adonis Male Club

This column was the meeting place of more homosexuals than Krafft-
Ebing or Kinsey ever dreamed of! Ostensibly a "pen pals" club, it became
notorious with the passing years and was finally discontinued . . . this,
to our knowledge, is the *first time in history the faggots have ever been
organized.*
—*Muscle Builder, 1957*

I N JANUARY 1961 the U.S. federal government indicted more than
fifty members of the Adonis Male Club on charges of conspiracy to
send obscene materials through the mail. After a six-month investigation, the U.S. Post Office had uncovered what Postmaster General Arthur
Summerfield called "one of the most vicious, filthy, and widespread operations"
of its kind.

Announced by a U.S. attorney in Chicago in front of television cameras and
the press, the indictments exploded in newspapers, in boardrooms, and on cam-
puses across the nation. The *Chicago Tribune* called this 750-member pen-pal
club "an international pornography ring" that targeted children. For the postmaster general, the indictments represented something larger than one pen-
pal club. "It is the climax of six years of concentrated effort by the Post Office
Department to cleanse the mails of hard-core obscenity," Summerfield boasted.
He considered it a crowning achievement of his war against smut, declaring
that he had "broken the back of a nation-wide organization whose contacts form
a network throughout the country. We've gotten to the very core and source of
this thing."[1]

The Adonis Male Club was founded by the editors of VIM, a popular physique magazine that, under new management in 1958, explicitly moved to appeal to a homosexual market. For years gay men had been using the pen-pal listings in mainstream magazines and, more recently, clamoring for both physique and homophile organizations to offer similar services targeted explicitly to them. The Adonis Male Club, launched in the summer of 1959, was among the first to venture into this market. It quickly amassed a membership of over six hundred men from around the country, particularly rural areas. Members varied in age from eighteen to sixty-two and included college students and high school teachers, an Iowa grain elevator manager, a congressional staff member, a truck driver, and a bank auditor. It was so successful that VIM editors had plans to offer a monthly newsletter, a members' yearbook, and annual summer camps. Instead, the magazine ceased publication, the publishers went to prison, and most of the men indicted were found guilty of federal conspiracy charges.

The indictments were the culmination of Postmaster General Summerfield's vigorous campaign to eliminate obscenity from the nation's mails. Launched in 1958 in response to a number of liberal Supreme Court decisions narrowing the legal definition of obscenity and the power of the Post Office, Summerfield's campaign called on citizens to help root out obscenity of all kinds but particularly targeted male nudes because of their perceived danger to society. As U.S. Attorney Robert Tieken explained when announcing the indictments, "Postal authorities have repeatedly said that the biggest increase in obscenity has occurred in the field of correspondence between males with deviate tendencies."[2]

To root out this evil, federal postal inspectors infiltrated mailing lists, raided physique studios, confiscated customer lists, and harassed individual buyers. Inspectors visited gay men around the country, threatened them with arrest, and forced them to turn over evidence or sign confessions. As word spread, first informally and then through the announcement of the indictments in Chicago, a panic ensued among gay men. They wrote frantic letters to physique magazines and homophile publications alike canceling subscriptions and demanding to be taken off incriminating mailing lists. Teachers in Illinois, Maine, Texas, and Michigan were suspended. A teacher caught up in the Adonis investigation in New York committed suicide, while another man in South Carolina fled the country.[3] Two more indicted Adonis Male Club members attempted suicide—a Harvard University senior did so quietly behind closed doors, while an Indiana

University professor threw himself in front of a car in Bloomington, resulting in broken bones and more headlines.

The four-week Chicago trial of the Adonis Male Club was the most public skirmish in an ongoing war between the U.S. Post Office and a gay community trying to connect through the mails. Carrying guns and badges, postal inspectors represented the federal government's oldest law enforcement agency, and gay men and lesbians in the postwar United States were extremely aware of their power. Whether a physique photographer, homophile publisher, or mere pen-pal member or physique magazine subscriber, they feared a visit from one of over one thousand postal inspectors.[4] It was fear of postal inspectors in 1947 that kept "Lisa Ben"—considered the "mother" of the gay and lesbian press—from distributing *Vice Versa*, a mimeographed lesbian-oriented newsletter, beyond her coterie of Southern California friends.[5] It was postal inspectors who tipped off the Massachusetts police to the physique magazine purchases of Newton Arvin, a Smith College professor whose arrest in 1960 caused a scandal in Northampton, making him perhaps the most well-known victim of Summerfield's campaign.[6] While the story of the Post Office's attempt to suppress *ONE* and the burgeoning homophile press has been well documented, its wider attack on the LGBT community and its commercial enterprises has received only anecdotal attention.[7]

PEN-PAL CLUBS

By the time of the Adonis club indictments in 1961, gay men had for decades been using commercial pen-pal clubs, classified ads, and lonely hearts advertising in mainstream publications to surreptitiously connect to one another. And prosecutors both in the United States and overseas had been shutting them down for nearly as long.

The first publication entirely devoted to lonely hearts advertising was the British magazine *Link*. Launched with the slogan "Social—Not Matrimonial" in 1915, it quickly became a conduit for homosexual liaisons. To signal their intent, gay men used classical allusions, the names of famous gay authors—Walt Whitman, Edward Carpenter, Oscar Wilde—and other well-known code terms for same-sex behavior, such as "artistic," "musical," and "temperamental." For example, twenty-four-year-old "Iolaus," who described himself as having a "peculiar temperament" and being "intensely musical," was in search of

a "tall, manly Hercules." A muckraking journalist and antiprostitution cam-
paigner easily saw through the code and alerted the London police. Soon *Link*
publisher Alfred Barrett was charged with "corrupting public morals," and several male correspondents were brought up on charges of conspiring to commit
"gross indecency." Barrett was sentenced to two years imprisonment with hard
labor, *Link* ceased publication, and other British weeklies quietly ended similar pen-pal classifieds.[8]

Gay men in the United States also used the classifieds in mass circulation
or specialty magazines to single their interest in other men.[9] In the 1930s gay
activist Henry Gerber ran *Contacts*, a correspondence club for the "mentally
marooned" that had a subset of homosexual followers—what Gerber called an
"inner sanctum." Gerber's own personal advertisement noted that he was
"favored by nature with immunity to female 'charms.'" After World War II, he
and a small group of fellow gay correspondents talked of reactivating it as a
potential vehicle to organize homosexuals to fight for their rights, envisioning
it as a potentially revolutionary "committee of correspondence."[10]

By the 1940s gay men were also among the more prominent subscribers to
the *Hobby Directory*, a forum for "men and boys" to correspond about their special interests. As historian Martin Meeker has argued, the magazine was filled
with ads from single men looking for companionship with like-minded men.
Gay men signaled their desires by mentioning an assortment of interests, such
as "collecting physical culture photos," sunbathing, naturism, ballet, interior
decoration, and the theater. Sometimes it was the combination of interests that
most clearly signaled homosexual desire. A typical ad from 1948 by a thirty-
three-year-old single man from California read: "Physical culture, wrestling,
outdoor life, music, particularly vocal; the theatre, arts and crafts; reading and
gardening. Visits N.Y.C., Chicago, Milwaukee, and Los Angeles. C[ontacts]
D[esired]: those who combine physical and cultural ideals with high standards
of friendship."[11]

Soon the *Hobby Directory* took on some of the characteristics of a physique
magazine, as it added photos of subscribers and cover art featuring naked boys
seen from behind. Publisher F. Willard Ewing featured an editorial against
"intolerance" for all types of minorities, including communists, the left-handed,
bachelors, and other people who are different because "circumstances and
birth—over which they have no control—made them what they are." By 1951
the membership's focus on physique photography became so dominant that
Ewing wrote a personal essay outlining his views on the topic—the only hobby

so honored. Ewing was quite clear about his preferences. Denouncing the "musclemen pictures" with overdeveloped bodies and "blank stares," he preferred graceful models that reflected the lines and proportions of classical sculpture. He also liked those with a smile, "natural handsomeness," and a "willingness to cooperate"—preferences reflected in the work of gay physique publishers such as Bob Mizer and Randolph Benson. This was also one of the *Hobby Directory*'s last known issues, suggesting the likelihood of a police crackdown.[12]

By 1946 postal inspectors launched an investigation of persons placing letters and pen-pal advertisements in the nudist magazine *Sunshine & Health*, suspicious that both heterosexuals and homosexuals were using it to exchange obscene photographs.[13] Even more notorious was the S & H Leaguers' Page, a classified ad section in the mainstream weightlifting magazine *Strength & Health*, which helped many gay men find one another in the 1940s. As the editors themselves revealed, "too many of the wrong kind, those with queer tendencies, took advantage of the league notes and it came very close to putting us out of business." Postal authorities had traced letters and photographs they considered obscene back to the S & H Leaguers' Page and threatened to withdraw the magazine's mailing privileges. A U.S. district attorney labeled the feature a "spawning ground . . . for unnatural sex practices."[14] Even after it was discontinued in 1946, its reputation among both fans and detractors endured. "This column was the meeting place of more homosexuals than Krafft-Ebing or Kinsey ever dreamed of!" derided a competing magazine editor. Bob Mizer, who during World War II had received an overwhelming three hundred responses to his own leaguer's notice, also saw it as an important early site of community formation. "It helped bring a broadened viewpoint of others' lives which could have been gained in no other way," Mizer fondly remembered.[15]

Pen-pal correspondences had become such a fixture of gay life that fictional representations considered it a rite of passage. In *The Divided Path*, the main gay character, Michael, established a deep bond with another sensitive young man through a correspondence club linked to a Hollywood actor's fan club. Gerald, who had beautiful penmanship and confessed he was "not athletically inclined," sent snapshots of himself, including one in a bathing suit. Michael felt an immediate and deep kinship. "This seemed to be the person he had always wanted to know, whom he had imagined in different guises . . . the solution of his problems, the answer to his most urgent need."[16] It was through this pen-pal club that Michael made his first contact with someone who shared his desires and offered solace from the antigay bullying he experienced in high school.

With the rise of homophile organizations such as the Mattachine Society and ONE in the 1950s, gay men and lesbians began clamoring for pen-pal registries specifically geared to them. These organizations received so many requests for such services that they called it "the topic immortal." ONE reported receiving several such queries every day.[17] Despite the clear need, homophile groups resisted, citing advice from their attorney that such an enterprise risked putting them in violation of obscenity laws. "It's not a pen-pal organization, nor an organization for homosexual contacts," insisted Hal Call in his first television appearance explaining the research and educational focus of the Mattachine Society.[18] "Under no circumstances do the editors forward letters from readers to other persons nor do they answer correspondence making such requests," echoed ONE editors in their letters to the editor column. But by 1959, aware that such clubs were now being offered by "inexperienced persons around the country, not knowing the serious legal issues involved," ONE editors thought it was time for a serious discussion and published a formal debate over the wisdom of offering gay pen-pal clubs (see fig. 4.1).[19]

Arguing for gay pen-pal clubs was thirty-six-year-old editor Jim Kepner. He cited numerous positive examples of pen-pal relationships, including a three-year correspondence he developed through a science fiction fan club with another gay youth. Kepner, who was just coming out, confessed that "our information trading helped us both," even though they never met.

Beyond stories of shared intimacies and long-term friendships, Kepner framed much of his argument using a rhetoric of political rights. He pointed out that if the editors of ONE had followed the cautious approach of their attorney, ONE magazine would not exist, since it, too, was charged with obscenity. As he put it, "Little that homosexuals do is safe today. As long as homosexuals continue to 'play it safe,' they will never know the true safety of public recognition of their rights." Gay men and lesbians had a "right" to these common forms of communication, just as California had ruled that gays had the right to assemble in bars, he argued. Both involved the constitutionally protected right of association. And as with bars, publishers would not be responsible for any illegal activity that might follow.

Acknowledging potential pitfalls to any facilitation of relationships between strangers, Kepner noted that American homophile groups were well behind their European counterparts, who placed "chief emphasis" on pen-pal clubs. Indeed, the widely circulated Swiss homophile magazine *Der Kreis* and

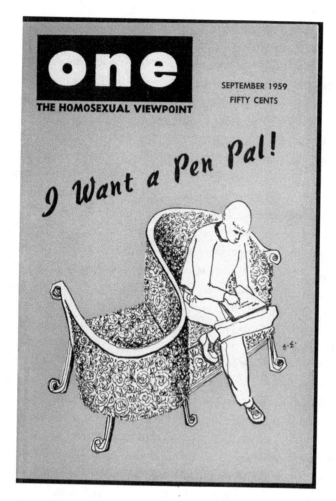

FIGURE 4.1 Calls for a pen-pal service from both gay men and lesbians were so insistent that the homophile magazine ONE published a debate on the subject in September 1959, just months before a police crackdown against such address exchanges.

Courtesy of ONE Archives at the USC Libraries.

the German *Der Weg* prominently featured entire sections of personal ads for members only. If ONE didn't provide this much needed service, someone else would.[20]

Opposing pen-pal clubs in this debate was fifty-five-year-old coeditor Dorr Legg. His stories of pen-pal relationships focused on the dangers of corresponding with strangers, starting with simple duplicity and disappointment but quickly escalating to blackmail and even robbery. He condemned the clubs as solely about sexual gratification, claiming mainstream cultural organizations could fulfill readers' other desires for community and intellectual stimulation. He portrayed pen-pal enthusiasts as daydreamers and escapists, always searching for a new adventure. To the many rural gay men and lesbians asking for local contacts, Legg's smug recommendation was that they flee to the city. He lashed out at the thousands of readers who wrote in clamoring for such services, calling them either too homely to meet people in person or "jaded satyriasts who have used up the local market." Rather than claiming political rights and "hiding behind the constitution," they needed to look internally for the reasons for their loneliness and unhappiness. Adopting a psychiatric language, he labeled the entire enterprise, "sick, sick, sick."[21]

Readers overwhelmingly favored pen-pal clubs—so much so that their letters took up much of ONE's next issue. They attacked Legg as bitter, patronizing, and fear-mongering. Older writers described finding pen pals through mainstream publications who became lasting gay friends or lovers. For many, it provided a bridge into a gay world. "I got a lucid view of what went on in the minds of other gay people," explained a man from Texas, "so by the time I went to New York and met gay people, I was somewhat prepared for the novel experience." A young writer from Oregon had begun the coming-out process by reading ONE, bleaching his hair, and using eye makeup. Now he was ready to take what he saw as the next step and have "a friend that has the same trouble as me." Even those who had negative pen-pal experiences pointed out the flaw in the cautious approach—to eliminate all potentially dangerous points of contact with strangers would necessitate the closing of all gay bars. Nor was the enthusiasm limited to those in rural areas. Those well immersed in an urban gay subculture also cried out for pen pals. "We're tired of going to bars," lamented Toby, a nineteen-year-old from Brooklyn.[22]

The political potential of pen-pal clubs was not lost on ONE's readers. Toby believed that by bringing people together, the clubs would foster not only romantic relationships but activism. "We won't be lonely anymore, and we will also feel stronger and fight for our rights," he argued. Lew Smith, who also frequented gay bars in New York City, saw the clubs as a way to transform the small homophile movement into something national, even international. "If you don't have a way for others to meet people, how the hell do you expect this homosexual society to come of age?" he complained. Acknowledging that there were "the few societies around the country," referring to the homophile organizations, he noted that they were limited to big cities. "But if you had pen pal clubs you'd have many boys and men and girls and women scattered all over the world," he proclaimed. "It seems like a damn good idea to me and I'm all for it."[23] It was an issue that even united gay men and lesbians. Amanda Schauberger, among the many lesbians who wrote in, suggested a pen-pal service sorted by sex and by city.

Even Dorr Legg, in his opposition to pen-pal clubs, envisioned their potential to expand the movement beyond its small cadre of dedicated activists and volunteers. "Stand back and watch ONE [Inc.] grow. It will be terrific!" Legg sarcastically imagined of a future ONE pen-pal service. "With the Constitution gleaming untarnished in the bright sunlight, flags waving in the breeze . . . the millennium will have come at last," he satirized. He preferred to keep the organization limited to serious, like-minded homophiles, rather than open it up to all those looking for companionship.

With young readers especially vehement in support of an exchange of addresses, it felt like a grassroots revolt against an entrenched establishment. "It is our magazine, isn't it?" asked a reader from New York. Without such a service, "the battle is lost," he warned. A sixteen-year-old self-proclaimed "homophile" from central Michigan wasn't waiting around for ONE to change its policy or allow those of his age to become members. Proclaiming "gay teenagers will be the leaders of the movement," he placed an ad in *Dig*, a teenage magazine that boasted an international "paper mates" pen-pal service.

With homophile organizations standing firm against any exchange of names and addresses, it would fall to their commercial counterparts to fill the void.[24] But even gay-operated physique magazines were reluctant to enter the business. Despite pleas from his own readers, Bob Mizer warned "There's Danger in Pen-Pal Clubs!" He cautioned all those who might respond to a typical pen-pal notice from a young man "interested in ballet, bodybuilding and physique pictures" to assume a pesky postal inspector would also be reading his letter.[25]

James Poulos, a forty-year-old high school teacher in Lansing, Michigan, was also not waiting around. Poulos was highly connected to the gay homophile and consumer culture networks. He was an avid reader of *ONE*, several physique magazines, and novels purchased through a gay book service. A frequent traveler who had taught in Japan and visited Fire Island, he ordered a directory of gay bars in Europe and wondered if there was one for the United States to replace the outdated "mimeographed list of places" he had acquired. Anxious to join a pen-pal club, he urged his friends at ONE to consider the idea. "I hope

ONE may soon be in a position to operate a pen pal club for gay boys," he implored. As if to pressure them, he noted that "one or two bodybuilding organizations (one around Chicago)" had begun offering clubs. But then he expressed his own reservations about these new ventures: "Illegally? I hope not," he commented ominously.

Poulos had reason to be concerned, since he had already joined the Adonis Male Club. What he didn't know, but suspected, was that he was already under investigation for sending obscene materials through the mail. Eighteen months later he would be one of many gay men indicted in Chicago, his name on the front page of local newspapers. Then he would frantically write again to ONE, this time to cancel his subscription. "Send no more copies. I am very sorry," was his only explanation. He had been caught in Summerfield's antismut campaign.[26]

VIM'S NEW LOOK

The Adonis Male Club was part of Jack Zuideveld's plan to turn the little physique magazine he edited into a huge financial success. From its debut in 1954, VIM had promised something different—no pill or product advertisements, just good pictures. The previous editor, William E. Bunton, had worked for Irv Johnson's *Tomorrow's Man*, which served as both inspiration and foil for VIM. Under Bunton's direction, VIM had already established a following as the campiest of the small physique magazines. It printed numerous articles satirizing the *Grecian Guild Pictorial* and muscle movies. It made fun of curious landladies who pry open plain brown envelopes that arrive for their young male tenants. A fake movie review of *The Potomac Affair* spoofed the notion that physique models (or gay men) might pose a threat to national security as undercover Soviet spies. As Bob Mizer noted, Bunton was a "witty, friendly" former ad executive who provided lively copy.[27]

Ironically it was a straight man who wanted to take VIM's campy reputation and make it more openly gay. In March 1959 Roger McCormick had tapped Zuideveld—a married sports writer and baseball radio announcer with two children—to run his two physique magazines, VIM and GYM. Fearing Zuideveld was too difficult (or too ethnic) a name for readers, he used the pseudonym Jack Walters. Zuideveld believed that a majority of his readership was gay—he even wrote a colleague that 40 percent of his thirty-five thousand readers had "homosexual tendencies." So he figured that articles dealing explicitly with homosexuality would raise sales and differentiate *VIM* from the growing field of physique magazines. Zuideveld first had to win over his more conventionally minded manager, who suggested that the magazine publish more legitimate bodybuilding material and workout tips. Zuideveld explained how this would alienate his key readership of homosexual men. His business plan included *more* articles on homosexuality. "Since the name homosexuality was avoided so much by people, he thought it would be appealing to the readers of the magazine *VIM* to bring it out in the open and deal with it directly," his manager testified.[28]

Zuideveld moved forward with his new strategy, even writing some articles himself, such as "Males, Morals and Mores," one of the most spirited defenses of "the true homosexual" to appear in an American magazine in 1959. A mish-mash of quotations from scholarly experts on human sexuality, it skewered the notion that homosexuals were contributing to the downfall of the nation. It paraphrased and exaggerated Alfred Kinsey's assertion that if laws against homo-sexual behavior were strictly enforced, "a majority of the male public would be in prison." More than any other physique publisher, Zuideveld openly discussed how men with a "homosexual bent" were attracted to bodybuilding—and had more time for it than did married men with families. As evidence he cited gym owners' claims that 40 percent of their clientele was gay (see fig. 4.2).[29]

Zuideveld envisioned the kind of explicitly gay magazine that would even-tually dominate the market—a mixture of enticing physique photo spreads and serious news and feature articles on gay topics. He solicited articles from Carl-son Wade, a New York–based writer of titillating gay pulps such as *Confessions of a Transvestite* and *Diary of a Homosexual*. From physique photographers he solicited suggestive dual poses or situations that would allow "good double entendre captioning." He even featured campy cartoons that suggested the "old school" muscle-bound weightlifter had been replaced by the "new school" of youthful, effeminate posers. He introduced the three-page pullout centerfold. When he included a photo of himself and a short biography, he pointedly made no mention of his wife and two children.[30]

By 1960 Zuideveld was publishing articles with provocative headlines such as "Homosexuality . . . on the Increase?" After noting Great Britain's Wolfen-den report and the movement to decriminalize homosexuality, the unnamed author (probably Zuideveld) heralded the flourishing of a gay subculture in the United States since the war—noting twelve gay bars on Chicago's Near North

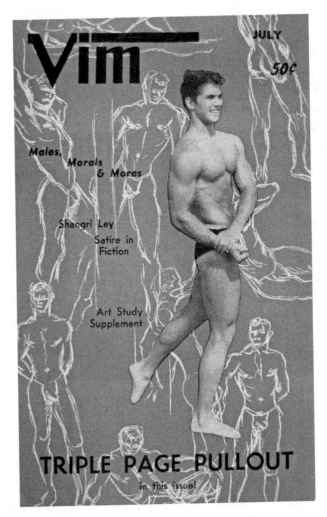

FIGURE 4.2 In 1959 *VIM* editor Jack Zuideveld launched a plan to make his physique magazine more explicitly gay, including favorable articles on homosexuality and bisexuality, along with pictorial centerfolds.

Side near *VIM*'s offices, calling them enviously "the most profitable type of saloon business in the city." He flattered his audience, asserting that most homosexuals were professionals and leaders in their communities, associating them with ancient Greek culture, intellectual conversation, and a highly developed aesthetic sense. A further sign that he was naively dealing in stereotypes was his assertion that few gay men ever came in contact with law enforcement. *VIM* also included a two-part series on "The Bi-sexual Male," which similarly posed a close correlation between bisexuality and high levels of intelligence and education.[31]

It was his wife Nirvana—*VIM*'s artistic director—who got the idea for a pen-pal club from reading customer correspondence. Like the readers of *ONE*, *VIM* readers were clamoring for ways to connect. Using the pseudonym Ed Nolan, she administered the club's parent organization, the International Body Culture Association.[32] Her first advertisement for the Adonis Male Club in June 1959 offered "a pen pal club that's for MALES ONLY!" that promised to be "the most truly DIFFERENT club in the world." For the stiff entry fee of $5 (the equivalent of $40 today), members would receive one new personal correspondent each month chosen by professional preferences—male model, truck driver, and wrestler were some of the most popular choices. "You'll exchange body-building photographs—relate interesting, personal experiences, get true enjoyment from swapping fascinating stories with males of unusual occupations and avocational pursuits," the advertising promised (see fig. 4.3).

The membership application included space for occupation, hobby, age, height, weight, and an ambiguous category for "measurements."[33] Noting that many applicants listed somewhere between 6 and 10 inches—clearly indicating penis size—prosecutors considered this a clear sign of homosexual intent. A twenty-five-year-old Utica College student admitted to prosecutors that he understood the club to be one for homosexuals from the moment he signed up. Referring to new names and addresses he received, an eighteen-year-old West Chester State College student remarked to a fellow member, "They're probably queer, all of them in this club are."[34]

The club soon had 750 members with an annual gross of $4,500. While the bulk of the membership was from the United States, the club had members from Mexico, Costa Rica, South Africa, and Ethiopia. Touting its success, a second advertisement featured the image of a mail carrier bending under the weight of his sack of letters. "Is he staggering to ring YOUR doorbell," the tagline asked (see fig. 4.4). Some eager members responded by writing in for a second membership so they could get more names.[35] Leveraging the surge in interest, Zuideveld decided to offer a "yearbook" listing members' occupations, hobbies, physical descriptions, and some physique photos for an exorbitant $20. The manager raised doubts about the project's appeal, since most of the photos were cheap reprints. "Do you really think those faggots are going to buy

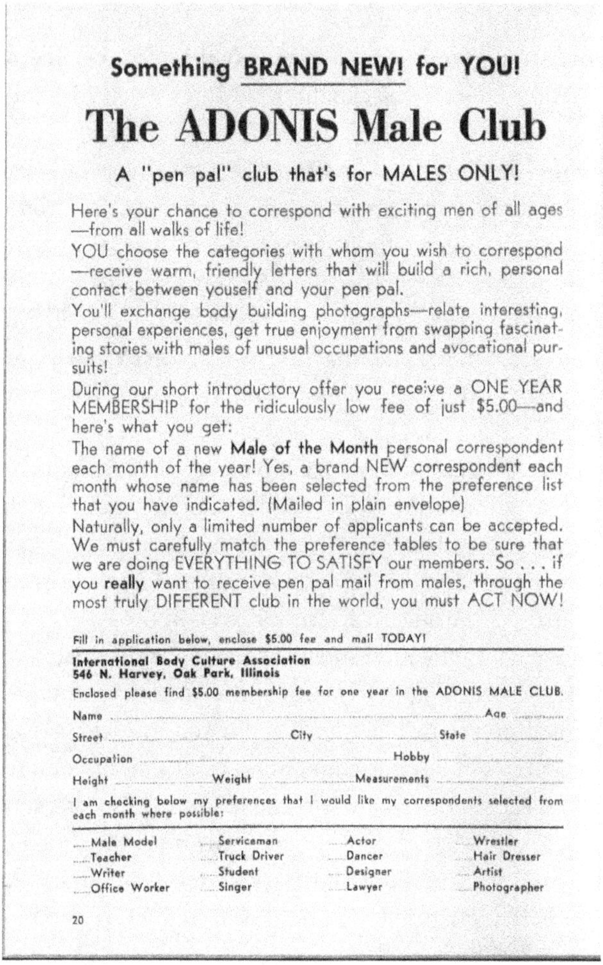

Something BRAND NEW! for YOU!

The ADONIS Male Club

A "pen pal" club that's for MALES ONLY!

Here's your chance to correspond with exciting men of all ages —from all walks of life!

YOU choose the categories with whom you wish to correspond —receive warm, friendly letters that will build a rich, personal contact between youself and your pen pal.

You'll exchange body building photographs—relate interesting, personal experiences, get true enjoyment from swapping fascinating stories with males of unusual occupations and avocational pursuits!

During our short introductory offer you receive a ONE YEAR MEMBERSHIP for the ridiculously low fee of just $5.00—and here's what you get:

The name of a new **Male of the Month** personal correspondent each month of the year! Yes, a brand NEW correspondent each month whose name has been selected from the preference list that you have indicated. (Mailed in plain envelope)

Naturally, only a limited number of applicants can be accepted. We must carefully match the preference tables to be sure that we are doing EVERYTHING TO SATISFY our members. So . . . if you **really** want to receive pen pal mail from males, through the most truly DIFFERENT club in the world, you must ACT NOW!

Fill in application below, enclose $5.00 fee and mail TODAY!

International Body Culture Association
546 N. Harvey, Oak Park, Illinois

Enclosed please find $5.00 membership fee for one year in the ADONIS MALE CLUB.

Name .... Age ....

Street .... City .... State ....

Occupation .... Hobby ....

Height .... Weight .... Measurements ....

I am checking below my preferences that I would like my correspondents selected from each month where possible:

....Male Model	....Serviceman	....Actor	....Wrestler
....Teacher	....Truck Driver	....Dancer	....Hair Dresser
....Writer	....Student	....Designer	....Artist
....Office Worker	....Singer	....Lawyer	....Photographer

20

FIGURE 4.3 Part of *VIM* editor Jack Zuideveld's plan to appeal to a gay audience was the opening of a pen-pal club called the Adonis Male Club, "the most truly DIFFERENT club in the world." Its first advertisement appeared in *VIM*, June 1959, and it quickly had a membership of 750 members.

that crap?" he protested. "You would be surprised at the expense and trouble those guys would go to and what appeals to them," Zuideveld responded.[36]

Zuideveld's strategy of appealing to gay men was initially so successful that he—like the founders of the Grecian Guild before him—tried to turn the virtual community of his magazine subscribers and pen-pal correspondents into

FIGURE 4.4 This second advertisement for the Adonis Male Club in the July 1960 edition of *GYM* suggested that members of the new pen-pal service were finding lots of friends with similar interests through the mail. "Why not give yourself the thrills and satisfaction of having a real pen pal . . . with whom you can exchange bodybuilding photographs, relate interesting personal experiences, get exciting pleasure from swapping stories with males of unusual interests and occupations."

face-to-face meetings and make more money. He planned "Body Beautiful contests" in Chicago to compete with AAU-sponsored events. In June 1960 he advertised a summer camp to take place on the "private, leased grounds" of the International Body Culture Association. For $50 (the equivalent of $400 today), members could enjoy a week of art classes, modeling, and photography, culminating in a bodybuilding contest. Members would arrive in Chicago and be bused to the facility in the Indiana Dunes, which promised opportunities for swimming, boating, and exploring "intriguing trails and delightful dells." It promised not only to be "completely different—unusual—stimulating!" but "the most wonderful week of your life." Twenty-five members immediately signed up.[37]

Zuideveld's new editorial strategy had not only increased sales but caught the attention of postal inspectors. By July 1959 the Post Office had declared *VIM* unmailable, interrupting its publication schedule for several months. But that was only the beginning of its efforts to shut the magazine down.[38]

"REPORT OBSCENE MAIL TO YOUR POSTMASTER"

As the Zuidevelds were starting the Adonis Male Club, the U.S. Post Office was in the midst of an aggressive campaign to eliminate smut from the nation's mails. In May 1959 Postmaster General Arthur Summerfield pledged a "war to the finish" against purveyors of obscenity and what he estimated was their half-billion-dollar industry. He invited lawmakers and civic groups to view an exhibit of confiscated materials in what became known as "the Chamber of Horrors." Some viewers, after their sex-segregated tour, became ill, according to newspaper reports. To enlist the help of average citizens, he created a new cancellation postmark for all first-class mail that urged Americans to "Report Obscene Mail to Your Postmaster." Summerfield justified such unusual tactics by arguing that if this industry continued unabated, it would result in "the moral breakdown of the entire nation" (see fig. 4.5).[39]

Arthur Summerfield was the most controversial postmaster general in U.S. history. As head of the Michigan delegation to the 1952 Republican National Convention, he had thrown his support to Dwight Eisenhower, who upon winning the nomination appointed him to chair the Republican National Committee. He was close to Tom Coleman, leader of the pro–Joseph McCarthy forces in Wisconsin, and helped the Republican Party reach out beyond its base of wealthy supporters to working-class voters. Although he had quit school after the eighth grade, he had been the owner of one of the largest Chevrolet car dealerships for over a decade. This business success was seen as qualification enough for President Eisenhower to appoint him to head the Post Office, then often labeled the largest business in the world. When Adlai Stevenson joked

FIGURE 4.5 In an attempt to overcome the effects of the Supreme Court's *Roth* decision in 1957 liberalizing American obscenity restrictions, Postmaster General Arthur Summerfield launched a sweeping crackdown on mail-order obscenity. To enlist the help of average citizens, he issued this postmark for all first-class mail: "Report Obscene Mail to your Postmaster."

after Eisenhower's election that "the New Dealers have all left Washington to make way for the car dealers," he was referring to Summerfield.[40]

Although often credited with modernizing the Post Office, Summerfield launched a spectacularly unsuccessful project termed "missile mail," a plan to transmit letters via submarine-launched Regulus missiles. "We stand on the threshold of rocket mail," he inaccurately predicted in 1959. His relations with Congress were also rocky. He once threatened to shut down mail delivery until Congress passed a budget favorable to his department. A few years later he threatened to impede mail service in the districts of members of Congress who voted to cut his budget. These were signs that Summerfield was willing to use unconventional, even illegal, tactics to reach his goals, particularly when he felt another branch of government was impeding his leadership of the Post Office.[41]

Summerfield was particularly incensed by recent Supreme Court decisions on obscenity, particularly its *Roth* decision in 1957, which he considered a threat to the nation.[42] According to the Supreme Court, the First Amendment allowed a work to be banned as obscene only if "to the average person, applying contemporary community standards, the dominant theme of the material taken as a whole appeals to prurient interest."[43] This was a major change from the prior *Hicklin* criteria, which required only a determination that some part of the work would corrupt the most vulnerable of citizens. It "must really 'smell,' not just be of slight 'odor,'" was how one appeals court judge deciphered the court's new intent.

Six months later the Supreme Court used this new, narrower, definition of obscenity to vindicate two publications the Post Office had been trying for years to shut down—the homophile magazine *ONE* and the nudist magazine *Sunshine & Health*.[44] After winning their legal victory, the editors of *Sunshine & Health* further antagonized Summerfield by publishing the image of a naked mail clerk from Homestead, Florida, noting that his nudism was "no threat to his job." Proving them wrong, postal authorities quickly dismissed the clerk for "conduct unbecoming a government employee." As these rulings gave rise to many new "nudist" magazines—many that clearly targeted a gay male audience—Summerfield's anger grew.[45] Despite what he saw as the "legal complications" of *Roth*, Summerfield felt a responsibility to prevent the use of the mails for what he considered harmful and indecent material.[46] Showing contempt for the Supreme Court, he was determined to continue to fight, even if it meant resorting to extralegal means.

Summerfield fought back at these judicial actions by urging lawmakers to strengthen the powers of the Post Office. Working with Senator Estes Kefauver (D–Tennessee) and his committee on juvenile delinquency, he helped Congress pass a law allowing obscenity prosecutions in the jurisdiction where the mail was received, not only from whence it was mailed, widening the government's enforcement power. Summerfield argued that such legislation would allow prosecutions where he believed most of the harm was inflicted—in rural areas, beyond the centers of production in New York and Los Angeles. But it also meant the Post Office could shop around for more sympathetic rural jurisdictions in hopes they would apply more parochial "community standards."

Working with local prosecutors, postal inspectors would even use this new law to expand their net beyond the traditional target of producers of pornography. Now the Post Office would take the unprecedented step of going after consumers as well. Chief Postal Inspector David Stephens was soon boasting how the new law helped the department "get around" the recent Supreme Court decisions and led to a doubling of arrests—a record 315 arrests for mail-order obscenity in 1959 alone. By 1964 there were over 800, with an 80 percent conviction rate, at least at the lower court level.[47]

Summerfield also worked with Rep. Kathryn Granahan (D–Pennsylvania), chair of the House Subcommittee on Postal Operations, which held a series of hearings throughout the country highlighting the dangers of mail order obscenity. New York Postmaster Robert K. Christenberry testified to a 300 to 500 percent increase in pornographic materials circulating through the mails. "Much of this material deals with sadism and homosexuality," he warned. Granahan claimed the situation was so extreme in Philadelphia that secret clubs of homosexuals used the mails to solicit teenagers and announce the times of their meetings.[48] A district attorney blamed the increase in "flagrant homosexuality" on the wide availability of "so-called strength magazines," which he noted were "never sold for strength purposes."[49]

Granahan further enhanced Summerfield's power by sponsoring a bill to allow the U.S. Post Office to seize the mail of anyone suspected of trafficking in obscenity. The initial bill, passed by the House of Representatives with only one dissenting vote, allowed the Post Office to withhold indefinitely the mail of suspected mailers of obscenity. Cooler heads prevailed in the Senate, which required the Post Office to first get a restraining order from the courts.[50]

Courting sympathetic lawmakers was only one of the tactics Summerfield used to circumvent the Supreme Court's liberal interpretation of obscenity.

Hoping to elicit the support of the American electorate, he launched a public relations crusade, urging civic and religious organizations, parents, and the media to join the fight against "racketeers mailing obscene material to children." As a distributor of an enormous number of patronage jobs around the nation, the postmaster general exerted considerable clout. Postmasters and postal inspectors fanned out across the nation giving speeches to civic groups on the dangers of obscene literature.

Summerfield offered newspaper editors prepared columns, resulting in many feature stories and editorials complaining of a "public subsidation of filth" and explaining how citizens could join the "war on obscenity." Abigail Van Buren, writer of the beloved "Dear Abby" column, visited Summerfield's Washington, D.C., exhibit and proclaimed it "vicious." "I don't know how anyone could confuse that stuff with art," she told readers. Columnist Jack Mabley ran a front-page story in the *Chicago Daily News* warning that pornographers were growing bolder. "Now they're going for the deviates . . . and recruiting to the ranks of perverts," he wrote, describing an offer to men for "artistic physique photos."[51]

Summerfield created a Citizen's Advisory Committee on Literature and packed it with a Catholic archbishop, a rabbi, and the editor of the *Christian Herald*. He hired women from the General Federation of Women's Clubs as "consultants" to further spread the word and pressure local newsstands to stop carrying objectionable magazines. Cecil M. Harden, a former Republican member of Congress from Indiana, served as "special assistant" to Summerfield and toured the country encouraging parents and church groups to take action against obscenity.[52]

ONE magazine derided these clubwomen consultants as "an army of antifreedom fighters," and some mainstream newspapers wondered if the Post Office was forgetting its main duty of delivering the mail. A *New Yorker* cartoon lampooned the seriousness with which such clubwomen took Summerfield's word. It featured a matronly woman in a bookstore declaring, "Before I buy a book these days, I ask myself a question: Would Postmaster General Arthur Summerfield want me to read this?" (see fig. 4.6).[53] Taking up Summerfield's call, one activist clubwoman wrote directly to Bob Mizer, "Oh, you think you are clever, but when I look at those pictures I know exactly the filthy intentions you have . . . your magazine is just about the worst of the lot—I buy them all just to see how rotten you people can get." She vowed to destroy Mizer's enterprise, promising, "with the help of God we will eventually rid the country of filth peddlers like yourself."[54]

"Before I buy a book these days, I ask myself a question: 'Would Postmaster General Arthur Summerfield want me to read this?'"

FIGURE 4.6 This Everett Opie *New Yorker* cartoon from July 30, 1960, reflects both the power Postmaster General Summerfield enjoyed and the ridicule he faced in his campaign against "smut" in the nation's mails.

Courtesy of Condé Nast.

To incite the American public to action, Summerfield and his surrogates made exaggerated claims about how pornographers targeted children. "Youngsters wrote in for model airplane catalogs, or a set of stamps, and later received materials on films portraying sex and perversion," claimed a typical postmaster in Indiana. Others argued that pornographers mined high school yearbooks to enlarge their mailing lists. "Their objective is to get the child hooked, as they say of the dope addict, and keep him hooked," Summerfield warned. "They feed him an array of trash carefully geared to successive stages of perversion," he told a religious group. A special Post Office pamphlet predicted that one million children would receive unsolicited "filth" through the mails in 1959 alone. Such early exposure to obscenity could lead to juvenile delinquency and even worse. "It is well known that almost all sex criminals prove to have a long record of obsession with pornographic and sadistic material," explained a post-master in Texas. FBI Director J. Edgar Hoover supported Summerfield's fight against "muck merchants" and "the forces of evil" who were "robbing our country and particularly our younger generation of decency." Calling for law enforce-ment across the nation to clean up America's newsstands, he warned of a link between obscene literature and a rising rate of "forcible rapes."[55]

Summerfield's public relations campaign falsely claimed that the Post Office was virtually powerless against such ruthless pornographers. Invoking the sanc-tity of first-class mail, postal authorities pretended that they could not act with-out the help of concerned citizens. "Control over [obscene] mail is totally dependent upon complaints made by the persons who receive it," explained a postal inspector before a Federation of Women's Clubs meeting. In fact, postal inspectors were actively involved in monitoring the mails, infiltrating mailing lists, raiding printing facilities, confiscating mailing lists, and intimidating cus-tomers. They worked with local prosecutors to seek indictments, either for violating federal mail laws or for violating a myriad of local obscenity statues (even though that was beyond their jurisdiction).

In announcing the Adonis Male Club indictments, prosecutors insisted that a concerned wife had found her husband's obscene letters and magazines and alerted them to this network. In fact, the Post Office was not nearly so passive. Postal inspectors had *VIM* under investigation and had already infiltrated the Adonis mailing list using the false name "Bob Ray." Soon inspectors all over the country were visiting Adonis members at their homes and offices, intimi-dating them into handing over letters and photographs and forcing them to sign statements or face stiff penalties and public exposure.[56]

The Adonis Male Club indictments represented an expansion of the Post Office's antiobscenity campaign—an attempt to widen the net to include not only producers but consumers. During this crackdown, postal inspectors raided the studios of many of the most prominent physique photographers, including Chuck Renslow, John Palatinus, Lynn Womack, Frank Collier, Al Urban, and Lon of New York.[57] But rather than just indict the photographers—as the Post Office sought to do in the past—it now confiscated mailing lists and combed through them to make further indictments.[58] "Thus the traffic in obscene photographs will be attacked in both directions," explained a newspaper editorial.[59]

"HOW TO MEET A POSTAL INSPECTOR"

Milan Roh was a twenty-seven-year-old auditor with the First National Bank of Morgantown, West Virginia, and a reader of *VIM*. In the summer of 1959 he saw the advertisement for the Adonis Male Club and immediately signed up. "We take this opportunity to welcome you to our fellowship," read the initial letter. "Shortly you will receive the name of your first correspondent and we hope that it will start a year filled with interest and stimulation." Over the course of the next year he engaged in an active correspondence with fifteen Adonis members. Most were other young professionals in the Midwest or Mid-Atlantic region—a music store owner in Lewistown, Pennsylvania, and a teacher in suburban Chicago were two of the more prolific.

Roh and Jack Mullen, an office worker who lived near Chicago, exchanged stories about meeting "interesting guys" at the YMCA. "I think we have a number of things in common, especially the tool we have to work with and what we like to do with it," Mullen wrote him. Roh was so excited by the explicit letter that he "had to jack off as I read it." He responded with his own description of his sexual tastes, which tended toward "straight" guys. "I go for the real masculine muscular type. I hate the sissy type," Roh confessed. Despite Mullen's request for a nude, Roh included only a "regular snapshot."

Within a few months of this frank letter exchange, Postal Inspector Edmond J. Stapleton visited Roh at his office in the First National Bank, flashed his badge, and showed him a copy of one of his letters—obtained from a similar visit to Mullen or another member (see fig. 4.7). Stapleton interrogated him for over an hour, trying to get him to confess to sending obscene letters and sign a prepared statement. Although Roh refused to cooperate at the bank, the postal inspector later came to his home, where Roh turned over twenty letters and photographs he received from club members. These would be used in similar postal inspector visits in other cities and later entered in evidence in the conspiracy case. Like most of the indicted Adonis members, Roh eventually plead guilty to sending obscene materials and was given two years probation. He was also subpoenaed to testify at the Chicago trial.[60]

Indictments were only one of the many tactics of federal officials in their fight against homosexual commercial enterprises. Because they were often stymied in the courts, postal authorities found other tactics to intimidate physique customers. In apologizing for not indicting the entire membership of the Adonis Male Club, prosecutors explained that they had already dealt with many

FIGURE 4.7 Postal inspectors, representing the federal government's oldest law enforcement agency, vigorously pursued physique photographers and publishers for allegedly sending obscene materials through the mail. With the confluence of Summerfield's crackdown and the rise of gay pen-pal services, they started harassing customers as well.

Courtesy of the National Postal Museum.

of the group members through what would become known as "educational visits" to their employers. Rather than arrest the correspondents, they contacted their employers and "obtained agreement that those involved would submit to psychiatrist treatment." They were more likely to take this more insidious, extralegal action in the case of middle-class "professional men."[61]

Such aggressive investigation tactics were not limited to the Adonis pen-pal investigation—they became standard operating procedure. The chief counsel of a congressional committee determined that "informing the employer of a suspect is such a common practice in these obscenity investigations that it can virtually be considered postal policy."[62] Bob Mizer called this campaign of harassment and intimidation "Inquisition, 1961 style." Many of his readers wrote to complain of being visited at their place of employment or school by postal authorities who threatened to search their homes and inform their families of their "difficulties." Under such duress, they gladly signed statements promising not to read or order such materials again.[63]

Homophile and civil liberties groups began to receive reports of postal inspector intimidation. "Last winter I had a rather upsetting experience," Adonis member Karl Thom, an unemployed hairdresser who lived on a farm in Minnesota, wrote to ONE magazine. "The local postal inspectors came without warning and took all letters written to me from pen pals . . . and asked questions about men I had been corresponding to."[64] H. E. Stokes from Hartsville, South Carolina, told the ACLU how postal inspectors had his mail under surveillance simply for receiving "an awful lot of mail from California." In November 1960 they called him into the post office to be interrogated. Postal inspectors forced him to open a letter he had only recently posted to a friend and, threatening a search warrant, to bring in copies of physique photos and magazines he had purchased. "Are you a homosexual?" the postal inspector asked. The ordeal left Stokes feeling "humiliated, harassed and insulted." Under constant threat of further interrogation, he complained to the ACLU that "my day by day life is a hell."[65]

In a statewide investigation into homosexual activity in Florida around the same time, a physique photographer complained to his attorney that postal inspectors were "interrogating him at length in his home against his will." By 1965 Playboy's "Forum" column featured so many letters complaining of postal inspector intimidation concerning private correspondence that Chief Postal Inspector Henry B. Montague felt compelled to respond and deny the charges.[66]

In its "educational visits" as well as its indictment of Adonis club members, the Post Office targeted one group more than any other: teachers and professors. Summerfield knew that this would keep the focus on the threat that pornography posed to children and thereby create the largest public firestorm. When announcing the Adonis indictments, Summerfield claimed the club targeted "young boys 13 and over." Of the defendants who would go on trial in Chicago, half were teachers. During the trial the prosecution brought out the young ages of several of the defendants' or coconspirators' sex partners to further incite the jury. U.S. Attorney Robert Tieken noted that sixty-five members of the organization were educators and seventy-seven were students. "It's about time the educational system and the boards of directors of educational institutions take an extremely serious look at this atrocious practice and bring a stop to it," Tieken cautioned. "We don't expect that we can stop the fundamental activities," he insisted, "but we'll do all we can to get it out of the schools."[67] Many newspapers concurred and emphasized the fate of local teachers. "Many Educators in 'Male Clubs'" blared a typical headline from Lincoln, Nebraska.[68]

Summerfield hoped the mass indictment in Chicago would serve as a wake-up call to American society of the dangers of homosexuality in the nation's schools. "Evidence gathered by Postal Inspectors shows conclusively that *organized* participation of so many confirmed homosexuals," he warned, "has a direct bearing and influence on formation of character of future generations." Playing on fears of pedophilia, Summerfield noted, "As a nation, we cannot allow such men to entrench themselves in areas where their evil can be brought to bear on character building of young boys. We must alert parents of America to dangers of this type of perversion."[69]

Summerfield was not alone in his concerns about homosexuality in the nation's schools. At the same moment gay and lesbian teachers were also under attack in Florida as that state's Legislative Investigation Committee was in the midst of a campaign to purge suspected homosexual teachers and state college professors. According to historian Karen Graves, the so-called Johns Committee interrogated eighty-one educators, many of whom lost their state teaching licenses. "The presence of even one homosexual teacher in our schools is not to be tolerated," asserted Florida's superintendent of public instruction.[70]

Leroy Miles was a thirty-seven-year-old civics teacher at Thomas Jefferson High School in suburban Dallas. Highly respected by both teachers and students, Miles had led a very quiet life far from gay bars. Like many gay men at the time, he led a sort of double life through marriage with a woman. According to one of his gay friends, he wouldn't subscribe to ONE or *Mattachine* for fear of getting on a suspect mailing list. But he had taken the chance of joining the Adonis club and started corresponding with a man who described himself as a wrestler. "I would like to get you in a wrestler's lock until something hard develops," he wrote Miles, who responded with similar sexually suggestive letters.

Miles pled guilty to sending obscene materials and received a three-year probated sentence. But the sentence was less important than the charge.

"Regardless of whether he is convicted or acquitted, his name is ruined," his friend explained to *ONE* magazine. "He will never again be able to teach in Dallas, and very probably not anywhere else," he complained. "Can the rest of us feel free? Which one of us will be next?" The Post Office held the sword of Damocles and aimed it at teachers.[71]

Rem Butterfield was a forty-four-year-old teacher in suburban Glencoe, Illinois, but lived on Chicago's North Side with a male roommate. As a member of the Adonis club, he carried on a lively correspondence with twenty-four other members, including a physique model from whom he ordered nude photographs. It was a pen pal from the tiny downstate town of Tolono, Illinois, who alerted him that he had been arrested for writing a "sex letter" and would have to suspend their correspondence. When postal inspectors came to Butterfield's apartment to question him, he claimed his interests were purely academic—part of his ongoing study of homosexual personalities. With a master's degree in sociology from the University of Wisconsin and classes in clinical psychology at Northwestern, Butterfield made a plausible claim, but postal inspectors thought his letters told a different story. Prosecutors noted that he talked about "making out" with his roommate and other male friends and freely discussed their penis sizes. As soon as the indictment was publicized, the Glencoe school board held a special meeting and suspended Butterfield, pending the outcome of the trial. "I have so much to lose," he wrote in a desperate plea to the ACLU, "and frankly it scares me."[72]

Teachers were the low-hanging fruit for a Post Office eager to get people off physique mailing lists and into the pages of local newspapers. A mere visit to a school principal by a postal inspector or an indictment on the flimsiest of charges would end in expulsion. Postal inspectors were known to leak information about such school visits to local media.[73] Ensuring conviction in the court of public opinion even without trial, this strategy was a means for prosecutors and the Post Office to circumvent the increasingly reluctant courts. Local courts were also more likely to convict teachers, sometimes even mandating that they seek psychiatric treatment.[74]

Teachers had little recourse, but many did write in to complain to *ONE* magazine. Historian Craig Loftin notes that "a disproportionate share" of its hundreds of reader letters complaining of postal harassment came from teachers.[75] It was "a kick in the pants," one gay teacher in Pittsburgh commented, traumatized by watching his friend lose his job on mere suspicion after postal inspectors visited his friend's principal. Appeals to the local school board were unsuccessful. "I was just sick about the whole thing," he remembered. Executives at the ACLU rightly feared that postal inspectors and federal attorneys were exceeding their authority by exerting governmental pressure on local schools. Postal inspectors' extralegal employer visits were creating both fear and a sense of injustice.[76]

One of the few teachers to fight his obscenity charge was Norman Blantz, a twenty-five-year-old single teacher at Myerstown High School in Maryland. His name appeared on a customer list of a Detroit physique studio raided by postal inspectors.[77] Blantz had sent away for photos from multiple studios, spending a total of $125 over the course of one year. He told postal inspectors that he had ordered the photos as aids to developing his art skills. His attorney pointed out that many of the studios advertised that their photos were legal—citing recent Supreme Court decisions—so Blantz could not have known he was breaking the law.

In the end the government could not prove that Blantz knowingly ordered obscene material, since each indictment was for an order from a different studio. Had they indicted him for ordering a *second* batch of photos from the same company, they might have been more successful. "Circumstances so clearly point to guilt," wrote the frustrated federal judge, clearly sympathetic to the Post Office's position. He marveled at "the depravity of a mind" that enjoys looking at the photos Blantz ordered. He was particularly concerned that Blantz, identified in court as wearing horn-rimmed glasses, was a teacher. "A fellow who engages in this thing is not qualified to deal with children," the judge ranted. Even though Blantz won his legal case, he lost his teaching job.[78]

THE CHICAGO TRIAL

When the federal trial involving the Adonis Male Club got underway in Chicago in January 1962, it would prove an exhausting and unwieldy event—one defense lawyer called it four weeks of "mass confusion." The government called sixty witnesses to testify over the course of twenty days. The prosecution placed fifty photographs in evidence and read over one hundred pen-pal letters into the record, which ran over four thousand pages. But beyond its size, the trial was unorthodox in a number of ways. Most of the original fifty-three people indicted had pled guilty, but the ten remaining defendants were tried in a single courtroom—two before a jury and eight before the presiding judge. The ten Adonis club members were tried together with the two club founders, who prosecutors argued had earned "substantial remuneration."

Although the jury was deciding the fate of only two men—Glen Willbern and James Poulos—it heard the case against all the club members and founders. Another forty nondefendant coconspirators served as witnesses. The multiple trials were so complex that the presiding judge had trouble remembering the names of the various defendants and attorneys. He frequently instructed the jury that some testimony was admissible only for certain conspiracy charges and should be disregarded for others. He tried to set ground rules to avoid "pandemonium"—to little avail.[79]

What united all of the defendants was the legal charge of conspiracy to mail obscene materials through the U.S. mail. The prosecution presumed that both the leaders and members held a common understanding that the club would be a place for gay men to exchange explicit photographs and letters. A pen-pal club designed to connect homosexual men, in their mind, could have no other purpose. To prosecutors, the association between homosexuality and obscenity was so close that they believed that demonstrating the homosexual nature of the club was prima facie evidence of a conspiracy to send obscene materials through the mail.

The U.S. Supreme Court had already ruled in *One v. Olesen* that homosexual magazines were not obscene per se, but Summerfield, his postal inspectors, and prosecutors continued to consider any overt reference to homosexuality to be an invitation to obscenity. Knowing the type of "faggots" who subscribed to these magazines, the U.S. attorney argued, "it is not much of an inference to infer what type of correspondence they are going to carry on." From a legal standpoint, it would have been much easier to prove that individual members sent individual pieces of obscene materials through the mail, but the prosecutors wanted to use the unconventional group trial to demonstrate a vast homosexual network. "This is a like a cancer—It starts out small and it gets bigger, and bigger, and bigger," explained Assistant U.S. Attorney William O. Bittman, who proposed submitting into evidence a "graphic illustration" to visually demonstrate the intricacies of the Adonis pen-pal network. By indicting and trying men from all over the country simultaneously—with each defendant getting prominent coverage in his hometown newspaper—they suggested an organized threat that justified their ongoing antismut campaign.[80]

In a way the government's charge of conspiracy was not far off the mark. As Judge Richard Austin explained to the jury, a conspiracy was a combination of two or more persons who together accomplish some unlawful purpose. The agreement did not have to be explicit—members might "through some contrivance, positively or tacitly come to a mutual understanding." The government merely had to demonstrate an unspoken common purpose among Adonis members. In short, the government's case rested on demonstrating that these defendants belonged to an imagined community or subculture in which illegal activity was central. Given the legal status of homosexuals and homoerotic materials in 1960, this was not difficult to do.[81]

To prove a conspiracy, the prosecution highlighted coded discussions of homosexual travel destinations and other references to gay culture. James—the Lansing, Michigan, high school teacher who had urged *ONE* to offer pen pals—had been cautious in his correspondence, speaking only in generalities and sending no nudes. So the Post Office made him sign a statement admitting that "most of the members who wrote to me discussed the subject of homosexuality and/or their homosexual experiences subtly or candidly." On the stand the prosecutor grilled Poulos about his discussion of Fire Island, noting that he put it in parentheses, suggesting it was some sort of code. "Isn't it a fact that Cherry Grove is a well-known spot in that area of the country that caters to homosexuals?" the prosecutor pressed. "When you wrote to [your pen pal] and gave the name of Fire Island wasn't it your intention to start to receive obscene correspondence from him? Wasn't it just a subtle way of saying 'I am one of the boys, let's go to it?'" The prosecutor noted that the recipient clearly wanted the salacious details—he underlined Cherry Grove and included three exclamation points.[82]

As regular subscribers to physique magazines, most of these Adonis club members shared an admiration for the male body and for ancient Greece, both of which served as code for their sexual interests. "You mentioned your admiration for the male body, and there's one place where we really agree. To me, the male body is one of the most beautiful things in the world," wrote Edward Dold, a twenty-eight-year-old business machine programmer from Lexington, Kentucky. "I cannot fully describe entirely what I feel when I see a well-developed male," he noted coyly. Both he and his pen pal, a twenty-four-year-old music teacher, invoked ancient Greece as a way to understand and normalize their interest in the male body. "You were right that the Greeks did understand it and in a lot of ways I think they must have had a wonderful life," he observed. He then mentioned a Mary Renault novel set in ancient Greece and featured by the Winston Book Service. "By the way, have you read *The Last of the Wine*?" he inquired. "It's a wonderful story. You should read it, if you haven't already."[83]

After the first two or three letters were exchanged, many members felt free to move beyond coded language and discuss their sexual experiences and desires. Judge Austin considered these discussions so pornographic that he barred the press and the public from the courtroom during the prosecution's reading of the letters.[84] But for the Adonis club members, their open correspondence represented a tremendous release. As a government clerk in Chicago put it, "I think we have both reached an understanding which is an admirable thing to have accomplished. If you write to other fellows as I have you have found that to be only too true. We all fear to drop our shields as we fear the blow of an antagonist to our pride. But what a wonderful feeling to drop the shield and find what you thought to be an adversary is in truth a friend."[85] Beyond sharing intimate stories, some achieved an even closer sense of intimacy by tape-recording their correspondence. Many would travel great distances on precious vacation time to visit one another. They shared gossip about other members and sometimes their addresses—a clever way of circumventing the slow process of waiting for additional addresses from club managers.

Most of the men expressed a sense of loneliness and a desire to meet like-minded men. They were certain that their common interest in the male body would paper over most other class or age distinctions. Boyd Giese, a twenty-six-year-old student at the University of North Dakota, wrote, "In a town as small as this it's pretty hard to find someone who admits to the same interests. That's one of the reasons I joined the club." Many expressed frustration with public cruising, what they derided as "latrine romances where it is just touch and go" or "five minute washroom sessions."[86]

Despite these men's desire to make a human connection, the language of desire they shared was rarely about pairing off into couples. More often they talked about meeting friends or buddies. James Thistle, a teacher from Massachusetts, complained "it has been months since I shared a bed with a friend" and talked of "friends with whom you shared sex," while others wrote of roommates with whom they shared sex. Another wrote of two friends he saw regularly—one every Tuesday night and one every Thursday night— "and we always have a ball."[87] If "friend" was the most common term used to describe a sexual partner, the terms boyfriend, partner, and husband were entirely absent. Even some of those who embraced the label "gay" and were sexually active contemplated heterosexual marriage. "Lots of gay fellows get married," one commented, noting his desire for security, a home, and children.[88] While prosecutors may well have chosen the letters from the most salacious and sexually adventurous members of the club to better make their case, the available letters from Adonis members suggest that gay men used the club not to find long-term monogamy but to construct a network of sexualized friendships—what the prosecutors used as further evidence of conspiracy.

Central to this shared cultural network was the taking and sharing of homoerotic images. Members shared photos of themselves and their friends and lovers just as others might of vacations or hobbies. They would meet up to take more photographs. "If I came to see you could we have a picture taking spree?" a man in Michigan asked his correspondent in suburban Chicago. Ironically it was the legal difficulties of acquiring nude photos that encouraged the club members to share photos and thereby got them in legal trouble. All wanted to receive photos, though not all were willing to take the risk of sending them. Many maintained private post office boxes and spent lavishly on nude and seminude studio photographs. Frank Semkoski of Lewiston, Pennsylvania, took art classes so he could acquire nude photos. As one member summarized, "Every person whom I have met in this club collects photos of the male body in the complete nude." It was the one thing that united them all.[89]

Within this community, the prized possession was a Polaroid camera, which circumvented any need to find a commercial film developer and therefore allowed full nudity.[90] Judge Austin noted how "self-photography" became a constant theme in their correspondence, with members offering various options, and the Polaroid camera became a central piece of the conspiracy. "Enclosed are pics of me . . . send one of yourself. Use your Polaroid. I'd like to see all of you with a hard-on," commanded a marine stationed in North Carolina to his pen pal in Pennsylvania. Members without a Polaroid described the difficulty of taking a revealing selfie. "I set [my Brownie Hawk Eye box camera] on a stool and tape it with a thin stick and maybe I can get myself in a position to get some sort of 'snaps,'" explained Jim Thistle, a young teacher in Massachusetts. Cornell Kirkeeng, an actor in San Diego, would borrow a friend's Polaroid but desperately wanted one of his own. "I won't be happy until I have my own Polaroid camera . . . maybe this Christmas," he wrote with hope.[91]

Benny Anderson, a farmer and grain elevator operator in Iowa, owned both a Polaroid and a photo-duplication machine, making him one of the most popular and prolific pen-pal club members. Erotic photos of him and a young man on a neighboring farm circulated throughout the country, from a government worker in Chicago to a teacher on Cape Cod. He loaned out not only his collection of erotica but even his prized Polaroid camera. "[He] hasn't lost it yet!" explained another Adonis member, marveling at the level of trust formed within the group.[92]

Where gay men saw an opportunity to find companionship, prosecutors saw a conspiracy to distribute pornography and encourage homosexuality. In closing arguments to the jury, Prosecutor Bittman compared physique magazines and pen-pal clubs to gateway drugs. As he told the jury, "When the man takes his first sniff and then goes on to smoking and then goes on to the real hard stuff, this is the same thing." Only with a guilty verdict would this moral menace "undermining the entire existence of this country" be stamped out. He thanked the postal inspectors, who had sat through the month-long trial, for making America safe. Because of their detective work, "your children and grandchildren won't walk by these newsstands and have to be afraid not only of the ads but the magazines themselves." Together they would shut down this threat to American morality for all future generations, just as they had tried to shutter ONE magazine, *Physique Pictorial*, the Little Blue Books, and other sources of information about homosexuality. "So you won't have to walk past a newsstand and pick up a physique magazine and page through it, asking, 'I wonder if the pen pals are still operating.'"[93]

All ten customer defendants in the Chicago Adonis trial were found guilty and received probation, joining scores of other convicted pen-pal members. Founders Jack and Nirvana Zuideveld were each sentenced to a year in federal prison, where they joined at least two other members of the club. One was Thomas Gorman from Owensboro, Kentucky, a married man whose wife apparently found his physique magazines and Adonis letters and notified postal authorities. It was probably a letter he sent describing a relationship with a newspaper delivery boy that accounted for his harsh sentence—six months in the federal prison in Terre Haute, Indiana. When he got out he was a broken man. Although only forty-four, he looked sixty-five, according to his aunt. Despite having spent many years in the seminary and in the army, he could find only occasional menial jobs in Owensboro. "Each day is a horror for me," he told his aunt. After someone gave him copies of the *Mattachine Review*, he started a correspondence with its manager, Don Lucas, hoping for advice on how to escape to San Francisco.[94]

For Summerfield, shutting down the Adonis Male Club represented the pinnacle of his antismut campaign. "Cracking of the Adonis Club broke the backbone of the largest group of homosexuals engaged in the distribution of obscene material through the mail," he boasted.[95] This legal victory also helped propel lead prosecutor William Bittman—then only three years out of law school—on to a high-profile career prosecuting conspiracies. A six-foot-tall former Marquette football linebacker and devout Roman Catholic, he developed a reputation as an aggressive prosecutor who "swarms over witnesses." After winning convictions in the Adonis case, he became special assistant attorney general in the U.S. Department of Justice and won another grueling Chicago-based conspiracy trial against Jimmy Hoffa, the Teamster Union president. He would again be in the news in the 1970s for accepting envelopes of cash from the White House as the attorney for Watergate burglar E. Howard Hunt.[96]

But while Summerfield won this skirmish, it was his last hurrah. The Adonis indictments came down just three days before the end of Summerfield's term of service and the inauguration of John F. Kennedy and a new Democratic postmaster general. In August 1965 the *New Republic* printed an exposé on the Post Office's extralegal tactics, including its "educational visits" to employers of persons receiving allegedly obscene mail. Claiming the tactic was "seldom used," Postmaster General Larry O'Brien ordered it stopped. A year later a congressional investigation uncovered postal surveillance of customers receiving gay magazines and continued "educational visits" to employers. The postmaster general *again* agreed to end the practice.[97] By then the Department of Justice had instructed U.S. attorneys that it was no longer willing to prosecute private correspondents for obscenity.[98] Although the Post Office would continue its aggressive attempts to suppress physique photographers, it largely ceased its campaign against consumers.

Publicly, postal authorities continued to claim that pornographers targeted children and that pornographic material was seeping into the homes of unsuspecting suburban families. But internal documents reveal that they knew this to be a lie. As Chief Postal Inspector Henry B. Montague wrote to the Post Office general counsel, "Obscenity dealers do not knowingly direct their mail order solicitations to minors. On the contrary, they bend every effort to avoid it and in the main succeed rather well." This explains why the Post Office, despite its continued campaign against obscenity, discouraged discussion of legislation specifically designed to criminalize sending obscene materials to minors.[99]

While successful at trial, the Post Office and prosecutors failed at their larger goal of shutting down gay pen-pal clubs and the physique magazines that sponsored them. Other clubs were already in business—several Adonis members reported being members.[100] Rogy's was a primitive mimeographed sheet of personal ads along with advertisements for campy books, greeting cards, and clothing run by Oscar Roganson out of a post office box in Hollywood, California.[101] Soon a gay couple in Minneapolis were offering a "Readers' Service" of personal ads as one of their many directories snatched up by a growing list of mail-order customers. By April 1963 *Tomorrow's Man* had a regular "Post Marks" page featuring photos and addresses of readers. Canadian entrepreneurs parlayed a classified ad for "Gay Partners" in a Toronto-based tabloid into Canada's first gay magazine.[102] Despite the government's efforts, personal advertisements and other forms of address exchange would become central features of the more openly gay press that emerged in the 1960s.

What both the members and prosecutors of the Adonis Male Club had in common was an understanding of the power of this commercial, physique-sponsored network to connect and affirm the desires of a large, national constituency. Buying magazines, writing letters, and exchanging photographs were central features of this network—what the Post Office saw as a conspiracy, gay men saw as a nascent community. Gay commercial enterprises fostered both those impressions by being the means by which this network formed. It brought the community together in a national way like nothing ever had before.

But the mailing lists that connected men around the country to this network and, with the rise of pen-pal clubs, to one another, also opened them up to intimidation, arrest, prosecution, and job loss. Summerfield's campaign underscored how putting oneself on a mailing list for either a homophile or a physique magazine was an act of courage. It politicized what had been for many a simple act of consumption. Many subscribers decided on a strategy of "retreat." Lon DeLaney in Clarksville, Indiana, had been a reader of both *ONE* magazine and several physique magazines. But as he began to hear of "clamp downs" by postal authorities, he wrote to cancel his subscriptions. "Because I have (somewhat stupidly I will admit) gotten my name on several 'Physique' studio's lists, I begin to fear that I am in danger." He asked that *ONE* remove him from their mailing list. "Frankly I want out," he implored *ONE* editors. He stuffed the envelope with dollar bills as a "bribe" to ensure their compliance.[103]

But while some chose discretion, others chose to fight. Ten of the Adonis members, for example, challenged their indictments, despite the risk of public humiliation and jail time. Many other physique readers corresponded with *ONE*, the Mattachine Society, the ACLU, or Bob Mizer to both express their outrage and seek legal advice. They shared information about the dangers involved in exchanging images, and how to avoid postal inspectors became a key topic of conversation—one of the common threads that tied them together. Physique subscribers were encouraged in their activism by physique publishers. In the face of the crackdown, publishers demonized Summerfield as the face of a "New McCarthyism," invoking a shared past of federal anti-gay witch hunting that many remembered. They founded new organizations that encouraged collective action and support for those who fell victim to Summerfield's campaign. Perhaps the most aggressive response came from the Guild Press, whose League for the Abolition of Postal Censorship promised to "fight this new menace" by offering financial support and expert legal counsel (see fig. 4.8).[104]

Given the high level of activism around the issue of pen-pal clubs, it's no surprise that several members went on to become minor figures in the gay rights movement. John Malzone was a thirty-year-old Catholic priest when he became an Adonis member; he was bold enough to use the address of his parish church in Elmhurst, Illinois, to receive club correspondence. He left the priesthood in 1970 and later served as president of the Chicago chapter of Dignity and was considered a "mover and shaker" in the local gay movement.[105] Benjamin Gardiner was a thirty-seven-year-old model and actor living in New York City

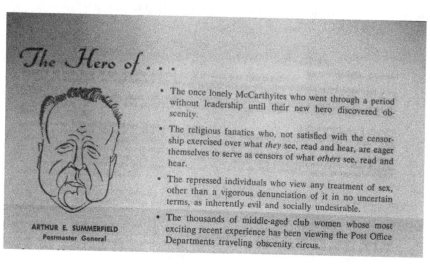

The Hero of . . .

- The once lonely McCarthyites who went through a period without leadership until their new hero discovered obscenity.

- The religious fanatics who, not satisfied with the censorship exercised over what *they* see, read and hear, are eager themselves to serve as censors of what *others* see, read and hear.

- The repressed individuals who view any treatment of sex, other than a vigorous denunciation of it in no uncertain terms, as inherently evil and socially undesirable.

- The thousands of middle-aged club women whose most exciting recent experience has been viewing the Post Office Departments traveling obscenity circus.

ARTHUR E. SUMMERFIELD
Postmaster General

FIGURE 4.8 To resist Postmaster General Summerfield's crackdown, physique publishers formed organizations such as the League for the Abolition of Postal Censorship, which demonized Summerfield as the successor to Joseph McCarthy and the hero of religious fanatics.

Courtesy of ONE Archives at the USC Libraries.

when he joined. He used the club to market "sexy pictures" of himself, which he claimed postal inspectors had cleared in advance, before they indicted him. Gardiner went on to serve as president of the Stonewall Democratic Club in San Francisco and to work on the political campaigns of Harvey Milk.[106]

The prosecution of Adonis members and founders was also not the end of VIM magazine. Three years later VIM reappeared, having been bought by Lynn Womack's Guild Press, which by the early 1960s was fast becoming the largest purveyor of magazines and books targeting a gay market. Under new gay ownership, VIM fulfilled the plans of the previous owners by becoming even more explicitly gay in both images and editorial content. Guild's VIM featured centerfolds of very young men lying on beds and naked duos touching each other. Guild Book Service bulletins alerted readers to the latest in gay books. Even VIM's travel articles entered the realm of gay politics. An article that asked the question "Is New York really gay?" warned readers of the pre–World's Fair crackdown happening in New York gay bars and cruising areas. They even proposed sky-writing "FAIR UNFAIR TO FAIRIES" above Flushing Meadows. By 1967 Guild founded a popular Friend-to-Friend pen-pal club, whose advertisements and member photographs took up half the editorial space of its flagship magazine, Grecian Guild Pictorial. Dubbed the world's largest male pen-pal club, it soon boasted its own magazine, the Male Swinger—all part of Lynn Womack's growing gay mail-order empire.[107]

5

DEFENDING A NAKED BOY

Lynn Womack at the Supreme Court

We will never again be at the mercy of a distributor, agent,
newsstand owner, or anyone else.
—Lynn Womack

But what a compulsion! What a peculiar goal
That led him to stand alone
Before the strongest power in the world
To defend with all his soul
A naked boy.
—George Haimsohn (a.k.a. Alexander Goodman)

AS PRESIDENT of the Mattachine Society of New York, Curtis
Dewees had a recruitment problem. He knew New York City in
the late 1950s and early 1960s was home to hundreds of thousands
of gay men and lesbians, but his organization never had an active membership
of more than a few hundred. Its newsletter's circulation hovered well below a
thousand. With a professional background in publishing, Dewees understood
the power of media companies to connect to readers, but he failed to translate
that expertise to increased participation in the homophile movement.

By the late 1960s he thought he found the answer in a media company owned
by Lynn Womack. "He had this gigantic warehouse in Washington, and at one
point he was selling literally thousands of copies a week of gay novels," Dewees
later remembered. Womack's Guild Press had begun as a publisher of physique
magazines but expanded to produce and market books and other consumer
items. "He simply reached out," Dewees explained, and discovered that his

magazine subscribers wanted more. "They read books as well as looked at pictures."

Dewees toured Womack's 16,000-square-foot warehouse on Capitol Hill and was spellbound by the deafening sound of the state-of-the-art Royal Zenith Press recently imported from Germany as it churned out tens of thousands of copies of promotional flyers. Dewees realized he could partner with Womack to transform the fledgling movement. "This man can really break ground," Dewees thought. "This man had access to a gay market, a gay audience far larger than the Mattachine had." Womack possessed what Mattachine had long coveted. He owned not only his own printing press and office facility but the holy grail of a gay rights organization: a mailing list of "thousands and thousands of gay names."[1] This had the potential to solve the homophile recruitment problem.

Historically homophile organizations had kept their distance from the physique world. The editors of ONE and Mattachine Review feared that including physique photography in publications explicitly devoted to the homosexual cause—as their European counterparts did—would further incite watchful postal inspectors, who had already tried to shut them down for merely providing information about how to purchase Der Kreis and other European homophile magazines. Featuring physique images or personal advertisements would also belie their claim that they were organizations about homosexuals, not of homosexuals. Their official target audience included authority figures as much as average homosexuals.

But beneath such seemingly rational calculations lay a deeper ambivalence. Homophile leaders publicly disdained physique magazines for their lewdness and superficiality while secretly coveting their popularity and their income stream. ONE magazine editors denounced physique photograph collectors as immature dreamers. "Homosexuals would do well to come down out of the clouds," they warned, "down from the romantic dream-world of the 'physique photo' to start wrestling with the far less glamorous, but considerably more adult job of trying to better their own lot in society."[2] They tended to see physique magazines as taking people away from activism, rather than leading them to it. But many homophile leaders were active participants in the physique world and kept close watch on its growing influence. The commercial and legal successes of Lynn Womack's Guild Press represented a new possibility for cooperation between these overlapping worlds.

Of the scores of physique entrepreneurs who preceded him, Lynn Womack was the only one to assemble the resources necessary to take an obscenity case to the U.S. Supreme Court and win, removing at least one of the homophile leaders' objections.[3] More businessman than artist, Womack created the first physique mail order empire, which encompassed a score of magazines, a book service, publishing house, travel guide, clothing line, and later one of the first LGBT newspapers. He assembled a veritable gay legal defense fund that would share information among and ensure legal protection for a coterie of artists and photographers. And he supported the increasingly politicized homophile community in Washington, D.C., earning their lasting support.

Womack's legal victories and vast business network allowed for an unprecedented merger of the physique and homophile worlds, establishing a model for gay publications that remained influential for decades. While much credit for the first magazine that combined gay news and homoerotic art usually goes to Clark Polak, a leader within the homophile movement, it was physique entrepreneur Lynn Womack who first brought these two strands of the community together.[4]

FROM PROFESSOR TO PUBLISHER

Herman Lynn Womack had always found refuge in books. As a Caucasian albino growing up in Hazelhurst, Mississippi, Womack was taunted by his school classmates. His father was an alcoholic tenant farmer who ended up in the Mississippi State Penitentiary at Parchman for murdering his best friend, some said for $300 cash. In response to this combination of harassment and neglect, Womack immersed himself in books. He was nearly expelled from high school for carrying to class a copy of Darwin's *The Origin of Species*—his first encounter with censorship.

By 1940, with the effects of the Great Depression still lingering, he began to put himself through the University of Mississippi by juggling multiple part-time jobs. But he heard from a friend that conditions were better in Washington, D.C., then a boomtown of New Deal agencies and war preparations. So Womack moved to the nation's capital, worked as a federal government clerk, and finished his B.A. degree at George Washington University. Always a good student, he decided to continue his studies, earned an M.A. in psychology, and served for a while as headmaster at Howell Academy, a boy's school in Maryland. By 1955 he had earned a Ph.D. degree in philosophy from Johns Hopkins University—alma mater of his liberal philosophical hero, John

Dewey—and secured an adjunct teaching position back at George Washington (see fig. 5.1).[5]

At the age of twenty-seven, after marrying two women and fathering one daughter, he decided that he was gay. His second wife divorced him on grounds of "mental cruelty." Rather than provide alimony for the rest of his life, he gave her a large cash settlement. He was ready to "face the world free, but broke."[6]

Womack's precarious financial situation only got worse when his adjunct position in George Washington's philosophy department abruptly ended.

**H. Lynn Womack, Head Master
Howell Academy for boys, and Director
CAMP APUSHIMATAHA**

FIGURE 5.1 Before he founded the Guild Press and established a physique magazine empire, H. Lynn Womack earned a Ph.D. degree from Johns Hopkins University and taught at Howell Academy for Boys, George Washington University, and Mary Washington College.

Courtesy of Division of Rare and Manuscript Collections, Cornell University Library.

Although he enjoyed the support of the chair and founder of the department, Charles Gauss, other colleagues considered him too liberal—some even accused him of being an atheist and a communist. Bypassing his application for a full-time position, they hired a graduate of Boston University, then a source of many "young Christian" faculty members for Methodist schools.[7]

After sending out a frenzy of application letters, Womack secured an academic appointment in Fredericksburg, Virginia, about an hour south of Washington, D.C., at Mary Washington College, then the women's college of the University of Virginia. He hated it. "I had forgotten what small town America was like. . . . There is absolutely nothing here—not even a decent movie." If it were not for the proximity of Washington, he wrote a male lover, "I should go mad." Soon he was back living in D.C. and commuting to Fredericksburg three days a week.[8]

Eager to be back in the city full-time and aware that both his liberal views and newly embraced sexuality could endanger his academic position, Womack was all ears when a friend called with a moneymaking proposal. It was 1957 and the Soviets had just launched *Sputnik*, the first artificial satellite, and Washington, D.C., was full of contractors eager to help the government compete in the space race. "Everything is research and development," his friend told him, "these people are crazy." He became part of a holding company that invested money in a start-up based in Silver Spring, Maryland. The stock price of Polytronics Research soared after the company claimed to land electronics contracts with the U.S. Navy. The Securities and Exchange Commission eventually revoked the licenses of three brokerage houses involved in the phony contract scheme but let Womack escape with a half-million-dollar profit. The SEC considered Womack a naïve academic who didn't understand finance. Whether he knew about the scheme remains unclear, but it was not the last time people underestimated his business savvy.[9]

Womack planned to invest his windfall in something that would provide enough income to allow him to leave academia forever while continuing to pursue his interest in books; as a budding scholar he had amassed a library of several thousand volumes. Somewhere along the way, the holding company acquired a printing company, a business that Womack soon learned from an accountant friend was the most secure and lucrative in Washington, D.C., a city that ran on government reports, policy papers, organizational newsletters, and other publications.

Like many academics, Womack already had considerable publishing experience as an editor. As president of Phi Sigma Tau, the newly formed philosophy honor society, he served as editor of *Dialogue,* its research journal for undergraduate and graduate students.[10] He had also served as business manager for the D.C. Library Association and thus editor of its publication, the *Potomac Review.* And since discovering his homosexuality, Womack had become a serious reader of *ONE* magazine—he had even written the editors asking for back issues, suggesting he was studying the field of gay publishing. But the publishing opportunity Womack found was in neither the academic nor homophile press.[11]

Womack, an avid reader of physique magazines, noticed an unusual advertisement in the November 1957 issue of *Grecian Guild Pictorial* (GGP). "Once-in-a-Lifetime Opportunity to Purchase a Successful National Magazine. Investigate Today!" read the banner headline. Familiar enough with the physique field to surmise that the mystery magazine was *GGP*'s sister publication, *TRIM,* Womack quickly submitted a series of detailed queries to publisher Randolph Benson concerning the magazine's advertising revenue, newsstand distribution, and printing costs. The letter signaled not only the seriousness of his inquiry but also his considerable knowledge of the publishing business.

Benson and Womack entered a lively correspondence and then met in Charlottesville over the Christmas break. Perhaps because of their mutual ties to the academy and to the South, the two hit it off and developed a mutual respect. Although Benson had a competing offer from a well-known physique photographer, he thought that Womack possessed better business skills and would be a better steward of an enterprise in which Benson intended to keep a small interest. "I've never met a man in whom I have greater confidence," Benson enthused. Womack purchased *TRIM* and began to work closely with Benson in solidifying the positions of both their magazines in a crowded and fragile field. The many strands of his life—his desire to leave academia, to invest his earnings, to manage this newfound printing company, to further his interest in publishing, and to pursue his gay desires—all seemed to meet in *TRIM.*[12]

ESTABLISHING A DISTRIBUTION NETWORK

As the owner and publisher of *TRIM,* Womack first had to solve an issue that had plagued nearly all physique magazines since their inception: newsstand distribution. Since the demise of the American News Company in the summer of 1957, the situation had grown direr. All physique magazines were at the mercy of smaller distributors who often objected to their content. Capital Distributing Company, which Benson had assured Womack would distribute *TRIM*, had pulled out of its agreement soon after the transfer. "There is, to put it mildly, a certain amount of resistance to physique photography publications at the top level of American magazine distribution," Womack quickly concluded. "Frankly all physique publications are on the brink of total ruin."[13] Only Lou Elson, a gay man who distributed *Tomorrow's Man*, along with several other physique, science fiction, and alternative magazines, had surmounted this obstacle by maintaining an independent distribution network, ACME. Womack found Elson to be untrustworthy but saw in ACME the model for a potential solution.[14]

So Womack took on the difficult task of setting up his own independent set of relationships with newsstands nationwide, holding conferences with every distributor he could identify and making himself known in the industry. "It means that some concrete system for covering every god damn city in every state will be worked out," he explained. "It means that I will check the galleys and see that additional copies go to stands that sold out and fewer to those with large returns." He would eventually institutionalize this labor-intensive process by establishing his own independent wholesale distribution company, Potomac News. By guaranteeing independent distribution of his magazine, Womack knew he had accomplished what no other physique magazine publisher had. "I will tell you very frankly, I would not even let my brother have the distribution lists which I have and am working up," he boasted to Benson about his newfound business relationships. "We will never again be at the mercy of a distributor, agent, newsstand owner, or anyone else," he vowed.[15]

Womack was committed to not only making a success of *TRIM* but to protecting and consolidating the entire field of physique magazines. "I intend to see that *TRIM* survives and that a decent physique publication remains in the field," he promised. Looking beyond his own publication, he began printing and distributing Benson's *Grecian Guild Pictorial*, eventually buying the magazine in 1960. By then he had also acquired *MANual*, a physique magazine originally published as a physique art catalog by SirPrise of Chicago. He also relaunched *Fizeek*, a publication originally produced by a group of physique photographers and artists who considered themselves the "Big Five"—Christopher, Quaintance, Delmonteque, Warner, and Vulcan Studios (Anthony Guyther). Womack felt that his distribution network could ensure that these publications were "distributed legitimately and openly." Womack's interest in protecting his personal investment simultaneously helped stabilize and expand the entire field.[16]

Beyond establishing his own distribution network and purchasing a coterie of magazines, Womack's unique business strategy involved assembling and supporting a stable of photographers that could ensure him a constant stream of quality images. He appreciated photographers who provided free photographs to his magazines in exchange for advertisements for their own mail-order businesses—a standard physique magazine practice. He considered such cooperative photographers shrewd business partners who knew how the market operated and how to get their models out before the public. He had little time for prima donna photographers who considered themselves "artistes" but had no business sense.

To further cement this alliance of successful photographers, he encouraged them to relocate near his Capitol Hill headquarters. One of these was G. Rodney Crowther, a photographer for luxury Washington, D.C., department stores, who had set up an independent photography studio in Chevy Chase, Maryland, in 1957. Forming a close alliance with Womack, Crowther gave up his day job, moved to Capitol Hill, and devoted himself full-time to physique photography. Postal authorities considered Crowther to be Womack's "technician."[17]

Anthony Guyther was another sought-after physique photographer who became a Womack protégé. He began doing layout for Condé Nast in New York City but left to become a freelance photographer, placing photo collages in store windows at Macy's and Bonwit Teller.[18] He photographed both male and female nudes and seminudes for publication but quickly found "easier money" in male images. "Girl models are very expensive and the prettiest girls won't pose nude," Guyther complained.[19] He could meet more willing male models, often street kids in Times Square, photograph them against simple backdrops in his Upper East Side apartment, and pay them ten dollars. Like hundreds of others, he began with small advertisements in the back of *Muscle Builder* and other mainstream bodybuilding magazines. Soon his $1 Vulcan Studio catalogs were producing between five hundred and a thousand pieces of mail each month. Unlike most physique photographers, Guyther used a street address, since he sold nudes to those who visited him in person. The volume of mail (and money) was so large that it caught the attention of his building's superintendent, who realized his tenant was running a lucrative mail-order business and broke into his mailbox to steal the cash. Only after this robbery did Guyther decide it was time to get a post office box.[20]

With his stylized images gracing the covers of *Grecian Guild Pictorial* and *Body Beautiful*, it was Guyther (as Vulcan Studios) who made the alliance with several other photographers to launch *Fizeek*. Like most such efforts, it produced only one issue, until Womack took over. Teaming up with Womack, Guyther found a stable patron, relocated to Washington, D.C., and became part of a collaborative effort with Womack's Capital Studio. "I got the most advertising space. [Womack] said I was the best," Guyther remembered. He not only supplied Womack with many cover images for *Trim* and the revitalized *Fizeek* but wrote and illustrated one of Womack's first special issue books, *How to Photograph the Male Nude*. He found Womack to be "very smart, cultured," as well as extremely persuasive.[21] "He can charm the paper off the walls," he told postal authorities. But his relationship with his benefactor was troubled. Describing him as a "con man," Guyther also testified that Womack "would come in like the whirlwind, look at my pictures and just snatch them away. He was a big, heavy, strong man." But by then Womack was Guyther's principal source of income. The business relationship was so close that postal authorities sometimes considered them a single enterprise.[22]

Womack offered photographers like Crowther and Guyther more than just access to his growing coterie of magazines and mailing list. Unlike any other physique publisher, he offered them legal defense, understanding that this would not only protect his supply of content but potentially expand civil rights protections. When the Post Office shut down Guyther's post office box, it was Womack's attorney Stanley Dietz who defended him. Dietz defended many of Womack's photographer allies when they fell victim to Postmaster General Arthur Summerfield's crackdown.[23] Womack also established a legal lending library on censorship for other publishers and photographers, the sort of central defense fund that Kinsey had suggested early on. "We have collected and maintain a large collection of bulletins, briefs, and other materials relating to both homosexuality and censorship," Womack boasted. "This collection is in constant use by attorneys from all over the country because we are in D.C. and both our cases and our attorney are well known."[24]

It is hard to estimate the impact of Womack defensive apparatus, but it's clear that many independent photographers, with no connections to this assistance, fell victim to federal prosecution. John Palatinus, for example, had a narrative much like those of Crowther and Guyther. He began as a designer for New York department stores but soon discovered that his physique photography business was more lucrative, especially when he started selling nudes. By 1958 his images were gracing the covers of *Tomorrow's Man*. But when his New York apartment was raided by postal authorities, and with no one to defend him in court, he was forced to abandon his mail-order business.[25] Unlike Palatinus, Womack and his coterie of photographers and attorneys would stay and fight in court.

ARRESTS BEGIN

The series of arrests and hearings that would bring Womack to the Supreme Court began in January 1960, when he and two of his photographers—G. Rodney Crowther and Frank Collier—were arrested for placing nude photos in the U.S. mail. They began like the scores of similar raids on physique photography studios organized by Postmaster General Summerfield's crackdown on mail-order pornography. First Womack was arrested by federal authorities for his mail-order business. Then the Post Office seized his magazines. Finally local vice officers raided his printing facility. As was often the case, federal and local authorities acted as a tag team to knock out their targets. Because of the numerous convictions and appeals, this series of cases would outlast Summerfield's tenure and be vigorously pursued by his successor, Edward J. Day. Although typical in many ways, these law enforcement operations would have a different outcome, one that would transform the field.

According to Chief Postal Inspector David H. Stephens, the raid of Womack's 14th Street printing plant and seizure of his forty-thousand-name mailing list was the culmination of a three-month campaign during which postal authorities had infiltrated the mailing list with decoy letters.[26] But the raid caught Womack by surprise. He had recently assured a colleague, "I am now more convinced that the P.O. is going to do nothing to us for simple nudes and I feel that we can settle down and put our operations on a systematic basis."[27] He had consulted with Post Office investigators about the legality of the photographs and received assurances of their mailability.[28]

Womack soon discovered that the Post Office, the press, and the courts considered him a threat to society. Headlines about the raid in local newspapers stressed that he was an "educator" and "ex-professor," raising the specter of Womack's potential nefarious influence on children. At the federal district court trial in Washington, D.C., prosecutors followed a similar strategy by calling teenage boys to testify that they had received Womack's mailings.[29] Seventy-four-year-old Judge Alexander Holtzoff was clearly unsympathetic to Womack's case. He refused to allow most of the defense witnesses to testify, insisting that only priests and rabbis were qualified to make determinations about "community standards." He barred Womack's attorney from presenting a replica of Michelangelo's statue of David to make a similar point. By contrast, the U.S. attorney was allowed to present seventeen witnesses from around the country.

In March the jury convicted Womack of multiple counts of obscenity and he was sentenced to one to three years in prison. Judge Holtzoff released him pending an appeal but promised to send him to prison if he continued publishing such images. Womack considered the entire process to be "legal harassment" and vowed "I intend to carry this up to the Supreme Court if I have to."[30]

Emboldened by Womack's conviction, the Post Office moved within weeks to impede the sale of his magazines. "Once Herman Womack was convicted in the federal court here," Womack's attorney explained, "the Post Office made up their mind that they were going to stop these magazines."[31] The postmaster in Alexandria, Virginia, just across the Potomac River, withheld six parcels containing Guild Press magazines, beginning the case that Womack would take to the Supreme Court. After a three-day administrative hearing, the Post Office found issues of *TRIM, MANual,* and *Grecian Guild Pictorial* to be obscene and unmailable. Assistant U.S. Attorney Robert J. Asman, Jr., promised to support the Post Office findings by prosecuting those who used the mail to promote "physique magazines" and material "appealing to homosexuals."[32] By August a federal district court judge affirmed the Post Office's findings. By the next year the U.S. Court of Appeals concurred.[33]

In November the Morals Division of the Washington, D.C., Police Department decided it was their turn to strike. They raided Womack's printing plant, arrested not only Womack but two of his employees—both former students—and carted away three hand trucks of materials. This led, a few days later, to a federal indictment on thirty-five counts of conspiracy to send obscene materials and advertisements in the mail.

These new charges had repercussions on Womack's first conviction, then coming up for appeal. Seeing this as a betrayal of their agreement, Judge Holtzoff revoked his earlier bond and ordered him to report to jail to serve his sentence of one to three years.[34] Then, when the U.S. Court of Appeals rejected his appeal, Womack opted to plead guilty to one count of conspiracy from the second indictment for an additional sentence of four to fourteen months. His protégé and accused coconspirator Alfred J. Heinecke also stood trial and was sentenced to fifteen months to three years in prison. "Gratified" by the convictions of these "serious offenders," Postmaster General Day used the occasion to announce, "the toughest crackdown ever conducted" against mailing obscene material. Although he promised to conduct the drive "without fanfare"—in contrast to his flamboyant predecessor—he vowed that the prosecution of obscenity would continue.[35]

Despite his now two- to four-year sentence, Womack used an ingenious legal strategy to stay out of prison: taking advantage of the widespread notion that homosexuals suffered from a psychological illness, he arranged to be confined to St. Elizabeths Hospital, the oldest federally operated psychiatric facility. A former student of psychology, Womack knew precisely what to say to the doctors to receive the proper diagnosis. He also had friends who worked at St. Elizabeths, and money to bribe other staff members. From this verdant campus near the Anacostia River, only a few miles from his printing plant and publishing headquarters, Womack continued to run his business. "It was very pleasant. I had a private room, TV, typewriter," Womack recalled of his stay on Ward 9.[36]

Womack remained defiant and continued to run and even expand his business. When the government confiscated his forty-thousand-name mailing list, he sued and won it back.[37] Labeling the government crackdown "the new McCarthyism," he and his attorney established the League for the Abolition of Postal Censorship and asked others to join the cause. He stamped his and his photographers' mailings with "Support the Supreme Court, Fight Postal Censorship" to counter Postmaster General Summerfield's "Report Obscene Mail to Your Postmaster" cancellation stamp.[38] Womack continued not only to publish his magazines but also to provoke the censors, as his images got more salacious and his models younger. The March 1961 issue of *Trim* featured a trio of naked men seen from behind, their hands and midsections overlapping, giving the impression they were fondling one another. By photographing them partly in shadow, with their faces all pointed down and away from the camera, Anthony Guyther, mimicking George Platt Lynes, accentuated the erotic nature of the encounter. A few months later Womack launched *Manorama*, a new physique magazine edited by Bob Anthony featuring photographs and artwork without the usual editorial accompaniment.[39]

If Womack was left unchastened by these legal setbacks, other publishers and photographers felt their effect as Womack's repeated convictions sent shockwaves through the industry. The Florida Model Guild warned customers that owing to recent federal court decisions it could not offer frontal nudes and reported that the Customs Department had been advised to confiscate such photos coming into the country.[40] Local police forces felt emboldened by the convictions. In their raids on a "homosexual pornography ring" in Miami, police noted that among their findings were national magazines "all declared obscene by a Federal judge in Washington."[41] The high-profile federal conspiracy trial against members of the Adonis club had just concluded in Chicago with all indicted participants found guilty. The Post Office's drive to smash physique magazines seemed to be working.

ARGUING BEFORE THE SUPREME COURT

When Womack's case against the Post Office reached the U.S. Supreme Court, his prospects looked dim.[42] Every court involved in his series of obscenity cases had ruled against him, including the Supreme Court, which had agreed to let his prison sentence for marketing mail-order photographs stand, along with that of his photographic coconspirator.[43] Indeed the Supreme Court had never entertained oral arguments in a case involving physique magazines, or gay material of any kind. And Stanley Dietz, Womack's lawyer, had never appeared there before.

When oral arguments began in *Manual v. Day*, Dietz's Brooklyn accent and halting speech were in sharp contrast to the dulcet tones and suave manner of his opponent, Assistant Solicitor General J. William Doolittle, who, like most of the justices and clerks, had an Ivy League background. Humble and colloquial, Dietz peppered his explanations with caveats such as "as I understand it." His approach seemed to exasperate eighty-year-old Justice Felix Frankfurter, who, after several unsuccessful queries, said, "I'm trying to find out what your case is." Frankfurter was interested in broad, theoretical implications of obscenity law. He asked Dietz whether, hypothetically, the Post Office might translate material from Sanskrit into English in order to determine mailability. But Dietz was more interested in the nuts and bolts of his client's business. "You can't sell a May magazine in June," he explained to prove that the Post Office was guilty of "prior restraint" in purposely delaying and preventing Womack from getting his merchandise to market. Responding to an inquiry about the size of the magazine circulation, Dietz editorialized, "Forty thousand or more a month. It's pretty good."[44]

It was a desire to protect minorities from police brutality that spurred Stanley Dietz's law practice. His real interest was business, but while an undergraduate at George Washington University he realized his business professors kept dodging questions by saying, "You'll have to ask your lawyer about that." So when he decided to get a law degree, it was with the intention of bettering his business acumen—not becoming an attorney. An incident in a Washington, D.C., taxicab changed his mind. "I got into this taxi with this cop who started telling me and my buddy how he'd shot this 'nigger' in an alley."[45] He decided to stay in Washington for six months and defend African Americans against such abuse. He ended up staying for three decades, expanding his practice to include gay men also harassed by the police. "I got a reputation as a defender of the underdog by counseling homosexuals arrested and beaten by the police in Lafayette Park, near the White House," he told a journalist. It was as a sort of lawyer to the gay community that Womack found him.[46]

Dietz was the first attorney to argue a case about gay rights before the Supreme Court. Although the court had ruled in 1957 that ONE magazine was not obscene, the ONE v. Olesen decision was decided without oral arguments in a one-sentence, unsigned decision. The court simply reversed the lower court's finding of obscenity, citing its own recent Roth decision. Although much touted by historians of the homophile movement, such a per curiam decision created what legal scholar Carlos Ball called "unavoidable uncertainty" because the court did not explain why it found the magazine not obscene. It, too, had been accused of obscenity both for a piece of romantic lesbian fiction and for an advertisement for more erotic European gay magazines. How much erotic content the court would allow was still an open question.[47]

While not an expert on the fine points of U.S. obscenity law, Dietz did know about the experiences of the homosexual community, and he used his unique opportunity to educate the court. Dietz told the court about the Kinsey reports, one of the few authoritative surveys available on American sexual behavior. Following Kinsey, he argued that the term homosexual applied to acts, not people, and that homosexual behavior was something practiced by a large percentage of the population. But he also offered a second argument that assumed that homosexuals were not only a discrete group but also Womack's intended audience. If this were true, Dietz argued, then the Post Office's refusal to mail their magazines "reduces a large segment of our society to second class citizenship."[48]

Applying such civil rights language to gay men in 1962 was virtually unprecedented and must have shocked the justices. Frank Kameny had only begun using similar language in his unsuccessful petition to the Supreme Court filed a year earlier, when he charged that the federal government had treated him as a "second-class citizen" by firing him for his homosexuality; several years later he would lead picketers in front of the White House with signs decrying the "second-class" status of gay men and lesbians. But Dietz got further than Kameny and his fellow protesters—he presented this argument to nine sitting Supreme Court justices. He explained to the justices that "there is no community that does not have homosexuals," but that many remained hidden because, he argued, "we keep these people suppressed." And since the Post Office considered any material that appealed to them to be obscene, he asked the justices, "Are we going to allow these second-class citizens to receive any literature?" As he summed up his case, "If we so-called normal people, according to our law, are entitled to have our pin-ups, then why shouldn't the second-class citizens, the homosexual group . . . why shouldn't they be allowed to have their pin-ups?" His was fundamentally a civil rights argument.[49]

Assistant Solicitor General Doolittle also focused his arguments less on the contents of the magazines then on their readership. He argued that these magazines were being "beamed" to a particular group of "deviates," and that the material caused them to engage in illegal acts, and therefore the Post Office had the right to consider them nonmailable. He also argued that they could lead young men and boys down a path to immorality. Obscenity, Doolittle seemed to argue, was not an immutable, abstract concept but varied depending on the audience. But several of the justices were skeptical of granting the Post Office the power to determine who may obtain what type of mail. "Do I understand you to say," Justice Hugo Black inquired, "that the Postmaster has the right to decide what person might be adversely affected by some pictures or some writers, and decline to deliver this to that person?" Another asked if the same magazines could legally be sent to medical professionals or academics. Summarizing this line of questioning, Justice William J. Brennan asked pointedly, "I take it, Mr. Doolittle, that . . . if all of these [magazines] were addressed to girls' colleges, you wouldn't be here, would you?" Doolittle responded, "I don't suppose I would," admitting that his case was really about same-sex desire.[50]

It was Womack himself who provided the evidence that physique magazine readers were overwhelmingly homosexual. Soon after purchasing TRIM in 1957, he had voluntarily met with Postal Inspector Harry Simon and according to Simon admitted that these magazines were purchased by homosexuals.[51] He had a similar exchange with the general counsel of the Post Office, who had tried to coerce an admission out of Womack about his readership. But coercion wasn't necessary, according to Dietz, who witnessed the exchange. Womack freely boasted about his business. "He was very proud of the fact that he could send this material [to homosexuals] and that the Post Office couldn't touch him," Dietz told the justices. Womack let the general counsel know that the Supreme Court had already decided that magazines targeting homosexuals were not obscene. "Have you ever heard of *ONE, Inc.?*" he asked pointedly. "This stuff is legal," he insisted to the general counsel. According to Dietz, "Dr. Womack had a lot of fun baiting the Post Office Department with this type of statement." Dietz made a similar argument to the nine justices, asking, if they banned Womack's magazine because it was intended for homosexuals, "then what does *ONE, Inc. v. Olesen* case stand for?"[52] If they found these magazines unmailable, they would effectively be overturning their earlier decision that cleared *ONE* magazine of obscenity.

It fell to Associate Justice John Marshall Harlan, a former Rhodes Scholar appointed by President Eisenhower, to write the Supreme Court's first formal opinion on the rights of gay people. Harlan first made it clear that the justices, like much of America, saw through the classical and bodybuilding alibis. He asserted categorically that Womack's magazines were not "physical culture or 'bodybuilding' publications, but are composed primarily, if not exclusively, for homosexuals" and "read almost entirely by homosexuals." Having established that these were gay magazines, he made it clear that he was disgusted by them, calling them "dismally unpleasant, uncouth, and tawdry." But in a 6–1 decision, he found that these Guild Press publications were not obscene because they were not "patently offensive."

The decision was a severe blow to the Post Office, calling into question its ability to single-handedly make determinations of obscenity. It established a new obscenity criterion—material had to be "patently offensive" to not enjoy protection under the First Amendment. Legal scholars came to refer to this as the "hard-core pornography test." As one legal analyst at the time argued, *Manual* represented "judicial impatience with the past practices of Congress and the postal authorities" and ushered in a "new phase" of diminished postal censorship.[53] Striking a clear and important blow for freedom of expression, Harlan and his fellow justices effectively called a halt to the procedures the Post Office had used to harass both gay and straight publishers and customers for decades.

Beyond its impact as a landmark obscenity case that hampered the powers of the Post Office, *Manual v. Day* was a pivotal gay rights case. It reinforced and clarified the right to publish material geared toward a gay audience first established by the *ONE v. Olesen* decision. More important, as legal scholar Carlos Ball has pointed out, it was the first time any court in the United States expressed an equivalency between homosexuality and heterosexuality. Womack's images, the justices concluded, "cannot fairly be regarded as more objectionable than many portrayals of the female nude that society tolerates." While the justices may have seen homosexuals as "unfortunates" and "sexual deviants," they did not use such moral judgments to separate homosexuals from their constitutional rights. Although they did not adopt Dietz's language, they seemed to agree with him that homosexuals could not be treated as second-class citizens, at least when it came to their First Amendment rights.[54]

It was a big and decisive win for the albino kid from Hazelton, Mississippi. He had taken on the federal government and won. In a letter to all Guild Press subscribers, Womack framed the case as a victory for the entire physique field over the campaign begun by Postmaster General Summerfield in 1959 to destroy it. "Our victory was total and complete," Womack enthused in bright red ink. "You are able to receive physique magazines today because we stood up and fought," he boasted. He let readers know that he had spent over $15,000 on the case while other publishers sat on their hands, criticized him, and made deals with the Post Office. He saw this as a historic rebuke to the Post Office and the "prior restraint activities" that it had practiced since 1865—all now declared illegal.[55]

The homophile press, reflecting its continued ambivalence to physique publishers, offered only minimal coverage of this first written Supreme Court decision on a gay issue. *Mattachine Review* first inaccurately reported that the Supreme Court had dismissed the case. Only by printing a corrective statement supplied by Womack did it alert readers to this major gay rights victory. *ONE* praised the court for recognizing the rights of "minorities" but lamented the timing of the decision. Because it came down on the same day as *Engle v. Vitale*—which found officially sanctioned school prayers to be unconstitutional—it led to headlines that conflated homosexuals and atheists. "Court Outlaws Prayer, Promotes Homosexuality" was one Catholic periodical's take on the court's rulings. *The Ladder* noted the decision only in passing as part of a speech by an ACLU representative at a Mattachine conference.[56]

Having won a decisive victory in the highest court in the land, Womack set about leveraging his newfound freedom. "I did not fight, spend money, go to jail, come to Saint Elizabeths to spend even one moment of my life living in fear of *anything*," Womack defiantly told one of his photographers.[57] Guild

Press's extensive line of magazines that had been suspended for much of 1962 started up again with the promise that they were now "solidly backed and soundly organized." Womack bought a new printing press from Germany and relocated to larger quarters on Capitol Hill. By the next year Guild acquired *VIM*, the campiest of the physique magazines that had been shut down in Summerfield's crackdown.[58]

Womack also helped other physique studios establish new magazines. He launched *Mars*, a leather-oriented publication to be edited by Chuck Renslow and his partner Domingo Orejudos, who had founded Kris Studios in Chicago in 1952. Renslow's physique photos and Orejudos's artwork—under the pseudonym Etienne—were well-known in the physique world, having graced the pages of *Tomorrow's Man* and many other publications. Both men were also leaders in the burgeoning leather community, having opened The Gold Coast, one of the first leather bars in the United States.[59]

In addition to expanding the variety of its offerings, Guild publications became increasingly bold in both imagery and editorial content. Images of physique models in posing straps were juxtaposed with images of the same model in drag.[60] The police became fodder for satire, as in a playful cartoon featuring a police officer glaring over a male couple wrestling (or cuddling) on the grass in a public park. "Do You Realize That You Guys Are Breaking the Law?" he asks, as he points at a "Keep Off the Grass" sign. The drawing reminded readers that although they might be arrested for other crimes, it would not be for obscenity.[61] Other treatments of law enforcement were less subtle. An Alfred Heinecke mailing asserted that "it has been clearly established, by the decisions of the Supreme Court of the United States," that nude art studies are legal. Police officers and postal inspectors who acted contrary to this decision would be met with "legal retaliatory measures," the studio threatened.[62] Gay rights arguments began creeping into editorials, such as one on overpopulation. In "Less Taxes for Bachelors," Womack suggested that "the public view toward homosexuals and lesbians will have to change" to encourage childlessness. "It will have to be more than acceptance—more like public approval. Homosexuals should be allowed to acknowledge their inclinations and be able to obtain public office."[63]

Readers seemed to notice "the boldness of recent months" and worried that the magazines were becoming reckless. A cautious *ONE* reader from Houston, Texas, wrote, "If Potomac [Press] meets with disaster, many homosexuals will be burned in the process."[64] Womack was pushing his business in bold new directions that even some in the gay community found threatening. But sales soared as Guild Press publications became more provocative and more openly gay. By 1965 Womack planned to launch a new magazine called "GAYBOY" with the goal of presenting "the homosexual world as it is today" with "realistic honesty."[65] Although the publication never got off the ground, it's new, more open, editorial policy informed all Guild Press operations.

GUILD BOOK SERVICE

It was within a year of the *Manual v. Day* victory that Guild Press made its most significant shift by expanding into the book-selling business. Despite "insistent demands" of his customers, Womack had been reluctant to venture into selling books since he considered himself "completely ignorant" of the publishing business. So he repeated the strategy he had used in entering the physique business—he learned all he could, allied himself with experts, and then used his considerable resources to transform the field.

Womack reached out to Curtis Dewees, who had recently stepped down as the head of Mattachine New York, after helping to establish a similar group in Washington, D.C. "I offered him my services because I thought what he was doing was so exciting," Dewees remembered. Womack called Dewees a "mentor" whose inside knowledge of the book industry was "invaluable" in helping him negotiate with mainstream publishers. Dewees, who worked for a book importer, also introduced Womack to the pioneer of gay book services, Donald Webster Cory, and to his successor, Elsie Carlton, allowing him to draw on more than ten years of experience in marketing gay and lesbian books.[66] Womack also formed a close alliance with Village Books & Press owner Howard Frisch, who would use his nearly encyclopedic knowledge of gay-related literature to help Womack identify gay books of interest and write summary reviews.[67]

The Guild Book Service (GBS) Bulletins that began appearing in all Womack's physique magazines read like gossipy letters from a friend and often assumed a great deal of familiarity with gay literature, comparing new books to classics in the genre. Reflecting Frisch's tastes and sensibilities, GBS would not resort to "extravagant endorsements" or "titillating advertisements" to sell books, at least initially. "We are selling books, not our integrity," the first issue informed readers. Instead it promised to cast a critical eye on the slew of books from a variety of disciplines that claimed to be scientific investigations into the homosexual problem. "The dull obscenities which certain psychiatrists are putting forth as case histories will be reviewed under the category of creative writing," it joked, suggesting its reviews would offer more judicious, informed commentary than slick marketing. It also promised to keep things light. "The above does not mean that we will not list and offer a certain amount of trash to our readers. However, this will be described for what it is and no pretense made that it is anything other than something with which to kill an otherwise dull evening."[68]

Appearing as four-page centerfold "pull outs" in Guild Press magazines, the book reviews became a major distinguishing feature. Over time the reviews also became franker, with lengthy excerpts of the racy passages. "Womack wrote great book reviews," Richard Schlegel remembered. "[He] knew how to review a book. . . . It may have had two erotic passages in it, but boy Womack could certainly inflate the significance of those passages."[69]

The response to the Guild Book Service was "overwhelming" and "an astonishing success," Womack gushed to customers by the end of 1963. "Today GBS is a highly organized, efficient and expanding service" offering hardcover and paperback books from the humorous to the serious, latest bestsellers and reprints of classics. By 1965 GBS had a full-time staffer who scanned issues of the *Times Literary Supplement, Publishers Weekly,* and *New York Times* for books with gay content and placed orders for thousands of copies from mainstream publishers.[70] GBS's first glossy catalog numbered over a hundred pages, with sophisticated graphics and pull quotes to entice customers. "There is no comparable service available anywhere in the world," Womack boasted. "There is no doubt that it will considerably strengthen the economic foundations of our entire operation."[71]

Guild Book Service offered not only serious literature but a rich variety of campy books and novelty items—cologne, jewelry, and posters. *The Gay Cook Book* offered campy tips on entertaining for the young gay bachelor on a budget in his New York City studio. *The Gay Coloring Book* followed Percy, a dandy who sported a chartreuse suit, bow tie, and bulging crotch as he decorated his apartment and cruised nearby parks, tearooms, bars, and bathhouses. *The Guild Dictionary of Homosexual Terms* was described as "THE FIRST COMPLETE HOMOSEXUAL DICTIONARY EVER OFFERED!!" The Flying Dick keychain promised "something to 'break the ice' with a just-met friend." *Fizeek* wall calendars featured America's "sexiest and handsomest physique models"—with no pretense that these images were about bodybuilding. Customers were encouraged to "order copies for yourself and all your friends." One brochure offered

20 x 24-inch posters and challenged customers to "be the first in your crowd to display them" (see fig. 5.2).

Guild not only was being more open in its approach to attracting gay customers, it was encouraging them to follow suit and publicly display the merchandise in their homes. As historian Stephen Vider has argued, "Such services

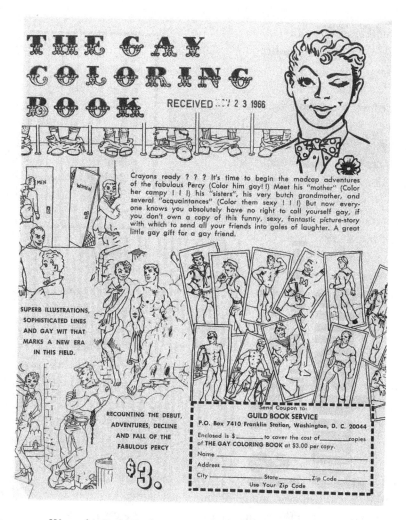

FIGURE 5.2 Womack's Guild Book Service sold a wide variety of novelty items. Cross-promotion between physique magazines and items like *The Gay Coloring Book* removed any doubt about the audience for these magazines.

Courtesy of ONE Archives at the USC Libraries.

transformed the home itself into a site of gay cultural consumption. You no longer needed to go to a bar to 'come out' into the gay world."[72]

Soon Guild launched its own publishing house, reprinting important early gay fiction, much of it first published by Greenberg before postal authorities stopped its pioneering efforts in gay publishing a decade earlier. At the suggestion of Donald Webster Cory, Womack reprinted Loren Wahl's *Invisible Glass* and Nial Kent's *The Divided Path*, noting that because of its hopeful ending it had been "'the most satisfying' to gay readers of the 1940s." Guild published new fiction as well, most notably *$TUD* by Samuel Steward (a.k.a. Phil Andros), whose erotic stories had become a staple of the Swiss gay journal *Der Kreis*. "You will not find in this book any trace of the sad-sick-sorry self-pity of the 'gay' boy for his plight," the dust jacket announced, promising something different from the fiction featured in American homophile publications.[73] With the capacity to publish original works of both serious and humorous gay fiction, to reprint classics, and to distribute them through its own network, Womack's enterprise had become, according to historian Philip Clark, "the most ambitious gay literary program the world had seen."[74] Guild Book Service's own marketing materials used the tagline "World's Largest Dealer in Homosexual Literature."[75]

Beyond sheer volume, Guild Press fiction and nonfiction publications offered gay men around the country and the world access to voices that not only described but celebrated a sexualized gay male culture. As Clark argues, they "present[ed] arguments about the ubiquity and normality of gay men and gay life" and thereby "contributed to the formation of a positive personal gay identity." As one character in the Guild original publication, *Handsome Is . . .* (1966) exclaims, "I just happened to like boys. And I'm not ashamed of it." Some of Guild's publication decisions were even more explicitly political, such as its reprint of *Homosexuality and Citizenship in Florida*, originally published by the Florida Legislative Investigation Committee as a warning to its constituents about the dangers of homosexuality. The "Purple Pamphlet" and its salacious illustrations had caused a scandal in the Sunshine State and was immediately suppressed—until Guild Press offered it for $2 a copy. "Our reprinting of the 'Purple Report' has made all of the Florida papers and is used as damning the Johns [Committee] even more," Womack exclaimed to a colleague. Within a year, the uproar over the pamphlet and its resale by a gay publishing house led to the demise of the committee and its campaign to oust gay public school educators (see fig. 5.3).[76]

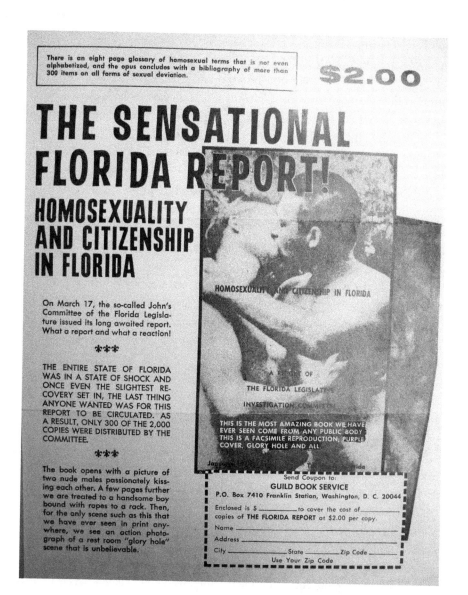

There is an eight page glossary of homosexual terms that is not even alphabetized, and the opus concludes with a bibliography of more than 300 items on all forms of sexual deviation.

$2.00

THE SENSATIONAL FLORIDA REPORT!

HOMOSEXUALITY AND CITIZENSHIP IN FLORIDA

On March 17, the so-called John's Committee of the Florida Legislature issued its long awaited report. What a report and what a reaction!

✳✳✳

THE ENTIRE STATE OF FLORIDA WAS IN A STATE OF SHOCK AND ONCE EVEN THE SLIGHTEST RECOVERY SET IN, THE LAST THING ANYONE WANTED WAS FOR THIS REPORT TO BE CIRCULATED. AS A RESULT, ONLY 300 OF THE 2,000 COPIES WERE DISTRIBUTED BY THE COMMITTEE.

✳✳✳

The book opens with a picture of two nude males passionately kissing each other. A few pages further we are treated to a handsome boy bound with ropes to a rack. Then, for the only scene such as this that we have ever seen in print anywhere, we see an action photograph of a rest room "glory hole" scene that is unbelievable.

HOMOSEXUALITY AND CITIZENSHIP IN FLORIDA

A REPORT OF THE FLORIDA LEGISLATIVE INVESTIGATION COMMITTEE

THIS IS THE MOST AMAZING BOOK WE HAVE EVER SEEN COME FROM ANY PUBLIC BODY THIS IS A FACSIMILE REPRODUCTION, PURPLE COVER, GLORY HOLE AND ALL.

Send Coupon to:
GUILD BOOK SERVICE
P.O. Box 7410 Franklin Station, Washington, D. C. 20044

Enclosed is $_____ to cover the cost of_____
copies of THE FLORIDA REPORT at $2.00 per copy.

Name _____
Address _____
City _____ State _____ Zip Code _____
Use Your Zip Code

FIGURE 5.3 Womack's Guild Book Service made a big sensation when it offered copies of the infamous "Purple Pamphlet" from the Florida Legislative Investigation Committee, then investigating homosexual teachers in the state. Publicity surrounding the pamphlet led to the demise of the committee.

Courtesy of ONE Archives at the USC Libraries.

The blending of Womack's book service and his physique empire represented a major change to both worlds. Making the gay content explicit, it removed any pretense that these were bodybuilding magazines and transformed many into gay lifestyle magazines. By 1965 some Guild magazines had added a "newsfront" section that included news of gay legal and cultural happenings from around the world.[77] Others offered travel advice. The "gay tourist" visiting Toronto was advised to visit two exciting clubs where "dancing on a boy-with-boy or girl-with-girl basis is the order of the day."[78] Paris, on the other hand, was panned. "I saw very few muscle-magazines in Europe, very few obvious queens, very few of the gay manifestations that abound in NYC. . . . For myself, who likes to go to bed with beautiful boys—[Paris] is dead."[79] For a more comprehensive list of gay bars in the United States, readers could order *The Guild Guide to the Gay Scene*.

Womack also ventured into the clothing business by offering a line of Guild fashions—mostly bathing suits and posing straps. He was inspired by Regency Square in New York and Ah Men in Los Angeles, clothiers whose brick-and-mortar stores and mail-order catalogs had developed a gay following.[80] "It was a new concept—we were the first gay-oriented business in West Hollywood," Don Cook boasted about Ah Men's first store on Santa Monica Boulevard in 1962. "We weren't trying to pull any punches, we aimed it that way." Featuring open mesh briefs, posing pouches, and tight pants, the catalogs offered almost as much male flesh as the physique magazines where they advertised, and generated as much sales as the storefront (see fig. 5.4).[81]

The association of tight pants and skimpy bathing suits with gay men became well entrenched in American culture. "They have their favored clothing suppliers who specialize in the tight slacks, short-cut coats and fastidious furnishings favored by many, but by no means all, male homosexuals," the *New York Times* helpfully explained to its readers. Columnist Lee Mortimer referred to "the boys-in-tight-pants set" to deride gay men who congregated in certain restaurants. The association was so keen that for some locales, sartorial laws became a way to keep gay men away. The City Council of Cape May, New Jersey, worried that an influx of the "gay set" to its beaches would turn it into a "Southern Fire Island," countered by passing an ordinance outlawing skimpy bikini bathing suits.[82]

Increasing cross-promotion between specialty clothing catalogs and physique magazines furthered the connection. Ah Men catalogs featured gay books such

FIGURE 5.4 Don Cook's Ah Men clothing store, the first gay-oriented business in West Hollywood in 1962, had a nationwide customer base thanks to its popular mail-order catalog, which resembled a physique magazine.

Courtesy of ONE Archives at the USC Libraries.

as *Mr. Madam* and *The Gay Cookbook* while one physique magazine featured a photo spread in the Ah Men store in West Hollywood.[83] Some of the most famous physique models, like Glenn Bishop and Mark Nixon, began offering their own lines of clothing, while Jim Stryker created "MascuLine" jewelry, including a "Lover's Ring" with two birthstones, "yours and his."[84] Advertisements for such clothing and jewelry further separated these magazines from their bodybuilding roots.

The final element that Womack added to his rich line of products—perhaps the one most desired by his gay male readership—was a correspondence club. *Grecian Guild Pictorial*, which had always positioned itself as fostering a fraternal order of Grecian brothers, started by printing the photos and addresses of members in its "From the Stoa" section. "Look forward to seeing you at our next convention," one member suggested, his photo showing him reclining nude on a bed. By 1967 Guild Press began its own "Friend-to-Friend Club" with its own magazine, *The Male Swinger*, which featured nearly fifty pages of classified ads (see fig. 5.5).[85]

FIGURE 5.5 By 1967 Guild Press offered a classified "Friend-to-Friend Club" for its customers.

IMITATORS RUSH IN

As Guild Press publications became more openly gay, its competitors followed suit. In his *Physique Pictorial*, Bob Mizer increasingly called for his readers to contribute to the defense fund of arrested physique photographers, join the ACLU, or contribute to the Mattachine Society.[86] In an open letter to those who opposed "Physical Culture Books," Mizer argued that they were no more likely to turn someone gay then girlie magazines will cause "queer boys" to start chasing girls.[87] Mizer became so uncharacteristically open that customers wrote in to suggest he should tone down some of the suggestive leering of the models to avoid the "wrath of censors." Mizer responded defiantly that these boys are happy and proud, unlike the dull censors, and why not show it off. And he included a coy plug for the new Guild Book Service, noting it provided "interesting books" now freely available without risk because of the owner's considerable "legal experience."[88]

The publications of fitness magazine publisher Joe Weider also became increasingly gay in the wake of *Manual v. Day*. Weider's *Young Physique* was a large-format color magazine that featured titillating images far removed from the world of bodybuilding. One cover featured a naked man reclining in a supine position on a rock, a delicate tulle fabric serving as a decorative, feminizing blanket.[89] Another featured a still image from what would become James Bidgood's film *Pink Narcissus* of a young man in white boots, stretch pants, and a fake fur jacket in a suggestive bedroom scene.[90] Editorial content featured travel tips for readers who "Search for Beauty with Gay Abandon." A guide to Nice, France, explained that "physiqultists"—which included both bodybuilders, their admirers, and all who search for happiness through the pursuit of Adonis—would enjoy the French Riviera and its "pantheon of godlike young men from all over the world." Gushing letters from readers about features on Fire Island and Acapulco were headlined "The Gay Resorts." A book review on Jean Marcade's *Eros Kalos* entitled "Homo-erotica from the Golden Age of Greek Civilization" noted that it was the subject of a U.S. Customs censorship battle and that the *Village Voice* dubbed it "The Book You Are Not Allowed to Admire."[91]

Copious use of the word "gay," peons to ancient Greece, and notes about police crackdowns marked *Young Physique*'s new editorial slant. And customers noticed the change. "I think by the time one graduated to the *Young Physique* (a treasured possession), one was aware of a shift of content," recalled a gay reader. "It was my first awareness that there were people like me out there, not just me" (see fig. 5.6).[92]

Even within the homophile movement, Womack had imitators. Clark Polak was elected to head the Janus Society of Philadelphia (the local homophile organization), promising to run it like a business. Owner of a personnel service, Polak had tried other moneymaking ventures, including a short-lived gay correspondence service, which the Post Office forced him to shut down. He saw *Manual v. Day* as "one of the most important homosexual court victories" and considered

FIGURE 5.6 Joe Weider's *Young Physique* became particularly daring in the wake of the Supreme Court's 1962 *Manual v. Day* decision. This cover from August 1964 features the work of James Bidgood, which would become part of the film *Pink Narcissus*.

Courtesy of ClapArt, New York City.

it "a testament to Womack's courage."[93] His meetings with Womack and Cory convinced him that the commercial and political sides of gay life could be mutually supporting. He wanted to get the sodomy laws in Pennsylvania and other states repealed, but he knew that would take money. "Change might be possible to buy for cold cash," he wrote a friend, with "donations to the right campaign funds." He considered Guild Press a potential model for political empowerment not only because of its large mailing list but because it could generate much-needed funds.[94]

Polak started his shake-up of the Janus Society with the group's lackluster newsletter. First he professionalized it, adding images and getting distribution on newsstands. It was gay magazine distributor Lou Elson who suggested that he add physique photos to get more circulation.[95] Soon his *Drum* magazine, combining gay news from a clipping service and physique photography, was among the hottest-selling gay magazines in the world. *Drum* irreverently promised "news for 'queers,' fiction for 'perverts,' photo essays for 'fairies,' and laughs for 'faggots.'"[96] Taking elements that Womack was experimenting with in his publication, Polak flipped the emphasis—stressing homophile news but providing enough physique photos and lifestyle articles to attract readership. "The success of *DRUM* was not due to its editorial content," Schlegel observed, "the success of *DRUM* was due to the photos." As *Janus*, a four-page newsletter, it enjoyed a circulation of 150 in 1963; as *Drum*, a slick, forty-page, physique-inspired magazine, it reached tens of thousands of subscribers by 1965.[97]

Polak initially worked with Womack, relying on Guild for printing services and editorial content, but soon the two became competitors. "Clark saw what he thought Womack was able to do with GBS and he was sure he could do it better," remembered Richard Schlegel. So he started a competing Trojan Book Service, which within a few short years made Polak an annual profit of a quarter million dollars. "I never made a Trojan [weekly bank] deposit that was less than $1,000," recalled one of Polak's employees.[98]

Having modeled his business on Womack's, Polak was soon pushing beyond it. It was Polak who inserted the first full-frontal male nudes into a gay publication, starting in 1965. "It's what's upfront that counts" read the suggestive tagline, accompanying an image of a nude man from behind. "The nude photo insert in *DRUM* magazine was the thing that swelled the mailing list," Schlegel recalled. "This was a quantum leap for Clark. This was the first time that a nude insert had been knowingly put through the mails. Womack never went that far."[99]

Drawing on Guild Press's *Gay Coloring Book*, Polak's other innovation was the first gay comic strip—featuring Harry Chess, the man from A.U.N.T.I.E., or Agents Undercover Network to Investigate Evil. A creation of *Drum's* art director, Pratt Art Institute graduate Allen J. Shapiro, Harry Chess spoofed the then-popular television series *The Man from U.N.C.L.E.* His muscular, hirsute body was rarely covered by more than a tank top and tight jeans. He was assisted by Big Bennie, a cigar-smoking old dyke bartender, and boy toy Mickey Muscle, a vapid, bodybuilding twink whose only utterance was "Gee." His crime solving began at the "Mr. Planetarium" bodybuilding contest, where physique model Bif Ripple had been kidnapped. He then investigates the theft of an "art lovers" collection of male nudes, during which he ends up in what he thinks is the Library of Congress but turns out to be the headquarters of Guild Press. The evil mastermind behind the kidnapping and thefts turns out to be a former postal inspector named "Seymour Summer-Feelzies," whose life of crime was attributed to beatings from his mother. More than just a frivolous gay comic strip, *The Man from A.U.N.T.I.E.* reflected major themes and conflicts of the gay male world—the glorification of the physique model, the centrality of erotica, and hypocrisy of governmental censorship. The strip became so popular that Polak was often introduced as "Harry Chess's daddy" (see fig. 5.7).[100]

With money rolling in, Polak began bankrolling gay court cases, including Clive Boutilier's challenge to the U.S. Immigration Service's exclusion of homosexual immigrants. When Boutilier lost his case at the Supreme Court, Polak vowed to find and support similar cases as well as challenges to state sodomy laws. He formed the Homosexual Law Reform Society and hired attorneys to write legal briefs. His legal defense of gay bars in New Jersey and Florida led to decisions upholding the right of gays to assemble in public. He also financed unemployed homophile leader Frank Kameny, who appeared on the *Drum* masthead for the first few issues. As Polak told *Drum* readers, responding to criticism that he was merely lining his own pockets, "The excess income—which comes from the homosexuals in America—is reserved for projects that eventually benefit those same homosexuals." Young and charismatic, he became a sought-after spokesperson for the gay movement, the first open homosexual to appear on the *Phil Donahue Show*.[101]

Polak's sex-positive message was widely popular, but it also had many detractors. "I wanted to put the sex back into homosexuality," Polak recalled. "I always felt it was important to affirm the sexual aspects." But this attitude got him and the Janus Society kicked out of the East Coast Homophile

FIGURE 5.7 Clark Polak's *Drum* magazine represented an integration of the physique and homophile magazines, featuring both news of the gay movement and nude male images. Its comic strip featuring Harry Chess was the first gay comic strip.

Organization (ECHO), a regional coalition of gay groups considered the most militant arm of homophile activism. Despite the financial boon he offered the homophile world, some thought he was sullying the cause. Members of his own Janus Society also mutinied and formed a separate organization, the Mattachine Society of Philadelphia. Mattachine of Washington passed a resolution condemning attempts to combine physique and homophile publications. The "old aunties" of Mattachine New York wouldn't allow *Drum* to be displayed or sold at its gatherings. Even Dick Leitch, who supported Womack, thought its only purpose was "to entertain faggots."[102]

Despite the homophile movement's official opposition, their publications, in the post-*Manual* context, adopted many of the characteristics of physique magazines. *ONE* and the *New York Mattachine Newsletter* began running advertisements for gay greeting cards, record albums, suggestive clothing, and other consumer items.[103] *ONE Confidential*, a newsletter for members, began a "Photo Feature" for members to submit photographs, most of which were in underwear, posing straps, or less.[104] *Mattachine Review*, in dire straits from a lack of subscribers, made a last-ditch attempt to increase circulation by running a cover that featured a pen-and-ink drawing of a locker room scene with men undressing, the focus clearly on crotches. In one of its last issues before folding, it announced plans for a new publication, *Dorian Vignettes*, which promised physique studio art and other "contents you have been asking for."[105]

ONE editor Jim Kepner tried to launch his own physique/homophile magazine hybrid. *Pursuit & Symposium*'s very name suggested its dual aims: part sexy space for "the pursuit of happiness" and part forum for serious literary and political discourse. "Beefcake for homosexual males needs to be just as acceptable as cheesecake for heterosexual males," Kepner explained, suggesting that, like Polak, he envisioned a homosexual *Playboy*, a national publication that had also overcome a censorship battle in the 1950s to become the center of a publishing empire. He included a cartoon figure of a weightlifting stud who was "mad about the boy"—a clear cousin to Harry Chess—suggesting *Drum* was Kepner's real model. After two expensive, glossy issues, however, the magazine folded, perhaps because it leaned more toward the highbrow "sophisticated reader" and left its promise of physique images largely unfulfilled.[106]

The merger of physique, homophile, and camp may have reached its apogee with the launch in 1966 of *Around the World with Kenneth Marlowe*. While ostensibly a physique magazine with the usual photo spreads from Bob Mizer, Mel Roberts, and others, it was edited by hairstylist and female impersonator Kenneth Marlowe, author of the autobiographical book *Mr. Madam*, which chronicled his exploits in a male brothel. The glossy, seventy-page, large-format magazine featured a Male à la Mode fashion section, photo shoots at the Ah Men storefront in West Hollywood, tips on gay bars in major cities, Hollywood gossip, and a Marlowe Mr. America model contest, with entries from every state.

The homophile movement gave its support with a half-page advertisement for *ONE* magazine, suggesting it offered "councils of friends in major cities." Considered something of an authority on homosexuality, Marlowe noted that he had not only lectured at *ONE* but also been interviewed on a television talk show about the decriminalization of homosexuality in the United Kingdom and suggested the United States should follow suit.[107]

That same year, physique and homophile worlds almost came together when Stuart Rosenberg, a physique photographer in Kansas City, offered his Troy Saxon studio for free as a centralized site for a proposed planning meeting to establish a national coalition of homophile organizations. Rosenberg had hosted a Grecian Guild Convention a few years earlier. While New York Mattachine leaders supported the idea, noting the potential cost savings, other homophile leaders vetoed it, feeling such a venue lacked "dignity" and might result in negative publicity. In the end the first meeting for what became the North American Conference of Homophile Organizations (NACHO) was held in a hotel in Kansas City. NACHO would go on to adopt a Homosexual Bill of Rights and endorse Frank Kameny's slogan "Gay Is Good" as the motto of the movement.[108]

BACK TO COURT

As his empire of products and imitators expanded, Womack continued the legal struggle that had transformed the marketplace. He got a second opportunity to prevail at the Supreme Court, this time against U.S. Customs. For years, customs officials had been intercepting mail from abroad that they deemed obscene, with a particular focus on homoerotic materials from Denmark and other countries with less government censorship. Individuals receiving such materials would be notified that their shipments had been detained. They could either agree to forfeit the materials or have them referred to a U.S. attorney "for appropriate action." Most customers demurred or occasionally complained to the ACLU.[109]

By 1965 Womack's Potomac News was importing tens of thousands of copies of *Hellenic Sun, Youth at Play* and similar Danish nudist magazines. Because of their questionable legality, Womack's markup was an astronomical 2,000 percent. When U.S. Customs officials moved to stop him, he took them to court, arguing, "If there are homosexual nudists, then these homosexual nudists are entitled to receive a homosexual magazine."[110] Ruling in his favor, the Supreme Court gave no explanation for the decision, simply citing an earlier ruling on similar "girlie" magazines. Guild Press's brochure boasted, "WE FOUGHT THE GOOD FIGHT IN 1962 AND WE HAVE FOUGHT THE GOOD FIGHT ONCE MORE." The evangelical language underscored that Womack saw his struggle against censorship as a moral crusade. By this time the Los Angeles Advocate, one of the new mixed magazines spawned in the wake of Manual v. Day, was around to cheer Womack's second Supreme Court victory on its front page.[111]

Perhaps because of his success in defeating them, postal authorities continued to hound Womack. In April 1970 they raided his Capitol Hill printing facility, along with bookstores he owned in five cities. They seized seventeen publications and arrested Womack, this time under a new charge that would prove harder to fight: using underage models. But when he went to court this time, Womack had the support of the local gay community. Lilli Vincenz, a local lesbian activist, wrote the judge asking for leniency, and longtime activist Frank Kameny and the Gay Activists Alliance gave him full-throated support. "We feel that not only has Dr. Womack not been doing harm to the community but he has supplied a valuable service to the community," GAA noted in an affidavit. Womack should be "commended not condemned," they argued.[112]

The Guild Press had been a major financial backer of Kameny's groundbreaking campaign for the District of Columbia's new seat in Congress, an event that galvanized the local LGBT community.[113] In addition to printing all Kameny's campaign literature for free, Womack had provided thousands of leaflets that Kameny and Barbara Gittings distributed at American Psychiatric Association conferences as they fought to get homosexuality removed from the Diagnostic and Statistical Manual of Mental Disorders. Kameny, who had become a regular contributor to Guild Press publications, testified at Womack's federal trial wearing a "Gay is Good" pin and claiming that Womack's publications were no more offensive then Playboy.[114] Womack's attorney Dietz tried to convince the judge that the prosecution was discriminating against the gay community by unfairly targeting its publications. "This is a cause. It's the cause of the homosexual," Dietz summarized in his closing argument. "He is entitled to his literature just as the heterosexual is entitled to read what he wishes."[115]

In October 1971 Womack launched Gay Forum, a newspaper he planned to distribute nationally, leveraging Guild's vast distribution network linking over a thousand newsstands. Although in a new, large newsprint format, Gay Forum retained key features of the company's physique magazines, such as cover photos of shirtless young men and graphic designs with Greek columns. It featured a "campus report" from colleges across the nation, a travel column on "Gay Fun Spots of the World," and gossipy news columns from San Francisco and Los Angeles. But what set it apart was a plan to have Frank Kameny serve as "editor-at-large on Capitol Hill," interviewing members of Congress and other political figures on gay issues. Imagining that such interviews would exert considerable political pressure, editors considered Kameny the first gay lobbyist and his column "a major breakthrough" for gay freedom.[116]

By the late 1960s Guild Press magazines and many of their competitors featured images of scantily clad men, often in erotic and suggestive poses, next to book reviews of gay books, fashion spreads, travel tips, political news, and classified ads. They offered a gateway to a cornucopia of consumer items tailored to a particular young gay male sensibility—in short, all the features of the magazines we associate with a post-Stonewall, gay liberationist era. It was Lynn Womack and his *Manual v. Day* victory in 1962 that made that possible.

But most historians of the LGBT movement, who generally privilege homophile politics over commercial enterprises, downplay Womack and his landmark Supreme Court decision. His *Manual v. Day* victory has been dismissed as "ambiguous" and of limited impact because several justices ruled on "procedural grounds."[117] Another historian suggested that it "hardly constituted a ringing endorsement of queer free expression" but instead "merely perpetuated the confusion surrounding obscenity."[118] But what these legal analyses fail to grasp is the revolutionary impact it had in the marketplace—how it was perceived at the time by entrepreneurs such as Womack, Mizer, Weider, and Polak and their hundreds of thousands of gay male customers.

To physique photographers like Dave Martin who had spent time in jail, *Manual v. Day* felt like vindication. "Womack's favorable verdict actually gave every photographer in the country a Bill of Rights for freedom of expression under the First Amendment which previously never existed," Martin asserted.[119] If it did not provide a final and decisive legal doctrine concerning gay words and images, that had less to do with the ambiguity of the Supreme Court's decision and more to do with the Post Office's relentlessness. Womack and his imitators certainly interpreted it as a green light and used it to revolutionize the gay media landscape. By creating a new genre of gay lifestyle magazines that combined physique and homophile elements, they made it a turning point in the history of the gay press.[120]

Womack certainly had his detractors. Many of his business associates claimed he was a cheapskate who rarely paid his bills or honored his contracts. He was a "shyster" according to Chuck Renslow, who never saw any money from his alliance with Womack to produce *Mars*. But Renslow admitted that *Mars* significantly raised the profile and income of Kris Studios.[121] Others questioned his sexual ethics. He was known for flaunting his wealth in exchange for sexual favors from young men. Some said he dispensed small amounts of stock in his numerous business interests to various tricks and lovers.[122] "[Womack] felt that all he had to was walk up to any guy he saw and when he offered him $100 the guy would fall all over him in gratitude," complained one observer from Washington, D.C. Dick Leitch, who stayed at Womack's Capitol Hill townhouse, said it was "full of boys, and Womack was the madam."[123] David Hurles, one of his photographers in the late 1960s, confessed he "had to trick with him" to get the job, but also called him "the wisest man I was ever blessed to meet."[124] Most significantly, today many could consider his publishing of images of teenagers to be a form of child abuse.

Although some found his business practices and ethics shoddy, he engendered a fierce loyalty from his employees. Angela Grimmer, who started working for Womack as an undergraduate from Mary Washington College, stayed with the business for over seventeen years, despite the constant threat of indictment. Grimmer found him to be "charming, dynamic, and thought-provoking" and objected to the press's characterization of him as a sleazy pornographer and a "fat, gay albino."[125] "There is no question that expanding the First Amendment was his central motivation," Grimmer recalled. "He knew that what he was doing would make a difference for a lot more people than just himself. He was fearless."[126]

The patrons at Washington's gay bars considered him a hero. He was honored for his contributions to the gay community at a "Groovy Guy" contest in Washington, D.C., where he challenged the younger members of the community to "carry on the fight." The audience gave him a standing ovation, recognizing his crucial role in winning them the right to read homoerotic materials.[127] Womack viewed himself a civil libertarian and champion of the First Amendment. "I'm not a martyr, but if homosexuals want a literature they have a right to it. They pay taxes and die. A hell of a lot of them died in Vietnam." Among his other causes, Womack contributed to the antiwar movement—he notably helped publish the antiwar newsletter *OM* put out by Roger Priest, an active member of the U.S. Navy.[128] Dick Leitch, president of Mattachine New York, considered

Womack "one of the foremost men in this movement for civil liberties and social rights." By taking his case to the Supreme Court at considerable expense, Womack, Leitch thought, had done more for the movement than all other East Coast homophile activists combined (see fig. 5.8).[129]

Womack's most prolific novelist, George Haimsohn, waxed eloquently about Womack as a gay rights pioneer. As "Plato," Haimsohn supplied many physique images, and as "Alexander Goodman," he supplied some of Guild's best-selling books. He would go on to write the book and lyrics for the off-Broadway musical *Dames at Sea*. Womack encouraged him in both photography and writing but paid him little, and they sparred often over money and deadlines.[130] A Guild

DR. WOMACK HONORED

CONTRIBUTIONS TO GAYS ARE CITED AT GROOVY GUY FINALS

A surprised Dr. H. Lynn Womack, titular head of Guild Press, Ltd., was the guest of honor at the Groovy Guy Finals, held at the Holiday Inn, Washington, D. C. on September 30, 1971.

Mr. J. J. Proferes, president of Galaxy Enterprises, Inc., introduced Dr. Womack and spoke of Womack's unparalleled contribution to the gay community. He then awarded the "Grooviest Guy" award to the former college professor-turned-pornographer.

Dr. Womack expressed surprise as he had not anticipated attending the affair, but when he called from New York City,

Dr. H. Lynn Womack (left) receives a plaque for his outstanding contribution to the gay community.

rushed back in order to receive the honor.

The audience received Dr. Womack's address enthusiastically, as he told of his past struggles and said that the "fight will have to be picked up by the younger members — those in GAA and GLF will have to carry on."

At the end of his talk, Dr. Womack received a standing ovation by the grateful audience.

FIGURE 5.8 Lynn Womack was honored for his contributions to the gay community at a Groovy Guy contest in Washington, D.C., in 1971. He received a standing ovation for his fight against censorship at the Supreme Court.

Courtesy of Rainbow History Project.

Press brochure promoting his first book, *The Soft Spot: Stories of the Homosexual Life*, described him as "a young writer who believes the only worthwhile literature is that which is bold and honest." His Guild author profile seemed to also capture the philosophy of the entire organization. "By frankly admitting his homosexuality, Goodman feels he can more deeply explore his own mind and personality and by doing so can find relevance and meaning for himself and his readers." His novel *A Summer on Fire Island* ends with the autobiographical protagonist, arrested in a police raid on the meat rack, making a passionate call for an end to police harassment and sodomy laws.[131]

Although Haimsohn knew his pulp fiction lacked "eternal value," he was grateful to Womack for giving him a platform to explore and articulate his sexuality and that of his contemporaries—"to give the gay a voice," as he put it in this unpublished ode to his benefactor:

> A peculiar Joan of Arc
> Round and white as a ball of snow
> Yet hard and braver than any man I know.
>
> He delights in finding dark corners
> And letting in fresh air.
> He works as though the land of Faggotry
> Was in his special care.
>
> He embarked on a solitary course, a mission
> To give the gay a voice.
> He says he was compelled,
> That it was really not his choice.
>
> But what a compulsion! What a peculiar goal
> That led him to stand alone
> Before the strongest power in the world
> To defend with all his soul
> A naked boy.[132]

Womack may not have solved the homophile recruitment problem, but he provided a positive, sexualized, and playful view of homosexuality more openly and to a larger audience than anyone had before. Through his business and legal successes, he provided his thousands of subscribers with images, stories, travel tips, bar guides, and ways to connect that homophile leaders feared to do. By meeting their desires as consumers, he helped connect them as a community. He helped transform both the physique and homophile presses, so each came to more resemble the other, enabling the sort of modern gay press that could nurture and support a broad-based gay rights movement. And by changing the definition of obscenity, he inspired more entrepreneurs to take up the fight.

6

CONSOLIDATING THE MARKET

DSI of Minneapolis

We made millions.
—Conrad Germain

IRECTORY SERVICES, Inc. (DSI) began in 1963 with a very simple business model: market directories of gay businesses to help customers navigate an increasingly dense field.

DSI founders Lloyd Spinar and Conrad Germain were both young men who had grown up in small towns in the Dakotas, where it was difficult to find gay books or magazines. They certainly could not consult the local librarian. Even buying a physique magazine at the local newsstand or drugstore posed a risk. If they were fortunate enough to travel to a big city, locating gay bars was detective work. So Spinar and Germain would help men like themselves all over the country locate physique photography studios, gay books, and bars by selling lists—hence the name Directory Services. "Compilers of the unusual in reference materials" was their modest early tagline.

Not photographers or artists or writers themselves, they had no products to offer. As savvy businessmen, they would sell information on the growing number of commercial outlets catering to gay men—a sort of gay mail-order clearinghouse. Long before there were gay yellow pages or online chatrooms or search engines, DSI was a pioneer in a gay information economy.[1]

Nothing better attests to the size and complexity of the gay market after the *Manual v. Day* Supreme Court decision in 1962 than that these two young entrepreneurs thought they could make money simply by providing *access* to this network—except, perhaps, how phenomenally and quickly their company grew.[2] One of the first items the two partners offered for sale was a directory of gay bars throughout the United States—a travel guide to "279 Places to Go for a Gay Time." As Germain remembered years later: "In mail-order, if you get a 5 percent response rate, you are a big success. But 80 percent of the people we offered this directory to bought it. That's when we knew there was a real need for this stuff."[3]

Soon their business model expanded to include books, records, jewelry, clothing, home furnishings, and greeting cards. They called their first merchandise catalog *Vagabond*—"the unusual catalog." DSI included a "Readers' Service"—a pen-pal club with classified ads where men could seek correspondents, friends, or lovers. They added a credit card for making catalog purchases, and a prepaid film development service that allowed customers to avoid embarrassment or even arrest at local photo labs.

They soon moved beyond merely providing addresses of physique photography studios to providing their own magazines. "We made millions," Germain confessed. According to their attorney, they were the single largest mail customer of the downtown Minneapolis post office. By 1967 the two partners had fourteen full-time employees with a purported annual gross income well over $1 million, making them arguably the largest gay-owned and gay-oriented commercial enterprise in the world. But their very success made them a target of federal prosecutors, who indicted them on charges of sending obscene materials through the mails. In 1967 they won one of the most important gay rights cases in the movement's early history—one almost entirely forgotten.[4]

DSI represents the integration and maturation of the network of gay consumer goods that developed in postwar America. It was the Sears Roebuck catalog of gay merchandise—a one-stop mail-order resource for information, products, and services for gay consumers. And like its more well-known mainstream antecedent, it was also a Midwest-based company connecting rural (and urban) consumers around the nation through the mail. Combining physique photographs, gay books, pen-pal services, and links to homophile organizations, DSI represented a major shift away from small, independent outfits such as Bob Mizer's Athletic Model Guild to a sort of gay corporate conglomerate that controlled numerous gay businesses and had the income to withstand and win obscenity challenges. Given its size and scope, DSI provided much more than gay merchandise—it provided community and connection. It served the same functions that in a digital age are provided by Google, Amazon, Facebook, Grindr, and a host of other web-based companies.[5]

Conrad Germain was born in 1939 into a farm family in rural North Dakota. His hometown of Hazelton had fewer than five hundred inhabitants. His mother managed to complete the eighth grade, but his father had only completed fourth grade. They would eventually have eighteen children. Hoping Conrad would become a priest, his mother sent him to St. John's Academy in Jamestown, two counties away. Instead, Germain left the area as soon as he graduated in 1957. He spent a few months in a business college in Spokane, Washington, which would prove to be the end of his formal education. With a friend, he enlisted in the U.S. Air Force and for the next four years traveled, experienced the world, and came out exuberantly as a gay man; he would later talk about this as the most wonderful time of his life.

After serving as a chaplain's assistant in Korea and earning an honorable discharge, he returned home to see his family for a few months before moving to Minneapolis, where he could lodge temporarily with his mother's relatives, all of whom were teachers. He had dreams of moving to New York, the business and gay capital of the nation, but in the meantime he got a job as a mail clerk with the stock brokerage firm Piper, Jaffray & Hopwood for $90 a week. One night he ventured downtown to visit a gay bar and saw a shy, handsome man sitting at the bar. They went home together that night. Germain decided to put his New York plans on hold.[6]

Lloyd Spinar had a similar background—raised in a farming community in South Dakota so far from the nearest town that he had to spend the night there during the week to complete high school. His first steady job was as an organist in the Methodist church. Like Germain, he also attended business school. After getting bored with his engineering studies at Rapid City School of Mines and Technology, he spent two years at a business college in Sioux Falls. Impressed with his abilities, the college president asked him to stay on to teach for two more years.

It was in Rapid City, thanks to the nearby Ellsworth Air Force Base, that he had his first sexual experience with another man, but it was an experience only infrequently and tentatively repeated. Coming out "took a long time" he later recalled. He was four years older than Germain when they met in 1962 and had a good job working for a truck manufacturer as an engineer's assistant. But he soon got bored with that. "I thought I'd explore the idea of learning how to set type, do paste up, to put together magazines," he later recalled. He went to work for a local woman who owned a shop that printed menus and corporate reports. It was the sort of creative, entrepreneurial work that he had been looking for, and that he would continue to do for the rest of his life. "He could sell anything to anyone," Germain boasted.[7]

Spinar was already "tinkering" on the side with an idea he had for a mail-order business—a directory of the myriad of physique photographers, artists, and clothing suppliers of interest to gay men. He used the equipment at work to do layout, until he got caught and had a falling out with his boss, which propelled him to work on the business full time. Within a year Germain quit his job as well so they could both work on what they were then calling Directory Services. They timidly called their first offering *Directory 84*—a title so bland that it would raise no suspicion. The first few issues looked equally innocuous—a simple 8 x 10-inch sheet folded into three columns. By the fifth edition it was twelve pages and sported a cardboard cover. By the sixth edition the next year they had their first photo of a showering bodybuilder—a hint of things to come.

Directory 84 embodied the overlapping network of gay publications and consumer items then available throughout the world. Companies such as Bob Mizer's Athletic Model Guild appeared in numerous categories since it offered a magazine, photographs, films, and clothing. Foreign physique photographers had their own category, with listings from Sweden, France, England, Chile, and South Africa. Their list of publications included not only the usual array of twenty to thirty physique magazines but both domestic and foreign homophile publications, identified with the tagline "deals with homosexual problems" (see fig. 6.1).[8]

If Spinar came up with the idea for the first directory, it was customers who provided the idea for more. In a 1960s mail-order version of crowdsourcing, they received not only hundreds of orders for *Directory 84* but ideas for new offerings. "They'd write back and say, 'Do you have a directory of books?'" Spinar remembered, "and pretty soon they'd write back, 'Do you have a directory of gay bars?'"

Responding to customer demand, soon they were offering *Directory 72*, a listing of "books that deal with the homosexual way of life." Customers could rent or buy copies of over 150 often rare or out-of-print titles. With the expansion from offering information to merchandise, they made the first of many moves to larger quarters—out of the apartment they shared to a place that could hold an inventory of two to three hundred books.[9]

Directory 43 was the third and most controversial offering, a listing of "279 Places to go for a Gay Time." At $5, it was not only the most expensive directory but also the most innovative. It was from the bar guide mailing that

FIGURE 6.1 Conrad Germain and Lloyd Spinar launched Directory Services, Inc. (DSI), in Minneapolis in 1963 by offering a series of directories of physique photography studios, gay books, and gay bars, as well as a "Readers' Service" of classified advertisements to connect customers.

Author's collection.

Germain recalled the phenomenal 80 percent response rate. While customers loved it—and helped to compile and update it by responding to DSI questionnaires—bar owners were less enthusiastic. "Boy did that cause controversy!" Spinar remembered. Unlike physique photographers, who were often listed in physique magazines, and gay mail-order book services, which had been advertising openly for more than a decade, gay bar guides had only circulated underground.[10] And although they were centers of gay life, most gay bars in much of the United States were owned by nongay people.[11] Many owners wrote demanding to be removed from the guide under threat of legal action. "Don't list me in your bar guide! People in town don't know we're here," they would complain.

Compiling gay bar guides was an effort by gay men to take some measure of control over these environments, an effort undertaken almost simultaneously by several other entrepreneurs. Also in 1963, Guy Strait offered the first edition of *The Lavender Baedeker*, a gay bar guide that was an outgrowth of his bar-oriented San Francisco newspaper *Citizen's News*. By the next year three more companies joined the field. A New York firm offered a *World Report Travel Guide*, Guild Press offered its first *Guild Guide to the Gay Scene*, and Bob Damron offered *The Address Book*, which survived all the others to become a standard resource for gay male tourists for decades. Perhaps as a sign of the impending competition, as well as their professionalism and long-term perspective, Spinar registered *Directory 43* with the U.S. Copyright Office.[12]

They purchased their first mailing list from Richard Fontaine, one of the first to make short 8 mm and 16 mm physique films marketed through *Tomorrow's Man* and *Physique Pictorial*. Soon they secured access to mailing lists from other physique firms. Germain took charge of acquiring and managing mailing lists, a vocation that became a lifelong passion. In the numerous depositions and court appearances he would make, Germain was often evasive about details, but he could always recall the size of his mailing lists. They placed a few advertisements in tabloids such as the *National Informer* with the ad copy, "For those looking for those hard to find physique photos." But the biggest source of new names was referrals. "[Customers] would pass on their literature to friends of theirs, and they would personally write in and ask to be put on the mailing list," Germain recalled. According to Germain, such word-of-mouth additions accounted for 75 percent of the growth of the mailing list, which within a year included ten thousand names.[13]

Robert Anthony, who ran a successful physique studio in New York, provided another early mailing list. Anthony got his start as a twenty-one-year-old darkroom assistant to Lon of New York and later worked as an editor for Lynn Womack. By 1962 he was publishing his own line of physique magazines—*Champ* and *Champ Annual*. Like many physique photographers, he increasingly encountered obstacles as printers and distributors refused his magazines and "police state clampdowns" cut into his business. His difficulties as an independent studio brought him into a closer alliance with the increasingly large printing and distribution network of DSI.[14]

Spinar and Germain experimented with various products and services and various formats for their publications, moving from directories to catalogs to magazines. "Because we are developing a new business in a long-neglected field," they explained to their customers, "there are no similar firms after which we can pattern our operations." They confessed to engaging in "trial-and-error" schemes that were sometimes "unprofitable or unwise." Their first catalog, *Vagabond*, offered music from Camp Records to play at parties. Customers could join the Movie Collector's Club to purchase short films from California "with the situations you've wanted." The Vagabond Photo-Finishing Service promised to develop or copy your "special photos." Customers could order a series of Halloween cards, Christmas cards, or just "everyday cards" to send to friends. If they would rather personalize their own stationery, customers could order a rubber stamp of their own revealing photo. Couples could order a "his and his towel set" or personalize a pack of male-model playing cards—the sample suggested "Don and Bill." Drag queens could purchase *Female Mimics*, a magazine of female impersonation from New York. There were Vagabond lotions for the bathroom and a "Sleeping Satyr" statuette with "detachable fig leaf" for the living room. A Vagabond coloring book featured a hunky model cavorting with his tricks, gym buddies, and "husband." Truly dedicated DSI shoppers could order a gold Vagabond ring with a "69" emblem, what the marketing materials described as "a most unique design of special significance" (see fig. 6.2).[15]

The heart of the DSI enterprise became the publication of a series of physique magazines, among the first to feature male frontal nudes. In 1965 DSI began offering *Butch*, with "the undraped front views you want." As DSI later boasted, it was "the first male nude magazine to be openly printed and sold in the US." The first issue was so popular it went through three printings that year alone. To capture a high-end market, DSI followed up with *Greyhuff*, with a leather-like cover, heavy paper stock, and artistic imagery. Continuing this effort at market segmentation, it began offering *Tiger*, a glossy magazine that featured full-color images. It changed formats in response to popular demand, experimenting with editorials against censorship, news stories of the homophile movement, and a commentary section with letters from customers. It drew some of its editorial content from Clark Polak's *Drum* magazine, although the emphasis remained squarely on the images, with an occasional article of homophile news. To increase circulation, DSI engaged the well-known New York advertising firm Diener & Dorskind. By 1966 it was printing fifty thousand copies of each issue of *Butch* and *Tiger* (see fig. 6.3).[16]

Soon DSI had such a wide distribution network that it began to acquire competing businesses or in some cases offer their products at steep discounts. To

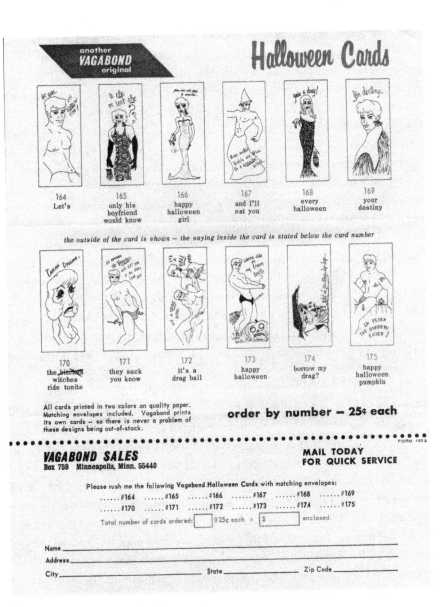

FIGURE 6.2 Through its Vagabond catalog, DSI offered a host of gay consumer items, including greeting cards, books, records, jewelry, toiletries, and a "his and his" towel set.

Author's collection.

FIGURE 6.3 In 1965 DSI began to offer a series of magazines featuring full-frontal male nudity.

Courtesy of ONE Archives at the USC Libraries.

expand its reach, it acquired several California firms, including DAK Products and Book Guild of America (BGA). It founded subsidiaries such as Commander Associates to handle layout and printing and Northern News to handle whole-sale distribution to newsstands. Like Guild Press, DSI acted as a sort of gay con-glomerate, reconfiguring a field that had been made up of small, independent sellers often working out of their homes or apartments.[17] Even Bob Mizer, one of the earliest and most famous of gay physique photo purveyors, was affected. As an inside observer commented in 1966, "Business at AMG is down to about a quarter of what it was before Directory Services and other nudies got into the business. What keeps AMG in business is wholesaling to Directory Services."[18] Filmmaker Pat Rocco also sold products wholesale to DSI but lived to regret it, since it undersold his products. "They are the biggest in the business therefore they can sell for less," he lamented.[19]

In 1966 DSI moved into a nearly 6,000-square-foot, state-of-the-art printing facility in a leafy neighborhood near the Minneapolis Institute of Art. It contained a reception area, separate offices for Spinar and Germain, two offices for typing clerks, a bookkeeper's office, a printing room, two stockrooms, an artwork room, a darkroom, and a mailroom. Another physique publisher who visited the plant described it enviously as an "up-to-date, modern, highly mechanized facility." By then the mailing list had fifty to sixty thousand names and was computerized on IBM punch cards.[20]

Like other large business conglomerates, DSI sometimes abused its position and engaged in questionable business practices toward its smaller suppliers and competitors. It was often accused of illegally reprinting images without crediting or paying photographers. A group of California physique photographers who started a competing nudist magazine charged it with exploitation.[21] Even if it paid for the images, DSI was undermining photographers' incomes since they were no longer the only source of male nudes. More important, DSI quickly came under the influence of mafia-controlled bookstores, which pressured it to offer increasingly revealing images. "The real money came in getting involved with the mafia," Spinar confessed. Especially in cities such as New York and Cleveland, the mafia controlled distribution of erotic materials through its own bookstores, which were largely immune from local prosecution. "They had the police and city officials under their thumb," Spinar explained. To negotiate bulk sales, Germain lunched regularly with a New York mob boss and his wife. As another industry insider confirmed, "The mafia had decided that male nudes were big business. . . . The mafia decided to put out magazines and photographers were told in no uncertain terms they had to provide the pictures."[22] As a result of these huge "mafia buys," both their incomes and spending were lavish. Germain and Spinar drove a Lincoln Continental and lived in a posh duplex apartment in one of the most exclusive high-rise buildings in the Twin Cities overlooking the Mississippi River. Celebrity columnist Abigail Van Buren was their downstairs neighbor.[23]

As successful businessmen, Spinar and Germain ran editorials to champion what they saw as a "New Era" of American capitalism and entrepreneurship. They applauded how both political parties realized that the ability of individuals and corporations to make financial profits made the country prosperous. "It is because this country drifted dangerously in the direction of socialism during the Thirties and Forties that we began to falter and fall behind," they opined. As proof of the power of the free market, they cited the economic success of West Berlin and Japan in contrast to what they saw as stagnation in the controlled economies of East Berlin and Cuba. Taking a libertarian perspective, they saw the government not as an ally but as a potential impediment to their economic success.[24]

POSTAL INSPECTOR EDGAR D. GOSNELL

DSI's customers were the first to alert Spinar and Germain that the Post Office had them under surveillance. A sign of how vigorously postal inspectors monitored the physique field, Minneapolis postal inspector Edgar D. Gosnell got test names on DSI's mailing list in April 1963, early enough to receive its primitive *Directory 84*, long before Spinar and Germain even contemplated male nudes. Gosnell would later claim that he was responding to a "complaint" from a postal patron. More likely he was alerted to a new firm in his territory when DSI rented Guild Press's mailing list, already infiltrated by other postal inspectors. He continued to quietly monitor mailings for the next four years.

Postal Inspector Gosnell also registered under a false name with DSI's Readers' Service of customer classified advertisements. If his response was like those of other subscribers, he probably received hundreds of letters from unsuspecting men. Soon he was visiting their homes, threatening them with arrest. And they started to write in to alert DSI. "They were being very much harassed from the postal inspectors throughout the country," Germain later testified. This convinced Germain and Spinar to discontinue the Readers' Service, at least for a while. But like ONE magazine and most other gay organizations, they would continue to receive mail from frightened customers about postal inspectors. "I have thousands of letters to indicate that," he told a federal prosecutor. "They are afraid that the Post Office is constantly snooping into their mail." DSI also received a warning from Bob Mizer, who editorialized in *Physique Pictorial* that our "Big-Brother government" would shut down their pen-pal club just like it did the Adonis Male Club and put its founders in jail.[25]

Robert L. Fox, a thirty-four-year-old doctor practicing medicine in Sioux City, Iowa, was one of the many DSI customers the Post Office had under surveillance. He ordered a copy of a Danish nudist magazine, *A Hundred Naked Rebels*, and placed an ad in DSI's Readers' Service. Among the many responses he received were letters from two men in nearby Sioux Falls, South Dakota. Both were junior high school teachers. In October 1964 both teachers were arrested for depositing "obscene, lewd, and lascivious" letters in the mail to Dr. Fox and were immediately relieved of their positions. The Post Office knew that whether it won or lost the legal case, the indictment alone would lead to local outrage about "perverts" teaching children. According to one report, the local U.S. attorney convicted thirty people for obscenity in connection with a single pen-pal ad Gosnell placed in the Readers' Service.[26] Charging that commercial pen-pal clubs do not care about the welfare of their gay clients, the editors of ONE snidely editorialized, "I told you so."[27]

The next sign that they were under investigation came from the U.S. Attorney's Office in Minneapolis. In 1964 Assistant U.S. Attorney Sidney Abramson subpoenaed Spinar and Germain and some of their employees to testify before a grand jury. Although Abramson requested that they bring DSI records with them, he would not allow them to be accompanied by an attorney. By then they had hired attorney Ronald Meshbesher, who suspected Abramson was trying to obtain evidence to be used against his clients. He challenged Abramson's refusal to allow Spinar and Germain to be accompanied by their attorneys but lost. The government continued to investigate for two more years.[28] But given Supreme Court liberal rulings on obscenity, it did not feel that prosecution would be successful. But all that changed one Monday in March 1966, when the Supreme Court offered several new surprise rulings.

For the first time since its 1957 *Roth* case establishing the legal definition of obscenity, the Supreme Court sustained two lower court obscenity convictions. In *Mishkin*, the court ruled that material was obscene if it was designed to appeal to the prurient interest of a particular deviant sexual group. This altered the *Roth* obscenity test, which focused on the effect on the "average person." Edward Mishkin had been sentenced to three years in prison for selling books that depicted sadomasochism and homosexuality. "The evidence fully establishes that these books were specifically conceived and marketed for such groups," Justice Brennan declared. In *Ginzburg*, the court found that the advertising of otherwise nonobscene material could render it obscene if it involved "pandering" to the public's prurient interest. Ralph Ginzburg had been sentenced to five years in prison for selling *Eros,* a magazine devoted to hetero-sexual "love and sex," which he promoted with millions of highly suggestive circulars.[29]

Prosecutors and antipornography advocates around the nation rejoiced at these decisions and their perceived broadening of the definition of obscenity. "It is a matter of profound gratification to all God-loving people," proclaimed a group of religious leaders, "that the Court has served notice that panderers of filth for profit will no longer be given a free hand in contaminating our soci-ety." The crackdown was almost immediate. Times Square booksellers began purging their shelves. "The bondage stuff is clearly out. I think the homosex-ual magazines showing genitals are going to have to go, too," cautioned one of their attorneys. DSI materials became more difficult to locate.[30] Physique stu-dios around the country were raided, including Guild Press in Washington, D.C., Troy Saxon in Kansas City, Times Square in New York, and David of Cleveland. The Post Office also seized copies of *Drum,* disrupting its produc-tion and distribution for months.[31]

Emboldened by *Ginzburg* and *Mishkin,* the U.S. attorney in Minneapolis decided to act. He agreed with Charles Keating, chairman of Citizens for Decent Literature, that the legal context was now "a different ballgame." He now pos-sessed what the chief postal inspector termed "a powerful new weapon." He met with Meshbesher and offered DSI a deal: if it would close the business and stop selling nude magazines to a gay market, the government would agree not to prosecute. At about the same time Meshbesher's law partner Mickey Robins flew to Washington to consult with government attorneys. He came away with the impression that the government still had no grounds to convict DSI. Consider-able uncertainty surrounded the *Mishkin* and *Ginzburg* decisions, partly because they had generated so many separate opinions from the bench. One lawyer saw "total confusion" surrounding the meaning of the decisions.[32]

So DSI refused the deal, and Abramson proceeded with an indictment from the Grand Jury. Having built up a relationship with the U.S. Attorney's Office, Meshbesher understood that his clients, local businessmen who were not a flight risk, would be issued a summons to turn themselves in.

Germain and Spinar knew they were going to be indicted, but they were still surprised on the frigidly cold Monday afternoon of February 6, 1967, when a large postal truck—with red, white, and blue Post Office colors—pulled up to their Minneapolis publishing plant. Several U.S. marshals, two U.S. district attorneys, and several postal inspectors arrested Spinar and Germain and charged them with twenty-nine counts of sending lewd materials through the mail.

Using the arrest warrant as cover, federal authorities ransacked their offices, seizing postage meters, business records, mailing lists, IBM cards, and eight cabinets full of addressograph plates. They took a thousand sealed envelopes of merchandise already prepared for mailing to customers. They also seized much of DSI's inventory of magazines and photographs. In their two-hour search, they even took playing cards, record albums, towels, and sheets—all DSI-advertised merchandise. The government confiscated so much material—ten tons, according to one reporter—that it had to order a second postal truck to haul it away. Federal authorities used none of the confiscated material at trial. Instead, they intended to impede DSI's operations even before any determination of guilt. Meshbesher unsuccessfully argued that it amounted to "illegal restraint of trade."[33]

To emphasize the reach of the DSI operation, federal agents simultaneously raided the apartment of Bob Anthony in New York and seized his mailing list, records, and inventory. Anthony had become one of the major suppliers of nude images for *Butch* and *Tiger* and would become one of the prosecution's major witnesses against DSI. He had not dealt in nudes until he started working with Germain and Spinar, who assured him that it was all legal. Prosecutors were able to bargain with him and play on his resentment that Germain had covered up knowledge that DSI was under investigation.

Federal agents had also alerted the local media, so when they brought Germain and Spinar into police headquarters for processing, photographers were on hand to capture the humiliating "perp walk." Front-page stories in both local newspapers the next day emphasized that this was the "biggest allegedly pornographic operation of its kind in the nation" and that DSI's annual gross income was several million dollars. By the end of the week Congressman Clement J. Zablocki (D–Wisconsin) cited the arrest in a congressional hearing on juvenile delinquency and mail-order pornography to highlight the extent of the problem (see fig. 6.4).[34]

JUDGE LARSON'S FEDERAL TRIAL

If found guilty on all charges, both men faced 145 years in prison and $145,000 in fines. As the case moved quickly toward a trial later that summer, Germain suffered from extreme anxiety. When a severe ulcer landed him in the hospital,

Minneapolis Tribune Photos by Donald Black

Indicted Monday Lloyd Spinar, 32, left, and Conrad Germain, 27, both living at 740 River Dr., St. Paul, were indicted Monday by the Minneapolis Federal Grand Jury for distributing allegedly obscene materials in the mail. The two were partners in Directory Services Inc., which was described by the assistant district attorneys as one of the largest distributors in the country. *(NEWS REPORT—Page 1.)*

FIGURE 6.4 On February 7, 1967, DSI publishers Lloyd Spinar and Conrad Germain were arrested in Minneapolis on twenty-nine counts of sending obscene material through the mail. Local newspapers captured the "perp walk" and claimed they represented "the biggest allegedly pornographic operation of its kind in the nation."

Courtesy of *Star Tribune*.

a doctor began prescribing him Valium and tranquilizers. Germain had wanted to hire Stanley Fleishman, an experienced First Amendment attorney from California. Instead, they decided to continue relying on local attorney Ronald Meshbesher, who had never handled a federal obscenity case. Having served as a county prosecutor, Meshbesher had been in private practice for just six years. The only encouraging news came when the case was assigned to U.S. District Court Judge Earl Larson, who had a reputation as a civil libertarian. Appointed to the bench by President Kennedy, Larson was a founder of the Minnesota Civil Liberties Union and former chairman of the Governor's Human Rights Commission.

But Germain's anxiety again increased when the trial opened in July and Larson began questioning potential jurors about their impression of the sexual content of magazines, films, and television. "I think it has a bad influence on young people," declared one man. Another woman thought they went "farther than they had to go" in depicting sex. Meshbesher quickly moved to waive his client's right to a jury trial so that Judge Larson would decide the case alone. Confident that the law was now on their side, the prosecution consented to the waiver, a decision that considerably complicated its burden.[35]

When the trial began in the summer of 1967, Assistant U.S. Attorney Stanley H. Green argued that DSI was operating under a "disguise." While it purported to be serving "artists, sculptors, and photographers," its real customer base was homosexuals. He pointed to *Directory 43*, the guide to gay bars, and how it was compiled from customer questionnaires. He noted the Readers' Service, with its accompanying photos and promise of companionship with other males. He highlighted *Greyhuff* articles on "Johns I Have Known and Loved" and "James I, Homosexual King." He tried to establish a connection between DSI and the homophile movement, pointing to overlap between their publications. Green even pointed to a DSI recruitment letter subtlety promising that gay employees would not have to hide their identities on the job. "The most wonderful advantage of a position with Directory Services," the letter promised, "is the elimination of that bothersome and worrisome business of pretending an interest in another way of life."

When Conrad Germain took the stand in his own defense, Green cross-examined him strenuously. Honing in on DSI's "69" logo, Green asked, "What is the value of 69 to an artist?" Raising the "his and his towels" available in the Vagabond catalog, Green demanded, "Who would buy that, an artist or a homosexual?" Germain held his ground, always claiming that he did not know the identity of his customers. The prosecutor was more successful with Bob Anthony, who testified that 80 percent of the mailing list he sold DSI was made up of homosexuals. Most of the witnesses conceded that the materials appealed to homosexuals. By the end of the trial, even DSI attorney Meshbesher conceded that, "for the sake of argument," DSI's customers were homosexuals.[36]

The government's argument was never really about the images themselves, although it did call an art professor to testify to the low quality of the images— "they are clearly awful," he pronounced. The trial instead focused on the place of homosexuality in American society. Green argued that homosexuality and any material dealing with it was considered obscene by the average American. He argued that by marketing to homosexuals, DSI not only was "pandering" to this group but sought to "promote homosexuality in our society." Arguing that many of the circulars went to unsuspecting members of the public, Green argued that DSI hoped to "stimulate others into becoming homosexuals" and thereby sell more merchandise.[37] "We learned a great deal about homosexuals," Green observed at the end of the trial. For him, it was that homosexuals were unhappy, lonely, guilt-burdened, and likely to be stimulated by DSI's nude images to commit illegal acts—sodomy was still illegal in every state but Illinois in 1967.

To support its claim that DSI was promoting homosexual behavior, the government forced several DSI customers to testify. Two juveniles claimed to have received unsolicited DSI mailings. A thirty-one-year-old real estate broker from Dallas claimed that when he ordered DSI magazines he was aroused enough to go out, several months later, to have a homosexual encounter. They acted as triggering devices, recalling experiences from his childhood. But he claimed that he was now heterosexual and disgusted by the images. The prosecution also called two openly gay men to establish that looking at magazines such as *Butch* and *Tiger* encouraged them to go out cruising for men and effectively caused homosexuality. Neither one, however, thought the DSI materials were particularly prurient or the genesis of their sexual orientation. "I have learned after buying material through the mail that a month later you could buy some of this same material on the newsstand at half the price," noted one unhappy customer.[38]

John R. Allsup, a forty-two-year-old mechanical engineer from Akron, Ohio, became a DSI customer after purchasing several nudist magazines on newsstands in New York's Times Square. He then ordered slides from a New York mail-order firm and soon was receiving DSI circulars, from which he purchased more slides, a movie, and an issue of *Butch* and placed a classified advertisement in the Readers' Service. Receiving over one hundred responses, he decided to mimeograph a form letter and send it out. That is when the postal inspector showed up at his door, threatening to show the letter to his employer if he did not "turn over pictures." The postal inspector worked with local law enforcement to charge Allsup with possession of obscene literature. Allsup alerted DSI to the surveillance. "It caused me a lot of worry, a lot of expense," he testified. Despite the controversy, he managed to hold on to his job of sixteen years.[39]

Although Allsup had agreed, under duress, to testify for the government, he proved a feisty witness. He confessed to "coming out" as a homosexual at the age of nineteen and having been twice arrested for homosexual activity, which had made it hard for him earlier in life to hold a job. He had no remorse about his homosexuality, had read widely on the subject (Kraft-Ebbing to Kinsey), and testified that he had known several thousand homosexuals in his life. Treating him as an expert witness, Green asked if *Butch* appealed to his prurient interest, specifying that this meant "an unwholesome, unhealthy appetite in sex or nudity." Allsup responded that it did arouse him but objected to the assumption of the question. "It is not unwholesome. I don't think it is unhealthy," he insisted. He freely admitted that DSI materials were clearly designed for men like him, "the homosexual in general," over defense attorney Meshbesher's vehement objection. But he insisted that this was only a matter of fairness. "For years you could buy female nude magazines, such as *Playboy*, and even years ago *Esquire* magazine, and up until recently all you could buy on the male part would be like muscle magazines, bodybuilding magazines," he complained.

In some ways the trial was a lengthy debate on the cause of homosexuality, with the prosecution arguing that it was caused by one's environment and thus could be prevented. To make this point, Green relied on the testimony of little-known Mexican American psychiatrist Hector Zeller, former head of the Hastings State Hospital in Minnesota. While Zeller asserted that DSI materials could turn a latent homosexual into an active one, he also admitted that boys swimming naked together, as was customary in Minneapolis schools, could also give them "the wrong idea." Similarly, a Roman Catholic priest testified that DSI magazines could be a "predisposing factor to a life of homosexuality," especially for teenagers. He particularly objected to DSI's editorial message that celebrated and normalized the desire to look at these images. A teenager might see this message and say, "I guess this is natural for me." But on cross-examination, Meshbesher got him to admit that he believed even masturbation to be unnatural and immoral, undercutting his case.

By the end, even Green had to acknowledge that he had not proven that homosexuality was caused by reading DSI magazines. "There is nothing concrete to support any opinion one way or another," he confessed about the conflicting testimony. Still, he urged caution: "I think that until enough is known there is good reason to believe that this material should be limited and out of the reach of people in these groups."[40]

Dissatisfied with the prosecution's psychiatrist, Judge Larson took the unusual step of calling his own witness. Donald Wilson was chair of psychiatry at Larson's alma mater, the University of Minnesota—a respected, local institution and one of the two major medical centers, along with Johns Hopkins, then doing research in sex-change operations. Wilson directly contradicted the priest's testimony, asserting that there was no data to support the notion that seeing nude photos was harmful to teenagers. "By age 16 or 17, the cycle of sexual development is completed and predominant orientation of this person, whether it be heterosexual or homosexual, is already a fact." Based on current scientific data, he considered homosexuality a learned behavior but predicted that in the future researchers might find genetic or endocrine factors.[41]

While the prosecution called average DSI customers, DSI called longtime gay activists and entrepreneurs like Hal Call, president of the Mattachine Society, and Larry Littlejohn, secretary of San Francisco's Society for Individual Rights (SIR). Call testified that his Adonis bookstore in San Francisco carried DSI materials and other nude male photographs with the knowledge of the local police. Littlejohn similarly testified that he showed nude male movies at his Big Basket coffeehouse in San Francisco, also with law enforcement approval. Among the well-credentialed defense witnesses was syndicated columnist Dr. Walter Alvarez of the prestigious Mayo Clinic in nearby Rochester, Minnesota. He railed against the unfairness of laws that criminalized homosexuality and encouraged blackmailers, noting that the United Kingdom was at that very moment decriminalizing homosexuality. "I wouldn't fuss about these things," he responded when asked about DSI's publications.[42]

Perhaps the most qualified of the defense witnesses was Ward Pomeroy, coauthor of the Kinsey reports. Alfred Kinsey had offered advice and encouragement to physique publishers such as Bob Mizer from the 1940s until his death in 1956. To anyone watching in the courtroom, Pomeroy was clearly Judge Larson's favorite witness. Larson took the unusual step of questioning Pomeroy personally, asking if he thought the DSI images were obscene. "No," he emphatically answered. "There was no action, there was no erection. This was a depiction of nudity." He dismissed the DSI movie *Blackie and the Pirate* as mere "camp." Unlike the prosecutor, who harped on society's prejudice against homosexuals, Pomeroy saw a "great shift in society's attitude about homosexuality over the past twenty-odd years." Pointing to the popularity of gay playwrights, the large amount of gay literature "on the market," and the rise of groups such as the Mattachine Society and ONE, he felt that "our whole standard is shifting in the direction of more understanding, more knowledge, and hence more acceptance of homosexuality."[43]

Judge Larson also posed direct questions to another important defense witness, the Rev. Ted McIlvenna, a heterosexual Methodist minister and community organizer from San Francisco. As director of the Young Adult Project at the Glide Urban Center, he counseled queer street kids in the city's Tenderloin neighborhood as well as hundreds of runaway youth who had come to the city for "the summer of love." His involvement with the queer community of San Francisco had led him to help found the Council on Religion and the Homosexual, putting him, according to historian Heather White, "at the front lines" of queer community empowerment. McIlvenna confessed amazement at the tameness of DSI materials and testified that young people would have little interest in them. When Judge Larson asked if he would show these images to his own children, he responded, "I would think it's helpful in some ways for them to see depicted what the human form is, to see it's a creation of God's." His only complaint was the need for more study and research on homosexuality. "We don't know that much yet. I think we have to find out," McIlvenna testified. Both Pomeroy's and McIlvenna's authoritative testimony found their way into Larson's decision.[44]

Confusion over the *Mishkin* and *Ginzburg* rulings played out in the courtroom. In his closing argument, Meshbesher asserted that the government was arguing the wrong case. He pointed out that in *Manual* the Supreme Court had found physique images not obscene; in *Sunshine* it found nude images not obscene; and in *ONE* it found homosexual magazines not obscene. But according to the prosecution, "somehow, by some stroke of magic, we combine nudity and homosexuality and get obscenity," Meshbesher summarized in exasperation. Because of the *Mishkin* decision, the task of the prosecution was to demonstrate that the material appealed to the prurient appeal *not* of the average American but of the average person in the recipient group—homosexuals. Instead, the prosecution had argued that the average American finds homosexuality to be "unwholesome, morbid, shameful, and unhealthy" and therefore that homosexuality was inherently obscene. It was actually to Meshbesher's advantage to admit that homosexuals were the intended recipient group, since none had testified that it appealed to a morbid, unhealthy interest in sex. Similar material was bought and sold at newsstands and bookstores all over America, so it clearly did not exceed community standards. And it even had some social value. Meshbesher pointed to the five hundred customers who were inspired enough to submit entries to DSI's art contest.[45]

To counter the prosecution's initial charge that DSI was operating under a "disguise," Meshbesher concluded his remarks by arguing that Spinar and Germain operated openly, using their own names, on a main thoroughfare in Minneapolis. Unlike Mishkin, who used aliases and hid in back alleys, "they hold their heads high when they walk into the office," he asserted. They were operating within the legal limits set by the courts and had nothing to hide. Meshbesher ended with a poetic flourish, quoting Romantic poet Robert Blake:

Children of a future Age
Reading this indignant page
Will know that in a former time
Love! Sweet love! was made a crime.

An early advocate of "free love," Blake opposed state sanctions that hindered the free expression of sexuality, including those against prostitution, adultery, and homosexuality. He had become the muse for Jim Morrison and the Doors, whose first album was that summer near the top of the Billboard chart and, ironically, would itself become the subject of a censorship battle. Despite weeks of testimony about sex, Meshbesher's invocation of Blake was the first time in the trial that anyone broached the notion of love.[46]

Outside the courtroom, tens of thousands of young Americans were making their way to San Francisco, hoping to become a part of the counterculture in a "summer of love." Many came as a way to protest the status quo and the Vietnam War, while others came for the drugs. In Newark and Detroit, some of the worst racial riots in American history were breaking out, as black citizens became fed up with their mistreatment by law enforcement. The unrest had spread to Minneapolis, where National Guard troops were mobilized. The prosecution considered DSI to be part of a rising tide of "smut" threatening the nation, yet another sign of increasing permissiveness reeking havoc on American values.

But Minneapolis citizens reading trial coverage in the local newspapers were led to sympathize with Spinar and Germain and their quest for personal freedoms. One reporter labeled Germain's rise from a South Dakota farm to mail clerk to founder of a business with a half million dollars in sales a "Horatio Alger Story." The editor of the *St. Paul Dispatch* criticized the government for depending on postal inspectors who disingenuously infiltrated correspondence club mailing lists and intimidated witnesses. He denounced this "entrapment" and "oversyping" as an infringement on the rights of homosexuals and heterosexuals. Though not commenting directly on the trial, the *Minneapolis Tribune* reprinted a *Washington Post* editorial praising the British Parliament for its progress toward freeing homosexuals from persecution for private, consensual acts.[47]

Larson's decision came quickly and decisively. Just two days after the trial ended, he shocked the government representatives by finding Spinar and Germain not guilty on all counts. "You never saw a couple of more disappointed people than the prosecutor and the postal inspector. They thought we were going to jail," recalled Spinar. Having infiltrated DSI's mailing list in 1963 and helped prosecute many of their customers, Postal Inspector Gosnell had sat next to prosecutor Green throughout the trial, anticipating victory. But Larson ruled that the government had failed each part of the three-part obscenity definition the Supreme Court had established. Citing John Allsup, the government's own witness, he ruled that the material did not appeal to the prurient interests of the intended recipient group. Since this material was available at stores all over the nation, it did not exceed the limits of contemporary community standards. And since it had some marginal value to commercial artists, it was not utterly without redeeming social value. He chastised the government for not grasping the implications of the *Mishkin* decision, holding on instead to an appeal to the views of the "average person."[48]

Larson's decision acknowledged that what the attorneys had really been debating was not obscenity in any abstract sense but homosexual rights. He acknowledged that DSI's customers were homosexuals and that their enjoyment of these materials was parallel to that of heterosexuals buying *Playboy*. His job was to balance the desires of those who wished to "maintain moral values" with the demands of the U.S. Constitution. Larson ruled that the Constitution included protections for DSI's homosexual customers. "The rights of minorities expressed individually in sexual groups or otherwise must be respected," he forcefully wrote. Echoing the words of Ward Pomeroy and Ted McIlvenna, Larson envisioned more enlightened days ahead: "With increasing research and study, we will in the future come to a better understanding of ourselves, sexual deviants, and others."[49]

Spinar and Germain held a victory party in their duplex apartment attended by celebrity attorney F. Lee Bailey and their neighbor Abigail Van Buren. They were so proud of this landmark legal achievement that they published summaries of the decision under the headline "A Major Victory" and included photographs of themselves—an unprecedented public display for publishers continually threatened with arrest. They wanted to show the world the "sweet kids" that the government was attacking. They noted how they had used "every resource at our command" to fight federal censorship in a struggle with implications far beyond their magazines. They had fought and won not only for themselves but also "for those others, less able to defend themselves, who also suffer intimidation and coercion at the hands of bigots, the censors, the enemies of freedom." Germain and Spinar contracted Victor Banis, one of the most well-known gay pulp novelists of the period, to write a book chronicling the DSI trial. All this publicity about the case "did not sit well with the U.S. Attorney's Office," Robins remembered. A federal district court decision was usually not published and did not have binding national precedent, but by publicizing the case, Spinar and Germain "provided a roadmap for all to follow" (see fig. 6.5).[50]

Although largely overlooked today, DSI's victory in federal district court was recognized at the time as a watershed moment: "an important step toward equal rights for homosexuals" and a "landmark case" gushed the *Advocate* on the cover of its inaugural issue. "The publishers and the distinguished witnesses who testified on behalf of sanity are to be congratulated on this victory for freedom of the press," announced the newsletter for the Winston Book Club, as it offered three DSI magazines for sale to commemorate the occasion. *Drum* magazine sold verbatim copies of the court's decision for one dollar.[51] Some of the full frontal nude images that had figured in the case soon turned up in physique magazines with the prominent caption "This photo was declared NOT obscene in a Federal Court."

After 1967 the artistic, bodybuilding, and classical alibis that had been used to justify male nudity fell away. Within a year publications appeared with cover photos of naked boys in bed, the sexual connotations no longer even thinly disguised.[52] Gay men throughout the country were grateful. Letters poured in to DSI telling them to "keep up the good work." As one man wrote from Rochester, New York, "Nobody needs to tell you guys about legal limits after what you have done for the country in your recent historic suit. We all owe you thanks for that." Within a few years gay men were comparing the DSI founders'

Conrad Germain

"We resolved to fight with every resource at our command this attempt by the federal government to suppress our magazines — not only for ourselves, but for those others, less able to defend themselves, who also suffer intimidation and coercion at the hands of the bigots, the censors, the enemies of freedom, who are forever attempting to reshape society — by fair means or foul — into their own twisted image of what it should be."

— The Publishers

Lloyd Spinar

FIGURE 6.5 When found not guilty in federal court in August 1967, Conrad Germain and Lloyd Spinar celebrated their victory by publishing their photographs in their own publications, including *Galerie 3*.

Author's collection.

pioneering efforts to those of astronauts, praising "Conrad Germain's walk in space."[53]

A major ally in the court victory was Hal Call of Mattachine of San Francisco, who was instrumental in helping DSI obtain expert witnesses. Call was one of the few homophile leaders who appreciated the advantages of an alliance with physique commercial interests. Germain was personal friends with Call, as he was with Dick Leitch at New York Mattachine.[54] But prior to the court victory, many homophile groups engaged in a politics of respectability and kept their distance from such enterprises. Richard Inman of Mattachine of Florida derided DSI for its "filthy Readers' Service," highlighting its legal troubles and warning readers of his newsletter to keep their names off its mailing lists.[55] After DSI won in federal court, these homophile groups became much more supportive. Mattachine of San Francisco sent out a two-page fundraising letter taking credit for the victory. *ONE Confidential* reprinted Judge Larson's decision in its entirety and began talking not of physique photography but "homophile photography," blurring the lines such groups had tried to keep distinct. Richard Inman became DSI's Miami distributor, opening a bookstore selling nudist magazines and homophile publications. The DSI victory brought the gay commercial and homophile worlds even closer together, continuing the work begun by Lynn Womack and Clark Polak.[56]

The post-1967 period was a heady time for DSI. Germain and Spinar moved to Los Angeles, purchased a mansion with a pool in the Hollywood Hills, and established business facilities in North Hollywood. "It's where the boys are," Germain explained, indicating that DSI needed to be closer to its photographers and models. Their grand plans included full-length movies and a new publication that would be the "gay *Playboy*"—Victor J. Banis would serve as editor. They wanted to expand the Vagabond Club to include private membership clubs in major cities featuring dining and entertainment. Their clothing catalog might become a chain of Vagabond Men's Shops. They even envisioned gay vacation resorts. "They would advertise to gay guys that this was a place that was private—no police to bother them," explained attorney Mickey Robins. "That was going to be a big economic success. . . . That was ahead of its time." Robins was certain that they had the resources to finance such deals.[57]

Despite all the celebrations and high hopes, DSI's victory proved to be pyrrhic. Germain and Spinar's personal relationship did not survive the move to California. Lavish spending included chauffeurs and hustlers. Lawsuits by their own attorneys and a former model, trying to cash in on their success, proved expensive. Bob Mizer reported that DSI was invaded at gunpoint and had its mailing list stolen.

But ironically it was the legal victory itself that proved most damaging to the business. By transforming the market, it opened up not only full-frontal male nudity but also open homoeroticism. Emboldened by DSI's own publicity about the case, scores of new companies entered the business, flooding the market with new magazines, photographs, and films. J. Brian teamed up with Bob Damron to form Calafran Studios, which published *Golden Boys* and opened a series of West Coast gay bookstores. Jim French had only recently started drawing physique artwork, but after the DSI decision, he began photographing models and opened Colt Studios, which became a major producer of gay erotica. "Competitors sprang up everywhere," Spinar recalled.[58]

As a sign that the physique era was over, even longtime physique photographers quickly switched to nudes. "His models had been caught with their pants *up*," some joked about Bob Mizer's supposed inability to keep up with the changing landscape. In fact, most older photographers had long envisioned a day when full-frontal male nudity would be legal and had a ready stock of images. Mizer began offering them almost immediately after the DSI decision, though not in his magazine. In Chicago, Chuck Renslow's Kris Studios began offering "Full-Nude Art Poses," a compromise term suggesting they were still skeptical of dropping the artistic pretense. By the next year Kris had started a new publication, *Rawhide Male*, featuring all nude photos and drawings. But now that such images were legal, they were not worth nearly as much as they had been during the physique era. DSI magazines that had sold for $10 were now lucky to bring $2.[59]

DSI tried to compete in this new marketplace and continued to push the limits of the law on censorship. A new version of the Vagabond Club promised to connect men using an IBM computer. They produced films with Pat Rocco and experimented with a new magazine, *Vagabond One*, "for those who think Gay." In 1968 they began offering *Tryst*, one of the first magazines to feature naked men together touching. By the 1970s they were offering hard-core action magazines and films. In this chaotic new marketplace, DSI itself became the victim of theft, as new publishers and printers hurried to produce new merchandise, often not bothering with the niceties of copyrights and fees.[60]

Meanwhile, the U.S. Post Office did not give up its attempts to put DSI out of business. "They harass people like crazy who beat them in court," Robins observed of government prosecutors. "They watch [them] like a hawk. . . . It becomes very personal." Indeed, by 1969 both Germain and Spinar were on the chief postal inspector's list of the fifteen most wanted purveyors of "smut" in the nation—of any kind, gay or straight. Working with the Department of Justice, Postmaster General Winston Blount formed teams to target each of the fifteen publishers to "run them into the ground" through multiple indictments.[61]

The government indicted DSI again in Fargo, North Dakota, on eight counts of obscenity and this time insisted on a jury trial. "The jury will convict even if the judge knows the material is not obscene," Assistant U.S. Attorney Jay Anthony confessed. Arguing that Germain and Spinar were "pandering" to their customers, Anthony got his guilty verdict and a sentence of eighteen months in prison—leading Conrad Germain to have a nervous breakdown. By this time they had hired the most famous First Amendment attorney then in practice, Stanley Fleishman, who won the case on appeal; as a constitutional lawyer, appeals were his main focus. But the financial damage was devastating. The Post Office tried a third time—raiding their North Hollywood offices, arresting Spinar, and seizing property without a search warrant. Even though the case was dismissed, the psychological damage, legal fees, and disruption of business effectively destroyed DSI. By then it was in default with printers and attorneys and Spinar was arrested again, this time for passing bad checks.[62]

Throughout the 1970s Germain operated a variety of gay mail-order houses under various names, most of which became known for the low quality of both their products and customer service. Bob Mizer complained about DSI's unreliability. The publisher of a gay erotic film buyer's newsletter singled Germain out for damaging the reputation of the entire industry. Hundreds responded to a "victims ad" in the *Advocate* asking for stories of customers burned by such mail-order companies.[63] The Post Office would not prosecute porn producers for fraud since that would encourage the efficiency of an industry it actively sought to suppress. But when Germain ventured into other questionable direct-mail practices, it pounced. In 1975 he was convicted of mail fraud in connection with a weight-loss scam. Although he could have plea-bargained his way to a misdemeanor, he was so enraged by the federal government's constant harassment that he fought and lost. After an unsuccessful appeal, he spent time in Terminal Island Federal Prison. His release was conditional on his not engaging in mail order.[64]

Conrad Germain and Lloyd Spinar and their company DSI represent the final stage of the physique era—the professionalization and consolidation of the market. Unlike the photographers and artists who inaugurated the era, they were business school–trained entrepreneurs looking for an opportunity. As gay men from the rural Midwest, they saw an underserved population and were able to cater to its desires, make lots of money, and defeat attacks from censors and prosecutors.

The physique era had begun more than a decade earlier with Bob Mizer, an independent gay artist and entrepreneur who was also wildly successful, at least for a while, in identifying and responding to a gay market. He helped to grow the market and create more centers of creativity and entrepreneurship, but the competition this fostered impeded efforts to collectively confront government censorship. Mizer fought the Post Office, mostly alone, and usually lost. More a crusader and champion of free speech than a profit-driven businessman, Mizer used his magazine to urge people to organize, to join the ACLU, to fight the fascist police state. He cultivated a sense of an "aesthetic" gay community. He made a good living but exhibited little interest in money.

As businessmen more concerned with profit than with making a statement, Germain and Spinar lived and spent extravagantly. They, of course, were also opposed to censorship, but their opposition was part of a larger conservative politics that championed free enterprise and individual liberty, not collective action. Both Mizer, the crusader, and DSI, the businessmen, were entrepreneurial, and both responded to and cultivated a gay market. But ultimately it was the DSI founders who created an organization large enough, and profitable enough, to take on the federal government and win the right to free expression.

7

THE PHYSIQUE LEGACY

The physical culture [magazines] have made continuing progress over the last fifteen years. . . . New physique titles are sprouting up like mushrooms. . . . This group will no longer be suppressed! Like the natives of the former colonial powers, they have tasted a little freedom and now they want full recognition and will settle for nothing less. . . . Only at a future time, possibly many years hence, will the tremendous and vital sociological importance of the movement created by these [magazines] be fully realized.

—Bob Mizer, 1964

EVERY MEMORIAL Day weekend, thousands of gay men gather in Chicago for three days of socializing, shopping, and sex. International Mr. Leather (IML) weekend began as a modest promotional event for Chuck Renslow's Gold Coast leather bar in 1972. But the amateur "Mr. Gold Coast" competition became so popular that by the end of the decade it outgrew the two-story bar and attracted a boisterous crowd that filled the sidewalks outside. So Renslow moved the event to a ballroom in one of Chicago's large Michigan Avenue convention hotels, where it quickly transformed into a holiday weekend of parties, commercial displays, and networking opportunities. "We began as a community effort and not a private endeavor," Renslow insisted.

Vendors from around the world display merchandise at booths during the day, while bars throughout the city offer special events at night. At the center of the weekend remains the selection of a contestant who best embodies the ideals of the leather community, both in physical appearance and in personality.

Bars and magazines from around the country and the world sponsor contestants for the title of Mr. International Leather. Judges over the years have included physique artist Tom of Finland and the Reverend Troy Perry, founder of the gay Metropolitan Community Church. In 1980 the winner hailed from Sydney, Australia; in 1984 an African American won the title. More recently both a trans man and a sixty-five-year-old cis man got the nod. Championing diversity, it has become one of Chicago's largest annual conventions in terms of both attendance and revenue—notable for a city famous for sponsoring large conventions. While its core participants are gay and bisexual men who are part of the leather subculture, it attracts a diverse group of men and women looking for a space to openly express their sexuality, whatever its form. It brings together what Renslow calls "a brotherhood and sisterhood of leather."[1]

IML is the culmination of Chuck Renslow's lifelong entrepreneurial efforts to both serve a gay market and foster community. And it has deep roots in the physique world. Renslow's first business venture was as a physique photographer. Like scores of other young gay photographers in the early 1950s, Renslow learned about the size of the gay market when he switched from taking portraits and cheesecake photographs to the more lucrative physique market.

To find models for his Kris Studios he frequented bodybuilding competitions and gyms, eventually becoming an AAU official in charge of the Mr. Chicago physique competitions. He teamed up with other physique photographers, sharing mailing lists and traveling to Los Angeles to photograph models at Bob Mizer's AMG studios. He became romantic and business partners with Domingo Orejudos, a physique artist who got his start publishing drawings in Irv Johnson's *Tomorrow's Man*. The two eventually bought Johnson's Triumph Gym, the first of many local business ventures that both enhanced Kris Studios—supplying a ready source for models—and simultaneously served as a social center for local gay men interested in bodybuilding.

With the help of Lynn Womack, Renslow began publishing *Mars*, a physique magazine with an emphasis on leather and Levi's. Seeking to provide this same audience a place to meet, he bought the Gold Coast bar, decorated it with Dom's physique artwork, and offered special Thursday spaghetti dinners and Sunday movie nights. By the 1970s the Mr. Gold Coast competition served as an updated, openly gay version of the bodybuilding contests that gay men like Renslow had been frequenting for decades. Today the annual IML gatherings carry clear echoes of the physique era and the bodybuilding contests and magazines where many gay men first found community.[2]

Like many of his physique studio peers, Renslow had almost been put out of business by the forces of censorship. Police raided Kris Studios during two nation-wide crackdowns on homosexual magazines; a 1958 raid occurred amid Postmaster General Arthur Summerfield's campaign against mail-order obscenity, and a 1966 raid coincided with the post-*Mishkin* crackdown that landed Directory Services in court. Renslow fought and won both cases in municipal court, which may say as much about the persuasiveness of his attorneys as their connections to the machine politics of Chicago.[3] So while physique entrepreneurs such as Lynn Womack, Clark Polak, John Palatinus, and others were forced out of business, Chuck Renslow survived as a successful entrepreneur into the postphysique era. He had diversified his holdings and opened gay bars, bathhouses, and other businesses, fulfilling what were only dreams for the founders of the Grecian Guild and DSI. All had tried to create opportunities for gay men to meet, socialize, and connect, whether it was through pen-pal clubs, conventions, summer camps, or other endeavors. But only Renslow managed to create and sustain one of the largest annual gatherings of gay men in the nation (see fig. 7.1).

Renslow was also the most successful physique entrepreneur at merging commercial success and political causes. As a business owner he had learned the value of political connections within the Chicago political machine. He

FIGURE 7.1 Tom of Finland, Chuck Renslow, and Dom Orejudos got their start as physique artists and photographers in the 1950s. Here they are enjoying International Mr. Leather contest in Chicago in 1986.

Courtesy of the Leather Archives & Museum.

had introduced himself and his cause so frequently to the legendary Mayor Richard J. Daley that by the end of his life Daley greeted him with, "I know. Chuck, gay rights." He became a loyal precinct captain, ran as an openly gay delegate to the Democratic National Convention in 1980, and was pushed to run for office but worried his bathhouse and leather connections would be a handicap. As the owner of *GayLife* newspaper, he convinced Mayor Jane Byrne to sign an executive order barring antigay discrimination in city hiring. Beyond his personal efforts, the mailing lists he had developed over the years as the owner of Kris Studios, *Mars* magazine, the Gold Coast bar, and Man's Country bathhouse proved useful in turning out votes for the Democratic Party in Chicago. A founder of Prairie State Democrats, he helped elect Illinois's first openly gay state representative in 1996, the same year Illinois voters sent Barack Obama to Springfield. As historian Timothy Stewart-Winter argues, Renslow was "a pioneer in the political incorporation of gay people into urban machine politics" (see figs. 7.2 and 7.3).[4]

FIGURE 7.2 Chuck Renslow was the gay physique photographer most successful at bringing his commercial success into mainstream partisan politics. After serving as precinct captain for Mayor Richard J. Daley in Chicago, he ran as an openly gay delegate to the Democratic National Convention in 1980 in support of Edward Kennedy.
Courtesy of the Leather Archives & Museum.

FIGURE 7.3 In 1982 Chuck Renslow, publisher of *GayLife* newspaper, convinced Mayor Jane Bryne to sign an executive order barring antigay discrimination in Chicago city hiring.

Courtesy of the Leather Archives & Museum.

Renslow may have been the physique photographer who was most successful at bringing gay men together and forming community, but he was not alone in that quest. The dream of uniting gay men through the marketplace, through a shared interest in images of the male body, had been a central aim of physique era entrepreneurs. It was an idea that animated Bob Mizer, who wanted to "help the homosexualists" by creating an open forum in his *Physique Pictorial* where entrepreneurs and consumers could safely buy and sell merchandise and see themselves as part of a distinct "aesthetic community." Donald Webster Cory, too, saw both his mail-order book service and Manhattan bookstore as ways to connect and educate a minority community through a common interest in books. With the *Grecian Guild Pictorial*, Randolph Benson and John Bullock created a fraternal order of physique enthusiasts throughout the country with local chapters, annual conventions, a chaplain, and a Grecian of the Month. The founders of the Adonis Male Club put members in direct contact with one another through a complex network of correspondence, until shuttered by the Post Office. By solving the dual problems of distribution and postal censorship, Lynn Womack ensured this network could grow to incorporate gay book services and homophile politics. Building on these successes, Lloyd Spinar and Conrad Germain dreamed of turning their wide offerings of merchandise, correspondence services, and travel guides into a nationwide series of Vagabond clubs and vacation resorts. All these entrepreneurs had tried to create opportunities for gay men to meet, socialize, and connect, first through the virtual medium of print, later through correspondence, and eventually in physical gatherings.

This hunger to connect remained largely at the level of a virtual or imagined community during the physique era, but it animated physique enterprises large and small. Physique customers responded to and encouraged these efforts as they came to understand themselves as part of a community of "physique enthusiasts" enjoying and being excited by the same images, and being marginalized for that desire—even if it went unnamed. Through these magazines, they learned there were other men out there collecting the same images, wearing the same clothes, reading the same books, decorating their apartments with similar paintings or statues. They enjoyed being part of an "imagined community," one that had noble roots in an ancient Greek and Roman culture, as these magazines informed them. Perhaps most important, they understood themselves as part of a minority group under attack by forces that considered their desires pathological and illegal. Through these periodicals, a community of men who enjoyed viewing other men's bodies literally became visible.

While many of these early attempts at community formation remained only virtually or partially fulfilled, two events in 1968 marked a kind of coming out of the physique world, a fulfillment of its long history of making the gay world visible to itself and the larger world. Less than one year after the DSI decision changed the landscape of obscenity law, a photographer who had only recently started shooting both still and moving physique images teamed up with the Park Theater in Los Angeles to offer the first regular public screenings of gay-oriented films.[5]

Pat Rocco was running a psychedelic head shop when he answered an ad in the *Free Press*, Los Angeles's alternative newspaper, looking for someone to take male physique photographs—itself a sign of the burgeoning physique market in 1967. Finding success with his still photos, Rocco started bringing along a film camera and shooting three-minute films. Under the name Bizarre

Productions, he offered the films and other items for sale through a mail-order catalog. "I was deluged with letters," Rocco latter recalled of the response to his first advertisements. Around the same time, Los Angeles's Park Theater was looking for a way to supplement its rather unsuccessful programming of heterosexual skin flicks. The theater's gay manager, Ed Kazan, suggested they start showing gay-oriented film. "There was a whole gay community around there and there wasn't a theater in that part of town, or Los Angeles, or the whole country, serving their needs," he told the owners. The theater owners liked the idea and, after seeing Rocco's films, offered him a public screening. "They were too good to be sold through the mail," they commented.[6]

Pat Rocco's "Male Nude Film Festival" was the first of its kind, the first gay film festival, but it also drew on a long tradition within the physique world. The primitive short films of Bob Mizer, Chuck Renslow, Dick Fontaine, and others had long been marketed and used as centerpieces for private gatherings of gay men. Their mail-order catalogs allowed customers to rent or buy films, suggested how to project them at parties, and even offered help in obtaining a film projector. By the 1960s a few gay bars in Los Angeles held screenings of Mizer's films, including bars where the Park Theater's Ed Kazan had worked. And a few intrepid movie houses had tried to screen experimental gay films, such as Kenneth Anger's *Fireworks* in 1958, only to be raided by the police. Building on these earlier attempts, the screenings in 1968 of Pat Rocco's films represented what historian Whitney Strub calls "an unprecedented visual spectacle in the public screening of American cinema" (see fig. 7.4).[7]

FIGURE 7.4 The Park Theater in Los Angeles offered the first regular public screenings of gay-oriented films in 1968, featuring the films of physique photographer Pat Rocco.

Not only the setting of the Park Theater but the content of Rocco's films suggested a new level of openness. Erotic yet without explicit sex scenes, they often featured two men meeting in a public place, flirting and cavorting in the woods, and culminating in a romantic, often naked, kiss. As ONE homophile activist Jim Kepner commented, Rocco's films were "exhilarating, fresh, ideal, basic and agonizingly beautiful—something homosexuals had never before found on screen."[8] Jack Nichols, a homophile activist then publishing GAY, one of the nation's first gay newspapers, also gushed over the romanticism he found in Rocco's use of nudity. "His main purpose . . . is to stir the heart, not the prick."[9] Nichols, leader of the first gay pickets in front of the White House in 1965, saw the political importance of this new sensibility. "Pat Rocco will do more to uplift the morale and self-image of American homosexuals than a thousand Mattachine orators," he enthused.[10]

Rocco's films were so popular they spawned not only the first gay film festivals but also a gay community organization: the Society of Pat Rocco Enlightened Enthusiasts (SPREE). Promising "entertainment with an emphasis on male nudity in a wholesome atmosphere," this gay social club and service organization held monthly meetings that attracted hundreds of participants, especially nondrinkers and others who felt uncomfortable in gay bars. SPREE organized outings, charity events, a repertory theater company, and published the SPREE News Pictorial. It held fundraisers for Troy Perry's Metropolitan Community Church, then getting its start in Los Angeles, with congregations forming all over the country. SPREE also allied itself with the homophile world, boasting ONE magazine's Jim Kepner as vice president and participating in the magazine's gay European tour, which became the subject of Pat Rocco's film ONE Adventure (1972).[11] Noting how members of the city council and other politicians had addressed the group, Bob Mizer praised SPREE as "a significant force in the Hollywood community."[12] SPREE demonstrated how a shared interest in images of naked men helped create community.

The other event in 1968 that marked a movement of the physique ethos into the public sphere was the first gay male beauty contest. Begun as a marketing tool by the newly founded Los Angeles Advocate, the contest was envisioned as a way to unite the city's gay community around a contest other than common drag events. Called the Groovy Guy contest, it offered an updated, openly gay version of a bodybuilding contest. "For many years we've had the Mr. America, Mr. USA, Mr. World, and Mr. Universe contests," a promotional film noted. "But now we're ready for a change, the younger generation is changing," and it was time for "a new kind of contest that fits the now happening of where it's at . . . the Groovy Guy Contest!"[13] Judging categories moved beyond bodybuilding's emphasis on physique to include personality, face, grooming, and carriage. Gay bars, stores, and other commercial outlets sponsored contestants, along with homophile community and religious organizations, including San Francisco's SIR, the Metropolitan Community Church, SPREE, and ONE, Inc. It was at one such contest in Washington, D.C., that Lynn Womack was honored for his success in fighting censorship.

The Groovy Guy contest became so popular it had to be moved from a local gay bar to the Sheraton-Universal Hotel, where it drew over a thousand spectators who could purchase a fifty-page souvenir program, complete with photos of contestants, many in the nude. Soon it seemed like every gay bar, bathhouse, and magazine offered a similar pageant, each one serving as a community-building event. In the South, *David* magazine sponsored the Mr. David competition, while *Queen's Quarterly*'s first Mr. Fire Island Body Beautiful Contest attracted nearly a thousand spectators, one of the largest gatherings in Cherry Grove history. Featuring professional International Federation of BodyBuilders "posers" mixing with "female impersonators," it offered a "decidedly gay brand of fun."[14] The Club Baths chain got each city where it operated to hold a local contest to send a representative to Chicago to be named Mr. Club Baths, with proceeds from ticket sales going to support local gay newspapers.[15] And Chuck Renslow's Mr. Gold Coast, building on this model as it expanded into International Mr. Leather, would outlast them all (see fig. 7.5).[16]

These gay pageants brought gay businesses and homophile groups together to engage in a ritual borrowed from the physique world but updated for the era of gay liberation. Bob Mizer, observing this from his AMG compound in Los Angeles, saw how these new gay beauty contests marked "a new era." Gone were the days, "many, many years ago," when he began taking physique photographs, when it was an "open secret" that gay men had filled the audiences at physique contests, suffering through the weightlifting events in anticipation of the bodybuilding competition organizers reluctantly used to close out the program. He was proud to now see that the contestants, the audience, and the sponsors were all openly gay.[17] Such contests became a prominent feature of gay pride events and floats, including the first such parade in Los Angeles in 1970.

The proliferation of gay beauty pageants was part of a larger explosion of gay-oriented newspapers, magazines, and commercial outlets in the late 1960s and early 1970s. Often attributed to the advent of gay liberation, or the

FIGURE 7.5 Gay male beauty pageants, inspired by bodybuilding competitions, proliferated starting in 1968, including the Mr. Groovy Guy, Mr. Fire Island, and Mr. David contests.

David, August–September 1972, courtesy of Peach Media Holdings.

increasing influence of the counterculture, publications like the *Advocate*, *Queen's Quarterly*, *David*, *Gay Scene*, *GAY*, and others would have been impossible without the legal victories of Guild Press and DSI.[18] Their free use of openly homoerotic images ensured they would reach a large market, sending their message of gay liberation far and wide. They represented a maturation of a gay market tied to male images that had been developing since 1951.

Like the beauty pageants they sponsored, these new magazines demonstrated the continuing legacy and influence of the physique world, both in content and in personnel. *Queen's Quarterly*, "the magazine for gay guys who have no hangups," followed in the footsteps of Guild Press by offering a variety of specialty magazines, including *Ciao!*, a "world of gay travel," and *Body*, a "male pictorial." Its editor, Bud Parker, had produced the Mr. America–Mr. Universe pageants to the delight of gay audiences for years. Hal Warner, former editor of Joe Weider's *Adonis* and *Body Beautiful* magazines, was a frequent contributor. *Queen's Quarterly* featured a regular "Muscle Contest News and Notes" about bodybuilding contests throughout the country, complete with images of the contestants and their recommended exercise routines. Such continuing coverage in openly gay magazines belied the notion that bodybuilding was simply an alibi behind which gay men took cover.[19]

Even as gay periodicals became more open in the wake of the DSI decision and the advent of gay liberation, the editorial format established in the physique era remained largely unchanged. With a mix of beefcake images, personal ads, travel advice and gay news, the *Los Angeles Advocate* resembled the combination physique/homophile magazines pioneered by Guild Press and perfected by *Drum*. Throughout the 1970s the *Advocate* featured male nude imagery, often on the cover, while its biggest early advertisers were gay book services and other mail-order companies.[20] *Drummer* magazine carried articles on the bodybuilding world next to fundraising advertisements to oppose Anita Bryant and her antigay crusade in Florida sponsored by Rush Poppers. The "Tough Customers" page of photographs of readers echoed the Grecian Guild's Grecian of the month and showed how the desire to connect with fellow readers continued. *Drummer* and many other 1970s gay periodicals also featured frequent nostalgic odes to physique artists and photographers.[21]

Perhaps the most significant innovation was the addition of female erotic photographs, often to accompany stories specifically targeted to lesbians. New York's GAY, which billed itself as the first gay weekly newspaper, began publishing in 1969 with a heavy emphasis on nude male images but soon added female nudes to accompany articles on lesbian culture. *David*, a regional publication targeting cities in the South, added a Venus section in October 1971 "where you girls can sound off, or show off." The new section featured pinups and customer profiles as well as a "Dear Venus" advice column (see fig. 7.6).[22]

Homophile organization publications had always looked at their more daring physique counterparts with envy.[23] In the wake of the *Manual v. Day* decision, they had already begun to resemble physique magazines. After 1967, with the threat of prosecution removed, they adopted a similar racy format. *Vector*,

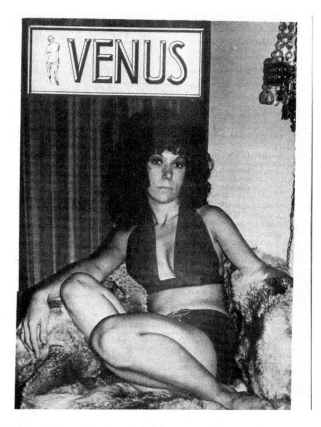

FIGURE 7.6 Gay magazines such as *David* began to offer "Venus" sections with female erotica to balance their beefcake imagery.

David, October 1971, courtesy of Peach Media Holdings.

published by San Francisco's Society for Individual Rights, offered its first nude male centerfold in June 1969, and a few months later full-frontal nudity had migrated to its cover.[24] Soon *Mattachine Times* in New York followed suit, featuring cover images of young men in posing straps.[25] ONE, Inc., entered contestants in the Groovy Guy contest and later teamed up with photographers of the male nude to offer *Spartan for Men*, providing factual reporting on the gay scene as well as "groovy guys for the healthy homosexual." Former editor Jim Kepner published collections of gay erotic stories lavishly illustrated with soft-core nudes, while ONE's Dorr Legg tried to sell Pat Rocco the copyright of homoerotic stories previously published in *ONE* so they could be adapted to film.[26]

This tendency to combine gay news, nude images, and raunchy classified advertising continued until magazines sought to attract large, mainstream advertisers. New York's GAY felt pressure early on from advertisers who objected to the use of nudes, particularly on the cover, forcing editor Nichols to moderate their use.[27] Thus began a movement away from a sexual liberation ethos to a more sanitized, corporate look. Like lots of gay periodicals, GAY abandoned its core gay businesses in search of mainstream acceptance.

The *Advocate* resisted this trend at first, keeping its racy classified ads but segregating them to a pullout section. "I like them; their fun," the *Advocate's* editor-in-chief Richard Rouilard proclaimed. "This is the way gays and lesbians talk to each other worldwide. And if you are going to compromise this community for advertisers or so that your mother can read the magazine, go buy yourself a copy of 'Catch-22.'" But even the *Advocate* eventually had to succumb to the demands of larger advertising dollars, spinning off its classifieds and naked images into a separate magazine. With the rise of upscale publications such as *Genre* and *Out* in the 1990s, the realms of homoerotic imagery and gay news have become increasingly divided. In many ways this represents a return to a politics of respectability practiced by the homophile organizations, a trend reinforced in the twenty-first century as the LGBTQ movement became dominated by the political struggle for gay marriage.[28]

This current bifurcation in LGBT media between the political and the erotic makes it difficult for us to see that the worlds of gay commerce, sex, and politics were once mutually reinforcing. Today gay men go to smart-phone apps like Grndr to hook up but to news websites or an LGBT advocacy organization to catch up on civil rights issues and community affairs. But historically it was the desire to connect and find one another that gave rise to such community publications. It was Bob Mizer's classified ad in *Strength & Health* that had alerted him to the large reservoir of gay men seeking contact with one another. Gay men had pleaded with physique and homophile organizations to allow them to connect, but the first tentative steps in that direction were met with swift and decisive state suppression. Gay men went to prison and others lost their jobs merely for participating in a gay pen-pal club. But thanks to physique entrepreneurs such as Lynn Womack, the correspondence club was able to thrive and morph into the classified ad, which was soon replaced with phone sex lines, followed by AOL chatrooms, and now hookup mobile applications such as Grndr and Scruff. The technology may have changed, but the business of connecting gay men has a long and rich history.

Today the term "gay power" is remembered as a political slogan shouted at the 1969 Stonewall Riots, but in the beginning it was understood largely in economic terms. Two years before the riots, *Vector* inaugurated a new column called "Gay Power" featuring information about its advertisers. The idea came from a young but vocal SIR member, Pat Hallinan, who suggested that it was time to invoke "our secret weapon, GAY POWER, upon the economic world." As the column advised, "When you visit our friends and advertisers, tell 'em you saw it in Vector—that's GAY POWER!"[29] A few months later, the founder of the *Los Angeles Advocate* similarly advised readers, "You can do much to strengthen and promote power in the gay community because you wield the great deciding weapon: The Almighty Dollar." He defined "gay power" as "buying power, selling power, voting power. . . . No dear, it isn't a queen with muscles," he joked.[30]

Gay magazine publishers were among the first to see the connection between economic and political clout, but they were not the only ones. Long before it was shouted at Stonewall, gay business owners used the term "gay power" to signal a new capacity to serve the needs of the community. A gay dating service in 1968 used it to highlight how modern technology was enhancing its ability to connect customers. Man-to-Man Inc. boasted that "gay power has now made available an I.B.M. 360 computer dating service designed by gay people for the exclusive use of the homosexual community." The *Detroit Free Press* was so impressed that it gave the company the "Dating Service of the Year" award. Craig Rodwell first used "gay power" to describe a proposed directory of gay-friendly businesses to be published by New York homophile organizations. The desire to connect and empower gay consumers through dating services and business directories was nothing new, but now it had a slogan: Gay Power.[31]

Even when shouted at Stonewall, the cry for gay power was largely about the desire of gay men and women to have control of their own commercial spaces. "Get the Mafia and the Police Out of Gay Bars," proclaimed one of the first pamphlets in response to the raid of the Stonewall Inn. Craig Rodwell called for "gay businessmen" to open bars and shops to create a healthier social atmosphere than bars like Stonewall. And he simultaneously encouraged customers to support them and "Buy Gay." Activist Marty Robinson suggested that a boycott of Bloomingdale's by New York's newly energized gay community would be a good exercise of "gay power."[32] Before they saw themselves possessing political clout, such gay activists felt and understood their capacity for exercising economic muscle.

For many gay liberationists, especially in New York City, physique maga-zines also came under attack as exemplary of the negative effects of a gay ghetto. In contrast to previous generations of young men who found comfort in images that glorified the male body, gay liberationists saw exploitation. "These maga-zines crudely showed men as nothing but sex objects; if they were objects, I could be one too," remembered John Murphy. "That frightened me then, and it infuriates me now," he wrote in 1971. Some worried that the "masculine mys-tique" depicted in these magazines was so inaccessible and exaggerated that it constituted a form of self-hatred. "Those male idols so worshiped cannot pos-sibly be faggots!" they complained. Following the Black Nationalist, Black Power, and feminist movements, they envisioned a world where gay men and women owned and managed their own, more equitable and inclusive, businesses.[33]

Despite his "Buy Gay" campaign, Craig Rodwell refused to sell "sexploit-ative" magazines in his own Oscar Wilde Memorial Bookshop, offended by both the high price-tag for nude male images and what he found to be an over-emphasis on sex. He was unaware of how physique publishers such as Bob Mizer were among the oldest gay businesses around and had been created with precisely the same goal of fostering community. But Mizer's crusading mission had waned as many straight and gay publishers had since entered the market with an eye toward making a quick buck. Rodwell and other gay liberationists tarred them all with the same brush. They did not appreciate the tremendous struggles they had encountered in the face of government censorship. They increasingly saw physique businesses as part of the problem of, not the solu-tion to, community empowerment.[34]

The buying, selling, and exchanging of images of the male body—whether one's own or someone else's—has been and continues to be central to gay cul-ture. It was the first and most crucial gay business in the formative years after World War II. It was an activity around which gay community and political consciousness formed. Started through mail-order and a network of print pub-lications, it expanded to include a host of products and services of interest to gay men and, by the 1960s, brick-and-mortar storefronts.

So it was no accident that Harvey Milk, the most influential gay political leader of the period, started his political career as the owner of a camera store in San Francisco's Castro neighborhood. Milk had intimate knowledge of how central the physique world was to gay culture from his early days in Los

Angeles after being discharged from the U.S. Navy. There, in 1955, he met his first lover, John Harvey, one of Bob Mizer's models at Athletic Model Guild. Milk was also involved with Craig Rodwell, who founded one of the nation's first gay bookstores in Greenwich Village in 1967 as a conduit for his political activism. As a financial analyst on Wall Street, Milk was fascinated by the possibility of combining commerce and activism and told Rodwell he wanted to open a similar bookstore when he moved to San Francisco.[35]

Although the story goes that Harvey Milk opened Castro Camera on a whim after receiving a spoiled roll of film from the local drug store, the decision also reflected his experiences with gay businesses like AMG and the Oscar Wilde Memorial Bookshop. His store assistant Daniel Nicoletta recalls that Milk soon realized that offering gay-friendly film-developing services could be a particularly profitable business because it fulfilled a special need within the burgeoning gay enclave. It solved a problem that preoccupied gay men in the physique era and beyond, one that some physique entrepreneurs had tried to address through mail-order film delivery systems. Gone were the days when gay men's favorite hobby was film developing, and their favorite possession an expensive Polaroid camera.

Now, at Castro Camera, customers felt at ease bringing in homoerotic images, sometimes letting the staff know a film was particularly juicy. "If they were hot, we'd mark the envelope to remember to look at them when they came back," Nicoletta recalled. Such nonchalance about images that had recently been illegal and that mainstream enterprises might still find objectionable marked a sea change and helped establish a sense of trust. "We are VERY open," announced a placard in the window. Like Rodwell's bookstore, Castro Camera became an informal gay community center. It was from there that Milk launched a gay boycott of Coors Beer, his first attempt at testing his idea of "achieving gay power through economic clout," followed by a "Buy Gay" movement to encourage patronage of similarly gay-owned businesses. It also made such a large profit from film developing—much of it erotic—that it did not actually sell cameras.[36]

Harvey Milk's political career was unprecedented in American politics, but his business had clear roots in the physique world. At Castro Camera, and thousands of other sites, the business of producing and disseminating homoerotic images helped forge a movement.

ACKNOWLEDGMENTS

THIS BOOK exists because of the generous support of a residential fellowship at the National Humanities Center (NHC) in Durham, North Carolina. Funded by the National Endowment for the Humanities (thank you, President Lyndon Johnson!), this fellowship year provided an ideal setting in which to write and think. I thank the amazing staff of the NHC, especially Cassie Mansfield, Brooke Andrade, Sarah Harris, Joel Elliot, Don Solomon, and Karen Carroll. My colleagues and friends from that year made this a better book, especially Ivan Penado, Kunal Parker, Lisa Levenstein, Nan Woodruff, Camille Serchuk, Yasmin Solomonescu, Robin Einhorn, Josephine McDonagh, Colin Jones, Bonna Wescoat, Lena Cown Orlin, David Ambaras, and Betty Collier-Thomas.

I also enjoyed a visiting scholarship at the Leather Archives and Museum in Chicago, which allowed me to research the papers of physique photographer Chuck Renslow, thanks to the help of Rick Storer and Mel Leverich. I was the lucky recipient of two Phil Zwickler Memorial Research Grants through the Rare and Manuscript Collections at the Cornell University Library. Many thanks to Brenda Marston for facilitating those trips, which allowed me to research the papers of Lynn Womack, founder of the Guild Press, and other materials in Cornell's pioneering Human Sexuality Collection.

The University of South Florida supported this work in important ways, including several research grants and a semester sabbatical. USF's College of Arts and Sciences provided an International Travel Grant and USF's Humanities Institute provided an important summer travel grant. USF's superb librarians and archivists, especially Andy Huse and Matt Knight, were of inestimable value. The History Department offered numerous opportunities to present my work as well as a warm and intellectually engaging home. I especially thank my colleagues Michael Decker, Fraser Ottanelli, Frances Ramos, Julia Irwin, Steve Prince, Brian Connolly, Philip Levy, and Giovanna Benadusi. My graduate students, particularly Keegan Shepherd, Chelsea Watts and Ron Arbisi, continue to inspire me with their scholarship. Judy Drawdy, Theresa Lewis, and Tami Davis make it all happen.

Research for this project took me to many professional archives throughout North America, where I depended on the kindness and expertise of numerous archivists. Kyle Morgan, Michael Oliveira, Joseph Hawkins, and Greg Williams helped me navigate the large holdings of ONE National Gay & Lesbian Archives at the University of Southern California Libraries. Alan Miller assisted me at the Canadian Gay and Lesbian Archives. Don Romesburg, Alex Barrows, Rebekah Kim, and Joanna Black all helped in various ways at the Gay, Lesbian, Bisexual, Transgender Historical Society in San Francisco. Glenn Longacre with the National Archives in Chicago helped me view transcripts of two key federal obscenity trials. Jessica Steytler and Cristina Prochilo helped me with the Robert Wood papers at the Congregational Library in Boston. Shawn Wilson tracked down materials at the Kinsey Institute in Bloomington, Indiana.

I also found my way into many private collections, basements, and even one high school. Dennis Bell at the Bob Mizer Foundation allowed me to view diaries and other early material of the Athletic Model Guild. Durk Dehner and S. R. Sharp allowed me to review materials at the Tom of Finland Foundation. Robert Mainardi and Marc Stein shared with me their personal collections, and Ethel Matlen and Lisa Blackwell helped me track down newspaper articles by and about Bob Mizer from Francis Polytechnic Senior High in Los Angeles.

As seems fitting for a project centered on entrepreneurs, the most complete, valuable, and accessible collection of physique magazines is a commercial site. Tim Wilbur's Vintage Physique Photography at http://timinvermont.com houses a database of 60 gigabits. Tim's dedication to preserving physique magazines, art, ephemera, and film is unparalleled, making a comprehensive review like this possible.

I relied on many oral histories to complete this story. I am grateful to all those who shared their personal recollections of physique magazines and early gay consumer culture. Thanks especially to Jack Croucher, Durk Dehrer, Michael Denneny, Drew Hanson, Jim Harper, Dick Leitch, Charles Leslie, Robert Mainardi, Daniel Nicoletta, Michael Syrjanen, Greg Weiss, and Robert Wood. I was also privileged to interview many physique entrepreneurs, their attorneys, and collaborators. Thanks particularly to Victor Banis, Don Cook, Conrad Germain, Anthony Guyther, Ronald Meschbesher, Jim Morris, Chuck Renslow, Mickey Robins, George Palatinus, and Lloyd Spinar. Thanks also to historians Philip Clark, John D'Emilio, Martin Duberman, and Marc Stein for sharing oral histories they conducted.

A special thanks to Bill Zewadski, who has not only supported my work and provided access to his own extensive personal archives but also been a leader in the support of LGBT history and art collections at institutions nationwide. Charles Francis of the Mattachine Society of Washington and Lisa Linsky of McDermott Will & Emory provided assistance in filing a freedom of information request to the National Archives in a vain search for Post Office records from this period.

I appreciate my many colleagues around the country and the world who provided helpful feedback and often gave me opportunities to publicly present my ideas at workshops, especially Justin Bengry, Simone Caron, George Chauncey, Rita Denny, Anthony Destafanis, Corey Fields, Gary Gebhardt, Andrew P. Mills, Kevin Murphy, Larry Rivers, Michael Sherry, Peter Stearns, Mitchell Stevens, Marc Stein, Marc Ventresca, and Timothy Stewart-Winter. Other generous colleagues helped with research leads and shared materials, especially Diane Hanson, Hans Johnson, Marc Stein, Craig Loftin, Estelle Freedman, and Julio Capó. James Mora and Mark Abraham helped with research in places I could not access.

Among the institutions willing to support earlier versions of this project were the *Journal of Social History*; the Ohio State University's Women's Gender and Sexuality Workshop and OSU's Queer Places, Practices and Lives Symposium; Otterbein University's Humanities Advisory Committee; Stanford University's Scandinavian Consortium for Organizational Research (SCANCOR); the University of Minnesota's Workshop in Comparative History of Gender and Sexuality; Wake Forest University's Social Science Research Seminar; and Yale University's Research Initiative on the History of Sexuality. Conferences where I had the opportunity to share my work included Brunel University London's Onscenity Sexual Cultures Conference, the Business History Conference, Gay American History@40 Conference, the European Social Science History Conference, and the Ethnographic Praxis in Industry Conference (EPIC).

The folks at Columbia University Press have been a joy to work with. Bridget Flannery-McCoy offered the kind of careful and thoughtful editing the likes of which I had never received. She helped me tell the story in a better and clearer way. Studies in the History of U.S. Capitalism series editors Bethany Moreton, Louis Hyman, Devin Fergus, and Julia Ott offered a terrific mix of encouragement and thoughtful criticism, pushing me to think about this material in new ways. The same is true of the two outside reviewers. Thanks to Christian Winting for help with numerous and complicated photo permissions.

Through it all were my friends, especially Keith Roberts, Rob Gottron, Paul Tabio, Jim Harper, David Ezell, Todd Richardson, Jack Croucher, Bob McCamant, Gary Gebhardt, Mitchell Stevens, Wallace Best, Mark Peco, and Steven Reigns. They let me share stories, photos, discoveries, and setbacks. They provided drinks, and meals, and get-aways. I could not have done it without them. Michael Benjamin and Justin Rocket helped me nurture body and soul. Tommy Voravong is the best of grinning comrades.

ABBREVIATIONS

ACLU Papers	American Civil Liberties Records, Mudd Library, Princeton University, Princeton, New Jersey
Adonis trial transcript	*U.S. v. Charles J. Anctil et al.*, trial transcript, RG 21, U.S. District Court, Northern District of Illinois, Chicago, Criminal Case Files, 61CR27, National Archives–Chicago Branch
AMG	Athletic Model Guild
ANC	American News Company
BGA	Book Guild of America
Carrington Papers	Glenn Carrington Papers, Schomburg Center for Research in Black Culture, New York Public Library
CBS	Cory Book Service
DOB	Daughters of Bilitis
DSI	Directory Services, Inc.
ECHO	East Coast Homophile Organization
Eccles Papers	John M. Eccles Papers, Special Collections, University of Washington, Seattle
Fleishman Papers	Stanley Fleishman Papers, University of California Los Angeles
GBS	Guild Book Service
GGP	*Grecian Guild Pictorial*
GLBTHS	Gay, Lesbian, Bisexual, Transgender Historical Society, San Francisco
Greenberg Papers	Greenberg Publisher Records, Rare Books and Manuscript Division, Columbia University Library, New York

IFBB	International Federation of BodyBuilders
IML	International Mr. Leather
KEC	Kinsey Era Correspondence, Kinsey Institute, Indiana University, Bloomington
Leather Archives	Leather Archives & Museum, Chicago
Mizer Diary	Bob Mizer Diary, Bob Mizer Permanent Collection, Bob Mizer Foundation, San Francisco
Mizer Foundation	Bob Mizer Foundation, San Francisco
NYPL	New York Public Library
ONE Archives	ONE National Gay and Lesbian Archives, USC Libraries, University of Southern California, Los Angeles
PP	*Physique Pictorial*
SIR	Society for Individual Rights
SPREE	Society of Pat Rocco Enlightened Enthusiasts
TM	*Tomorrow's Man*
U.S. v. Spinar	*U.S. v. Spinar and Germain*, RG 21, U.S. District Court, Fourth Division of Minnesota, Minneapolis, Criminal Case Files, 1966–1969, National Archives–Chicago Branch, Box 11, Case 4-67CR15.
USPSHOF	United States Postal Service, Historians Office Files
Womack Papers	H. Lynn Womack Papers, Human Sexuality Collection, Division of Rare and Manuscript Collections, Cornell University, Ithaca, N.Y.
Wood Papers	Rev. Robert Wood Papers, Congregational Library & Archives, Boston

NOTES

PREFACE

1. David K. Johnson, *The Lavender Scare: The Cold War Persecution of Gays and Lesbians in the Federal Government* (Chicago: University of Chicago Press, 2004).

2. Pioneering exhibit at Jan Kesner Gallery reviewed in Christopher Knight, "The Male Animal," *Los Angeles Times*, August 14, 1990; Christopher Knight, "Fun to Be Had in Works of Bob Mizer and Tom of Finland," *Los Angeles Times*, December 5, 2013; Holland Cotter, "Bob Mizer: 'Artifacts,'" *New York Times*, January 17, 2013.

3. F. Valentine Hooven, *Tom of Finland* (Cologne: Taschen, 1992); F. Valentine Hooven, *Beefcake: The Muscle Magazines of America 1950–1970* (Cologne: Taschen, 1995); Micha Ramakers, *Tom of Finland: The Art of Pleasure* (Cologne: Taschen, 2002); Dian Hanson, *Bob's World: The Life and Boys of A.M.G.'s Bob Mizer* (Cologne: Taschen, 2009); Dian Hanson, *Tom of Finland XXL* (Cologne: Taschen, 2009); Dian Hanson and Reed Massengill, *George Quaintance* (Cologne: Taschen, 2010).

4. Between 1995 and 2007, the European publisher Janssen published seven volumes of the series *American Photography of the Male Nude 1940–1970*, each featuring the works of a major physique photographer: Bruce of Los Angeles (1995), Lon of New York (1996), Douglas of Detroit (1998), Dave Martin (1999), Pat Milo (2001), Al Urban (2002), and Bob Mizer (2007).

5. David Chapman, *Mountain Men: The Male Photography of Don Whitman* (London: Aubrey Walter, 1991); David Chapman, *Hollywood Nudes: The Physique Photos of Fred Kovert* (London: Aubrey Walter, 2000); Walter Kundzicz, *Champion* (Frankfurt: Goliath Verlag, 2003); Reed Massengill, *The Male Ideal: Lon of New York and the Masculine Physique* (New York: Universe, 2003); Reed Massengill, *Uncovered: Rare Vintage Male Nudes* (New York: Universe, 2009); Petra Mason, *Beefcake: 100% Rare, All-Natural* (New York: Universe, 2015).

6. Tom of Finland Foundation, http://www.tomoffinlandfoundation.org.

7. Thomas Waugh, *Hard to Imagine: Gay Male Eroticism in Photography and Film from Their Beginnings to Stonewall* (New York: Columbia University Press, 1996), 217–19; Richard Meyer, *Outlaw Representation: Censorship and Homosexuality in Twentieth-Century American Art* (New York: Oxford University Press, 2002). Important work on gay pulp fiction similarly focused on the various stories in relative isolation. See Michael Bronski, *Culture*

Clash: The Making of Gay Sensibility (Boston: South End Press, 1984); Michael Bronski, *Pulp Friction: Uncovering the Golden Age of Gay Male Pulps* (New York: St. Martin's Press, 2003); and Drewey Wayne Gunn and Jaime Harker, eds., *1960s Gay Pulp Fiction: The Misplaced Heritage* (Amherst: University of Massachusetts Press, 2013).

8. Tracy D. Morgan, "Pages of Whiteness: Race, Physique Magazines, and the Emergence of Public Gay Culture," in *Queer Studies: A Lesbian, Gay, Bisexual, and Transgender Anthology*, ed. Brett Beemyn and Mickey Eliason (New York: New York University Press, 1996) , 280–97; Daniel Harris, *The Rise and Fall of Gay Culture* (New York: Hyperion, 1997), 86–90; Christopher Nealon, *Foundlings: Lesbian and Gay Historical Emotion Before Stonewall* (Durham, N.C.: Duke University Press, 2001).

9. Dennis Altman, *The Homosexualization of America, The Americanization of the Homosexual* (New York: St. Martin's Press, 1982), 21; John D'Emilio, "Capitalism and Gay Identity," in *Powers of Desire: The Politics of Sexuality*, ed. Ann Snitow, Christine Stansell, and Sharon Thompson (New York: Monthly Review Press, 1983), 74–87.

10. Among historians focusing on bar culture are George Chauncey, *Gay New York: Gender, Urban Culture, and the Making of a Gay Male World, 1890–1940* (New York: Basic Books, 1994); Elizabeth Kennedy and Madeline Davis, *Boots of Leather, Slippers of Gold: The History of a Lesbian Community* (New York: Routledge, 1993); and Nan Boyd, *Wide-Open Town: A History of Queer San Francisco to 1965* (Berkeley: University of California Press, 2003). Historians focusing on the homophile movement include John D'Emilio, *Sexual Politics, Sexual Communities: The Making of a Homosexual Minority in the United States, 1940–1970* (Chicago: University of Chicago Press, 1998); Marc Stein, *City of Sisterly and Brotherly Loves: Lesbian and Gay Philadelphia: 1945–1972* (Chicago: University of Chicago Press, 2000); Marcia M. Gallo, *Different Daughters: A History of the Daughters of Bilitis and the Rise of the Lesbian Rights Movement* (New York: Carroll & Graf, 2006); and Craig Loftin, *Masked Voices: Gay Men and Lesbians in Cold War America* (Albany, N.Y.: SUNY Press, 2012).

11. Cornell University's Human Sexuality Collection, ONE National Gay & Lesbian Archives at the University of Southern California, and the GLBT Historical Society are three prime examples.

12. Marc Stein, "Canonizing Homophile Sexual Respectability: Archives, History and Memory," *Radical History Review* 120 (Fall 2014), 52–73; John D'Emilio, remarks at GayAmericanHistory@40, May 2016; John D'Emilio, *Making Trouble: Essays on Gay History, Politics, and the University* (New York: Routledge, 1992).

13. Rodger Streitmatter ignores physique because he argues "they never identified themselves as targeting gays, although their physique photographs attracted a large gay readership—or at least viewership." Rodger Streitmatter, *Unspeakable: The Rise of the Gay and Lesbian Press in America* (Boston: Faber and Faber, 1995), xi. Using the notion of "communication networks" developed by historian Robert Darnton, Martin Meeker astutely argues that the rise of gay mass circulation periodicals shows "a homosexual identity forming into a collective sense of itself." Yet he dismisses physique magazines as "publishers of pornography," questions their circulation figures, and turns his attention to San Francisco–based magazines and the tiny homophile press. Martin Meeker, *Contacts Desired: Gay and Lesbian Communications and Community, 1940s–1970s* (Chicago: University of Chicago Press, 2006), 9, 56.

14. Amy Gluckman and Betsy Reed, eds., *Homo Economics: Capitalism, Community, and Lesbian and Gay Life* (New York: Routledge, 1997); Alexandra Chasin, *Selling Out: The Gay and Lesbian Movement Goes to Market* (New York: Palgrave, 2000); Katherine Sender, *Business, Not Politics: The Making of the Gay Market* (New York: Columbia University Press, 2005), 38. Sender devotes only one sentence to physique magazines and suggests that direct-mail marketing to a gay audience began in the 1980s with catalogs such as Shocking Gray and International Male. Chasin limits her discussion of physiques to their alleged racism.

15. Lillian Faderman and Stuart Timmons, *Gay L.A.: A History of Sexual Outlaws, Power Politics, and Lipstick Lesbians* (New York: Basic Books, 2006), 232.

16. Herbert A. Otto, " 'The Pornographic Fringeland' on the American Newsstand," *Journal of Human Relations* 12 (1964), 375–90.

17. While circulation figures vary and are subject to exaggeration, they can be verified through a number of sources, including court testimony given under oath and private correspondence. On *VIM*, see *U.S. v. Charles J. Anctil et al.*, trial transcript, RG 21, U.S. District Court, Northern District of Illinois, Chicago, Criminal Case Files, 61CR27, National Archives–Chicago Branch, 2505 and 2868. On Guild Press's forty-thousand-person mailing list, see Leon Friedman, *Obscenity: The Complete Oral Arguments Before the Supreme Court* (New York: Chelsea House, 1970), 131; Womack to Tom Men's Shop, August 2, 1966, H. Lynn Womack Papers, Human Sexuality Collection, Division of Rare Books and Manuscript Collections, Cornell University, Ithaca, N.Y.; and *Washington Post*, January 7, 1960. On *Physique Pictorial*, see Micha Ramakers, *Dirty Pictures: Tom of Finland, Masculinity, and Homosexuality* (New York: Stonewall Inn Editions, 2001), 78; *Strength & Health*, May 1961, 15.

18. Ronald Meshbesher, interview by author, April 30, 2013; *U.S. v. Spinar and Germain*, RG 21, U.S. District Court, Fourth Division of Minnesota, Minneapolis, Criminal Case Files, 1966–1969, National Archives–Chicago Branch, Box 11, Case 4-67CR 15.

19. Clark Polak, "The Story Behind Physique Photography," *Drum*, October 1965, 8–15.

20. Sources labeling this an "underground" economy include Faderman and Timmons, *Gay L.A.*, 74; Jean-Francois Monette (director), *Eye on the Guy: Alan B. Stone and the Age of Beefcake* (Montreal, 2006).

21. *Confidential*'s first issue featured a story on a gay wedding. Henry E. Scott, *Shocking True Story: The Rise and Fall of Confidential, "America's Most Scandalous Magazine"* (New York: Pantheon, 2010); "Magazine Goldmine: Run an Article on Queers!" *ONE*, June 1953, 2–12; "Fight for the Gay Dollar," *Citizens News*, September 1964; Meeker, *Contacts Desired*, 151–52; Justin Bengry, "Profit (f)or the Public Good: Sensationalism, Homosexuality and the Postwar Popular Press," *Media History* 20 (2014), 146–66.

22. "The Homosexual Viewpoint," *ONE*, August 1960, 4; Lambert to Holton, August 29, 1955, H folder, ONE Correspondence Files, ONE National Gay and Lesbian Archives, USC Libraries, University of Southern California, Los Angeles.

23. Robert Wood, *Christ and the Homosexual: Some Observations* (New York: Vantage, 1960), 54.

24. Friedman, *Obscenity*, 133.

25. David Halperin, *Gay Shame* (Chicago: University of Chicago Press, 2009), 42; Freddie Francis, "We're a Movement, Not a Market," *Media*, June 7, 2013. Virginia Apuzzo, former director of the Gay and Lesbian Task Force, similarly lamented that she did not fight

all those years "just to be a market niche." Virginia Apuzzo, interview with Kelly Anderson, June 2, 2005, Voices of Feminism Oral History Project, Smith College, Mass.

26. On the importance of lists to both political and commercial enterprises, see Sean Strub, *Body Counts: A Memoir of Politics, Sex, AIDS, and Survival* (New York: Scribner, 2014), 283–302. On the importance of lists to conservative grassroots organizing in the 1980s, see Marvin Leibman, *Coming Out Conservative: An Autobiography* (San Francisco: Chronicle Books, 1992); Dennis W. Johnson, *Democracy for Hire: A History of American Political Consulting* (New York: Oxford University Press, 2016), 192.

27. D'Emilio, *Sexual Politics*, 5.

28. Fritz Peters, *Finistere* (New York: Farrar, Straus, 1951), 47; James Barr, *Quatrefoil* (New York: Greenberg, 1950), 166–69; Victor J. Banis, *The Man from C.A.M.P.* (Albion, N.Y.: MLR Press, 2008). On gay use of classified advertising, see Meeker, *Contacts Desired*; and Justin Bengry, "Films and Filming: The Making of a Queer Marketplace in Pre-Decriminalisation Britain," in *British Queer History: New Approaches and Perspectives*, 244–66 (Manchester, UK: University of Manchester Press, 2013).

29. Victor J. Banis, *Spine Intact, Some Creases: Remembrances of a Paperback Writer* (San Bernardino, Calif.: Borgo Press, 2007), 228–30. Tomoz Associates in Ohio offered to develop film for fellow Grecian Guild members. *Grecian Guild Pictorial*, January 1960, 45. Spectra Photo advertised "Confidential Photo Finishing" in *In Touch*, March–April 1976, 77; Daniel Nicoletta, telephone interview by author, July 3, 2013. For more on Harvey Milk's Castro Camera, see chapter 7.

30. David Steigerwald, T. H. Breen, and Lizabeth Cohen "Exchange: American Consumerism," *Journal of American History* 93 (2006): 385–414; Meg Jacobs, "State of the Field: The Politics of Consumption," *Reviews in American History* 39 (2011), 561–73; Lawrence B. Glickman, ed., *Consumer Society in American History: A Reader* (Ithaca, N.Y.: Cornell University Press, 1999); William Leach, *Land of Desire: Merchants, Power, and the Rise of a New American Culture* (New York: Vintage, 1994); Susan Strasser, *Satisfaction Guaranteed: The Making of the American Mass Market* (Washington, D.C.: Smithsonian Institution Scholarly Press, 1989).

31. T. H. Breen, *The Marketplace of Revolution: How Consumer Politics Shaped American Independence* (Oxford: Oxford University Press, 2004), 496; Daniel Boorstein, *The Americans: The Democratic Experience* (New York: Random House, 1973), 89–164. See also Colin Jones, "The Great Chain of Buying: Medical Advertisements, the Bourgeois Public Sphere, and the Origins of the French Revolution," *American Historical Review* 10 (1996), 12–40.

32. Julia Kirk Blackwelder, *Styling Jim Crow: African American Beauty Training During Segregation* (College Station: Texas A&M University Press 2003); Kathy Peiss, *Hope in a Jar: The Making of America's Beauty Culture* (New York: Metropolitan Books, 1998); Kathy Peiss, *Zoot Suit: The Enigmatic Career of an Extreme Style* (Philadelphia: University of Pennsylvania Press, 2011); Robert Weems, *Desegregating the Dollar: African American Consumerism in the Twentieth Century* (New York: New York University Press, 1998); Adam Green, *Selling the Race: Culture, Community, and Black Chicago, 1940–1955* (Chicago: University of Chicago Press, 2006).

33. Joshua Clark Davis, *From Head Shops to Whole Foods: The Rise and Fall of Activist Entrepreneurs* (New York: Columbia University Press, 2017); Bethany Moreton, *To Serve God*

and Wal-Mart: The Making of Christian Free Enterprise (Cambridge, Mass.: Harvard University Press, 2009).

34. Lizabeth Cohen, *A Consumers' Republic: The Politics of Mass Consumption in Postwar America* (New York: Vintage, 2003), 295–309.

35. Lorraine Baltera, "No Gay Market Yet, Admen, Gays Agree," *Advertising Age*, August 28, 1972; Blaine J. Branchik, "Out in the Market: A History of the Gay Market Segment in the United States," *Journal of Macromarketing* 22, no. 1 (2002), 86–97; Gluckman and Reed, *Homo Economics*.

36. John Howard, *Men Like That: A Southern Queer History* (Chicago: University Of Chicago Press, 1999); Meeker, *Contacts Desired*.

37. Elizabeth Fraterrigo, *Playboy and the Making of the Good Life in Modern America* (New York: Oxford University Press, 2001); Brian Hoffman, *Naked: A Cultural History of American Nudism* (New York: New York University Press, 2015).

38. Elizabeth Heineman, *Before Porn Was Legal: The Erotica Empire of Beate Uhse* (Chicago: University of Chicago Press, 2011); Justin Bengry, "Courting the Pink Pound: Men Only and the Queer Consumer, 1935–39," *History Workshop Journal* no. 68 (2009); Justin Bengry, "Queer Profits: Homosexual Scandal and the Origins of Legal Reform in Britain," in *Queer 1950s: Rethinking Sexuality in the Postwar Years*, ed. Heike Bauer and Matt Cook (New York: Palgrave Macmillan, 2012), 167–82; Whitney Strub, "Challenging the Anti-Pleasure League: *Physique Pictorial* and the Cultivation of Gay Politics," in *Modern Print Activism in the United States*, ed. Rachel Schreiber (Burlington, Vt.: Ashgate, 2013); Stephen Vider, "'Oh Hell, May, Why Don't You People Have a Cookbook?': Camp Humor and Gay Domesticity," *American Quarterly* 65, no. 4 (December 2013), 877–904.

39. Deidre McCloskey, "Queer Markets," in *Media/Queered: Visibility and its Discontents*, ed. Kevin G. Barnhurst (New York: Peter Lang, 2007), 83–87.

40. Lisa Duggan, *The Twilight of Equality: Neoliberalism, Cultural Politics, and the Attack on Democracy* (Boston: Beacon Press, 2003), 50; Nan Alamilla Boyd, "Sex and Tourism: The Economic Implications of the Gay Marriage Movement," *Radical History Review* 2008, no. 100 (Winter 2008), 223–35.

41. See Martin Meeker, "Behind the Mask of Respectability: Reconsidering the Mattachine Society and Male Homophile Practice, 1950s and 1960s," *Journal of the History of Sexuality* 10, no. 1 (January 2001), 78–116. In arguing for the radical nature of homophile activism, Meeker emphasizes its commercial endeavors, particularly Hal Call's Pan-Graphic Press. For a satirical look at this complicated relationship, see "The Body Beautiful," *ONE*, June 1955, 4–6.

INTRODUCTION

1. David L. Chapman and Brett Josef Grubisic, *American Hunks: The Muscular Male Body in Popular Culture 1860–1970* (Vancouver: Arsenal Pulp Press, 2009), 8. Chapman asserts that Chula Vista possessed "enough urbanity" that its magazine shop carried such magazines. This perpetuates the flawed notion that such items were found only in cities.

2. Paul Monette, *Becoming a Man: Half a Life Story* (New York: Harper Collins, 1992), 82–83. *Tomorrow's Man* started publication in 1952 but might not have been distributed

in Andover until later. By 1961 there were well over a dozen similar periodicals, so Monette might be remembering a different magazine. He remembers buying his first copy of *Muscleboy*, which debuted in 1963, in Boston a few years later.

3. Michael Denneny, interview by author, July 29, 2012; *Physique Pictorial (PP)*, Spring 1957; Owen Keehnen, "Tom of Finland: Exposed! Talking with Biographer F. Valentine Hooven III," *Out in Albuquerque*, October 1993, http://www.queerculturalcenter.org/Pages /Keehnen/vanHooven.html. See also F. Valentine Hooven III, *Tom of Finland: His Life and Times* (New York: St. Martin's Press, 1993), 87.

4. Michael Denneny, interview by author, July 29, 2012; *VIM*, May 1957. Denneny discussed the impact of these images in Mingus, "Through the Looking Glass," *New York Native*, July 7–13, 1986. Denneny went on to become an editor at St. Martin's Press, responsible for its extensive gay fiction and nonfiction list. See Donald Weise, "The History of Gay Publishing in One Career: Interview with Michael Denneny," Slate.com, October 27, 2014.

5. John Waters, *Role Models* (New York: Farrar, Straus & Giroux, 2010), 220; Charles Leslie, interview with author, March 18, 2011; Kevin Clarke, *The Art of Looking: The Life and Treasures of Collector Charles Leslie* (Berlin: Bruno Gmuender, 2015), 41; Edmund White, *The Beautiful Room Is Empty* (New York: Knopf, 1988), 171; "Edmund White on Writing About Gay Sex," *Creative Independent*, November 3, 2016, https://thecreativeindependent.com /people/edmund-white-on-writing-about-gay-sex/. See also Jennifer Kroot (dir.), *To Be Takei* (Starz Digital Media, 2014); Ron Williams, *San Francisco's Native "Sissy" Son: A Coming Out Memoir*, Blurb.com, 2013; Ilppo Pohjola (dir.) *Daddy and the Muscle Academy* (Finland: Zeitgeist Films, 1991).

6. Michael Syrjanen, interview with author, October 24, 2011. Syrjanen's father ran a drug store in Florence, Wisconsin, in the 1950s that carried physique magazines. Little scholarship exists on magazine distribution, which was dominated by the American News Company until 1957. See Gerald Jones, *Men of Tomorrow: Geeks, Gangsters and the Birth of the Comic Book* (New York: Basic Books, 2005), 279.

7. Monette, *Becoming a Man*, 96; Jerry Weiss, comment on "A Short History of Physique Magazines," by Jesse Monteagudo, *Belerico Project*, February 11, 2011, http://www.bilerico.com/2011 /02/a_short_history_of_physique_magazines.php. See also Berry Werth, *The Scarlet Professor: Newton Arvin: A Literary Life Shattered by Scandal* (New York: Nan A. Talese, 2001).

8. *U.S. v. Spinar and Germain*, RG 21, U.S. District Court, Fourth Division of Minnesota, Minneapolis, Criminal Case Files, 1966–1969, National Archives–Chicago Branch, Case 4-67CR15, 765, July 26, 1967.

9. Previous scholarship that has argued that physique magazines helped create community includes Larry Gross, *Up From Invisibility* (New York: Columbia University Press, 2001), 222; F. Valentine Hooven, *Beefcake: The Muscle Magazines of America 1950–1970*, (Cologne: Taschen, 1996); and Steve Hogan and Lee Hudson, eds., *Completely Queer: The Gay and Lesbian Encyclopedia* (New York: Holt, 1998), 440.

10. Gail Bederman, *Manliness & Civilization* (Chicago: University of Chicago Press, 1995); John F. Kasson, *Houdini, Tarzan and the Perfect Man: The White Male Body and the Challenge of Modernity in America* (New York: Hill and Wang, 2001); David L. Chapman, *Sandow the Magnificent: Eugene Sandow and the Beginnings of Bodybuilding* (Urbana: University of Illinois Press, 2006).

11. Joe Weider and Ben Weider, *Brothers of Iron: Building the Weider Empire* (Champagne, Ill.: Sports Publishing, 2006); John D. Fair, *Mr. America: The Tragic History of a Body-building Icon* (Austin: University of Texas Press, 2015); John D. Fair, *Muscletown U.S.A.: Bob Hoffman and the Manly Culture of York Barbell* (State College: Pennsylvania State University Press, 1999); Randy Roach, *Muscle, Smoke, and Mirrors*, vol. 1 (Bloomington, Ind.: AuthorHouse, 2008); Peary Rader, "Are You a Bodybuilder or a Weightlifter?" *Iron Man*, August–September 1956, 7. The dispute between Hoffman and Weider even led to litigation, *Weider v. Hoffman*, 238 F. Supp. 437 (1965).

12. George Chauncey, *Gay New York: Gender, Urban Culture, and the Making of a Gay Male World, 1890–1940* (New York: Basic Books, 1994); John Donald Gustav-Wrathall, *Take the Stranger by the Hand: Same-Sex Relations and the YMCA* (Chicago: University of Chicago Press, 1998).

13. *PP*, April 1961, 25, and April 1973, 25. Jim Kepner and Glenn Carrington were also big fans. See Jim Kepner Papers, folder 4, box 28, ONE National Gay and Lesbian Archives, USC Libraries, University of Southern California; Glenn Carrington Papers, Schomburg Center for Research in Black Culture, New York Public Library (NYPL).

14. Lurie quoted in Roach, *Muscle, Smoke, and Mirrors*, 273; Jim Morris, interview by author, June 4, 2008; Chuck Renslow, interview by author, May 24, 2008; Dian Hanson and Reed Massengill, *George Quaintance* (Cologne: Taschen, 2010); Reed Massengill, *The Male Ideal: Lon of New York and the Masculine Physique* (New York: Universe, 2003).

15. On the dangers of male-to-male glances, see "Jonathan Ned Katz: Turning from History to Art," *Gay and Lesbian Review*, January–February 2010, 34–35.

16. *PP*, June 1954.

17. Jim Edwards to Etienne, December 25, 1963, and January 8, 1964, correspondence files, Chuck Renslow Collection, Leather Archives & Museum, Chicago.

18. *Strength & Health*, June 1957, 17; *Iron Man*, September 1956, 47–49, and April–May 1958, 25.

19. *Rave*, September, 1957, 12–15, and January 1958, 48–51; *Hush-Hush*, September 1961, 13.

20. Stephen Birmingham, "For Love of Muscle," *Sports Illustrated*, August 3, 1959, 61–64; *New York Times*, December 17, 1963, 1.

21. Donald Webster Cory, *The Homosexual and His Society: A View from Within* (New York: Citadel Press, 1963), 83–87; Robert W. Wood, *Christ and the Homosexual: Some Observations* (New York: Vantage, 1960), 65; Jim Harper, interview with author, July 14, 2013.

22. Ira Wallach, *Muscle Beach* (New York: Dell, 1959), 128, 134; Bud Clifton, *Muscle Boy* (New York: Ace Books, 1958).

23. William Asher (dir.), *Muscle Beach Party* (American International Pictures, 1964). The Jack Fanny character is based on Vic Tanny, owner of a chain of gyms in Southern California. See Chapman and Grubisic, *American Hunks*, 315.

24. Charles Gaines and George Butler, *Pumping Iron: The Art and Sport of Bodybuilding* (New York: Simon & Schuster, 1981); George Butler, *Arnold Schwarzenegger: A Portrait* (New York: Simon and Schuster, 1990), 50–52; Daniel Delis Hill, "Men in Briefs," *Gay and Lesbian Review*, November–December 2011, 23.

25. Christopher Nealon, *Foundlings: Lesbian and Gay Historical Emotion Before Stonewall* (Durham, N.C.: Duke University Press, 2001); Thomas Waugh, *Hard to Imagine:*

Gay Male Eroticism in Photography and Film from Their Beginnings to Stonewall (New York: Columbia University Press, 1996), 222. Waugh provides considerable counterevidence of his claim that this "open secret" was never articulated, but largely in footnotes (433).

26. Jackie Hatton, "The Pornography Empire of H. Lynn Womack," *Thresholds: Viewing Culture* 7 (Spring 1993), 8–32; Tracy D. Morgan, "Pages of Whiteness: Race, Physique Magazines, and the Emergence of Public Gay Culture," in *Queer Studies: A Lesbian, Gay, Bisexual, and Transgender Anthology*, ed. Brett Beemyn and Mickey Eliason (New York: New York University Press, 1996), 280–97.

27. Wayne Stanley, *The Complete Reprint of Physique Pictorial: 1951–1990* (Cologne: Taschen, 1997). Tim Wilbur's "Vintage Physique Photography" subscription website at http://Tim invermont.com is now the most comprehensive venue for accessing these magazines, including nearly twenty thousand gay and/or bodybuilding magazines from the 1890s through the 1990s and over fifty thousand images from nearly six thousand photography studios.

28. One of the best collections to give a sense of the scope of this consumer network is the John M. Eccles Papers, 1946–1977, at the University of Washington, Seattle.

29. Sources who ignore or obscure these legal battles include Chapman and Grubisic, *American Hunks*, 336; Jeffrey Escoffier, *Bigger than Life: The History of Gay Porn Cinema from Beefcake to Hardcore* (Philadelphia: Running Press, 2009), 19; and Morgan, "Pages of Whiteness." Tracy Morgan argues that physique publishers ignored censorship issues and were powerless to do anything. For more astute political interpretations, see Whitney Strub, *Perversion for Profit: The Politics of Pornography and the Rise of the New Right* (New York: Columbia University Press, 2011); and Rodger and John C. Watson Streitmatter, "Herman Lynn Womack: Pornographer as First Amendment Pioneer," *Journalism History* 28 (Summer 2002): 56–66.

30. Justin Spring, *Secret Historian: The Life and Times of Samuel Steward, Professor, Tattoo Artist, and Sexual Renegade* (New York: Farrar, Straus and Giroux, 2010), makes a similar argue about the change in censorship laws.

31. Anonymous drawings, "Old School" and "New School," folder 6, box 2, Eccles Papers. See also GYM, June 1959, 44.

32. PP, June 1954; Jennifer Evans, "Queer Beauty: Image and Acceptance in the Expanded Public Sphere," in *Globalizing Beauty: Consumerism and Body Aesthetics in the Twentieth Century*, ed. Hartmut Berghoff and Thomas Kühne (New York: Palgrave Macmillan, 2013), 91–107. See also David M. Halperin, *Saint Foucault: Towards a Gay Hagiography* (New York: Oxford University Press, 1995), 115–18.

33. Kilfoyle to McInnis, n.d., and McGinnis to Kilfoyle, September, 26, 1967, Womack Papers, Cornell University; *Tomorrow's Man* (TM), April 1963; *Grecian Guild Pictorial* (GGP), September 1966; VIM, February 1966.

34. Johnny A. Pitts to *Fizeek Art Quarterly*, June 21, 1967, George Fisher Papers, Cornell University, Ithaca, N.Y.

35. PP, Winter 1955.

36. Carrington Papers, NYPL.

37. Mingus, "Through the Looking Glass," *New York Native*, July 7–13, 1986.

38. *PP*, Summer and Fall 1955.

39. *PP*, Fall 1956.

40. "Beefcake: Physique Photography of Dave Martin" curated by Michele Kraus, exhibit at Cantor Center at Stanford University, 2007, http://tusb.stanford.edu/2007/01/beefcake_cantor.html.

41. Letter to Editor, *GGP*, August 1959, 44. Scholars who insist on the erasure of black men from physique magazines have relied on an extremely small source base. See Morgan, "Pages of Whiteness"; and Rahul K. Gairola, "White Skin, Red Masks: 'Playing Indian' in Queer Images from *Physique Pictorial*, 1957–67," *Liminalities: A Journal of Performance Studies* 8 (2012), 1–17.

42. Quaintance complained of a "constant stream of letters" in *GGP*, Spring 1956, 12–22. Conrad Germain testified under oath to having "thousands" of customer letters indicating postal authority abuses. *U.S. v. Spinar* trial transcript, 827. Mizer considered his customers letters so incriminating that he gave them to the Kinsey Institute for safekeeping. Mizer to Kinsey, August 5, 1955, Kinsey Era Correspondence (KEC), Kinsey Institute, Indiana University, Bloomington.

43. Jess Stearn, *The Sixth Man* (New York: MacFadden-Bartell, 1961), 15.

44. Spring, *Secret Historian*, 202.

45. Thor Studio Correspondence, 1953–1955, Kinsey Institute, Indiana University, Bloomington. Although many of the letters in the Kinsey Era Correspondence Files indicate that Kinsey collected customer letters and surveys from Bob Mizer and many other physique publishers, the Kinsey Institute cannot locate them.

46. *Frontier Athletic Club Newsletter* no. 7, 1960, folder 9, box 1, Eccles Papers.

47. *TM*, December 1956; *GGP*, July 1957; John Palatinus model sheet, n.d., http://timinvermont.com.

48. See Elija Cassidy, *Gay Men, Identity and Social Media: A Culture of Participatory Reluctance* (New York: Routledge, 2018).

49. Heather Murray, "Free for All Lesbians: Lesbian Cultural Production and Consumption in the United States During the 1970s," *Journal of the History of Sexuality* 16 (May 2007), 251–75; Victoria A. Brownworth, "Barbara Grier: Climbing the Ladder," in *Before Stonewall: Activists for Gay and Lesbian Rights in Historical Context*, ed. Vern L. Bullough (New York: Harrington Park Press, 2002), 253–64. See also Lynn Cornella, *Vibrator Nation: How Feminist Sex-Toy Stores Changed the Business of Pleasure* (Durham, N.C.: Duke University Press, 2017).

50. Bonnie Morris, "Olivia Records: The Production of a Movement," *Journal of Lesbian Studies* 19, no. 3 (July 2015), 290–304; Judith A. Peraino, *Listening to the Sirens: Musical Technologies of Queer Identity from Homer to Hedwig* (Berkeley: University of California Press, 2006), 163–65.

51. Kinsey's research suggested that men are much more responsive than women to nude images. Alfred Kinsey, *Sexual Behavior in the Human Female* (Bloomington: Indiana University Press, 1998), 652; Cindy Patton, "Unmediated Lust? The Improbable Space of Lesbian Desires," in *Stolen Glances: Lesbians Take Photographs*, ed. Tessa Boffin and Jean Fraser (London: Pandora, 1991); Rebecca Beirne, *Lesbians in Television and Text After the Millennium* (New York: Palgrave Macmillan, 2008).

52. M. V. Lee Badgett, *Money, Myths and Change: The Economic Lives of Lesbians and Gay Men* (Chicago: University of Chicago Press, 2001); Alexandra Chasin, *Selling Out: The Gay and Lesbian Movement Goes to Market* (New York: Palgrave, 2000), xvii.

1. EMERGING FROM THE MUSCLE MAGAZINES: BOB MIZER'S ATHLETIC MODEL GUILD

1. Bob Mizer Diary, March 18 and April 23, 1940, Bob Mizer Foundation Permanent Collection, Bob Mizer Foundation, San Francisco, Calif.; *Poly Optimist*, March 14, 1940; Boris Brasol, *Oscar Wilde: The Man, the Artist, the Martyr* (New York: Scribner, 1938); Dian Hanson, *Bob's World: The Life and Boys of AMG's Bob Mizer* (Cologne: Taschen, 2009); Bob Mizer, interview by Pat Allen, February 17, 1992, ONE National Gay and Lesbian Archives, USC Libraries, University of Southern California, Los Angeles (hereafter ONE Archives). Mizer's use of the term "Urning" underscores how widely he read in the field of sexology, but it also demonstrates his early ability to use coded language to speak to an insider audience while confounding outside authority figures.

2. Hart Crane quoted in William J. Mann, *Behind the Screen: How Gays and Lesbians Shaped Hollywood, 1910–1969* (New York: Viking, 2001), 87. On Pershing Square, see Daniel Hurewitz, *Bohemian Los Angeles and the Making of Modern Politics* (Berkeley: University of California Press, 2007), 49–52. For another gay man who first came out in Pershing Square and later went on to publish a physique-style magazine, see Kenneth Marlowe, *Mr. Madam: Confessions of a Male Madam* (New York: Sherbourne Press, 1964).

3. Mizer Diary, February 4 and May 12, 1940. Gay parties with models in posing straps or in the nude were not uncommon. Alfonso Hanagan held similar parties in New York in the 1940s and 1950s. See Reed Massengill, *The Male Ideal: Lon of New York and the Masculine Physique* (New York: Universe, 2004), 41.

4. *Strength & Health*, April 1945, 49.

5. Bob Mizer, "Pros and Cons of Pen Pal Clubs," *Grecian Guild Pictorial* (GGP), March 1961, 7–9; *Strength & Health*, May 1945, 46; *Physique Pictorial* (PP), Summer 1957.

6. Mizer Diary, May 24 and June 25, 1945; David Chapman, ed., *Hollywood Nudes: The Physique Photos of Fred Kovert* (London: Heretic Books, 2000); Reed Massengill, *Uncovered: Rare Vintage Male Nudes* (New York: Universe, 2009), 27. Kovert's legal name was Covert.

7. Harold Zinkin, *Remembering Muscle Beach: Where Hard Bodies Began; Photographs and Memories* (Santa Monica, Calif.: Angel City Press, 1999); Hanson, *Bob's World*, 185; Bob Mizer, interview by Pat Allen, February 17, 1992, ONE Archives.

8. Massengill, *Male Ideal*.

9. Jason Goldman, "'The Golden Age of Gay Porn': Nostalgia and the Photography of Wilhelm von Gloeden," *GLQ: A Journal of Lesbian and Gay Studies* 12, no. 2 (2006), 237–58; Thomas Waugh, *Hard to Imagine: Gay Male Eroticism in Photography and Film from Their Beginnings to Stonewall* (New York: Columbia University Press, 1996), 72–77.

10. Robert Mainardi, interview by author, November 12, 2011; Robert Mainardi, *Strong Man: Vintage Photos of a Masculine Icon* (San Francisco: Council Oaks Books, 2001), 24; David L. Chapman and Brett Josef Grubisic, *American Hunks: The Muscular Male Body in Popular Culture, 1860–1970* (Vancouver: Arsenal Pulp Press, 2009), 118, 159, 179; John Hernic ad in

Strength & Health, July 1935, 83; Ritter ad in *Strength & Health*, December 1935, 39; Waugh, *Hard to Imagine*, 208.

11. John D. Fair, *Muscletown USA: Bob Hoffman and the Manly Culture of York Barbell* (University Park: Pennsylvania State University Press, 1999), 42; David L. Chapman, *Sandow the Magnificent: Eugen Sandow and the Beginnings of Bodybuilding* (Urbana: University of Illinois Press, 2006); Mark Adams, *Mr. America: How Muscular Millionaire Bernarr Macfadden Transformed the Nation Through Sex, Salad, and the Ultimate Starvation Diet* (New York: Harper, 2009).

12. The model agency legend seems to have originated with Timothy Lewis's short biographical essay in Winston Leyland, *PHYSIQUE: A Pictorial History of the Athletic Model Guild* (San Francisco: Gay Sunshine Press, 1982), the first coffee-table book of Mizer's work. It is repeated in F. Valentine Hooven, *Beefcake: The Muscle Magazines of America, 1950–1970* (Cologne: Taschen, 1995), 26; Wayne E. Stanley, introduction to *The Complete Reprint of "Physique Pictorial": 1951–1990* (Cologne: Taschen, 1997), 11; and Thom Fitzgerald (dir.), *Beefcake* (Strand Releasing, 1998). David Hurles, who knew Mizer well, also debunks the legend. See Volker Janssen, ed., *Bob Mizer: Athletic Model Guild, American Photography of the Male Nude, 1940–1970*, vol. 7 (London: Janssen, 2007). Mizer printed "Special Privileges of AMG Models" cards, but these seem to have functioned as a recruiting tool to get models to pose. Later in life he acted as "Hollywood pimp" for wealthy "amateur photographers" who were looking for models, which may have been the origin of the legend. See Charles Casillo, *Outlaw: The Lives and Careers of John Rechy* (Los Angeles: Advocate Books, 2002), 100.

13. Chapman and Grubisic, *American Hunks*, 132; Daniel Delis Hill, *History of Men's Underwear and Swimwear* (n.p.: Daniel Delis Hill, 2011); Lena Lencek and Gideon Bosker, *Making Waves: Swimsuits and the Undressing of America* (San Francisco: Chronicle Books, 1989), 70.

14. *Look*, November 17, 1942; Bruce H. Joffe, *A Hint of Homosexuality? "Gay" and Homoerotic Imagery in American Print Advertising* (Philadelphia: Xlibris, 2007), 83–89; Robert Hofler, *The Man Who Invented Rock Hudson: The Pretty Boys and Dirty Deals of Henry Willson* (New York: Carroll & Graf, 2005), 120; Massengill, *Male Ideal*, 42.

15. Randy Shilts, *The Mayor of Castro Street: The Life and Times of Harvey Milk* (New York: St. Martin's Press, 1982), 3–4. Shilts titled his first chapter "The Men Without Their Shirts." In 1961 a fifty-one-year-old stage manager and his twenty-one-year-old friend were arrested in Riverside Park for "sunbathing with bared chests." News clipping, June 28, 1961, box 16, George Fisher Papers, Cornell University, Ithaca, N.Y..

16. Mizer Diary, July 23 and 25, 1945. Much of the considerable literature on Mizer highlights his arrests in 1947 and 1954, but none discusses this 1945 raid on his house. This may have been part of what historians have identified as a 1940s crackdown on magazine and mail-order obscenity by the postmaster general. Lee Kennett, *For the Duration: The United States Goes to War, Pearl Harbor–1942* (New York: Scribner, 1985), 162; Jean Preer, *"Esquire v. Walker*: The Postmaster General and 'The Magazine for Men,'" *Prologue* 23 (Spring 1990).

17. Mizer specifies in contemporary court documents that he began a commercial photography business on September 1, 1946, after "having it as a hobby since 1944." *California v. Mizer*, Superior Court of California, Probation Officer's Report, May 1, 1947, Kinsey

Institute, Indiana University, Bloomington. Mizer considered 1946 the beginning of his business since he celebrated its twentieth anniversary in 1966. See *AMG Bulletin* 66-B, n.d., Mizer Foundation.

18. Album C, Mizer Foundation, n.d. (circa October 1946); Mizer to Kinsey, May 25, 1948, Kinsey Era Correspondence (KEC), Kinsey Institute, Indiana University, Bloomington; *Strength & Health*, September 1946, 29, and February 1947, 26; *PP*, Spring 1956. AMG's images of Forrester Millard (a.k.a. Forrester D'Orlac) continued to be popular with physique customers. See *GGP*, November 1957; and *Muscles à Go-Go*, March 1967.

19. Album W, 1948, Mizer Foundation; Mizer to Kinsey, May 25, 1948, KEC. Based on a cursory examination of only a few issues of *Physique Pictorial*, cultural critic Daniel Harris argues that Mizer emphasized the working-class heterosexuality of models and encouraged gay male readers to feel "self-contempt." Daniel Harris, *The Rise and Fall of Gay Culture* (New York: Hyperion, 1997), 86–90.

20. Albums B and N, Mizer Foundation.

21. Album C, Mizer Foundation.

22. *People of California v. Robert H. Mizer*, C-14164, Probation Officer's Report, May 1, 1947, Superior Court of California, Kinsey Institute.

23. *People of California v. Robert H. Mizer*, C-14164, Probation Officer's Report, May 1, 1947; *PP*, January 1961, 2; Bob Mizer to mother, Mizer Foundation, http://bobmizerfoundation.org, accessed September 23, 2014. In numerous popular histories of AMG, this 1947 arrest is misidentified as one for disseminating obscene materials. Stanley, introduction to *Complete Reprint*, 12.

24. *AMG Bulletin* 16, January 1950, Mizer Foundation.

25. Album V, July 1948, Mizer Foundation.

26. Album K, Mizer Foundation.

27. *Physique Photo News* 1, no. 1, May 1951; *PP*, November 1951. The other five studios were Spartan, Russ Warner, Bruce of Los Angeles, Richard Caldwell, and Al Urban. Only with the third issue in May 1952 did Mizer begin to charge fifteen cents.

28. *Iron Man*, September 1949, 34, and March 1953, 42; *PP*, Summer 1957, 4 (a typographical error suggests the censorship effort was in 1956 instead of 1946). *Strength & Health* continued to carry physique photo ads throughout much of the 1950s, but Post Office pressure was a recurring threat. See Chapman and Grubisic, *American Hunks*, 279.

29. Mizer to Kinsey, January 1952, August 13, 1951, and November 5, 1951, KEC; Bob Mizer, interview by Pat Allen, February 17, 1992, ONE Archives; Jim Dolinsky, *Bruce of Los Angeles* (Berlin: Bruno Gmünder, 1989); Victor J. Banis, *Spine Intact, Some Creases: Remembrances of a Paperback Writer* (San Bernardino, Calif.: Borgo Press, 2007), 228.

30. Mizer to Gebhard, April 30, 1964, Gebhard correspondence, Kinsey Institute. Mizer recommended the Kinsey reports to readers, suggesting "your whole life might be changed." *PP*, Spring 1958, 10.

31. Kinsey to Mizer, November 21, 1951, KEC. Through his close collaboration with Mizer, Kinsey also had occasional correspondence with physique photographers Ralph Kelly, Bruce Bellas, Don Whitman, Russ Warner, and Bob Delmonteque.

32. Bob Mizer, interview by Pat Allen, February 17, 1992, ONE Archives; Herbert Clement to AMG, n.d. (circa 1949), KEC; Ben Sorenson quoted in Hanson, *Bob's World*, 185. The Clement letter seems to be the only customer letter preserved in the Kinsey records.

33. Bob Mizer, interview by Pat Allen, February 17, 1992, ONE Archives.

34. *AMG Bulletin* 16, January 1950, Mizer Foundation.

35. Chuck Renslow, interview by author, May 24, 2008; Bob Mizer, interview by Pat Allen, February 24, 1992, ONE Archives; *PP*, Winter 1957, 5, and January 1960, 5; Womack to Benson, March 29, 1958, H. Lynn Womack Papers, Human Sexuality Collection, Division of Rare and Manuscript Collections, Cornell University.

36. *AMG Bulletin* 67-A, March 1967, Mizer Foundation; *Young Adonis* 1, no. 1, 1963.

37. See John D'Emilio, *Sexual Politics, Sexual Communities* (Chicago: University of Chicago Press, 1983), 68.

38. *PP*, October 1953, 2. Kris Studio sent an early mass mailing addressed to "Dear Physique Pictorial subscriber." Kris Studio Business Files, Chuck Renslow Collection, Leather Archives & Museum, Chicago. Editors of *Art & Physique* from Louisiana in 1960 thanked Athletic Model Guild, "who have in the past helped us so much to make *Art & Physique* a success." *Art & Physique*, series 8 (1960), 28, New York Public Library (NYPL).

39. Mizer discussed disagreement with Quaintance in *PP*, Spring 1956, and with Fontaine of Apollo Studios, *PP*, November 1961, 2, and October 1963, 8.

40. *PP*, Winter 1957.

41. *Art & Physique*, series 8, 1960, NYPL; *PP*, Fall 1954; *PP*, Winter 1954–55; European tours, *PP*, March 1962, 13.

42. Artists whom Mizer promoted included Ray Richardson, Andy Kozak, David Damon, Arthur Lewis, Kenneth Kendall, and Lloyd Steel.

43. *PP*, March 1954.

44. Reed Massengill, *George Quaintance*, ed. Dian Hanson (Cologne: Taschen, 2010); Quaintance to Cory, April 27, 1953, Mattachine NY Microfilm, NYPL; Robert Wood, interview with author, July 7, 2014, Concord, N.H..

45. Michael Bronski, "Blatant Male Pulchritude: The Art of George Quaintance and Bruce Weber's Bear Pond," *Art Papers* 16, no. 4 (August 1992), 26–29; Massengill, *Quaintance*, 144; Micha Ramakers, *Dirty Pictures: Tom of Finland, Masculinity, and Homosexuality* (New York: Stonewall Inn Editions, 2001); Nayland Blake, "Tom of Finland, an Appreciation," *Out/Look*, Fall 1988, 36–45.

46. *PP*, Summer 1956, 14, 28.

47. *AMG Bulletin* 57, October 1961, and 66, 1966, Mizer Foundation.

48. *PP*, June 1954; Mizer Diary, February 2, 1940; Christopher Reed, *Art and Homosexuality: A History of Ideas* (New York: Oxford University Press, 2011), 93–106.

49. Michael Sherry, *Gay Artists in Modern American Culture: An Imagined Conspiracy* (Chapel Hill: University of North Carolina Press, 2007), 17–25; Laurel Brake, "'Gay Discourse' and *The Artist and Journal of Home Culture*," in *Nineteenth-Century Media and the Construction of Identities*, ed. Laurel Brake, Bill Bell, and David Finkelstein (New York: Palgrave, 2000), 271–94; *PP*, Spring 1955, 15, 27.

50. "Revlon Buys 'Confidential' as Fall Bow," *Billboard*, September 18, 1954, 5; Jack Holland, "Man of Controversy," *TV-Radio Life*, July 31–August 6, 1954, 4; "Slice of Life," *Time*, August 2, 1954, 37; "The TV Show That Made America Gasp," undated clipping from Don Lucas Papers, Gay, Lesbian, Bisexual, Transgender Historical Society (GLBTHS), San Francisco; Edward Alwood, *Straight News: Gays, Lesbians, and the News Media* (New York: Columbia University Press, 1996), 31–32; Stephen Tropiano, *The Prime Time Closet:*

A History of Gays and Lesbians on TV (New York: Applause Theatre & Cinema Books, 2002), 3–4.

51. Paul V. Coates, "Well, Medium and Rare," *Los Angeles Mirror*, May 4, 1954.

52. Paul V. Coates, "Well, Medium and Rare," *Los Angeles Mirror*, May 18 and 21, 1954; *PP*, Fall 1955 and Winter 1957; Mizer to Kinsey, October 26, 1954, and July 14, 1955, KEC. On the Chandlers's influence, see Robert Gottlieb, *Thinking Big: The Story of the Los Angeles Times, Its Publishers and Their Influence on Southern California* (New York: Penguin, 1977).

53. *People v. Robert H. Mizer*, trial transcript, no. 23722, Municipal Court of Los Angeles; and Philip E. Grey, deputy city attorney, CRA 3216, Los Angeles (1954), both in Mizer Legal Documents, Kinsey Institute; Mizer to Kinsey, October 26, 1954, KEC; Kenneth Frank, "America on Guard! Homosexuals, Inc.," *Confidential*, May 1954.

54. Mizer to Kinsey, October 26, 1954, February 1955, and July 18, 1955, KEC.

55. U.S. Congress, Senate, Juvenile Delinquency (Obscene and Pornographic Materials), Hearings Before a Subcommittee of the Committee on the Judiciary, 84th Cong., 1st sess., 1955, 385; Mizer to Kinsey, July 14, 1955, KEC.

56. *PP*, Spring 1956, 13, and Fall 1957, 5; "Ex-Policeman Convicted of Molesting Girl, 13," *Los Angeles Daily Mirror*, June 6, 1957, "Ex-Kefauver Aide Quits Job Over Sex Movies," *Los Angeles Times*, September 1, 1957. For the Kefauver hearings, see Whitney Strub, *Perversion for Profit: The Politics of Pornography and the Rise of the New Right* (New York: Columbia University Press, 2010), 25–27.

57. D'Emilio, *Sexual Politics*, 77–87. Like most historical accounts of Paul Coates's sensational coverage of homosexuality, D'Emilio ignores his attack on *Physique Pictorial*.

58. Mizer to Kinsey, October 26, 1954, and July 14, 1955; Kinsey to Bruce Bellas, July 16, 1956; Mizer to Kinsey, October 15, 1948, KEC.

59. *PP*, Fall and Winter 1955, Fall and Winter 1957, and January 1969. Among the censorship texts Mizer referenced was Robert Kramer, ed., *Obscenity and the Arts*, special issue of *Law and Contemporary Problems* (Duke University School of Law, Autumn 1955). Whitney Strub, one of the few historians to see how Mizer "cultivated a politically conscious counterpublic" in his editorials, dates Mizer's politicization to his arrest in 1954. Whitney Strub, "Challenging the Anti-Pleasure League: *Physique Pictorial* and the Cultivation of a Gay Politics," in *Modern Print Activism in the United States*, ed. Rachel Schreiber (Burlington, Vt.: Ashgate, 2013), 161–77.

60. *PP*, Fall 1956, 2.

61. *Iron Man*, May–June 1949 and September 1956, 47–49. *Physique Photo News*, May 1951, encouraged readers to support *Iron Man*; Mizer to Kinsey, February 25, 1952, KEC. *Iron Man* published a second indictment of homosexuals in bodybuilding: Richard Alan, "Bodybuilding 1958," *Iron Man* 17, April–May 1958, 25.

62. "Homosexuality and Bodybuilding," *PP*, Fall 1956, 17. A few years later Mizer penned a second editorial on the subject, "Muscle-He-Men vs. Sissies," *PP*, June 1960, 13. Martin Meeker reports that Hal Call at the Mattachine Society was happy with the referral and quickly received a dozen inquiries. Martin Meeker, *Contacts Desired: Gay and Lesbian Communications and Community, 1940s–1970s* (Chicago: University of Chicago Press, 2006), 273. On Liberace, see Darden Asbury Pyron, *Liberace: An American Boy* (Chicago: University of Chicago Press, 2000).

63. Letters from Our Readers, *PP*, Spring 1957, 4.

64. Mizer to Kinsey, August 5, 1955, KEC. The only surviving letter in the Kinsey collection asked Mizer to be more upfront about homosexuality.

65. Rebecca Peabody et al., eds., *Pacific Standard Time: Los Angeles Art, 1945–1980* (Los Angeles: Getty Research Institute and J. Paul Getty Museum, 2011); Richard Meyer, *Outlaw Representation: Censorship and Homosexuality in Twentieth-Century American Art* (Boston: Beacon Press, 2002); Rachael Thomas, *Jack Pierson: Angel Youth* (Dublin: Irish Museum of Modern Art, 2008); Daniell Cornell, ed., *Backyard Oasis: The Swimming Pool in Southern California Photography, 1945–1982* (Palm Springs, Calif.: Palm Springs Art Museum and Delmonico Books, 2012).

66. Manuel boyFrank to Barton Hovarth, quoted in Manuel boyFrank to Henry Gerber, April 16, 1944, Manuel boyFrank Papers, ONE Archives. The best-known depiction of Mizer as naive and isolated is the fictionalized docudrama by Thom Fitzgerald (dir.), *Beefcake* (Strand Releasing, 1998). Diane Hanson suggests a more sexually and politically aware Mizer in *Bob's World*.

67. Mizer to Kinsey, July 14, 1948, KEC.

68. Author interview with Durk Dehrer, April 11, 2015; Hanson, *Bob's World*; *PP*, August 1960, 28, and Fall 1957, 1.

69. Noel Gillespie, "A Remembrance of Bodies Past," *Washington Blade*, July 8, 1983, 19.

70. David Hurles, "It All Happened So Fast," *Outcome Magazine* 12 (1992), http://models.badpuppy.com/archive/amg/mizer1.htm.

2. SELLING GAY BOOKS: DONALD WEBSTER CORY'S "BUSINESS WITH A CONSCIENCE"

1. Nial Kent, *The Divided Path* (New York: Greenberg, 1949); press releases and undated publicity materials, August 5 and September 28, 1949, Nial Kent folder, Greenberg Publisher Records, Rare Books and Manuscript Division, Columbia University Library, New York (Greenberg Papers). In 2015 dollars, this would be a $4,000 contest. Among the many publications where the contest appeared, see "Book Section," *Los Angeles Daily News*, September 24, 1949.

2. Nial Kent Folder, Greenberg Papers; on Gore Vidal's success, see Christopher Bram, *Eminent Outlaws: The Gay Writers Who Changed America* (New York: Twelve, 2012), 9.

3. *Writers' Journal*, January 1950; Harry Zollars to Greenberg, August 27, 1949; Daniel S. Mead Literary Agent, "Staff Report," Spring and Summer 1950; "Psychopath," *New York Times Book Review*, November 10, 1949; royalty statement, June 3, 1955, all in Nial Kent folder, Greenberg Papers; C. Todd White, *Pre-Gay L.A.: A Social History of the Movement for Homosexuals Rights* (Urbana: University of Illinois Press, 2009), 69.

4. Tony Makos, n.d., Cory folder, Greenberg Papers.

5. Eric Marcus, *Making History: The Struggle for Gay and Lesbian Equal Rights, 1945–1990: An Oral History* (New York: HarperCollins, 1992), 45; Drewey Wayne Gunn, *The Golden Age of Gay Fiction* (Albion, N.Y.: MLR Press, 2009), 117; Michael Bronski, *Pulp Friction: Uncovering the Golden Age of Gay Male Pulps* (New York: St. Martin's Griffin, 2003);

Victor J. Banis, *Spine Intact, Some Creases: Remembrances of a Paperback Writer* (San Bernardino, Calif.: Borgo Press, 2007), 179, 207; Bram, *Eminent Outlaws*, 1, 48. Bram erroneously suggests that Greenberg's books "were rarely promoted and never reviewed."

6. "Jae Greenberg, Publisher, Dead," *New York Times*, November 27, 1974; Anthony Slide, *Lost Gay Novels: A Reference Guide to Fifty Works from the First Half of the Twentieth Century* (New York: Harrington Park Press, 2003), 4, 168. Slide suspects that Greenberg must have had a gay editor but is unable to identify him.

7. Harford Powel and Brandt Aymar, *The Deck Chair Reader: An Anthology for Travelers* (New York: Greenberg, 1938); "U.S. Treasury Man to Address Mail Advertisers," *Montreal Gazette*, September 23, 1941; "Advertising News and Notes," *New York Times*, October 3, 1942; "Books–Authors," *New York Times*, March 30, 1946; "Harford Powel, Satirist, Was 68," *New York Times*, August 18, 1956; Aymar to *Yale Daily News*, September 20, 1949, Divided Path folder, Greenberg Papers.

8. "Obvious" comment in Walter Breen to Stephen Foster, September 6, 1975, Letters of Stephen Wayne Foster, http://www.williamapercy.com; James Barr to Dorr Legg, November 5, 1954, James Barr Papers, ONE National Gay and Lesbian Archives, USC Libraries, University of Southern California, Los Angeles (ONE Archives); Brandt Aymar, *Cruising Is Fun* (New York: Greenberg, 1941); Brandt Aymar, *The Complete Cruiser* (New York: Greenberg, 1946); Brandt Aymar, *Treasury of Snake Lore: From the Garden of Eden to Snakes of Today* (New York: Greenberg, 1956); Brandt Aymar, *The Personality of the Bird* (New York: Crown, 1965).

9. Nial Kent folder, Greenberg Papers. This five-page list of approximately 225 names and address of contestants in the Divided Path Contest suggests that the claim of five hundred entries may have been an exaggeration. Andrew Wagner, "Archiving the Male Body: Leroy Ebert's 'Male Physique' Scrapbooks," *Broad Recognition: A Feminist Magazine at Yale*, August 31, 2013.

10. Fugate to Greenberg, May 13, 1949, and undated, untitled list of bars, both in James Barr folder, Greenberg Papers; James Barr to Dorr Legg, February 10, 1954, Barr Papers, ONE Archives. Often considered the first modern homosexual novel to portray homosexuals "positively," *Quatrefoil* became the name for the first LGBT community library in Minneapolis in the 1980s. See Quatrefoil Library, http://www.qlibrary.org, accessed December 12, 2014.

11. Royalty statement, Wahl folder, Greenberg Papers; Loren Wahl, *If This Be Sin* (New York: Avon, 1952).

12. Cory folder, Greenberg Papers; Jim Kepner, interview by Martin Duberman, September 16 and 20, 1996, Martin Duberman Papers, New York Public Library (NYPL); "Inside Report on Homosexuality in America," *People Today*, March 26, 1952, 2–7; Martin Duberman, "The 'Father' of the Homophile Movement," *Left Out: The Politics of Exclusion: Essays 1964–2002* (Cambridge, Mass.: South End Press, 2002), 59–94; Jim Kepner, "Gay Los Angeles: The Early Years," Tangents, January 1, 1988, http:// https://www.tangentgroup.org/gay-los-angeles-early-days/.

13. Donald Webster Cory, "Preface to the Second Edition," *The Homosexual in America: A Subjective Approach*, 2nd ed. (New York: Castle Books, 1960), xix; Donald Webster Cory, "From the First to the Second Report," *ONE*, October 1963.

14. Donald Webster Cory, *The Homosexual in America: A Subjective Approach* (New York: Greenberg, 1951).

15. *James Fugate v. Greenberg*, 189 N.Y.S. 2d 948 (1959); Barr, "Warts and All," Barr Papers, ONE Archives; Cory to Kinsey, May 10, 1952, Sagarin Correspondence, Duberman Papers, NYPL; Greenberg to William Thomas, October 26, 1951, Nial Kent folder, Greenberg Papers. Greenberg was "afraid" to publish novelist Samuel Stewart's fiction in 1953 because of "three lawsuits . . . in southern states." See Justin Spring, *Secret Historian: The Life and Times of Samuel Steward, Professor, Tattoo Artist, and Sexual Renegade* (New York: Farrar, Straus and Giroux, 2010), 181. The censorship cases didn't discourage Greenberg from publishing Cory's *21 Variations on a Theme* (1953), a collection of classic works with a homosexual theme, nor Pyramid Books from issuing a paperback edition of *The Divided Path* (1952).

16. "The Deviate," *Newark News*, October 1, 1950; Britton to Greenberg, October 7, 1951, Cory folder, Greenberg Papers; for sales figures, see folder 12, Barr Papers, ONE archives; Fugate to Aymar, July 6, 1951, Derricks folder, Greenberg Papers. Ralph Foster Daigh, editor at Fawcett, which published *Women's Barracks*, thought the State Department homosexual investigations fueled the interest in gay literature. See U.S. Congress, House, Select Committee on Current Pornographic Materials, *Investigation of Literature Allegedly Containing Objectionable Material*, 82nd Cong, 2nd sess., December 1, 1952, 32.

17. Business certificate, Cory Book Service, August 5, 1952, Jim Kepner Papers, ONE Archives; Cory Book Service circular, September 2, 1952, Don Lucas Papers, Gay, Lesbian, Bisexual, Transgender Historical Society (GLBTHS); Cory to Kinsey, October 3, 1952, Sagarin Correspondence, Duberman Papers, NYPL; David Bergman, "Selling Gay Literature Before Stonewall," in *A Sea of Stories: The Shaping Power of Narrative in Gay and Lesbian Cultures: A Festschrift for John P. De Cecco*, ed. Sonya L. Jones (New York: Routledge, 2000), 47.

18. R.E.L. Masters, *The Homosexual Revolution* (New York: Belmont Books, 1962), 54; Barr Papers, ONE Archives; "A Word of Explanation from the Cory Book Service," n.d. Book Service Files, Phyllis Lyon and Del Martin Papers, GLBTHS; Elsie Carlton, interview by Martin Duberman, September 1, 1996, Duberman Papers, NYPL.

19. Janice A. Radway, *A Feeling for Books: The Book-of-the-Month Club, Literary Taste, and Middle-Class Desire* (Chapel Hill: University of North Carolina Press, 1999), 154–86; Christine D'Arpa, "The Corporate Development of Middlebrow Reading: The Peoples Book Club of the Sears Roebuck Mail Order Catalog, 1943–1959," poster, ALISE Conference, 2014; Hellmut Lehmann-Haupt, *The Book in America: A History of the Making and Selling of Books in the United States* (New York: Bowker, 1952), 378; Hugo Gernsback to Brandt Aymar, February 13, 1950, Cory folder, Greenberg Papers. The letter was accompanied by two undated New Book Company solicitation letters, one on "abnormal psychology theme books" and a later one on "homosexual theme books." See also Larry Steckler, ed., *Hugo Gernsback: A Man Well Ahead of His Time* (Marana, Ariz.: Poptronix, 2007).

20. Donal MacNamara, interview by Martin Duberman, October 16, 1996, Duberman Papers, NYPL.

21. Cory to Quaintance, October 15, 1952, and Quaintance to Cory, October 8, 1952, folder 4, box 4, Mattachine Society Records, NYPL. Cory does not identify from whom he rented

the mailing list of "5,000 names," but given his inquiry to Quaintance, it seems likely that
it was a physique studio, possibly Lon of New York.

22. David Bergman, who has written extensively on the history of early gay pulp novels, claims
that the Cory Book Service went out of business within a year for lack of books, arguing
that Greenberg's federal obscenity conviction had a chilling effect on mainstream publishers. His assertion that it lasted less than a year is based on an oral history interview
with a very feeble Brandt Aymar in 1996. David Bergman to the author, June 17, 2011; David
Bergman, "Selling Gay Literature Before Stonewall." At the other end of the spectrum,
novelist Christopher Bram downplays the role of censorship, arguing, "The patchwork of
state and local obscenity laws didn't prevent the distribution of adult novels." See Bram,
Eminent Outlaws, 47.

23. Cory Book Service circular, October 1, 1953, Cory folder, Kepner Papers, ONE Archives;
James Barr to Eric, February 19, 1955, Barr Papers, ONE Archives.

24. Cory, *The Homosexual in America* (1951), 172, 297.

25. FBI informants suggested the group was called "Homosexuals Anonymous." Douglas M.
Charles, *Hoover's War on Gays: Exposing the FBI's "Sex Deviates" Program* (Lawrence: Uni-
versity Press of Kansas, 2015), 219–23. On the Veterans Benevolent Association, see Allen
Berube, *Coming Out Under Fire: The History of Gay Men and Lesbians in World War II*
(Chapel Hill: University of North Carolina Press, 2010); and *Charles Kaiser, The Gay
Metropolis, 1950–1996* (New York: Houghton-Mifflin, 1997).

26. Robert W. Wood, *Christ and the Homosexual: Some Observations* (New York: Vantage,
1960), 77; Robert Wood, interview with the author, July 7, 2014, Concord, N.H.; Edward
Sagarin, *Structure and Ideology in an Association of Deviants* (New York: Arno Press, 1975).

27. Cory to Kinsey, May 10, 1952, Sagarin Correspondence, Duberman Papers, NYPL.

28. Cory Book Service circular, April 6, 1953, Kepner Papers, ONE Archives; Cory Book Service to George Quaintance, April 16, 1953, folder 4, box 4, Mattachine Society Records,
NYPL; Brandt Aymar, interview with Charles Kaiser, May 1, 1995, quoted in Kaiser, *The
Gay Metropolis*, 126; Kaiser is one of the only writers to note the existence of Cory's bookstore but incorrectly calls it "The Book Seller." It is not clear how long the shop lasted at
237 E. 56th Street, but Rev. Wood wrote to Cory in the fall of 1955 asking to meet him at
his bookshop. See Robert Wood to Donald Cory, October 29, 1955, box 1, Wood Papers,
Congregational Library & Archives, Boston.

29. Cory folder, Kepner Papers, ONE Archives; *Homosexuals Today: A Handbook of Organizations & Publications*, ed. Marvin Cutler (Los Angeles: ONE, 1956), 95. Most accounts
of Cory's life note that he became an editor of ONE but miss his key role in enhancing its
mailing list. See Duberman, "'Father' of the Homophile Movement."

30. Marcia M. Gallo, *Different Daughters: A History of the Daughters of Bilitis and the Rise of
the Lesbian Rights Movement* (New York: Carroll & Graf, 2006), 5.

31. Jim Kepner, interview by Martin Duberman, September 1996, Duberman Papers, NYPL;
Cory to Lambert, August 25, 1953, Kepner Papers, ONE Archives. On the meeting with
Maxey, see also Whitney Strub, "The Homophile Is a Sexual Being: Wallace de Ortega
Maxey's Pulp Theology and Gay Activism," *Journal of the History of Sexuality* 25, no. 2
(2016): 337–38.

32. His many coedited anthologies include Brandt Aymar and Edward Sagarin, *The Personality of the Horse* (New York: Crown, 1963); Brandt Aymar and Edward Sagarin, *The*

Personality of the Dog (New York: Crown, 1964); Brandt Aymar and Edward Sagarin, *A Pictorial History of the World's Great Trials* (New York: Bonanza, 1967); Brandt Aymar and Edward Sagarin, *Laws and Trials That Created History* (New York: Crown, 1974). On his investment in a "weightlifting firm," see Donal MacNamara, interview by Martin Duberman, October 16, 1996, Duberman Papers, NYPL.

33. Cory to Lambert, January 27, 1954, Kepner Papers, ONE Archives. Years later, Cory listed Winston Book Service, the successor to the Cory Book Service, as a homophile group in one of his many writings on the movement. See Sagarin, *Structure and Ideology*, 424.

34. Elsie Carlton, interview by Martin Duberman, September 1, 1996, Duberman Papers, NYPL.

35. Cory to Lambert, January 27, 1954, Kepner Papers, ONE Archives.

36. Notes from speech by Robert Veit Sherwin, "Homosexuals in America: Their Organizations and Literature," *Mattachine Review*, February 1959, 36.

37. "The Cory Book Service Reactivated," *Mattachine Review*, March 1957.

38. SAC New York to J. Edgar Hoover, May 27, 1953, FBI 100-109371-5; Charles, *Hoover's War on Gays*, 224.

39. Toby Marotta, *The Politics of Homosexuality* (Boston: Houghton Mifflin, 1981), 19; John P. LeRoy, "The Anti-Homosexual in America: Donald Webster Cory," *Gay*, April 20, 1970, 8; Duberman, "'Father' of the Homophile Movement," 76.

40. Business certificate, Cory Book Service, September 14, 1954, Kepner Papers, ONE Archives; Segura to Olson, August 14, 1956, New York Area Correspondence, Call Papers, ONE Archives, cited in Sears, *Behind the Mask of Mattachine*, 378n55; "Arthur Richmond," *New York Times*, January 7, 1956, 17. See also Arthur Richmond, *Modern Quotations for Ready Reference* (New York: Dover, 1947); M. Oldfield Howey, *The Cat in the Mysteries of Religion and Magic* (New York: Arthur Richmond, 1955); M. Oldfield Howey, *The Encircled Serpent* (New York: Arthur Richmond, 1955). Both Aymar and Richmond published commercial and pictorial books on cats and serpents.

41. Elsie Carlton, interview by Martin Duberman, September 1, 1996, Duberman Papers, NYPL; Ronnie Carlton Barker to David Johnson, May 24, 2018; Winston Book Service circular, n.d., Phyllis Lyon and Del Martin Papers, GLBTHS.

42. Tram Combs to Preston Dettman, May 22, 1959, Tram Combs Papers, Mandeville Special Collections Library, University of California, San Diego. Combs ordered five thousand flyers for his book *Ceremonies in Mind* to be included in a Winston Book Service mailing; that figure also appears in *Mattachine Review*, February 1959, 36; Egam to Wood, July 11, 1959, Correspondence: Rev. Edward Egan folder, Wood Papers.

43. Elsie Carlton, interview by Martin Duberman, September 1, 1996, Duberman Papers, NYPL; James Barr, "Warts and All," Barr Papers, ONE Archives. Carlton holds the copyright to James Barr, *The Occasional Man* (New York: Paperback Library, 1965) and *Quatrefoil* (New York: Paperback Library, 1965); Bread Loaf Writers' Conference, "1963 Enrollment," *Gray Books*, Middlebury College Registrar, Middlebury College Special Collections and Archives, Middlebury, Vt.; see also David Haward Bain, *Whose Woods These Are: A History of the Bread Loaf Writer's Conference, 1926–1992* (Hopewell, N.J.: Ecco Press, 1993).

44. Elsie Carlton, interview by Martin Duberman, September 1, 1996, Duberman Papers, NYPL; author interview with Richard Carlton, September 17, 2015; Roland G. Carlton, Letters, *PM*, April 14, 1942.

45. Elsie Carlton, interview by Martin Duberman, September 1, 1996; Winston Book Service brochure, n.d. circa 1960, H. Lynn Womack Papers, Human Sexuality Collection, Division of Rare and Manuscript Collections, Cornell University.

46. Elsie Carlton, interview by Martin Duberman, September 1, 1996; *New York Mattachine Newsletter*, September 1961, April 1962, and December 1964; "Homosexuality: Current Research Trends," Annual Convention Program, Mattachine Society of New York, September 1–3, 1961, Frank Kameny Papers.

47. "DOB on New York Radio in September," *Ladder* 5, no. 11, August 1961, 7, quoted in Gallo, *Different Daughters*, 74; Ronnie Carlton Barker to David Johnson, Mary 24, 2018; Leticia Kent, "Getting Arrested Is Not as Easy as It Seems," *Village Voice*, February 23, 1967, 1.

48. Arthur Richmond to Roy T. Hyre, January 7, 1955, Thor Studio Correspondence, 1955 series, Kinsey Institute; *PP*, Summer 1957, 23. CBS sold "such items as Christmas cards and shaving lotions, especially designed for the invert market," according to Masters, *The Homosexual Revolution*, 54.

49. Undated Winston Book Club newsletters, Canadian Gay and Lesbian Archives.

50. Whitney Strub makes a similar argument in "Historicizing Pulp: Gay Male Pulp and the Narrative of Queer Cultural History," in *1960s Gay Pulp Fiction: The Misplaced Heritage*, ed. Drewey Wayne Gunn and Jaime Harker (Amherst: University of Massachusetts Press, 2013), 47–48.

51. Guild Book Service (Washington, D.C.), Trojan Book Service (Philadelphia), Village Books and Press (New York), House of Clark (Los Angeles), Directory Services (Minneapolis), and Cosmo Book Sales (San Francisco) were among the gay book services that proliferated by the 1960s. Guy Strait's *Citizens News* in San Francisco also had a book service.

52. *ONE*, June 1955; *ONE Confidential*, December, 1960; "Book Notes from ONE," April 1958, ONE, Inc., Papers, ONE Archives.

53. Howard Frisch obituary, September 4, 2007, www.millspaughcamerato.com/obituary /Howard-J.-Frisch/_/1382630; the largest selection of Village Book circulars, all undated, is in Womack Papers.

54. Hugh Hagius identifies Noel I. Garde as Edgar H. Leoni in Hagius, *Swasarnt Nerf's Gay Guides for 1949* (New York: Bibliogay Publications, 2010). In his bibliography, Garde identifies material similarly to Frisch's Village Books newsletter, specifying whether it is of primary or secondary gay interest. See Noel I. Garde, *The Homosexual in Literature: A Chronological Bibliography, Circa 700 B.C.–1958* (New York: Village Press, 1959). Frisch also published a series of cat books, starting with George Freedly, *Mr. Cat* (New York: Frisch, 1960). Freedly had been the theater librarian at the New York Public Library.

55. "Winston Reactivates Cory Book Service," *Ladder* 1, no. 6 (March 1957), 15; "Beginning— DOB Book Service," *Ladder* 4, no. 8 (May 1960), 9; Gallo, *Different Daughters*, 59–60, 90; Book Service files, Phyllis Lyon and Del Martin Papers, GLBTHS.

56. *Dorian Book Service Quarterly*, January 1960; *Mattachine Review*, February, 1961; Strub, "Historicizing Pulp," 50.

57. MacNichols to McDowell, April 15, 1951, Cory folder, Greenberg Papers; Cosmo Book Sales, Studio and Distributor Marketing Ephemera, ONE Archives; Ken Furtado, *Quaintance: The Short Life of an American Art Pioneer* (Smashwords, 2015).

58. Bern to Bill, April 3, 1960, folder 15, box 5, Don Lucas Papers, GLBTHS; Hal Call to John Eccles, March 18, 1963, Eccles Papers; Dorian Book Service catalog, hardcover edition, 1963, Eccles Papers; *Mattachine Review*, July 1960.

59. *Free Press*, July 21, 1967, Kepner Papers, ONE Archives; *Golden Boys #1*, 1967; testimony of Hal Call, *U.S. v. Spinar*, 654–69; Sears, *Behind the Mask of Mattachine*, 519.

60. Jim Downs, *Stand by Me: The Forgotten History of Gay Liberation* (New York: Basic Books, 2016), 68; Oscar Wilde Memorial Bookshop's mail-order catalog in 1976 was just one page. Box 16, folder 1, George Fisher Papers, Cornell University, Ithaca, N.Y.

61. Martin Duberman, *Stonewall* (New York: Dutton, 1993), 165; Martha E. Stone, "After Many a Season Dies the Oscar Wilde," *Gay & Lesbian Review Worldwide*, July–August 2009, 9; Downs, *Stand by Me*, 65–88.

62. Despite his pioneering target marketing to gays and lesbians, Aymar's obituary was completely silent on his role. "Brandt Aymar," *Publisher's Weekly*, December 1 1997, 16.

63. For a more modern case of gay mailing lists, direct-mail campaigns, and the intermixing of business and activism, see Sean Strub, *Body Counts: A Memoir of Politics, Sex, AIDS, and Survival* (New York: Scribner, 2014), 283–302.

3. THE GRECIAN GUILD: IMAGINING A GAY PAST, AND FUTURE

1. *Tomorrow's Man* (TM), August 1955; *VIM*, August 1955.

2. *Grecian Guild Pictorial* (GGP), Fall 1955. Within a few years, this first issue became a collector's item and sold for four and then eight times the initial retail price. *GGP*, June 1959, 37, and July 1964. "Gay as pink ink" was a common expression in gay circles in the 1940s and 1950s. See James Barr, "Warts and All," James Barr Papers, ONE National Gay and Lesbian Archives, USC Libraries, University of Southern California, Los Angeles (ONE Archives). For uses of the term by contemporaries, see Allan Bérubé, *My Desire for History: Essays in Gay, Community, and Labor History* (Chapel Hill: University of North Carolina Press, 2011), 116; and Steve Estes, *Ask and Tell: Gay and Lesbian Veterans Speak Out: Gay and Lesbian Veterans Speak Out* (Chapel Hill: University of North Carolina Press, 2009), 42.

3. *GGP*, Fall 1955, 42. The first several issues contain fairly sophisticated appreciations of classical Greek sculpture, suggesting a familiarity with art history.

4. "The Glory That Was . . . ," *VIM*, May 1954, 8–11.

5. A 1957 Grecian Guild flyer in the Studio and Distributor Marketing Ephemera Collection at the ONE Archives included sufficient biographical data on both Benson and Bullock to allow me to begin to piece their lives together through other sources. The ephemera is also available through Tim Wilbur's Vintage Physique Photography commercial website, http://timinvermont.com. Obituary of C. W. Randolph Benson, *Roanoke Times*, March 9, 2007; obituary of John F. Bullock, Jr., http://Robesonian.com, accessed February 28, 2012. According to the *University of Virginia Record, College of Arts and Sciences, Announcements 1946–47*, Benson made the dean's list three out of four semesters. Carl W. Randolph Benson, "Family Organization and Disorganization in Virginia," M.A. thesis, University of Virginia, 1948; telephone interview with anonymous relative of John Bullock, October 14, 2014. For more on World War II military artists, see Edward Reep, *A Combat Artist in World War II* (Lexington: University Press of Kentucky, 1987).

6. Grecian Guild advertisements appeared in *TM*, December 1953, August and November 1954, and January and February 1955; *VIM*, August 1954; *GGP*, Fall 1955; and *Physique Pictorial* (PP), Spring 1957, 2.

7. Scholars who associate the Grecian Guild only with Womack include Richard Meyer, *Outlaw Representations: Censorship and Homosexuality in Twentieth Century American Art* (Boston: Beacon Press, 2002); and David Bergman, "The Cultural Work of Sixties Gay Pulp Fiction," in *The Queer Sixties*, ed. Patricia Juliana Smith (New York: Routledge, 1999). One of the few scholars to acknowledge Benson's foundational role is Philip Clark, "Accept Your Essential Self: The Guild Press, Identity Formation and Gay Male Community," in *1960s Gay Pulp Fiction: The Misplaced Heritage*, ed. Drewey Wayne Gunn and Jamie Harker (Amherst: University of Massachusetts Press, 2013), 86.

8. "College Fraternities," *Life*, February 6, 1950, 86–98; *GGP*, July 1958, 13. For how Benson's fraternity Sigma Chi adopted a creed, pledge pin, and prayer, see http://history.sigmachi .org, accessed October 17, 2014.

9. Will Roscoe, ed., *Radically Gay: Gay Liberation in the Words of Its Founder* (Boston: Beacon, 1997), 47, 70; interview with Harry Hay in Jonathan Ned Katz, *Gay American History* (New York: Avon Books, 1978), 406–20; Stuart Timmons and Lillian Faderman, *Gay L.A.: A History of Sexual Outlaws, Power Politics, and Lipstick Lesbians* (New York: Basic Books, 2006), 109–12. Mattachine is listed as a fraternity in a 1950s underground guide, "Gay Girl's Guide to the U.S. & The Western World," reprinted in Hugh Hagius, *Swasarnt Nerf's Gay Guides for 1949* (New York: Bibliogay Publications, 2010), 126. For a perspective that stresses the CPUSA cell structure model, see John D'Emilio, *Sexual Politics, Sexual Communities: The Making of a Homosexual Minority in the United States, 1940–1970* (Chicago: University of Chicago Press, 1983), 64. The Knights of the Clock, a short-lived Los Angeles–based organization largely of interracial gay couples, had initiation rituals similar to those of the Masons.

10. Linda Dowling, *Hellenism and Homosexuality in Victorian Oxford* (Ithaca, N.Y.: Cornell University Press, 1994).

11. Alan Helms, *Young Man from the Provinces: A Gay Life Before Stonewall* (New York: Faber & Faber, 1995), 52.

12. William Alexander Percy, *Lanterns on the Levee: Recollections of a Planter's Son* (New York: Knopf, 1941); Benjamin E. Wise, *William Alexander Percy: The Curious Life of a Mississippi Planter and Sexual Freethinker* (Chapel Hill: University of North Carolina Press, 2012).

13. Paul Brandt [Hans Licht, pseud.], *Sexual Life in Ancient Greece* (London: Routledge, 1932).

14. David Halperin, John J. Winkler, and Froma Zeitlin, eds., *Before Sexuality: The Construction of Erotic Experience in the Ancient Greek World* (Princeton, N.J.: Princeton University Press, 1990), 10–12; Robert Aldrich, *The Seduction of the Mediterranean: Writing, Art and Homosexual Fantasy* (London: Routledge, 1993), 14, 82.

15. Alfred Kinsey, *Sexual Behavior in the Human Male* (Philadelphia: W. B. Saunders, 1948), 660; folder 4, box 28, Jim Kepner Papers, ONE Archives; Norman Arlington, "The Grecian Ideal," *GGP*, November 1959, 14. Quoting Licht and ascribed to a nonexistent "American Novelist, Norman Arlington," the article was likely penned by Benson.

16. John Addington Symonds, *A Problem in Greek Ethics: Being an Inquiry into the Phenomenon of Sexual Inversion* (1901; repr. New York: Haskell House); D. H. Mader, "The Greek Mirror: The Uranians and Their Use of Greece," *Journal of Homosexuality* 49, nos. 3–4 (2005): 377–420.

17. During World War II Wally Jordan and some of his pen-pal correspondents discussed forming or reactivating "Sons of Hamidy," a group named for the Greek hero Harmodius, who killed the tyrant Hipparchus. Although an unrealized vision, it suggests that the notion of organizing around the trope of Ancient Greek heroes was not unique. Faderman and Timmons, *Gay L.A.*, 109; Marvin Cutler, ed., *Homosexuals Today: A Handbook of Organizations & Publications* (Los Angeles: ONE, 1956), 88–89.

18. Letters to the Editor, *ONE*, July 1960, 31; Rodwell quoted in Kay Tobin and Randy Wicker, *The Gay Crusaders* (New York: Paperback Library, 1972), 67.

19. Blair Niles, *Strange Brother* (New York: Liveright, 1931), 186, 235; the protagonist is based on Niles's friend Leland Pettit, a gay man from Milwaukee, later the organist at New York's Grace Church. See Eric Garber, "A Spectacle in Color," in *Hidden from History: Reclaiming the Gay and Lesbian Past*, ed. Martin Duberman, Martha Vicinus, and George Chauncey (New York: Dutton, 1989), 329; George Chauncey, *Gay New York: Gender, Urban Culture, and the Making of the Gay Male World* (New York: Basic Books, 1994), 283–85. On these novels' popularity, see David K. Johnson, "Kids of Fairytown: Gay Male Culture on Chicago's Near North Side in the 1930s," in *Creating a Place for Ourselves: Lesbian, Gay, and Bisexual Community Histories*, ed. Brett Beemyn (New York: Routledge, 1997), 99–100.

20. James Vincent Nash, *Homosexuality in the Lives of the Great* (Girard, Kans.: Haldeman-Julius Publications, n.d.); "Dime Literature," *New Republic*, September 20, 1922, 87–88.

21. Emanuel Haldeman-Julius, *The First Hundred Million* (New York: Simon & Schuster, 1928), 19–23; Mark Scott, "The Little Blue Books in the War on Bigotry and Bunk," *Kansas History* 1 (Autumn 1978), 155–76.

22. Eric Marcus, *Making History: The Struggle for Gay and Lesbian Equal Rights, 1945–1990* (New York: Harper Collins, 192), 45. Homophile activist Bruce Scott also recalls first learning of homosexuality through the Little Blue Books. Author interview with Bruce Scott, October 24, 1992.

23. Sigmund Freud, "Letter to an American Mother," *American Journal of Psychiatry* 107 (1951), 787; William Billings, October 1, 1945, quoted in Heather Murray, *Not in This Family: Gays and the Meaning of Kinship in Postwar North America* (Philadelphia: University of Pennsylvania Press, 2012), 2; Marcel Martin (Ross Ingersoll), "A Matter of Language," *ONE*, November 1961, 7.

24. See Amy Richlin, "Eros Underground: Greece and Rome in Gay Print Culture, 1953–65," *Journal of Homosexuality* 49 (2005), 421–61. Many homophile publications in Europe favored classical names, such as the French *Arcadie*, the German *Hellas*, and the Danish group Ganymedes.

25. Benson folder, ONE, Inc., records, ONE Archives. Benson supplied ONE with contact information for an attorney who handled homosexual solicitation cases, offered to volunteer in the office when he lived in nearby Laguna Beach, and contributed at least one piece of fiction. See Richard Rand (a.k.a. Randy Benson), "Courage," *ONE*, August 1960, 6. Both magazines ran maps of the United States to demonstrate their wide national circulation, and *ONE*'s seasonal banquets may have inspired the Grecian Guild's conventions. See *ONE*, December 1954 and January 1958.

26. "America's Greatest Physique Artist Tells His Own Story," *GGP*, Spring 1956, 12–22; Reed Massengill, *Quaintance*, ed. Dian Hanson (Cologne: Taschen, 2010). For a literary critic's somewhat differing interpretation of Quaintance's bizarre autobiographical story, see

Christopher Nealon, *Foundlings: Lesbian and Gay Historical Emotion Before Stonewall* (Durham, N.C.: Duke University Press, 2001), 132–35.

27.   Byrne R. S. Fone, ed., *The Columbia Anthology of Gay Literature: Readings from Western Antiquity to the Present Day* (New York: Columbia University Press, 1998), 39; Margaret Werth, *The Joy of Life: The Idyllic in French Art, Circa 1900* (Berkeley: University of California Press, 2002), 2.

28.   Eric Hobsbawn and Terence Ranger, eds., *The Invention of Tradition* (Cambridge: Cambridge University Press, 2012); Chauncey, *Gay New York*, 286.

29.   Helms, *Young Man from the Provinces*, 52.

30.   Matthew Rettenmund, "Striking Poses: Photographer Lon of New York and the Rebirth of Beefcake," *Torso*, December 1996, 78–82; Reed Massengill, ed., *The Male Ideal: Lon of New York and the Masculine Physique* (New York: Universe, 2003).

31.   Bob Mizer Diary, March 16, 1940, Bob Mizer Permanent Collection, Bob Mizer Foundation, San Francisco; *PP*, June 1960; *GGP*, July 1957, 5.

32.   Nial Kent, *The Divided Path* (New York: Greenberg, 1949), 15–17, 278, 351.

33.   Martin, "A Matter of Language," *ONE*, November 1961, 7; Lon of New York, *Star Models*, n.d.

34.   Craig Loftin, "Unacceptable Mannerisms: Gender Anxieties, Homosexual Activism, and Swish in the United States, 1945–1965," *Journal of Social History* 40 (2007), 557–96; John Howard, *Men Like That: A Southern Queer History* (Chicago: University of Chicago Press, 1999), 202.

35.   *GGP*, July 1957, 4; Benson to Womack, March 25, 1958, H. Lynn Womack Papers, Human Sexuality Collection, Division of Rare and Manuscript Collections, Cornell University. For scholarship on rural gay life, see Mary L. Gray, Colin R. Johnson, and Brian J. Gilley, eds., *Queering the Countryside: New Frontiers in Rural Queer Studies* (New York: New York University Press, 2016); Colin R. Johnson, *Just Queer Folks: Gender and Sexuality in Rural America* (Philadelphia: Temple University Press, 2013); Scott Herring, *Another Country: Queer Anti-Urbanism* (New York: New York University Press, 2010); Brock Thompson, *The Un-Natural State: Arkansas and the Queer South* (Fayetteville: University of Arkansas Press, 2010).

36.   *Drum*, nos. 18–19, September 1966, 11–12; *PP*, Summer 1955, 17.

37.   *GGP*, December 1956. Coleman, a Harvard graduate who served in the marines, returned from Japan the next year and hanged himself in his parents' home near Baltimore. *Daily Times* (Salisbury, Maryland), July 2, 1957, 16.

38.   *Daily Mail* (Hagerstown, Maryland), August 5, 1940, 9. Benson's later correspondence continues to use religious language. See Randy Benson to Robert Wood, March 4, 1960, box 1, Correspondence, 1940–1960, Rev. Robert Wood Papers, Congregational Library & Archives, Boston.

39.   Aldrich, *Seduction of the Mediterranean*, 38; E. M Forster, *Maurice: A Novel* (New York: Norton, 2005), 70. Forster originally wrote the novel in 1913. See David M. Halperin, *One Hundred Years of Homosexuality and Other Essays on Greek Love* (New York: Routledge, 1990).

40.   Robert Wood, interview with author, July 7, 2014; box 2, Wood Papers; Wood to Quaintance, March 25, 1954, in the possession of Rev. Robert Wood. For more on Wood, see

Heather R. White, *Reforming Sodom: Protestants and the Rise of Gay Rights* (Chapel Hill: University of North Carolina Press, 2015), 63–68.

41. *GGP*, Summer 1956; Hildebrand to Wood, June 9, 1956, and Wood to Hildebrand, July 20 and August 21, 1956, box 1, Wood Papers.

42. Wood to Thorwaldsen, August 2, 1956, and Thorwaldsen to Wood, July 28, 1956, box 1, Wood Papers. For Wood's view of gay culture, see Robert W. Wood, *Christ and the Homosexual: Some Observations* (New York: Vantage, 1960). For the relationship between gay and lesbian bars and the sacred, see E. Patrick Johnson, "Feeling the Spirit in the Dark: Expanding Notions of the Sacred in the African American Gay Community," in *The Greatest Taboo: Homosexuality in Black Communities*, ed. Delroy Constantine-Simms (Los Angeles: Alyson, 2000); and Marie Carter, *Baby, You Are My Religion: Women, Gay Bars, and Theology Before Stonewall* (New York: Routledge, 2014).

43. Rev. Thorman Alderson, "The Grecian Guild and America Today," *GGP*, February 1959, 42. Alderson is clearly a pseudonym. Unlike the other chaplains featured in the magazine, no biographical information or photograph is offered. "I Am a Grecian," *GGP*, January 1957, 15.

44. The creed first appears in *GGP*, Winter 1955; a second version appears December 1956–May 1957; the final version begins in July 1957 and continues through to the late 1960s. Tracy Morgan's often-quoted version of the Grecian Guild creed, which emphasizes its Cold War rhetoric, is from a pledge called "I Am a Grecian" printed only once, *GGP*, January 1957. See Tracy D. Morgan, "Pages of Whiteness: Race, Physique Magazines, and the Emergence of Public Gay Culture," in *Queer Studies: A Lesbian, Gay, Bisexual, and Transgender Anthology*, ed. Brett Beemyn and Mickey Eliason (New York: New York University Press, 1996), 289.

45. *VIM*, November 1955, 44–45.

46. *VIM*, September 1956, 7–10.

47. *PP*, Summer 1956, 14; *VIM*, January 1956 and November 1956, 36; *TM*, February 1956.

48. Wood to Thorwaldsen, August 2, 1956, box 1, Wood Papers.

49. Although letters to the editor should be considered with some skepticism, the editors' practice of including names and addresses (with permission) suggests the letters were genuine. George U. Lyon would later found his own physique photography studio. P.C.P., *GGP*, Winter 1955, 47; George U. Lyon, *GGP*, Spring 1956, 47; B.N.K., Texas, E.R., Ohio, and R.C.P., New York, *GGP*, Summer 1956, 48; G. H. Gauthier, Quebec, *GGP*, April 1958; Edward A. Schultz, Tampa, *GGP*, January 1953.

50. *GGP*, April 1959; *TM*, November 1957.

51. *GGP*, Summer 1956.

52. *GGP*, April 1958. In the 1940 census Ordway was forty-four years old, unmarried, and lived with his mother and sister; http://www.ancestry.com.

53. *GGP*, January, May, and November 1960; Grecian Guild Directory at http://timinvermont .com. By the mid-1960s the editors would recommend that those looking to make contacts purchase the International Guild Guide "to meet others with similar Grecian interests" or "meet compatible Greek brothers." McInnis to Purcell, April 28, 1966, Indianapolis, in 1.56 Letters—Grecian Guild, Womack Papers.

54. *GGP*, Summer 1956, 11, and December 1956, 7; Thorwaldsen to Wood, December 10, 1956, box 1, Wood Papers.

55. Thorwaldsen to Wood, December 10, 1956, box 1, Wood Papers; *VIM*, November 1955; *ONE Confidential*, August 1957; "Dear Fellow Grecian," April 17, 1957, http://timinvermont.com.

56. "Report to Members," *GGP*, January 1958, 10.

57. "The Grecian Guild Convention," *GGP*, February 1959; "The San Francisco Convention," *GGP*, January 1960; Dear Brother Grecian letters, n.d., http://timinvermont.com. Writing in 1996, Thomas Waugh only knew of the first convention in 1958 and asserts that their plans "very quickly fizzled out." Waugh, *Hard to Imagine*, 219. By comparison, the first Mattachine convention in 1954 drew forty-two members. D'Emilio, *Sexual Politics*, 86.

58. "Important Notice," *GGP*, July 1960, 17; Robert Collins to Grecian Guild, ca. 1965, 1.56 Letters—Grecian Guild, Womack Papers. Collins seems to have written two letters asking about conventions. The first was published in *GGP*, March 1965. At the time the new editors were unaware of the West Coast convention held six years earlier.

59. *GGP*, February 1959 and January and September 1960; Letter to Editor, *GYM*, July 1959; *Fizeek*, December 1964; "Elden Moore: Resident of the Month," *Good News Letter* (Bellaire, Minn.: Meadow Brook Medical Care Facility, November/December 2008), http://www.meadowbrookmcf.com/publications/nov_dec08.pdf. On the history of gay men as flight attendants, see Phil Tiemeyer, *Plane Queer: Labor, Sexuality and AIDS in the History of Male Flight Attendants* (Berkeley: University of California Press, 2013).

60. *GGP*, January and March 1960.

61. Scott Bravmann, *Queer Fictions of the Past: History, Culture and Difference* (Cambridge: Cambridge University Press, 1997), 67; Morgan, "Pages of Whiteness"; membership collage in *GGP*, July 1957.

62. Letter to Editor, *GGP*, August 1959.

63. Diversifying by offering multiple magazines or studio names was common. B&B Photos, headquartered from a post office box in Los Angeles, was likely another Benson and Bullock enterprise. Its dates of operation and pool of models overlaps with those of Grecian Guild, including exclusive model Dick Norman. The layout of B&B's advertisements in *GGP* also suggests co-ownership. See *GGP*, November 1957 and July 1958; *TRIM*, May 1958; B&B ephemera at http://timinvermont.com.

64. *Fizeek*, 1, no. 1; *Fizeek* ephemera in Tim Wood Collection, Gay, Lesbian, Bisexual, Transgender Historical Society. The five studios were Christopher, Quaintance, Delmonteque, Vulcan, and Warner.

65. Joe Weider and Ben Weider, *Brothers of Iron: Building the Weider Empire* (Champaign, Ill.: Sports Publishing, 2006), 116–19; "Let Me Tell You a Fairy Tale . . .," *Strength & Health*, June 1957, 17.

66. Womack counts fifteen magazines. Womack to Benson, November 12, 1957; Benson to Womack, February 11, 1958; Benson to Womack, March 25, 1958, all in Womack Papers. An advertisement for "French briefs" in *TRIM* got 130 orders.

67. *PP*, Spring 1955, 2, 15.

68. *PP*, Summer 1955, 21; and "All Aboard!" Grecian Guild flyer, circa 1955, http://timinvermont.com.

69. Womack to Benson, March 29, 1958, Womack Papers.

70. Benson to Womack, March 25 and 27, 1958, Womack Papers. Although early Grecian Guild images had painted-on posing straps, indicating models were photographed in the nude, there is no evidence that the guild sold nudes. Bodybuilding fans also reported police raids

on Detroit newsstands in 1957–1958. See John D. Fair, *Muscletown U.S.A.: Bob Hoffman and the Manly Culture of York Barbell* (University Park: Pennsylvania State University Press, 1999), 178.

71. *Serving the Reading Public: America's Leading Distributor of Books, Magazines, and Newspapers Celebrates 80 Years of Growth* (New York: American News Company, 1944); Michael Feldman, "How Men's Magazines Got to the Masses," in *History of Men's Magazines*, vol. 1, ed. Dian Hanson (Cologne: Taschen, 2004). Newsstand distribution is a topic worthy of further study.

72. Benson to Womack, January 10, 1958; and Womack to Benson, March 18 and 29, 1958, all in Womack Papers; *PP*, Fall 1957. *TM* offered a combined February–March 1958 issue. The Union News Company in New York refused to carry physique magazines according to Stephen Birmingham, "For Love of Muscle," *Sports Illustrated*, August 3, 1959, 63.

73. *GGP*, September 1958.

74. Statement of J. E. Hessert, postal inspector, "Obscene Matter Sent Through the Mail," Hearings Before Subcommittee on Postal Operations, Committee on Post Office and Civil Service, House, 87th Cong. 1st sess., November 18, 1961, 193. Hessert describes the arrest of two physique studio operators in Arizona; C.W.R. Benson to ONE, Inc., February 7, 1961, ONE Archives.

75. Carl W. Randolph Benson, "Sociological Elements in Selected Writings and Works of Thomas Jefferson," Ph.D. diss., Louisiana State University and Agricultural and Mechanical College, 1966; Meeting Minutes, Roanoke City Council, September 28, 1981; telephone interview with Greg Weiss, November 3, 2014; email correspondence with John Leachtenauer, October 3, 2014.

76. Dionysus is first referenced in *ONE*, June 1962, 18; *PP*, January 1960, 2; *Romans* 1, no. 1 (September 1964), in Womack Papers. For more on the use of classical names, especially for gay and lesbian homophile groups in Europe, see Richlin, "Eros Underground," 421–61.

77. "Greeks Go Hollywood," *VIM*, October 1954, 7–10; Maria Wyke, "Herculean Muscle! The Classicizing Rhetoric of Bodybuilding," in *Constructions of the Classical Body*, ed. James I. Porter (Ann Arbor: University of Michigan Press, 1999), 366; G. T. Wallace, "Richard Fontaine: Pioneer Gay Filmmaker," *Inches*, October 1996, 88–91.

78. Meyer, *Outlaw Representations*, 179; Wise, *William Alexander Percy*, 200; for pen-pal correspondence, see *U.S. v. Charles J. Anctil et al.*, trial transcript, U.S. District Court, Northern District of Illinois, Chicago, Criminal Case Files, 61CR27, RG 21, National Archives–Chicago Branch.

79. Critiques of this nostalgic view include Halperin, *One Hundred Years of Homosexuality*; Morgan, "Pages of Whiteness"; Jason Goldman, "'The Golden Age of Gay Porn': Nostalgia and the Photography of Wilhelm von Gloeden," *GLQ: A Journal of Lesbian and Gay Studies* 12, no. 2 (2006): 237–58; Daniel Mendelsohn, "The Stand: Expert Witness and Ancient Mysteries in a Colorado Courtroom," *Lingua Franca* (September/October 1996): 34–46. The nostalgic view was still reflected in a radical 1990 broadside, "Queers Read This—I Hate Straights," which attributed democracy, the arts, and the very concept of love to "our ancient Greek Dykes [and] Fags." http://www.qrd.org/qrd/misc/text/queers.read.this, accessed June 13, 2016.

80. Maria Wyke, "Herculean Muscle!" claims the classical alibi disappears when no longer necessary to evade censors. On the history of *David* magazine, see http://outhistory.org;

on the lambda, see *The Whole Gay Catalog #1* (Washington, D.C.: Lambda Rising, 1982); on the Dorian Group, see Dudley Clendinen and Adam Nagourney, *Out for Good: The Struggle to Build a Gay Rights Movement in America* (New York: Simon and Schuster, 1999), 253. For a novel that uniquely blends ancient Greek myth and modern-day gay life, see Mark Merlis, *An Arrow's Flight* (New York: St. Martin's Press, 1998).

81. *The Mighty—Happy and Healthy*, n.d., folder 9, box 1, John M. Eccles Papers, Special Collections, University of Washington, Seattle; Frontier Athletic Newsletter C, 1961, clippings files, ONE Archives; George Grieg, "A Short Frontier Club History," *Fizeek*, August 1964, 6–9.

82. *H&H Club Journal*, June–July 1960, folder 10, box 1, Eccles Papers.

83. GGP, Spring 1956; Underwood ephemera from http://timinvermont.com; Frontier Athletic Club newsletters in "Frontier Athletic Club," clippings files, ONE Archives, and Eccles Papers.

84. Michael Denneny, interview with author, July 29, 2012; Mingus (a.k.a. Michael Denneny), "Through the Looking Glass," *New York Native*, July 21–27, 1986, 10.

4. "I WANT A PEN PAL!" POSTMASTER GENERAL ARTHUR SUMMERFIELD AND THE ADONIS MALE CLUB

1. "Obscenity Laid to 'Pen Pals,'" *Washington Star*, January 18, 1961; "U.S. Indicts 53 in Breakup of 'Smut' Club," *Chicago Tribune*, January 17, 1961, 1; U.S. Department of Justice, *United States Attorneys Bulletin* 10, no. 7 (April 6, 1962), 206–7. Among the newspapers that featured the story on the front page were the *Chicago Tribune, Southern Illinoisan, Tucson Daily Citizen, Simpson Leader-Times* (Kittanning, Pa.), *Naugatuck (Conn.) Daily, Daily Pantagraph* (Bloomington-Normal, Ill.), and *Kingston (N.Y.) Daily Freeman*.

2. Associated Press, January 17, 1961.

3. "Twelve in Obscenity Cases Enter Innocent Pleas," *Anderson (Ind.) Sunday Herald*, May 28, 1961 (United Press International).

4. John N. Makris, *The Silent Investigators: The Great Untold Story of the United States Postal Inspection Service* (New York: Dutton, 1959); "Post Office Will Not Use New Tool Like Club in Fighting Obscenity," *Times Daily* (Florence, Ala.), May 8, 1966.

5. Vern L. Bulloughs, ed., *Before Stonewall: Activists for Gay and Lesbian Rights in Historical Context* (Binghamton, N.Y.: Harrington Park Press, 2002), 64; Rodger Streitmatter, *Unspeakable: The Rise of the Gay and Lesbian Press in America* (Boston: Faber and Faber, 1995), 5.

6. Berry Werth, *The Scarlet Professor: Newton Arvin: A Literary Life Shattered by Scandal* (New York: Nan A. Talese, 2001).

7. Among the few historical treatments that discuss the role of postal inspectors are John D'Emilio, *Sexual Politics, Sexual Communities: The Making of a Homosexual Minority in the United States, 1940–1970* (Chicago: University of Chicago Press, 1983), 47; and Gay Talese, *Thy Neighbors Wife*, (New York: Dell, 1980), 443–44. Historian Whitney Strub chronicles an antismut campaign but traces its origins more to grassroots organizations and politicians, not Summerfield or the Post Office. Whitney Strub, *Perversion for Profit* (New York: Columbia University Press, 2011), 29.

8. H. G. Cocks, *Classified: The Secret History of the Personal Column* (London: Random House, 2009).

9. See David K. Johnson, "Kids of Fairytown: Gay Male Culture on Chicago's Near North Side in the 1930s," in *Creating a Place for Ourselves: Lesbian, Gay, and Bisexual Community Histories,* ed. Brett Beemyn (New York: Routledge, 1997), 110; author interview with Bruce Scott, April 21, 1994.

10. Gerber to boyFrank, March 28, 1944, Gerber-boyFrank Correspondence, ONE National Gay and Lesbian Archives, USC Libraries, University of Southern California (ONE Archives) (much of this correspondence is also available in box 160, James T. Sears Papers, Duke University Libraries); James T. Sears, *Behind the Mask of Mattachine: The Hal Call Chronicles and the Early Movement for Homosexual Emancipation* (Binghamton, N.Y.: Harrington Park Press, 2006), 73–102.

11. Martin Meeker, *Contacts Desired: Gay and Lesbian Communications and Community, 1940s–1970s* (Chicago: University of Chicago Press, 2006), 23–26; *Hobby Directory,* June 1951, 4–5, Gay, Lesbian, Bisexual, Transgender Historical Society (GLBTHS). See also Daniel Harris, *The Rise and Fall of Gay Culture* (New York: Hyperion, 1997), 40.

12. "Total Democracy," *Hobby Directory,* March, 1950, 1; "Physique Photography," *Hobby Directory,* June 1951, 4–5, GLBTHS.

13. Box 25, Fraud and Mailability Division, Policy and Precedent Docket Case Files, 1913–1953, RG 28, Records of the Post Office, NARA; Brian Hoffman, *Naked: A Cultural History of American Nudism* (New York: New York University Press, 2015), 119, 122, 172.

14. *Strength & Health* (hereafter *S & H*), April 1946, 5.

15. *Muscle Builder,* December 1957, 56. Bob Mizer, "Pros and Cons of Pen Pal Clubs," *Grecian Guild Pictorial* (GGP), March 1961, 8.

16. Nial Kent, *The Divided Path* (New York: Greenberg, 1949), 30–33.

17. Historians who have reviewed these organizations' surviving mail report that a request for an exchange of addresses was one of the most common requests. Craig M. Loftin, *Letters to ONE: Gay and Lesbian Voices from the 1950s and 1960s* (Albany, N.Y.: SUNY Press, 2012), 96–101; Angelia R. Wilson, "Getting Your Kicks on Route 66! Stories of Gay and Lesbian Life in Rural America, c. 1950–1970," in *De-Centering Sexualities: Politics and Representations Beyond the Metropolis,* ed. Richard Phillips, Diane Watt and David Shuttleon (New York: Routledge, 2000), 198.

18. John W. Reavis, "The Rejected," *KQED,* San Francisco, September 11, 1961.

19. Lyn Pedersen, "Why Not a Pen Pal Club?" *ONE,* September 1959, 5–9.

20. Kepner wrote under the pseudonym Lyn Pedersen. See Pedersen, "Why Not a Pen Pal Club?"; Hubert Kennedy, *The Ideal Gay Man: The Story of Der Kreis* (New York: Routledge, 2000), 32–33; Clayton J. Whisnant, *Male Homosexuality in West Germany: Between Persecution and Freedom, 1945–69* (New York: Palgrave Macmillan, 2012), 93–94.

21. Dorr Legg wrote using the pseudonym William Lambert, "Sick, Sick, Sick," *ONE,* September 1959, 9–13.

22. *ONE,* January 1960; Loftin, *Letters to ONE,* 87.

23. *ONE,* January 1960.

24. Loftin, *Letters to ONE,* 20, 70. On another gay teenager who advertised in *Dig,* see "Pen Pals," *Retired in Delaware* blog, March 16, 2011, http://retiredindelaware.blogspot.com/2011/03/pen-pals.html. Members of Dionysus, a homophile group in Orange County, also

wanted to exchange addresses with others in their area, but leaders of the organization refused. "Dionysus Not Address Exchange," *Dionysus Newsletter*, March 1963, Eccles Papers, University of Washington.

25. *Physique Pictorial* (PP), August 1960, 21; Bob Mizer, "Pros and Cons of Pen Pal Clubs," *GGP*, March 1961, 7.

26. U.S. v. Charles J. Anctil et al, trial transcript, RG 21, U.S. District Court, Northern District of Illinois, Chicago Criminal Case Files, 61CR27, National Archives–Chicago Branch (Adonis trial transcript), 3782; Poulos correspondence, ONE, Inc., Records, ONE Archives; letter to the editor, ONE, October 1959, 31; "Pornography Ring Broken; 52 Indicted," *Holland (Mich.) Evening Sentinel*, January 17, 1961, 1.

27. "A Publisher's Statement," *GYM*, July 1959; "The Potomac Affair," *VIM*, October 1955. "The Landlady Died of Curiosity," *VIM*, May 1956. Bob Mizer's *Physique Pictorial* is the best source to uncover the career of the former editor William Bunton, the first editor of Irv Johnson's *Tomorrow's Man*. Bunton moved to *VIM* in May 1954 and was there until the spring of 1959, when, under the name WEB Enterprises, he launched *Manual*, also in Chicago. Within a year *Manual* was bought by Guild Press. *PP*, March 1954 and Spring 1959.

28. Adonis trial transcript, 2688–95, 3679–83.

29. *VIM*, July 1959; *GYM*, June 1959.

30. *GYM*, June 1959, 44.

31. *GYM*, April 1960; *VIM*, September 1959 and April 1960.

32. *U.S. v. Zuideveld*, 316 F.2d 873 (7th Circuit, 1963); Brief for Appellee, *U.S. v. Zuideveld*, U.S. Court of Appeals, 7th Circuit, Nos. 13771–2, in Adonis trial transcript.

33. Advertisements appeared in *VIM*, June and July 1959 and September 1960; and *GYM*, June and July 1959 and March 1960. The club was also advertised in two other magazines Zuideveld briefly offered, *Vigor* and *Vitality*—magazines with physique photos but no editorial content.

34. "Utica Man Indicted in Obscene Mail Case," *Rome (N.Y.) Daily Sentinel*, January 17, 1961; Adonis trial transcript, 3835.

35. *GYM*, July 1960; international members mentioned in Brief for Appellee, 54.

36. Adonis trial transcript, 2738.

37. *GYM*, March 1960, 32, and June 1960, 13; Adonis trial transcript, 3546, 4671.

38. Adonis trial transcript, 3954–76. After this declaration of unmailability, Chicago financier scion Roger McCormick, the owner of Victory Printing, transferred ownership of the business to Zuideveld, who later claimed that U.S. Attorney Tieken protected McCormick from prosecution.

39. "Post Office Forms Unit on Obscene, Fraudulent Mail," *Washington Star*, May 3, 1958; "Mailmen Told of Smut Peril," *Washington Star*, August 13, 1959; "Panel Asks Towns to Combat Smut," *New York Times*, October 11, 1959; "Summerfield Tells Gains in War on Smut," *Los Angeles Times*, December 8, 1959. For an early critical analysis of Summerfield's campaign, see James C. N. Paul and Murray L. Schwartz, *Federal Censorship: Obscenity in the Mail* (Glencoe, N.Y.: Free Press, 1961); for a more sympathetic narrative, see Dorothy Fowler, *Unmailable: Congress and the Post Office* (Athens: University of Georgia Press, 1977).

40. John Bartlow, *Adlai Stevenson and the World* (New York: Doubleday, 1977).

41. Arthur Summerfield, *U.S. Mail: The Story of the United States Postal Service* (New York: Holt, Rinehart and Winston, 1960); *St. Petersburg (Fla.) Times*, April 6, 1957; *Reading (Pa.) Eagle*, February 23, 1960.

42. Statement of Herbert Warburton, General Counsel, Post Office Department, "Obscene Matter Sent Through the Mail," Hearings Before the U.S. Congress, House, Committee on Post Office and Civil Service, Subcommittee on Postal Operations, 86th Cong. 1st sess., April 23, 1959, 17.

43. *Roth v. United States*, 354 U.S. 476 (1957); *Eastman Kodak v. Hendricks*, 9th Circuit (1958) 262 F.2d 392; see also Whitney Strub, *Obscenity Rules: Roth v. United States and the Long Struggle Over Sexual Expression* (Lawrence: University Press of Kansas, 2013).

44. *One, Inc. v. Olesen* 355 U.S. 371, 78 S.Ct. 364 (1958); *Sunshine Book Co. v. Summerfield* 355 US. 372 (1958) 78 S. Ct. 365.

45. "The Unkindest Cut," *Newsweek*, June 27, 1960; "Postmaster General Fires Nudist Postman," *Censorship Scoreboard*, August 1960, 2; Talese, *Thy Neighbor's Wife*, 131; Hoffman, *Naked*, 198–202.

46. Statement of Postmaster General Arthur Summerfield Before the House Post Office and Civil Service Subcommittee Investigating the Mailing of Obscene and Pornographic Material, April 23, 1959, Obscenity File, United States Postal Service, Historians Office Files (USFSHOF).

47. August 28, 1958, Public Law 85–796, Amendment to Title 18, section 1461; "President Signs New Law Barring Obscene Matter," *Washington Star*, August 29, 1958; Fowler, *Unmailable*, 178; John N. Makris, *The Silent Investigators: The Great Untold Story of the United States Postal Inspection Service* (New York: Dutton, 1959), 307–9; *ONE*, November 1960, 16. U.S. Attorney Bernard J. Brown indicated that the law was passed in reaction to *Roth* in *U.S. v. Norman V. Blantz*, No. 13394 Criminal, U.S. District Court, Middle District of Pennsylvania, NARA–Mid-Atlantic Region.

48. "Rise in Smut Mail to Youth Reported," *New York Times*, November 18, 1961. For more on the police and postal inspector raid of a 1960 Philadelphia homophile meeting where physique movies were shown, see Marc Stein, *City of Sisterly and Brotherly Loves: Lesbian and Gay Philadelphia, 1945–1972* (Chicago: University of Chicago Press, 2000), 179–84.

49. "Obscene Matter Sent Through the Mails," U.S. Congress, House, Committee on Post Office and Civil Service, Subcommittee on Postal Operations, 87th Cong., 1st sess., November 13, 1961, 26.

50. "Obscene Matter Sent Through the Mail," April 23, 1959; statement of Arthur Summerfield, House Post Office and Civil Service Subcommittee Investigating the Mailing of Obscene and Pornographic Material, April 23, 1959, Obscenity File, USPSHOF; Paul and Schwartz, *Federal Censorship*, 176–78, 235; Fowler, *Unmailable*, 179.

51. Post Office Press Release No. 261 and Walter to Editor, October 9, 1959, Obscenity File, USFSHOF; "Drive on Smut Urged," *New York Times*, May 25, 1959, 34; "The War on Obscenity," *Anderson (Ind.) Herald*, May 6, 1959; "12 in Obscenity Case Enter Innocent Pleas," *Anderson Herald*, May 28, 1961; "Abby Jolted as She Views Mailed Smut," *Washington Star*, March 31, 1960; Jack Mabley, "Pornography Sellers Bolder," *Chicago Daily News*, May 29, 1959, 1.

52. Summerfield, *U.S. Mail*, 146; "Cousins Advisor in Fight on Smut," *Milwaukee Sentinel*, December 9, 1959; "Women's Clubs Blast 'Merchants of Filth,'" *Los Angeles Examiner*, June 3, 1959; Andrea Friedman, "Sadists and Sissies: Anti-Pornography Campaigns in Cold War America," *Gender and History* 15, no. 2 (August 2003), 213–39.

53. *ONE*, January 1960, 18; Alvin Shuster, ". . . Nor Gloom of Censorship," *New York Times*, August 2, 1959; *New Yorker*, July 30, 1960.

54. *PP*, January 1961, 2.

55. "Post Office Declares War on Mail Order 'Merchants of Filth,'" *Monon (Ind.) News*, May 7, 1959, 7; "City Children Unwittingly Being Sent Pornography," *Victoria (Tex.) Advocate*, June 11, 1959, 18; Roscoe Drummond, "Obscenity and the Mails," *New York Herald Tribune*, September 9, 1959, 18; "Post Office Maps Smut Committee," *New York Times*, November 25, 1959; J. Edgar Hoover, *FBI Law Enforcement Bulletin*, January 1960.

56. "Smut Mail Shocks Women Leaders," *Denver Post*, October 15, 1959; Adonis trial transcript, 343. During the trial an Adonis member inadvertently revealed his correspondence with a postal inspector using the alias "Bob Ray."

57. "Mailing Lewd Pictures Charged to Two Here," *Washington Post*, January 7, 1960; "Lewd Ring Is Reported Smashed," *Washington Star*, January 9, 1960. On Al Urban arrest, see *PP*, January 1961; on Lon of New York arrest, see Reed Massengill, *The Male Ideal: Lon of New York and the Masculine Physique* (New York: Universe, 2003), 48.

58. "Obscene Matter Sent Through the Mail," April 23, 1959; "Postmaster Levels Attack on Mail's 'Barons of Obscenity,'" *Great Bend (Kans.) Daily Tribune*, May 3, 1960; "Cops Raid Ring Selling Lewd Male Photos," January 30, 1959, http://johnpalatinus.com; interview with John Palatinus, December 7, 2011, Miami, Florida.

59. James and Ann Free, "The National Whirligig," *Bridgeport (Conn.) Telegram*, February 14, 1962.

60. Adonis trial transcript, 90–110.

61. UPI story, January 16, 1961, reported on page 1 of scores of newspapers, including *San Mateo (Calif.) Times*.

62. "The Playboy Forum," *Playboy*, August 1966, 44; U.S. Congress, Senate, Committee on the Judiciary, Subcommittee on Administrative Practice and Procedure, *Hearings on Invasion of Privacy*, 89th Cong., 1st sess., 1965.

63. *PP*, April 1961, 21, and May 1962, 16; see also "How to Meet a Postal Inspector," Guild Press, n.d., Womack Papers, Cornell University.

64. Karl Thom to *ONE*, June 10, 1961, ONE, Inc. Correspondence File, ONE Archives. Of the sixty-six Adonis club members I have been able to identify, eight were *ONE* subscribers or readers, based on files in the ONE, Inc., Correspondence File. One other corresponded with Mattachine, and another had a friend write to *ONE*.

65. Stokes to ACLU, February 2, 1962, MC#001, box 788, folder 14, American Civil Liberties Records, Mudd Library, Princeton University, Princeton, New Jersey (ACLU Papers).

66. Detective Division to Juvenile Division, December 10, 1960, Series 1486, box 13, Florida Legislative Investigation Committee Files, Florida State Archives; "Playboy Forum," September 1966, Obscenity folder, USPSHOF; "The Playboy Forum," *Playboy*, December 1965, 79–80.

67. *Herald-Telephone* (Bloomington, Ind.), January 17, 1961, 1.

68. *Lincoln (Neb.) Star*, January 17, 1961, 14.

69. Frank A. White, "The Hoosier Day: Don't Gloss It Over," *Vidette Messenger* (Valparaiso, Ind.), January 25, 1961. White's column was syndicated in over forty Indiana newspapers. See *Indianapolis News*, November 19, 1970; Reitman to Knight, January 31, 1961, MC#001, box 786, folder 17, ACLU Papers.

70. *Homosexuality and Citizenship in Florida: A Report of the Florida Legislative Investigation Committee* (Tallahassee: Florida Legislative Investigation Committee, 1964); Karen L. Graves, *And They Were Wonderful Teachers: Florida's Purge of Gay and Lesbian Teachers* (Urbana: University of Illinois Press, 2009), 98.

71. *Corpus Christi (Tex.) Times*, January 17, 1961, 5, and March 8, 1961, 8; Philip Johnson to ONE, January 23, 1961, quoted in Craig Loftin, *Masked Voices: Gay Men and Lesbians in Cold War America* (Albany, N.Y.: SUNY Press, 2012), 126.

72. Butterfield to Malin, April 6, 1961, folder 17, box 786, ACLU Papers; Adonis trial transcript, 4606-4631.

73. "The Playboy Forum," *Playboy*, January 1966, 64–65.

74. "Principal Sentenced on Obscenity Charge," *Anniston (Ala.) Star*, February 7, 1960.

75. Loftin, *Masked Voices*, 126. Loftin attributed the disproportionate number of complaints from teachers to their sense that communicating via the mail was safer than going to gay bars, but it is now clear that the Post Office targeted teachers. Attorney Ronald Meshbesher noticed how the Post Office tended to target teachers in the later investigation of DSI. See *U.S. v. Spinar*, trial transcript, 424.

76. Ed to ONE, January 30, 1963, ONE General Correspondence, cited in Loftin, *Masked Voices*, 126.

77. The Detroit studio was probably that of Douglas Juleff, known professionally as Douglas of Detroit. Volker Janssen, *Douglas of Detroit: American Photography of the Male Nude 1940–1970*, vol. 4 (Berlin: Janssen, 2001).

78. *U.S. v. Norman V. Blantz*, No. 13394 Criminal, U.S. District Court, Middle District of Pennsylvania, NARA–Mid-Atlantic Region, Opinion, March 20, 1962, found in Schlegel Correspondence, Lucas Papers, GLBT Historical Society; interview with Drew Hanson, April 25, 2015. The judge in *U.S. v. Blantz* cited three prior unreported successful customer prosecutions, all with guilty pleas: *U.S. v. Lee Winters Douglas* (middle Alabama), *U.S. v. Warren Lee Stonecipher* (eastern Illinois), and *U.S. v. Stephen T. Kolodziejski* (middle Pennsylvania). At least one of these victims, Lee W. Douglas, was also an educator. See "Principle Sentenced on Obscenity Charge," *Anniston Star*, February 7, 1960. Another case of a federal obscenity conviction for a private letter with homosexual content is *U.S. v. John Darnell*, III, 316 F2d 813 (2nd Circuit, 1963).

79. Adonis trial transcript, 16–22, 94–95, 4293; U.S. Department of Justice, *United States Attorneys Bulletin*, vol. 10, no. 7, April 6, 1962, 206–7. Willbern and Poulos demanded new trials but were denied. *Rushville (Ind.) Republican*, February 7, 1962, 6.

80. Adonis trial transcript, 275–80, 3844, 4377–84.

81. Adonis trial transcript, 4415.

82. Adonis trial transcript, 3810, 4119.

83. Dold to Green, Adonis trial transcript, 3412–51; Winston Book Service newsletter, n.d. circa 1957, Book Service Files, Phyllis Lyon and Del Martin Papers, GLBTHS.

84. *Chicago Tribune*, January 19, 1962, 14.

85. Adonis trial transcript, 3000.

86. Adonis trial transcript, 2648–55, 2993.

87. Adonis trial transcript, 2993, 3012, 4123.

88. Adonis trial transcript, 3831.

89. Adonis trial transcript, 2976, 3812.

90. On the history of the Polaroid and its use for sexualized photos, including those by Robert Mapplethorpe, see Christopher Bonanos, *Instant: The Story of Polaroid* (New York: Princeton Architectural Press, 2012), 71–73; and Peter Buse, *The Camera Does the Rest: How Polaroid Changed Photography* (Chicago: University of Chicago Press, 2016), 68–69.

91. *U.S. v. Zuideveld*, 316 F.2d 873 (7th Circuit, 1963), 9; *U.S. v. Zuideveld*, Brief for Appellee, 23; Adonis trial transcript, 3871, 3751, 3008.

92. Adonis Trial transcript, 3001–03.

93. Adonis trial transcript, 4404. For how those behind the Little Blue Books were indicted and put out of business, see Oliver B. Pollak, "Obscenity in Kansas: Big Blue Books," *Journal of the West* 51, no. 1 (Winter 2012), 77–83; *Henry J. Haldeman v. U.S.*, 340 F2d 59, 10th Circuit, 1965.

94. Gorman to Lucas, April 16, June 13, and October 5, 1962; and Gorman relative to Call, September 28, 1963, all in Don Lucas Papers, GLBTHS; *Mattachine Review*, May 1962, 25. See also Meeker, *Contacts Desired*, 72–74. Frank Semkoski, a thirty-eight-year-old bandleader and music store owner, was another Adonis member sentenced to a year in the U.S. penitentiary in Lewisburg, Pennsylvania. Semkoski had also written letters that discussed a sexual relationship with a teenager. Adonis trial transcript, 2939.

95. AP story, January 18, 1961, *Alton Evening Telegraph* and *Daily Gazette* (Rockford, Ill.).

96. "Hoffa Prosecutor Has 58–2 Record," *Oakland Tribune*, July 29, 1964; "A Fighting Prosecutor," *New York Times*, January 30, 1967; John Dean, *Blind Ambition* (New York: Simon & Shuster, 1976.); E. Howard Hunt, *Undercover: Memoirs of an American Secret Agent* (New York: Berkley/Putnam, 1974).

97. "Mail Snooping," *New Republic*, August 21, 1965; Note, August 19, 1965, Obscenity Files, USFSHOF; "Post Office to Stop Spying," *Vector*, August 1966, 4.

98. *Redmond v. U.S.* 384 U.S. 264, 1966.

99. Chief Inspector H. B. Montague to David Nelson, General Counsel, March 11, 1969, Pornography File, USPS Historians Office.

100. Tom Mulliken, an Adonis club member, wrote, "I have a whole mess of names that Henry Jr. keeps sending me from another club." William Broadgate was a member of a Canadian pen-pal club. Adonis trial transcript, 3674.

101. Rogy's brochures, box 4, Womack Papers; "Homosexual Smut Found, Man Jailed," *Sun-Sentinel* (Pompano Beach, Fla.), March 25, 1966; Steven Barney, "She Fights Smut Aimed at the Kids," *Wisconsin State Journal*, May 1, 1966.

102. Donald W. McLeod, *A Brief History of Gay: Canada's First Gay Tabloid, 1964–1966* (Toronto: Homewood Books, 2003), 16–17.

103. Lon Delany to ONE, October 30, 1960, ONE, Inc., Papers, ONE Archives.

104. "You Must Help Fight the New McCarthyism Now," League for the Abolition of Postal Censorship, Eccles Papers. The Matttachine Society responded with a Freedom to Read Committee, and its leader Hal Call offered a special publication, *Sex and Censorship*. *Frontier Athletic Club Newsletter* established a "Defense Against Suppression Fund."

105. Adonis trial transcript, 3954; "Passages—John D. Malzone," *Windy City Times* (Chicago), March 5, 2008; John Malzone file, ONE, Inc., Files, ONE Archives.

106. Adonis trial transcript 328–60; Marisa Lagos, "Ben Gardiner Dies: Gay Rights Activist, Actor," *SFGate*, February 27, 2010, http://www.sfgate.com/bayarea/article/Ben-Gardiner -dies-gay-rights-activist-actor-3271651.php.

107. *VIM*, October 1963, June 1964, and August 1964; *GGP* no. 65 (1967); Philip Clark, "Accept Your Essential Self: The Guild Press, Identity Formation, and Gay Male Community," in *1960s Gay Pulp Fiction: The Misplaced Heritage*, ed. Drewey Gunn and Jaime Harker (Amherst: University of Massachusetts Press, 2013), 108–9.

5. DEFENDING A NAKED BOY: LYNN WOMACK AT THE SUPREME COURT

1. Interview with Curtis Dewees, September 27, 1996, Martin Duberman Papers, New York Public Library (NYPL).

2. *ONE*, January 1961, 16. See also "the body beautiful," *ONE*, June 1955, 4–6, a satirical one-act play of an encounter between a homophile leader and a physique publisher.

3. Womack has received considerable praise for his defense of the First Amendment. See Jackie Hatton, "The Pornography Empire of H. Lynn Womack: Gay Political Discourse and Popular Culture 1955–1970," *Thresholds: Viewing Culture* 7 (Spring 1993), 9–32; Rodger Streitmatter and John C. Watson, "Herman Lynn Womack: Pornographer as First Amendment Pioneer," *Journalism History* 28 (Summer 2002), 56–66; Joyce Murdoch and Deb Price, *Courting Justice: Gay Men and Lesbians v. The Supreme Court* (New York: Basic Books, 2001).

4. Marc Stein, *City of Sisterly and Brotherly Loves: Lesbian and Gay Philadelphia, 1945–1972* (Chicago: University of Chicago Press, 2000); Marc Stein, "Canonizing Homophile Sexual Respectability: Archives, History and Memory," *Radical History Review* no. 120 (Fall 2014), 52–73; Streitmatter and Watson, "Herman Lynn Womack," sees the importance of *Manual v. Day* but argues that it was Polak, not Womack, who used it to revolutionize gay publishing.

5. James Larder, "A Pornographer's Rise, Fall," *Washington Post*, January 12, 1978; James Griffin, "Dr. Womack and the Nudie Magazines," *Washington Daily News*, April 30, 1970. For a portrait of Washington, D.C., as a progressive, tolerant boomtown in the 1930s, see David K. Johnson, *The Lavender Scare: The Cold War Persecution of Gays and Lesbians in the Federal Government* (Chicago: University of Chicago Press, 2004).

6. Womack to Benson, December 1, 1957, H. Lynn Womack Papers, Human Sexuality Collection, Division of Rare and Manuscript Collections, Cornell University (Womack Papers).

7. Womack to George, April 30, 1956, and George to Womack, August 15, 1956, Womack Papers. Why they considered him too liberal is unclear, but he was close friends with philosopher Harry McFarland Bracken, known for his friendship with Noam Chomsky and his later anti–Vietnam War activism.

8. Womack to Glenn, May 21, 1957, and Womack to George, September 30, 1956, and May 20, 1957, Womack Papers.

9. Womack to Benson, December 1, 1957, Womack Papers; "Violations Charged to Four Firms," *Securities and Exchange Commission News Digest*, June 30, 1959, 2; James Lardner, "A Pornographer's Rise, Fall," *Washington Post*, January 12, 1978; Paul Dickson, *Sputnik: The Shock of the Century* (New York: Bloomsbury, 2001).

10. Womack to George, April 30 1956, Womack Papers; Phi Sigma Tau Honor Society, https://phi-sigma-tau.org/history.html, accessed January 4, 2017.

11. Lambert to Womack, February 10, 1955, ONE, Inc., Papers, ONE National Gay and Lesbian Archives, USC Libraries, University of Southern California (ONE Archives).

12. GGP, November 1957, 17; Womack to Grecian Guild, October 13, 1957, and Benson to Womack, January 10, 1958, Womack Papers. Womack would later claim that he discovered physique magazines only after acquiring the printing company and *GGP* became one of his better-paying clients. The archival record shows that his decision to get into the physique business was much more calculated and thoughtful. James Lardner, "A Pornographer's Rise, Fall," *Washington Post*, January 12, 1978.

13. Womack to Benson, February 7 and March 23, 1958, Womack Papers; Clark Polak, "The Story Behind Physique Magazines," *Drum*, October 1965, 8–15.

14. Little is known about Lou Elson and ACME. See Reed Massengill, *The Male Ideal: Lon of New York and the Masculine Physique* (New York: Universe, 2004), 45, 50; Donald W. McLeod, *A Brief History of Gay: Canada's First Gay Tabloid, 1964–1966* (Toronto: Homewood Books, 2003), 54–55, 65–68; interview with Richard Schlegel, May 11, 1993, Marc Stein personal papers.

15. Womack to Benson, February 7, March 18, and March 23 1958, Womack Papers.

16. Womack to Benson, February 7, 1958, Womack Papers.

17. Womack to Benson, March 29, 1958, Womack Papers; *Washington Post*, January 7, 1960.

18. "Artist Profile: Anthony Guyther," *Martha's Vineyard (Mass.) Times*, June 24, 2015; "Anthony Guyther," *Martha's Vineyard Times*, April 25, 2017; author interview with Anthony Guyther, December 19, 2016.

19. *Matter of Capital Studio*, Initial Decision of Hearing Examiner, P.O.D. Docket No 2/47, March 16, 1962. The original trial transcript, quoted in the initial decision, exceeded four hundred pages. Neither the U.S. Postal Service nor the National Archives retains any of these original records, nor do they have any record of their destruction.

20. *Muscle Builder*, September 1955, 54; author interview with Guyther, December 19, 2016.

21. Author interview with Guyther, December 19, 2016.

22. *Matter of Capital Studio*, Initial Decision of Hearing Examiner, P.O.D. Docket No 2/47, March 16, 1962.

23. *Matter of Alfred J. Heinecke*, Departmental Decision, P.O.D. Docket 1/281, November 28, 1960; *Matter of Capital Studio and Anthony Guyther*, Initial Decision of Hearing Examiner, P.O.D. Docket 2/47, March 16, 1962; *Alfred J. Heinecke v. U.S.*, 294 F.2d 727.

24. Womack to National League for Social Understanding, August 15, 1963, Womack Papers.

25. Author interview with George Palatinus, December 7, 2011; "Cops Raid Ring Selling Lewd Male Photos," *New York Daily News*, January 30, 1959. With a resurgence of interest in physique images, Palatinus was rediscovered in the twenty-first century and began exhibiting internationally. See http://john-palatinus.com, accessed May 15, 2017.

26. Indictment, *U.S. v. Herman L. Womack*, U.S. District Court for D.C., Criminal No. 41–60, Womack Papers; "Lewd Ring Is Reported Smashed," *Washington Star*, January 9, 1960; "3 Indicted on Lewd Mail Charge," *Washington Post*, January 14, 1960.

27. Womack to Benson, March 29, 1958, Womack Papers.

28. "4 Experts Testify on Nude Photos," *Washington Post*, March 18, 1960.

29. "Boys Testify at Obscene Mail Trial," *Washington Post*, March 19, 1960; "Educator Convicted of Sending Obscene Literature Through Mail," *Washington Post*, March 22, 1960; "Ex-professor Is Sentenced in Morals Case," *Washington Post*, April 15, 1960.

30. *Womack v U.S.*, 294 F.2d 204; *Washington Post*, January 7 and March 22, 1960; *Washington Star*, March 17, March 22, and October 7, 1960.

31. Leon Friedman, ed., *Obscenity: The Complete Oral Arguments Before the Supreme Court in the Major Obscenity Cases* (New York: Chelsea House, 1970), 99.

32. *Matter of Manual Enterprises, Inc.*, Departmental Decision, P.O.D. Docket No 1/246, April 28, 1960; *Washington Post*, April 14 and August 16, 1960; *New York Times*, August 16, 1960.

33. *Manual Enterprises, Inc. v. J. Edward Day*, 289 F.2d 455, 110 U.S. App. DC 78; *Washington Post*, March 24, 1961.

34. *Washington Star*, November 11, 1960; *Washington Post*, December 9 and December 16, 1960.

35. *Heinecke v. U.S.*, 294 F.2d 727 (1961); *Washington Post*, January 28, 1961; *Washington Star*, January 28, 1961.

36. Larder, "A Pornographer's Rise, Fall," *Washington Post*, January 12, 1978. The insanity defense also eventually got his convictions overturned. "Insanity Acquittal Cited by Womack in Appeal," *Washington Star*, September 8, 1962; *U.S. v. Womack*, 211 F Supp. 578 (1962); Thomas Otto, *St. Elizabeths Hospital: A History* (Washington, D.C.: General Services Administration, May 2013).

37. *Washington Star*, January 30, 1960.

38. Heinecke brochure, September 14, 1960, Tim Wood Collection, Gay, Lesbian, Bisexual, Transgender Historical Society, San Francisco (GLBTHS).

39. *Trim*, March 1961; *Manorama*, December 1960; Womack and Anthony to Friend, October 12, 1960, http://timinvermont.com.

40. Statement of Policy on Complete Nude Photographs, Florida Model Guild, Tim Wood Collection, GLBTHS.

41. Detective Division to Post Office Department, December 15, 1960, Series 1486, box 13, Florida State Archives.

42. R.E.L. Masters, *The Homosexual Revolution* (New York: Belmont Books, 1964), 58. Masters predicted in the original edition (1962) that Womack would lose his court case but had to admit his prediction was wrong in the preface to the paperback edition (1964).

43. *Womack v. U.S.*, 365 U.S. 859 (1961); *Heinecke v. U.S.*, 386 U.S. 901 (1961).

44. Friedman, *Obscenity*, 89–142. President Kennedy's solicitor general, Archibald Cox, choose not to argue the case himself.

45. Judith Valente, "Making a Living Defending the Pornographers," *Washington Post*, January 11, 1978.

46. Jerry Oppenheimer, "Smut Merchants Go Establishment," *Washington Daily News*, December 7, 1970.

47. *ONE v. Olesen*, 355 U.S. 371 (1958); Carlos A. Ball, *The First Amendment and LGBT Equality: A Contentious History* (Cambridge, Mass.: Harvard University Press, 2017), 37. This *per curiam* decision was later revealed to be a slim 5–4 ruling in Murdoch and Price, *Courting Justice*, 46.

48. Friedman, *Obscenity*, 306.

49. *Kameny v. Brucker*, Petition for Writ of Certiorari, no. 676, U.S. Supreme Court, October 1960 term, NARA; Friedman, *Obscenity*, 91–93.

50. Friedman, *Obscenity*, 127.

51. *Matters Concerning Manual Enterprises, Inc.*, Departmental Decision, P.O.D. Docket No 1/246, April 28, 1960.

52. Friedman, *Obscenity*, 129–35.

53. *Manual Enterprises Inc. v. J. Edward Day*, 370 US 478 (1962); Jay A. Sigler, "Freedom of the Mails: A Developing Right," *Georgetown Law Journal* 54 (1965), 36; Louis Henkin, "Morals and the Constitution: The Sin of Obscenity," *Columbia Law Review* 63 (1963), 391.

54. Ball, *The First Amendment and LGBT Equality*, 40.

55. Potomac Press "dear friend" letter, December 1962, John M. Eccles Papers, Special Collections, University of Washington, Seattle (Eccles Papers).

56. *Mattachine Review*, July 1962, 34, and August 1962, 2; *ONE*, September 1962, 12; *Ladder*, November 1962, 5; Craig Loftin, *Letters to ONE: Gay and Lesbian Voices from the 1950s and 1960s* (Albany, N.Y.: SUNY Press, 2012), 78.

57. Womack to Haimsohn, April 8, 1963, quoted in Reed Massengill, "Carnal Matters: The Alexander Goodman Story," in *1960s Gay Pulp Fiction: The Misplaced Heritage*, ed. Drewey Wayne Gunn and Jaime Harker (Amherst: University of Massachusetts Press, 2013), 172.

58. *VIM*, October 1963.

59. *Mars*, May 1963; author interview with Chuck Renslow, May 24, 2008; Tracy Baim and Owen Keehnen, *Leatherman: The Legend of Chuck Renslow* (Chicago: Prairie Avenue Productions, 2011), 56–57; Joseph W. Bean, ed., *Kris: The Physique Photography of Chuck Renslow* (Las Vegas: Nazca Plains, 2007); Sukie De La Croix, *Whispers: A History of LGBT Chicago Before Stonewall* (Madison: University of Wisconsin Press, 2012), 186–88.

60. *VIM*, December 1964.

61. *MANual*, October 1964, 34.

62. Notice, Alfred Heinecke, n.d., Willie Walker Papers, GLBTHS; Notice, Alfred Heinecke, n.d., Eccles Papers.

63. *Grecian Guild Pictorial* (GGP), July 1964.

64. *ONE*, October 1964, 31.

65. Wright to Priam, July 14, 1965, Tim Wood Collection, GLBTHS; *Manorama*, July 1965.

66. Womack to Call, July 2, 1964, Sears Papers, Duke University; Martin Duberman interview with Curtis Dewees, September 27, 1996, NYPL; John D'Emilio interview with Curtis Dewees, January 24, 1979, http://outhistory.org.

67. *ONE*, August–September 1957 and October 1959; Village Books & Press circulars, all undated, Womack Papers; Howard Frisch obituary, www.millspaughcamerato.com/obituary/Howard-J.-Frisch/_/1382630, accessed August 22, 2012.

68. Guild Book Service, Bulletin no. 1. Bulletins began appearing in *GGP*, May 1963.

69. Richard Schlegel interview with Marc Stein, May 11, 1993. Frisch probably wrote or drafted the book reviews.

70. Angela Grimmer to Pocket Books, May 13, 1965, George Fisher Papers, Cornell University, Ithaca, N.Y.; Guild Book Service, Bulletin no. 24.

71. "A History of Guild Press," Guild Press Book Service Catalog, 1963–1964; Guild Press to friend, November 1, 1963, http://timinvermont.com.

72. Brochures in Womack Papers; Stephen Vider, "'Oh Hell, May, Why Don't You People Have a Cookbook?' Camp Humor and Gay Domesticity," *American Quarterly* 65, no. 4 (December 2013), 877–904.

73. Phil Andros, *$TUD* (Washington, D.C.: Guild Press, 1966); Justin Spring, *Secret Historian: The Life and Times of Samuel Steward, Professor, Tattoo Artist, and Sexual Renegade* (New York: Farrar, Straus and Giroux, 2010), 315–18; Michael Bronski, *Pulp Friction: Uncovering the Golden Age of Gay Male Pulps* (New York: St. Martin's Press, 2003), 84, 199.

74. Philip Clark, "The First King of Pornography: H. Lynn Womack and Washington, D.C.'s Guild Press," in *The Golden Age of Gay Fiction*, ed. Drewey Wayne Gunn (Albion, N.Y.: MLR Press, 2009), 87–95. Because the history of these book services has been obscured, Clark and other historians erroneously credit Womack with offering the first gay book service.

75. *Model of the Month Club Magazine* no. 6, n.d.

76. Womack to Call, July 2, 1964, Fisher Papers; "Purple Pamphlet Again . . .," *Miami News*, November 15, 1964. See also Stacy Braukman, *Communists and Perverts Under the Palms: The Johns Committee in Florida, 1956–1965* (Gainesville: University Press of Florida, 2012).

77. *Manorama*, July 1965 and January 1966; *GGP*, November 1966; *Male Swinger* no. 2, 1967.

78. *Manorama*, November 1965.

79. Alexis Johns, "The GAY European Tour!" *Manorama*, July 1966.

80. H. Lynn Womack to TOM Men's Shop, August 4, 1966, Womack Papers; clothing advertisements in *Mars*, September 1964 and January 1965.

81. Don Cook interview with author, November 14, 2011; Ah Men Catalogs in vertical files, Leather Archives & Museum, Chicago; "Ah Men Cruise Time," *Male Figure* no. 31, 1964, 2; *Mars*, January 1965, 43; Shaun Cole, *Don We Now Our Gay Apparel: Gay Men's Dress in the Twentieth Century* (New York: Oxford, 2000). Womack may also have been inspired by Vince Man's Shop in London, one of the first such menswear stores cultivating a gay clientele, founded by a former physique photographer. See Justin Bengry, "Peacock Revolution: Mainstreaming Queer Styles in Post-War Britain, 1945–1967," *Socialist History* 36 (2010), 55–68.

82. *New York Times*, December 17, 1963, 33; Lee Mortimer, *New York Mirror*, February 24, 1962; Charles V. Mathis, "'Gay Set' Influx Worries Cape May," *Variety*, April 28, 1965, quoted in *DRUM*, August 1965; Daniel Delis Hill, "Men in Briefs," *Gay & Lesbian Review*, November–December 2011, 20–24.

83. *Around the World with Kenneth Marlowe*, April–May, 1966: Ah Men "House Party" Catalog, 1966, vertical files, Leather Archives.

84. Ephemera, Willie Walker Papers, GLBTHS.

85. *GGP*, May 1965, *Male Swinger* no. 1, 1967.

86. *PP*, February 1963, 8; May 1964, 17; July 1964, 22 and 26. Mattachine New York thanked Mizer for his "favorable mention." Hodges to *Physique Pictorial* editor, August 27, 1964, folder 4, box 4, New York Mattachine Microfilm, NYPL.

87. *PP*, July 1964, 2.

88. *PP*, October 1963.

89. *Young Physique*, May 1963.

90. *Young Physique*, August–September 1964.

91. *Young Physique*, August–September 1963; James Bidgood, *Bidgood* (Cologne: Taschen, 1999).

92. Noto Dante, "Miniaturization, Marginalization and Desire: The Boy's Physique Magazines of the 1950s–1960s," M.A. thesis, Duke University, 1995, 25.

93. Polak, "The Story Behind Physique Photography," 9.

94. Richard Schlegel interview with Marc Stein, May 11, 1993.

95. Schlegel interview with Stein, May 11, 1993; Clark Polak interview with John D'Emilio, October 5, 1976, http://outhistory.org.

96. ECHO Conference Program, 1964, quoted in Stein, *City of Sisterly and Brotherly Loves*, 232; *Atheneum Review*, October 1964, NYPL.

97. Report of Chief Postal Inspector, July 7, 1965, Oshtry Papers, Marc Stein personal papers; *Janus* 4, no. 4 (April 1964), Eccles Papers.

98. *DRUM*, March and April 1965; Schlegel interview with Stein, May 10, 1993.

99. Janus Society announced it was considering running full-frontal nudes in *DRUM*, October 1965, and inaugurated them in *DRUM*, December 1965. *DRUM* brochure, n.d., Schlegel to 1966 folder, Marc Stein personal papers.

100. Harry Chess debuted in *DRUM* in April 1965. The strip was so popular it survived into the postphysique era in *Queens Quarterly* starting in 1969, and after 1977 in *Drummer* and other publications. A. Jay, *The Uncensored Adventures of Harry Chess* (Philadelphia: Trojan Book Service, 1966); A. Jay, *The Super Adventures of Harry Chess* (San Francisco: Leyland, 1989); Jack Fritscher, "The Passing of One of *Drummer's* First Daddies: Al Shapiro," *Drummer* 107 (August 1987), 34–40; Drewey Wayne Gunn, *The Gay Male Sleuth in Print and Film: A History and Annotated Bibliography* (Lanham, Md.: Rowman & Littlefield, 2013), 222.

101. "Court Ruling Attacked," *News Journal* (Mansfield, Ohio), May 25, 1967; *Drum*, December 1966. Kameny is listed as a staff member in *Drum*, November and December 1964; Stein, *City of Sisterly and Brotherly Loves*, 282–302; Charles Kaiser, *Gay Metropolis*, 207; *ONE Archives Bulletin*, Fall 1983, 16. Later in life Polak continued to support gay rights causes, including the ACLU Gay Rights Chapter and the ONE Archives. In a will that was not honored, he left his $2 million estate to the LGBT community.

102. Leitch to Polak, March 23, 1965, Mattachine Papers, NYPL; Editorial, *Eastern Mattachine Review*, November–December 1965.

103. *New York Mattachine Newsletter* to Gentlemen, April 5, 1964, folder 7, box 4, Mattachine Papers, NYPL; *New York Mattachine Newsletter*, November 1964, 12.

104. *ONE Confidential*, January 1964.

105. *Mattachine Review*, March 1964.

106. *Pursuit & Symposium*, March–April 1966 and June 1967; *Bag One: A Pursuit Newsletter*, July 1966, ONE Archives. Art Enterprises of Hamilton, Ontario, was the only

physique studio included. The cartoons are signed "Jonas" but seem to be the work of A. J. Shapiro.

107. *Around the World with Kenneth Marlowe*, June–July 1966 and August–October 1966.

108. Inman to Leitch, January 24, 1966, box 5, folder 1, Mattachine Papers, NYPL; *Kansas City Times*, February 21, 1966; John D'Emilio, *Sexual Politics, Sexual Communities: The Making of a Homosexual Minority in the United States, 1940–1970* (Chicago: University of Chicago Press, 1983), 197–99. Troy Saxon was featured in *Grecian Guild Studio Quarterly* 12 (Winter 1965).

109. *Drum*, April 1966, 4; Collector of Customs to Sam Steward, February 14, 1958, Sam Steward Papers, Yale University; Editorial, *Body Beautiful*, December 1961. Among the many cases referred to the ACLU, see folders 16 and 18, box 787; folder 19, box 793; and folder 10, box 794, ACLU Records, Princeton, N.J.

110. "OK's Nudist Magazines," *Chicago American*, October 23, 1967; "Court Lifts Ban on Nude Pictures," *New York Times*, October 24, 1967. Womack bought the magazines for twenty-four cents and sold them for five dollars. U.S. Customs had allowed all male nudist magazines coming from Denmark after *Manual v. Day*, but in March 1966, probably in response to the more restrictive *Mishkin* decision, it began stopping them again. See "Customs Backs Down," *Dorian Book Quarterly*, October 1962, 2.

111. "Danish Nudie Mags Get the Nod," *Los Angeles Advocate*, December 1967, 1; "Potomac News Co. Wins Again," flyer, n.d., Womack Papers; *U.S. v. Potomac News Co.*, 373 F.2d 635 (1967); *Potomac News Co. v. U.S.*, 389 U.S. 47 (1967).

112. *Gay*, September 27, 1971, 8; Vincenz to Parker, August 13, 1971, Lilli Vincenz Papers, Library of Congress, Washington, D.C.

113. Paul Kuntzler, interview by Philip Clark, May 8, 2012.

114. Dr. Franklin Kameny, "Gay Pride," *Mark II Theatre Bulletin* no. 2, n.d.; Dr. Franklin E. Kameny, "In Case of Emergency, Don't Panic," *Mark II Theatre Bulletin* no. 3, n.d., Womack Papers.

115. Sanford J. Unger, "Homosexual 'Cause' Seen as Issue in Trial," *Washington Post*, July 21, 1971. In August a jury found fifteen of the seventeen seized Guild Press publications to be obscene. Womack was sentenced to six months in prison, but in exchange he agreed to sever all ties with Guild Press and leave Washington, D.C.

116. *Gay Forum*, October 15–31, 1971, 8. In addition to advertisements from gay bars and bathhouses, *Gay Forum* boasted at least one national chain: Omaha Steaks.

117. Marc Stein, *Sexual Injustice: Supreme Court Decisions from Griswold to Roe* (Chapel Hill: University of North Carolina Press, 2010), 39, 57, 224–25; see also Marc Stein, *Rethinking the Gay and Lesbian Movement* (New York: Routledge, 2012); and William N. Eskridge, Jr., and Nan D. Hunter, *Sexuality, Gender, and the Law* (Westbury, N.Y.: Foundation Press, 2011), which make only passing mention of *Manual v. Day* while focusing attention on *ONE v. Olesen*.

118. Whitney Strub, *Perversion for Profit: The Politics of Pornography and the Rise of the New Right* (New York: Columbia University Press, 2011), 66; Whitney Strub, *Obscenity Rules: Roth v. United States and the Long Struggle Over Sexual Expression* (Lawrence: University Press of Kansas, 2013), 193.

119. Dave Martin, "A Brief History of the Male Nude in the U.S.A., 1996," http://models.badpuppy .com/archive/davem/dave1.htm, accessed January 17, 2013. See also Dave Martin, *Dave*

Martin: *American Photography of the Male Nude 1940–1970*, vol. 3 (Berlin: Janssen Verlag, 1996); Jim Provenzano, "Dave's Letterman," *Bay Area Reporter* (San Francisco), December 14, 2006.

120. Legal research indicates that *Manual v. Day* is cited three times more frequently than *ONE v. Olesen* in subsequent Supreme Court decisions. Thanks to James Mora for this analysis.

121. Chuck Renslow interview with Jack Rinella, 1995, Leather Archives.

122. Schlegel interview with Stein, May 11, 1993.

123. V-M-P Yahoo Group via http://timinvermont.com; Dick Leitch interview with author, July 31, 2012.

124. John Waters, *Role Models* (New York: Farrar, Straus and Giroux, 2010), 220; David Hurles, *Outcast* (San Francisco: Green Candy Press, 2010).

125. James Lardner, "A Pornographer's Rise, Fall," *Washington Post*, January 12, 1978.

126. Streitmatter and Watson, "Pornographer as First Amendment Pioneer," 59.

127. "Dr. Womack Honored," *Gay Forum*, October 15–31, 1971, 3.

128. Griffin, *Washington Daily News*, April 30, 1970; James Lewes, *Protest and Survive: Underground GI Newspapers During the Vietnam War* (New York: Greenwood, 2003), 81–88.

129. Leitch to Kameny, September 29, 1964, Frank Kameny Papers, Library of Congress, Washington, D.C.; *New York Mattachine Newsletter*, September 1964.

130. *New York Times*, January 25, 2003; Massengill, "Carnal Matters."

131. Guild Press flyers, Womack Papers; Alexander Goodman, *A Summer on Fire Island* (Washington, D.C.: Guild Press, 1966).

132. Poem quoted in Massengill, "Carnal Matters." Massengill offers a more cynical, less sympathetic interpretation of both Womack and Haimsohn.

6. CONSOLIDATING THE MARKET: DSI OF MINNEAPOLIS

1. Elija Cassidy, *Gay Men, Identity and Social Media: A Culture of Participatory Reluctance* (New York: Routledge, 2018). On the development of gay yellow pages, see Stephen O. Murray, *American Gay* (Chicago: University of Chicago Press, 1996), 191; Larry Gross, *Up from Invisibility* (New York: Columbia University Press, 2001), 245; "Gay Yellow Pages" episode, *Ellen DeGeneres Show* (1997).

2. On the post-*Manual* expansion of the market, see *Physique Pictorial* (*PP*), August and October 1963, including its first mention of DSI.

3. Conrad Germain, interview by author, June 6, 2008, West Hollywood, Calif.; Mickey Robins, interview by author, June 12, 2007, Santa Monica, Calif.

4. Ronald Meshbesher, interview by author, April 30, 2013. Spinar and Germain may have borrowed the catalog's name from the *Vagabond*, a popular men's or "girlie" magazine of the 1960s.

5. Robin Cherry, *Catalog: The Illustrated History of Mail-Order Shopping* (New York: Princeton Architectural Press, 2008); David Blanke, *Sowing the American Dream: How Consumer Culture Took Root in the Rural Midwest* (Athens: Ohio University Press, 2000).

6. Germain, interview by author, June 6, 2008; Robins, interview by author, June 12, 2007; Deposition of Conrad Germain, April 10, 1972, Spinar & Germain adv Robins & Meshbesher folder, box 114, Stanley Fleishman Papers, University of California Los Angeles

(Fleishman Papers); U.S. Census, 1940, Emmons County, North Dakota, population schedule, sheet 2B, enumeration district (ED) 15-5, family 30, line 44, Willard Germain; *U.S. v. Spinar and Germain*, RG 21, U.S. District Court, Fourth Division of Minnesota, Minneapolis, Criminal Case Files, 1966–1969, National Archives–Chicago Branch, Box 11, Case 4-67CR 15, 765 (*U.S. v. Spinar*).

7. Lloyd Spinar, interview by author, June 16, 2009, Henderson, Nev.; Germain, interview by author, June 6, 2008. Spinar first operated under his own name and the designation "marketing and printing services" before forming a partnership with Germain in May 1963 as Directory Services. Spinar to *TRIM*, February 7, 1963, H. Lynn Womack Papers, Human Sexuality Collection, Division of Rare and Manuscript Collections, Cornell University, Ithaca, N.Y. (Womack Papers); Stipulation of facts, July 11, 1967, *U.S. v. Spinar* trial transcript.

8. The earliest edition I have found is *Directory 84*, third edition (1963), Womack Papers; Mizer first mentions DSI and *Directory 84* in *PP*, October 1963, 19.

9. Spinar, interview by author, June 16, 2009; *U.S. v. Spinar* trial transcript, 770.

10. For examples of early underground gay travel guides, see Hugh Hagius, *Swasarnt Nerf's Gay Guides for 1949* (New York: Bibliogay Publications, 2010); "International List of Gay Bars," courtesy of Michael Williams, "Obscene Diary: The Secret Archive of Samuel Steward, Professor, Tattoo Artist and Pornographer" exhibit, Museum of Sex (New York, 2011). Ganymede Press offered a *Gay Guide to Europe* as early as 1960. See ONE, May 1960.

11. Bob Damron, who began publishing guides to gay bars in 1964, suggests that in the 1960s most gay bars in the East were mafia owned, while in San Francisco "25 to 30 percent" of gay bars were gay owned. See Wayne Sage, "Inside the Colossal Closet," in *Gay Men: The Sociology of Male Homosexuality*, ed. Martin P. Levine (New York: Harper & Row, 1979), 150; Nan Alamilla Boyd, *Wide-Open Town: A History of Queer San Francisco to 1965* (Berkeley: University of California Press, 2003), 127–32.

12. Martin Meeker, *Contacts Desired: Gay and Lesbian Communications and Community, 1940s–1970s* (Chicago: University of Chicago Press, 2006), 207–17; "1964 World Report Travel Guide" brochure, folder 22, box 1, John M. Eccles Papers, Special Collections, University of Washington, Seattle (Eccles Papers); Guild Guides from 1964 to 1972, in Womack Papers; Catalog of Copyright Entries: Books and Pamphlets. ser. 3 pt.1 vol. 17, July–December, 1963, 1450. The *World Report Travel Guide* was published by Martin W. Swithinbank of Book Horizons in New York. See Howard Frisch to Martin Swithinbank, June 9, 1964, Womack Papers.

13. *U.S. v. Spinar* trial transcript, 54, 768–77; Spinar to Cox, September 11, 1963, Womack Papers. On Richard Fontaine, who ran R.A. Enterprises, Zenith Films, and Apollo Productions, see G. T. Wallace, "Queer Shorts: Richard Fontaine, Pioneer Gay Filmmaker," *Inches*, October 1996, 88–91; and "Richard Fontaine: Pioneer of Gay Films Since 1949," *Victory News* 35 (March 1990), 5. *Victory News*, which called itself "Ohio's Gay Entertainment Magazine," put a naked model from Fontaine's films on its cover and offered an address for buying videos of his vintage films, underscoring the continuity between 1950s physique magazines and post-Stonewall gay periodicals.

14. His real name was Robert Anthony Dabrowski. Reed Massengill, *The Male Ideal: Lon of New York and the Masculine Physique* (New York: Universe, 2004), 39; Bob Anthony folder, Clippings Files, ONE National Gay and Lesbian Archives, USC Libraries, University of Southern California (ONE Archives); http://timinvermont.com.

15. This summary is based on numerous, mostly undated circulars and Vagabond catalogs in Womack Papers, ONE Archives, and the Canadian Gay and Lesbian Archives. *Female Mimics*, 1963, in Eccles Papers.

16. *U.S. v. Spinar* trial transcript, 226, 854; *Greyhuff* is advertised in *Drum*, January 1966, as "a work of art."

17. DSI subsidiaries included Commander Associates, Commander Books, Conrad Associates, DSI Sales, Greyhuff, Northern News, and Vagabond Sales. Stipulation of Facts, July 11, 1967, in *U.S. v. Spinar*, Criminal Case Files; DAK folder, ONE Archives.

18. George Scithers to Dom Orejudos, September 24, 1966, Chuck Renslow Papers, Leather Archives.

19. Rocco sold his films for $10; DSI sold them for $8. Pat Rocco to Benjamin McNeal, July 26, 1968, Pat Rocco Papers, ONE Archives.

20. Deposition of Conrad Germain, April 10, 1972, Spinar & Germain adv Robins & Meshbesher folder, box 114, Fleishman Papers; Judge Larson, Order No 4-67-Crim. 15, *U.S. v. Spinar*; *U.S. v. Spinar* trial transcript, 294, 763.

21. Editorial, *Golden Boys* no. 1, 1967.

22. Spinar, interview by author, June 16, 2009; John Michael Cox, Jr., to author, November 14, 2006. Cox owns Champion Studios. A presidential commission determined that there was "insufficient data" to conclude that organized crime controlled the pornography business. Earl Kemp, ed., *The Illustrated Presidential Report of the Commission on Obscenity and Pornography* (New York: Greenleaf Classics, 1970), 33.

23. Robins, interview by author, June 12, 2007. They lived at 740 River Drive in the Highland Park neighborhood of St. Paul.

24. "A New Era Is Upon Us," *Butch* 3 (1967), 44–48. Spinar later identified as a Republican, while Germain was known to contribute to progressive causes. Spinar, interview by author, June 16, 2009. Clark Polak editorials also followed a libertarian line. See "Liberty in the Defense of Vice Is No Extreme," *Drum* 4, no. 9 (November 1964), 1.

25. *Spinar v. U.S.* trial transcript, 105, 419, 777, 827; "The Danger in Pen Pal Clubs," *PP*, July 1964, 12.

26. Fox is named in count 2 of indictment, February 15, 1967, *U.S. v. Spinar*, Criminal Case Files; *Daily Plainsman* (Huron, S.D.), October 27, 1964, 3; *Minneapolis Tribune*, February 7, 1967.

27. *ONE*, October 1964, 4–5.

28. *Directory Services, Inc. v. U.S.*, 353 F.2d 299 (8th Circuit, 1965); *U.S. v. Spinar* trial transcript, 1157.

29. *Ginzburg v. U.S.*, 383 U.S. 463 (1966); *Mishkin v. U.S.*, 383 U.S. 502 (1966).

30. "Booksellers Here Staging a Cleanup," *New York Times*, March 23, 1966; O. K. Armstrong, "A Victory Over the Smut Peddlers," *Reader's Digest*, February 1967, 147–52. On *Mishkin* and the police crackdown, see Whitney Strub, *Perversion for Profit: The Politics of Pornography and the Rise of the New Right* (New York: Columbia University Press, 2011), 75; and Marc Stein, *Sexual Injustice: Supreme Court Decisions from Griswold to Roe* (Chapel Hill: University of North Carolina Press, 2010), 35–44.

31. *Washington Star*, June 30, 1966; *Frontier Athletic Club Newsletter* no. 5, 1966, ONE Archives; box 795, folder 4, ACLU Papers, Princeton; *ONE*, May 1966, 19.

32. Lewis Patterson, "Two St. Paul Men Arrested by U.S. on Smut Counts," *St. Paul Pioneer Press*, February 7, 1967; Stipulation of Facts, July 26, 1967, *U.S. v. Spinar*, Criminal Case Files; *U.S. v. Spinar* trial transcript, 741, 816; "confusion" in *Drum*, September 1966, 30–31. Debate surrounding the *Mishkin* decision continues. See Stein, *Sexual Injustice*, 39, 224–25.

33. Brief in Support of Motion to Suppress, *U.S. v. Spinar and Germain*, folder 13, box 1, Womack Papers; Affidavit of Ronald Meshbesher, March 13, 1967, Affidavit of Lloyd Spinar, May 8, 1967, and Order, May 12, 1967 in *U.S. v. Spinar*, Criminal Case Files; *St. Paul Dispatch*, July 10, 1967.

34. Patterson, "Two St. Paul Men Arrested by U.S. on Smut Counts," *St. Paul Pioneer Press*, February 7, 1967, 1; "Grand Jury Indicts 3 on Charge of Mailing of Obscene Material," *Minneapolis Tribune*, February 7, 1967, 1; U.S. Congress, Senate, Committee of the Judiciary, Juvenile Delinquency: Hearings Before the Subcommittee to Investigate Juvenile Delinquency, 90th Cong., 1st sess., February 9, 1967, 3946.

35. *History of the U.S. District Court for the District of Minnesota* (1989), 17; "Earl Larson Award," *St. Paul Star Tribune*, November 7, 2007; Finlay Lewis, "Obscenity Trial Defendants Waive Jury," *Minneapolis Tribune*, July 12, 1967; *U.S. v. Spinar* trial transcript, 13; Lloyd Spinar deposition, April 10, 1972, Spinar & Germain adv. Robins & Meshbesher folder, box 114, Fleishman Papers; Hal Call, interview by Paul Cain, 1994, Hal Call Papers, Duke University, Durham, N.C. Robins testified at the trial about the legal advice he gave DSI on its publications over the years, but at Germain's request he played no other substantive role in the trial.

36. *U.S. v. Spinar* trial transcript, 820–50.

37. *U.S. v. Spinar* trial transcript, 23.

38. *U.S. v. Spinar* trial transcript, 160–96.

39. *U.S. v. Spinar* trial transcript, 82–140.

40. *U.S. v. Spinar* trial transcript, 1123–24; "Smut Trial Told Nude Swimming May Harm Boys," *St. Paul Dispatch*, July 17, 1967.

41. *U.S. v. Spinar* trial transcript, 1090–95. The University of Minnesota Medical School established a Gender Committee in 1966. See Joanne Meyerowitz, *How Sex Changed: A History of Transsexuality in the United States* (Cambridge, Mass: Harvard University Press, 2002), 222.

42. *U.S. v. Spinar* trial transcript, 870–87; Walter C. Alvarez, *The Incurable Physician: An Autobiography* (Englewood Cliffs, N.J.: Prentice-Hall, 1963).

43. *U.S. v. Spinar* trial transcript, 579.

44. *U.S. v. Spinar* trial transcript, 991; Heather R. White, *Reforming Sodom: Protestants and the Rise of Gay Rights* (Chapel Hill: University of North Carolina Press, 2015), 73–87.

45. *U.S. v. Spinar* trial transcript, 1154. Meshbesher was referencing *ONE, Inc. v. Olesen*, 355 U.S. 371 (1958); *Sunshine Book Co. v. Summerfield*, 355 U.S. 372 (1958); and *Manual Enterprises Inc. v. Day Postmaster General*, 370 U.S. 478 (1962).

46. William Blake, "A Little Girl Lost," *Songs of Innocence and of Experience* (London: Urban Romantics, 2014), 26; Stephen D. Cox, *Love and Logic: The Evolution of Blake's Thought* (Ann Arbor: University of Michigan Press, 1992); Stephen Davis, *Jim Morrison: Life, Death, Legend* (New York: Penguin, 2005).

47. "A Sensible Law for Homosexuals," *Minneapolis Tribune*, July 28, 1967; William Sumner, "Postal Inspectors Tend to Overspy," *St. Paul Dispatch*, July 18, 1967.

48. Spinar, interview by author, June 16, 2009.

49. Decision, July 26, 1967, *U.S. v. Spinar*, Criminal Case Files. The decision was not formally published by the court but was reported elsewhere, including *Minneapolis Tribune*, July 27, 1967, 1; *St. Paul Pioneer Press*, July 27, 1967, 1; *ONE Confidential* 12, no. 7, July 1967, 1; *Los Angeles Advocate*, September 1967, 1; and *Butch* 9, 1967. Larson would be remembered for cases in which he opened up the computer industry and free agency in the National Football League. See Alice Rowe Burks, *Who Invented the Computer? The Legal Battle That Changed Computing History* (Amherst, N.Y.: Prometheus Books, 2003).

50. Robins, interview by author, June 12, 2007; *Galerie* 3, 1967; Victor Banis, interview by author, February 18, 2015; Mickey Robins email to author, May 1, 2007.

51. *Los Angeles Advocate*, September 1967, 1; *Drum* 27, October 1967, 7; *Winston Book Club Newsletter*, n.d., Canadian Lesbian and Gay Archives. Thomas Waugh is one of the only scholars to discuss the DSI case. Thomas Waugh, *Hard to Imagine: Gay Male Eroticism in Photography and Film from Their Beginnings to Stonewall* (New York: Columbia University Press, 1996), 280–83. Multiple writers mistakenly attribute the emergence of full-frontal male nudity to a nonexistent Supreme Court case involving *Drum* magazine. See F. Valentine Hooven, III, *Beefcake: The Muscle Magazines of America 1950–1970* (Cologne: Taschen, 1995), 122–24; and Jeffrey Escoffier, *Bigger than Life: The History of Gay Porn Cinema from Beefcake to Hardcore* (Philadelphia: Running Press, 2009), 19.

52. Among the publishers that started to offer nudes soon after September 1967 was the Frontier Athletic Club. George Greig to Guild Press, October 16, 1967, Womack Papers.

53. *Male Nudist Portfolio* 7, 1967; Germain, interview with author, June 6, 2008; Robert G. Hobstetter to DSI, n.d., Pat Rocco Papers, ONE Archives; "A History of Collecting Erotica," *Market Reports Newsletter* 4, no. 2 (April 6, 1976), 3. See also "Ten Years Ago: Anniversary of a Landmark," *Market Reports Newsletter* 5, no. 5 (July 12, 1977), 1.

54. Germain, interview with author, June 6, 2008; Spinar to Leitch, October 12, 1964, folder 7, box 4, *New York Mattachine Newsletter*, New York Mattachine Papers, New York Public Library.

55. *ONE*, January 1961, 16; Richard Inman, *Antheneum Review*, September 1964, 14.

56. *ONE Confidential* 12, no. 7 (July 1967), 1; Hal Call to Friend, n.d, Eccles Papers; Inman to Vincenz, February 18, 1968, Lillie Vincenz Papers, Library of Congress, Washington, D.C. Thanks to David Carter for calling the Inman letter to my attention.

57. Germain C. dba Craig Folder, box 80, Fleishman Papers; *Los Angeles Advocate* 3, no. 1 (January 1969), 3; Victor J. Banis, *Spine Intact, Some Creases: Remembrances of a Paperback Writer* (San Bernardino, Calif.: Borgo Press, 2007), 182; Robins, interview by author, June 12, 2007; Vagabond Club application, 1967, DSI folder, Ephemera Collection, ONE Archives. Germain and Spinar purchased a home at 2745 Outpost Drive.

58. David Hurles interview with Dian Hanson, August 26, 2014; Spinar & Germain adv. Robins & Meshbesher folder and DSI Inc. adv. Travis Marin County folder, box 114, Fleishman Papers; "Hearing on Nude Deputy," *San Francisco Examiner*, October 23, 1968; *PP*, Dec 1971, 4; Robert Mainardi, ed., *Jim French Diaries: The Creator of Colt Studios* (Berlin: Bruno Gmunder, 2011).

59. AMG Bulletin 67-F; *PP*, February 1968, 8; Leonard Riefenstahl, "Out of Vogue, Bob Mizer Movies Stand Between Porn and Pretense," *Los Angeles Advocate*, August 19–September 1,

1970, 23; "Full-Nude Art Poses" brochure (postmarked December 8, 1967), Chuck Renslow Collection, Leather Archives; *Rawhide Male* no. 1, September 1968; author interview with Chuck Renslow, May 24, 2008, Chicago.

60. DSI, "We've Moved," October 1968; Vagabond Club, "Letters Now Being Accepted," July 1969; and DSI, "8 Albums of All Male Action," August 1971, all in DSI folder, Ephemera Collection, ONE Archives; "Nudie Kidnappers Plague Photo Studios," *Los Angeles Advocate*, January 1969, 2.

61. Memo for the record, W. J. Cotter, Chief Inspector, on Meeting with Assistant Attorney General, July 15, 1969; Statement of Winton M. Blount before United States Attorneys' Orientation Conference, July 30, 1969; and Chief Postal Inspector to Postmaster General, May 14, 1969, all in Pornography File, USPSHOF; Robins, interview with author, June 12, 2007.

62. "Post Office Still After DSI," *Los Angeles Advocate*, September 1969, 9; "Jury Convicts DSI Owners of Obscenity," *Los Angeles Advocate*, August 5, 1970, 1; *DSI Sales v. U.S.*, 440 F2d 1241. U.S. App., 8th Circuit (1971). On Stanley Fleishman, see Gay Talese, *Thy Neighbor's Wife* (New York: Dell, 1980), 481–512; and Stanley Fleishman, "Obscenity and Post Office Censorship," *Law in Transition* 22 (Winter 1963), 222–30.

63. *PP*, January 1974, 4; box 80, Fleishman Papers; among the names Conrad Germain was doing business under in the 1970s were the Photographer's Guild, Books Unlimited, Studio 9, Odyssey Club, Mark IV, Outpost Development, KG Enterprises, and Conrad Germain Designs.

64. "Firm Convicted," *Press-Courier* (Oxnard, Calif.), August 15, 1975, 8; *U.S. v. Outpost Development*, 552 F.2d 868 (U.S. App., 9th Circuit, 1977); *Market Reports Newsletter* 6, no 2 (September 12, 1978), 8; Germain, interview with author, June 6, 2008. Despite his agreement to not engage in mail order, Germain was later the target of a Federal Trade Commission crackdown on fraud for advertisements claiming to provide winning lottery numbers. See *Los Angeles Times*, October 2, 1997, 1.

7. THE PHYSIQUE LEGACY

1. Joseph W. Bean, *International Mr. Leather: 25 Years of Champions* (Las Vegas: Nazca Plains, 2004).

2. Chuck Renslow interview with author, May 24, 2008; Tracy Baim and Owen Keehnen, *Leatherman: The Legend of Chuck Renslow* (Chicago: Prairie Avenue Productions, 2011); Joseph W. Bean, ed., *Kris: The Physique Photography of Chuck Renslow* (Las Vegas: Nazca Plains, 2007).

3. *Physique Pictorial* (PP), Winter 1958; *Chicago Tribune*, May 21, 1966; Baim and Keehnen, *Leatherman*, 258–60. Like any astute Chicago businessman engaging in the sale of regulated merchandise, Renslow knew how to pay off the police. See Timothy Stewart-Winter, *Queer Clout: Chicago and the Rise of Gay Politics* (Philadelphia: University of Pennsylvania Press, 2015), 24.

4. Baim and Keehnen, *Leatherman*, 264; Stewart-Winter, *Queer Clout*, 111–13, 127.

5. *Vector*, August 1968, 29.

6. Paul Siebenand, "Beginnings of Gay Cinema in Los Angeles: The Industry and the Audience," Ph.D. dissertation, University of Southern California, 1975, ONE Archives; Escoffier, *Bigger than Life*, 47–52.

7. Whitney Strub, "Mondo Rocco: Mapping Gay Los Angeles Sexual Geography in the Late-1960s Films of Pat Rocco," *Radical History Review* 113 (Spring 2012): 13–34.

8. Jim Kepner, "The Films of Pat Rocco," *Tangents*, November–December–January 1968/69.

9. *Spree News Pictorial* 1, no. 3, n.d. (circa 1969).

10. "Homosexual Citizens," *Screw*, September 8, 1969. Quotation noted in Pat Rocco Papers, ONE Archives.

11. *SPREE News Pictorial*, January 1973.

12. *PP*, May 1974, 3.

13. Pat Rocco (dir.), *Man Happenings: Groovy Guy* (1968).

14. *Queen's Quarterly*, Fall 1970, 25.

15. "Mr. Club Baths Named," *Washington Blade*, October 1976, 1.

16. Outhistory.org; *Gay Blade* (Washington, D.C.) 1, no. 11 (August 1970), 2; *SPREE News Pictorial*, September 1971.

17. *PP*, April 1973, 25.

18. Rodger Streitmatter, *Unspeakable: The Rise of the Gay and Lesbian Press in America* (Boston: Faber and Faber, 1995), 80–99.

19. *Queen's Quarterly*, January–February 1972, 13, and January–February 1971, 23–25. On Bud Parker's move to *Queen's Quarterly*, see Rick Wayne, *Muscle Wars: The Behind the Scenes Story of Competitive Bodybuilding* (New York: St. Martin's Press, 1985), 109–10; Lucas Hilderbrand, "A Suitcase Full of Vaseline, or Travels in the 1970s Gay World," *Journal of the History of Sexuality* 22 (2013), 373–402.

20. Streitmatter, *Unspeakable*, 88.

21. *Drummer* 1, no. 10 (1976), and 2, no. 14 (1977).

22. J. Louis Campbell, *Jack Nichols, Gay Pioneer "Have You Heard My Message?"* (New York: Harrington Park Press, 2007), 122; *David*, October 1971.

23. "The Body Beautiful," *ONE*, June 1955, 4.

24. *Vector*, June and October 1969; Ron Williams, *San Francisco's Native "Sissy" Son: A Coming Out Memoir* (Blurb.com, 2013), 133–37.

25. *Mattachine Times* (New York), February 1974. On the same trend in Mattachine-San Francisco, see Lucas Hilderbrand, "The Uncut Version: The Mattachine Society's Pornographic Epilogue," *Sexualities* 19 (2016): 449–64.

26. *Spartan for Men* 1, no. 1 (1969); *Kepner Omnibus* (North Hollywood, Calif.: House One, 1975); *Six by Jim Kepner* (Rotterdam: Omega International, 1975); Dorr Legg to Pat Rocco, December 3, 1968, Pat Rocco Papers, ONE Archives.

27. Campbell, *Jack Nichols, Gay Pioneer*, 122.

28. Streitmatter, *Unspeakable*, 315; Deidre Carmody, "The Advocate's Makeover for Madison Ave.," *New York Times*, May 25, 1992, 37.

29. Cindy Claire Lewis, "Gay Power," *Vector*, September 1967, 23.

30. P. Nutz, "Gay Power $$$," *Los Angeles Advocate*, September 1967, 8.

31. *Vector*, September 1968; *Detroit Free Press*, December 28, 1968, 13; *Insider*, February 1969, quoted in Lillian Faderman, *The Gay Revolution: The Story of the Struggle* (New York: Simon & Schuster, 2016), 682.

32. Clendenin, *Out for Good*, 30; "Get the Mafia and the Cops Out of Gay Bars," Craig Rodwell Papers, New York Public Library.

33. Carl Wittman, "A Gay Manifesto," and John Murphy, "Queer Books," in *Out of the Closets: Voices of Gay Liberation*, ed. Karla Jay and Allen Young (New York: Pyramid Books, 1972); Allen Young, "No Longer the Court Jesters," in *Lavender Culture*, ed. Karla Jay and Allen Young (New York: Jove/HBJ, 1978), 28.

34. Craig Rodwell Papers, New York Public Library; Jim Downs, *Stand by Me: The Forgotten History of Gay Liberation* (New York: Basic Books, 2016), 65–88.

35. Martin Duberman, *Stonewall* (New York: Dutton, 1993), 165.

36. Telephone interview with Daniel Nicoletta, July 3, 2013; Lillian Faderman, *Harvey Milk: His Lives and Death* (New Haven, Conn.: Yale University Press, 2018), 72; Randy Shilts, *The Mayor of Castro Street: The Life and Times of Harvey Milk* (New York: St. Martin's Press, 1982), 83; Harvey Milk, "Gay Economic Power," *Bay Area Reporter* (San Francisco), September 15, 1977, reprinted in *An Archive of Hope: Harvey Milk's Speeches and Writings* (Berkeley: University of California Press, 2013), 162.

INDEX